QUALITY CIRCLES

QUALITY AND RELIABILITY

A Series Edited by

Edward G. Schilling

Center for Quality and Applied Statistics
Rochester Institute of Technology
Rochester, New York

Additional volumes in preparation

QUALITY CIRCLES

SELECTED READINGS

Edited by

Roger W. Berger

Industrial Engineering Department
Iowa State University
Ames, Iowa

David L. Shores

Seminar Clearing House International
St. Paul, Minnesota

Contributing editor

Mary C. Thompson

Iowa State University
Ames, Iowa

MARCEL DEKKER, INC.   New York and Basel
ASQC QUALITY PRESS   Milwaukee

Library of Congress Cataloging-in-Publication Data

Quality circles.
  (Quality and reliability ; 9)
  Includes index.
  1. Quality circles. I. Berger, Roger W. II. Shores,
David L. III. Thompson, Mary C. IV. Series: Quality
and reliability ; vol. 9.
HD66.Q35 1986   658.4'036   86-4590
ISBN 0-8247-7614-3

MARCEL DEKKER, INC.
270 Madison Avenue, New York, New York 10016

American Society for Quality Control
230 West Wells Street, Milwaukee, Wisconsin 53203

Current printing (last digit):
10 9 8 7 6 5 4 3 2 1

PRINTED IN THE UNITED STATES OF AMERICA

PREFACE

Statistical Process Control.

Quality Control Circles.

Quality Circles.

Zero Defects.

Participative Management.

Quality of Work Life.

Pride Circles.

Involvement Teams.

Names . . . all assigned by managers and workers . . . intended to create improvement in the quality of work life, attitudes, productivity, and cost savings. The techniques used to accomplish the goals established by the work group also vary, but have many common features. Managers and workers also hold in common cultural ideas about what makes up work and their roles in the workplace based on ethnicity, geographic location, religion, and political ideology.

What are quality circles? Where did they originate? Do they have any place in your organization? Will they work? Will you make more money, have more satisfied employees, improve production? That depends — on you, your attitudes, the attitudes of your immediate supervisor, the support for the concepts of quality circles from the top people in the organization through the lowest echelons of employees.

As more and more of our manufactured products are imported from other countries you must take a closer look at the reasons behind corporate choices to move the manufacturing facilities to foreign countries. You must consider the meaning of standards and evaluate the costs of quality as practiced by manufacturers in other nations. You, the reader, must draw your own conclusions about the effect of quality circles on the future of manufacturing in the United States.

Roger W. Berger
David L. Shores

ACKNOWLEDGMENTS

We appreciate and thank the authors who have granted permission to reproduce their articles as part of our reader. We thank Julie Muckler for initiating the project.

Chapter One: Overview and History

The QC Phenomenon
  J.M. Juran
© 1967 American Society for Quality Control. Reprinted by permission.

What Happened in Japan?
  W. Edwards Deming
© 1967 American Society for Quality Control. Reprinted by permission.

Learning from the Japanese: Prospects and Pitfalls
  Robert E. Cole.
©1980 Robert E. Cole. Reprinted by permission. All rights reserved.

Quality Circles: A Tool for the '80s
  Edwin G. Yager
Copyright 1980 *Training and Development Journal*, American Society for Training and Development. Reprinted with permission. All rights reserved.

Can We Adopt the Japanese Methods of Human Resources Management?
  Kae H. Chung and Margaret Ann Gray
Reprinted from the May, 1982 issue of *Personnel Administrator*, copyright 1982, The American Society for Personnel Administration, 606 North Washington Street, Alexandria, VA 22314, $30 per year.

Chapter Two: Implementing Quality Circles

Implementing Quality Circles in Your Organization
  Donald L. Dewar
"Reprinted with permission from the 1980 IAQC Conference Transactions, a publication of the International Association of Quality Circles."

Predictable Developmental Stages in the Evolution of a Quality Circle
  Vivian C. Comstock and Gerald E. Swartz
"Reprinted with permission from the 1980 IAQC Conference Transactions, a publication of the International Association of Quality Circles."

QC Circles' Success Depends on Management Readiness to Support Workers' Involvement
  Keith A. Brooke
Reprinted with permission from *Industrial Engineering* magazine, Vol. 14, No. 1, January 1982. Copyright © Institute of Industrial Engineers, 25 Technology Park/Atlanta, Norcross, GA 30092.

Diagnosing Readiness
  Edmund J. Metz
"Reprinted with permission from *The Quality Circles Journal*, Vol. 4, No. 1, the quarterly publication of the International Association of Quality Circles."

Avoiding Problems in Developing Quality Circles
  Roger W. Berger
Reprinted with permission from the January 1983 issue of the *Quality Circle Digest*, published by Quality Control Institute, P.O. Box Q, Red Bluff, CA 96080. Copyright 1983.

Quality Circles and Corporate Culture
  William B. Werther, Jr.
© National Productivity Review
Executive Enterprises, Inc. New York, NY
Reprinted with Permission

Implementing Quality Circles: A Hard Look at Some of the Realities
  Gerald D. Klein
Reprinted, by permission of the publisher, from PERSONNEL, November/December 1981, © 1981 by AMACOM, a division of American Management Associations. All rights reserved.

Chapter Three: Training and Tools

Quality Control Circle Programs — What Works and What Doesn't
  Matthew Goodfellow
© 1981 American Society for Quality Control. Reprinted by permission.

A Trend in the Wrong Direction
  Jeff Dewar
Reprinted with permission from the 1982 issue of the *Quality Circle Digest*, published by Quality Circle Institute, P.O. Box Q, Red Bluff, CA 96080. Copyright 1982.

What Are the Tools of QC Circles?
  Virgil Rehg
© 1976 American Society for Quality Control. Reprinted with permission.

QC Circle Workshop: Application
  Virgil Rehg
© 1976 American Society for Quality Control. Reprinted with permission.

Problem Solving Comparisons: QC Circles, KT, etc.
  Robert T. Amsden
© 1978 American Society for Quality Control. Reprinted with permission.

QC Circle Training Process Should Cover Relating, Supporting, Problem-Solving Skills
  Scott M. Sedam
Reprinted with permission from *Industrial Engineering* magazine, Vol 14, No. 1, January 1982. Copyright © Institute of Industrial Engineers, 25 Technology Park/Atlanta, Norcross, GA 30092.

How to Be a Good Group Member
  Michael Doyle and David Straus
Reprinted by permission of the Berkley Publishing Group from HOW TO MAKE MEETINGS WORK by Michael Doyle and David Straus. Copyright © 1976 by Michael Doyle and David Straus.

Chapter Four: Measurement and Evaluation

Quality Control Circles: They Work and Don't Work
  Kenichi Ohmae
"Reprinted by permission of The Wall Street Journal © Dow Jones & Company, Inc. 1982. All Rights Reserved."

Designing Quality Circles Research
  Robert P. Steel, Russell F. Lloyd, Nestor K. Ovalle, and William H. Hendrix
"Reprinted with permission from *The Quality Circle Journal*, Vol. 5, No. 1, the quarterly publication of the International Association of Quality Circles."

To Measure or Not to Measure
  Donald L. Dewar
Reprinted with permission from the July 1982 issue of *The Quality Circle Digest*, published by Quality Circle Institute, P.O. Box Q, Red Bluff, CA 96080. Copyright 1982.

What's Good for Japan May Not Be Best for You or Your Training Department
  Ron Zemke
Reprinted with permission from the October 1981 issue of TRAINING, The magazine of Human Resources Development. Copyright 1981, Lakewood Publications, Inc., Minneapolis, MN (612) 333-0471. All rights reserved.

Chapter Five: Case Studies

Quality of Work Life — Learning from Tarrytown
  Robert H. Guest
Reprinted by permission of the *Harvard Business Review*. "Quality of Work Life — Learning From Tarrytown" by Robert H. Guest (July/August 1979). Copyright © 1979 by the President and Fellows of Harvard College; all rights reserved.

The Topeka Story: Teaching an Old Dog Food New Tricks
  Richard E. Walton
Reprinted with permission from "The Topeka Story: Teaching an Old Dog Food New Tricks" by Richard E. Walton, *The Wharton Magazine*, Vol. 2, Nos. 2, © by Wharton School of the University of Pennsylvania.

The Topeka Story: Part Two: What's the Bottom Line?
    Richard E. Walton

"Awakening a Sleeping Giant . . ." Ford's Employee Involvement Program
    Gerard Tavernier

Participative Management at Motorola — The Results
    Walter B. Scott

Hewlett Packard's Quality Team Program
    Ross Redeker

Circles
    Dian Sprenger

Banking on High Quality
    Charles A. Aubrey II and Lawrence A. Eldridge

Quality Circles at Hughes Aircraft
    Mary T. Kohler and Everett R. Wells

Chapter Six: Supportive Literature from Behavioral Sciences and Human Resource Development

The Principle of Supportive Relationships as an Organizing Concept
    Rensis Likert

An Improvement Cycle for Human Resource Development
    Rensis Likert

Work Innovations in the United States
    Richard E. Walton

A Changing View of the Union-Management Relationship: Scientific Management vs. Human Development
    Irving Bluestone

The Quality Circle Explosion
    Edwin G. Yager

Integrating Quality Control and Quality of Work Life
    Sidney P. Rubinstein

CONTENTS

CONTRIBUTORS

Robert T. Amsden, Ph.D., Wright State University, Dayton, OH

Charles A. Aubrey II, Continental Illinois National Bank & Trust Company, Chicago, IL

Roger W. Berger, Iowa State University, Ames, IA

Irving Bluestone, United Auto Workers, Detroit, MI

Keith A. Brooke, General Motors Corp., Detroit, MI

Kae H. Chung, Wichita State University, Wichita, KS

Robert E. Cole, University of Michigan, Ann Arbor, MI

Vivian C. Comstock, Westinghouse Electric Corp., Baltimore, MD

W. Edwards Deming, Consultant in Statistical Survey, Washington, D.C.

Donald L. Dewar, Quality Circle Institute, Red Bluff, CA

Jeff Dewar, Quality Circles Institute, Red Bluff, CA

Michael Doyle, Interaction Associates, San Diego, CA

Lawrence A. Eldridge, Continental Illinois National Bank & Trust Company, Chicago, IL

Matthew Goodfellow, University Research Center, Chicago, IL

Margaret Ann Gray, Wichita State University, Wichita, KS

Robert H. Guest, Amos Tuck School, Dartmouth College, Hanover, NH

William H. Hendrix, Air Force Institute of Technology, Wright-Patterson Air Force Base, OH

J. M. Juran, Juran Institute, New York, NY

Gerald D. Klein, Rider College, Montclair, NJ

Mary T. Kohler, Hughes Aircraft Company, Culver City, CA

Rensis Likert, University of Michigan, Ann Arbor, MI

Russell F. Lloyd, Air Force Institute of Technology, Wright-Patterson Air Force Base, OH

Edmund J. Metz, Management Development Consultant, Stanford, CT

Kenichi Ohmae, McKinsey and Company, Tokyo, Japan

Nestor K. Ovalle, Air Force Institute of Technology, Wright-Patterson Air Force Base, OH

Ross Redeker, P.E., Hewelett-Packard, Palo Alto, CA

Virgil Rehg, U.S. Air Force Institute of Technology, Wright-Patterson Air Force Base, OH

Sidney P. Rubinstein, Participative Systems, Inc., Princeton, NJ

Walter B. Scott, Motorola Co., Schaumberg, IL

Scott M. Sedam, Wilson Learning Corp., Minneapolis, MN

David L. Shores, Seminar Clearing International, Saint Paul, MN

Dian Sprenger, University of Missouri, Columbia, MO

Robert P. Steel, Air Force Institute of Technology, Wright-Patterson Air Force Base, OH

David Straus, Interaction Associates, San Diego, CA

Gerald E. Swartz, Westinghouse Electric Corp., Baltimore, MD

Gerard Tavernier, Management Review, N.Y., NY

Mary C. Thompson, Iowa State University, Ames, IA

Richard E. Walton, Harvard Business School, Cambridge, MA

Everett R. Wells, Hughes Aircraft Company, Culver City, CA

William B. Werther, Jr., Arizona State University, Phoenix, AZ

Edwin G. Yager, Consulting Associates Inc., Southfield, MI

Ron Zemke, Performance Research, Minneapolis, MN

A COMPARISON OF MANAGEMENT TECHNIQUES

	Quality Circles	Scanlon Plan	M.B.O.	Organization Development	Job Enrichment	Profit-Sharing
Date of Inception	1970's	1930's	1960's	1960's	1960's	1700's
Type of Program	Participative Problem-Solving	Gain Sharing Plan	Performance Appraisal	Improvement of Organizational Health & Effectiveness	Work Design	Gain Sharing Plan
Purposes	To increase worker involvement; To improve product quality; To increase productivity	To improve plant efficiency; To reduce production costs; To increase productivity through lower labor costs	To enhance employer/employee relationships; To improve motivational climate	To direct organizational climate towards one which supports worker participation; To improve organizational effectiveness	To increase worker involvement and commitment; To improve worker satisfaction, productivity, and job performance through change of job assignment	To share profits with worker; To motivate employees to increase productivity
Rationale	Reduced production costs will result from participative problem-solving by workers	Passing on labor cost savings to workers will result in increasing worker productivity	Enhancing relationships through joint goal development improves motivational climate	Valuing the worker leads to more participation and collective decision-making which benefits both the individual and organization	Increased growth and advancement in job responsibilities will improve job satisfaction and result in improved productivity	Creating a self-interest in the organization and work itself will motivate the employee to work harder to increase profits
Scope	Small groups of workers within same department	Organization-wide participation of individual workers	One-on one involvement between superior and subordinate	Organization-wide participation of individual workers as teams	Individual worker and job	Organization-wide participation of individuals
Benefits	Increased involvement in solving production problems for workers; Improved product quality and increased productivity for organization through employee contribution of ideas	Monthly bonus passed on to workers (based upon labor savings); Reduced production costs for organization	Achievement of individual goals for workers; Improved motivational climate; Achievement of organizational goals	Increased worker involvement in planning, controlling, and managing the organization; Organization becomes more effective through better communication, improved decision-making and increased openess	Worker receives more responsibility in planning and controlling own work; Improved organizational morale and increased productivity	Yearly distribution of profits to workers; Lower production costs to organization; Creates a feeling of ownership on the part of the employees
Key Features	Voluntary participation; Requires support from all levels; Groups of workers meet to identify and solve production problems; Workers implement solution with management support	A formal mechanism to develop and evaluate cost-saving ideas; A suggestion system; Bonus based upon percent of labor savings	Requires support from all levels; Requires a trusting environment; Employee/employer jointly agrees upon job duties, work goals, and job evaluation criteria	Requires support from all levels; A long-range effort to improve problem-solving consisting of diagnosis, action, and maintenance; Each organization is unique	Wholeness in job; Job can be expanded vertically to include more control, planning and directing; Job can be expanded horizontally to include more duties or tasks; Ownership in results	Requires support of all levels; The plan must be in writing; A predetermined formula is used to allocate bonus; A trust fund is established where bonuses are deposited

CHRONOLOGY

JAPAN

1940s: Post-War Era
— products made in Japan were know for poor quality
— government began its commitment to improve product quality
— government permitted 'JIS' symbol for high quality

1950s: The Seeds of Q.C. Circles are Planted
— Dr. W. E. Deming, U.S. Statistician, lectured on statistical methods for the Union of Japanese Scientists & Engineers (J.U.S.E.)
— J. M. Juran taught courses on Management of Quality Control (quality control is the responsibility for all levels)
— Deming Application Prize was established to promote quality
— a weekly radio series on quality began

1960s: Quality Control Circles are Formed
— Dr. Karou Ishikawa conceived the idea of Quality Control Circles from U.S. management theories
— a Quality Control Circles Headquarters was established
— 1st Quality Control Circle was registered with J.U.S.E.
— "Quality Control for Foreman," a magazine published for the foreman, was started

1970s: Continued Expansion of Quality Control Circles
— one out of eight workers belonged to Q.C. Circles
— "Fundamentals of Quality Control Circles" was published
— Japan took the world lead in product quality and productivity

1980s: Quality Control Circles are Exported
— over 100,000 Circles registered with J.U.S.E.

UNITED STATES

1950s: A New Form of Management Begins to Appear
— Harwood Manufacturing used worker participation to manage the workers
— Sidney P. Rubinstein developed his "Participative Management System"
— University of Michigan conducted research in the area of worker participation

1960s: Continued Interest in Participative Management
— Douglas McGregor published his management theories of Theory X and Theory Y
— Rensis Likert published research from the Institute of Social Sciences and his 4 Systems approach to management
— Fredrick Herzberg developed his Motivator-Hygiene Theory

1970s: Quality Control Circles are Formed
— Lockheed Missile and Space formed the 1st Quality Control Circle
— GM-UAW began a Quality of Work Life program at Tarrytown, NY
— Pet Foods revamped their management at their Topeka plant
— the International Association of Quality Circles (I.A.Q.C.) was formed
— the American Society for Quality Control formed a division for Quality Circles
— 1st I.A.Q.C. conference held

1980s: Quality Circles Spread throughout the United States
— over 500 major organizations implemented Quality Circles
— seminars on Quality Circles and Japanese management grew at a rapid rate
— Quality Circles entered into the service industries and public sector
— two journals, *The Quality Circle Journal* and *Quality Circle Digest*, began publication

QUALITY CIRCLES

INTRODUCTION: CHAPTER ONE
OVERVIEW AND HISTORY

The readings contained in this reader were selected from a large number of publications to define, illustrate approaches to, and evaluate the concept of quality circles and statistical process control. They cover the philosophy of quality circles, describe the thinking of the originators of the quality circle concepts, and describe the success story of how statistical process control and quality circles have turned the Japanese work force into a highly successful economic team producing top quality products and competing in an international market for world trade.

Experts in initiating, evaluating, and participating in quality circles describe their satisfactions and frustrations with using participative management techniques in these readings. They offer some ''how-to'' approaches to successfully organizing and operating quality circle groups in the work place. Many different opinions and ideas are covered to provide you with definitive information on what is being viewed as the basis for Japan's success in an intensely competitive market.

The Japanese culture lends itself to the concept of quality control and standards because of its paternalistic and hierarchical structure. Japanese employees view their role in the workplace as vital in the production of a product or the delivery of services because each worker makes a contribution to the company's goals ultimately its profit. The concept of participative management is an acceptable management technique in Japan because the concept fits the societal patterns of status and strata.

The six basic principles of quality circle activity, according to Robert E. Cole, are:

- trust your employees
- build employee loyalty to the company
- invest in training and treat employees as resources which, if cultivated, will yield economic returns to the firm
- recognize employee accomplishments
- decentralize decision making
- work should be seen as a cooperative effort with workers and managers doing the job together.

These are not new ideas to the U.S. blue collar work force nor to middle management, but they are not widely practiced. All six principles can be found in almost any behavioral science literature in the U.S. Most interesting is that, while these basic ideas were developed in the U.S., the Japanese have institutionalized them nationally and practice them daily in their organizations.

The development of the quality circle concept resembles that of the development of the transistor. Cole points out that the transistor was invented in the U.S. but initially commercialized most successfully in Japan. Once more we are taking credit for the ideas and competing with the results. It is, he says, a terrible mistake to downplay the creativity needed to take an invention and adapt it to commercial possibilities.

Quality circles are being hailed as a management tool for the '80s. A great deal of attention is being given to consideration of whether or not we can change the ideas cherished by managers during the organization and development of powerful unions — that workers were determined to perform at the lowest level of efficiency, to sabotage company products, to demand the highest pay, to give the least and expect the most in return. There is great concern about whether we can adopt the Japanese methods of human resource management to American industries. The consensus appears to be that the concept of quality circles as practiced by the Japanese can be adapted to fit American industry — but not adopted in the form presently used in Japan. The technique can be successful only when there is commitment at the top levels to support the concept and when appropriate public relations, recognition, training, and reinforcement is present at all levels.

Many futurists and management consultants are strong advocates of more participative management. They declare a new style of leadership is needed in the '80s. They liken the changes in today's industry to those during the industrial revolution and credit the computer and information explosion with creating the change. Workers desire an environment where they can take their concerns directly to the supervisors for resolution.

Proponents of the quality circle techniques relate their thinking to the work of McGregor, Herzberg, and Likert. Most managers, at all levels, are quite familiar with the concept of "Theory Y" which promotes democratic human resource management but they find it very difficult to put into practice. They may, instead, apply the more coercive "Theory X" techniques because theory is not always easy to apply in work environments. In American industry, however, the general consensus is that there are as many management styles as there are managers.

Are quality circles just another management fad? Can they really create a work environment where employees have feelings of belonging to the decision making team, feelings of importance for their part in making the company a success in the marketplace, feelings that they have some control over the quality of life in the workplace, and feelings of deep satisfaction about meaningful work experiences? The readings in this book will give you a variety of views.

THE QC CIRCLE PHENOMENON
J. M. Juran

The QC Circle is a small group of departmental work leaders and line operators who have volunteered to spend time outside of their regular hours to help solve departmental quality problems. The QC Circle movement orginated in Japan about four years ago. A phenomenal rate of growth has taken place. The effect of the movement on the Japanese drive toward quality leadership may well be dramatic.

On the afternoon of Wednesday, April 20, 1966, a Westerner visiting the Daiichi Seimei Hall in central Tokyo would have witnessed a remarkable sight. The meeting in progress in this historic auditorium (General Douglas MacArthur staged his large conferences here) was billed as the 14th QC Circle Conference. It had started at 1:00 p.m., and, after some ceremonial addresses, the technical program got under way. Seven Japanese companies presented reports on improvements they had made on a variety of company problems. For example, the first report, by Takenosuke Kakegawa of the Stereophonic plant of Tokyo Sanyo Electric Company, was on "Finding a Solution to Trouble About Solder." The seventh report was by a trio, Shoko Yazawa, Reiko Yamada, and Mitsuko Yamazaki, from the Car Radio Division of Matsushita Communication Industrial Company, who reported on "Decrease of Car Radio Defects in Final Assembly." Each report was allowed 15 minutes, with 7 added minutes for discussion from the floor.

To understand what was so remarkable about the conference, let us look in detail at the presentation made by the trio from Matsushita. They had taken on a project to reduce final assembly defects in the radios which Matsushita makes for sale and export to automobile companies. From information of assembly rejections and customer troubles, the trio prepared a Pareto analysis,[1] and established that the number one defect was loose control knobs. This "public enemy number one" accounted for 80 percent of all final assembly defects. The number two defect, missing mounting brackets, comprised 13 percent of all defects. The remaining 7 percent were assorted minor defects. Collectively, all defects ran at a level of 2.2 percent of the product.

Next, the trio considered each of the two principal defects (loose control knobs and missing mounting brackets) as a project requiring a breakthrough to a new level.

The control knob is designed with a blind hole to mate with the control shaft. To provide enough friction to hold the knob tight, the shaft is slotted to create two springy sides which are then spread with a screwdriver during the final assembly operation. However, there was a difference of opinion as to the cause of loose control knobs — was it parts, operators, tools, methods? The trio mapped out the variables on an Ishikawa diagram, as shown in Fig. 1. This is described in Reference 2.

From analysis and from some experimentation, it was established that the two main causes were:

1. Variation in slot size when enlarged by different operators.
2. Screwdriver not well suited for the operation.

A solution was found by providing screwdrivers with a parallel-sided blade instead of a tapered blade.

The missing mounting brackets were the second project. (These brackets are used in the car factory to mount the radio to the automobile dashboard). The cause of missing brackets was "operator error." Radio assemblers in a prior stage of manufacture have a wide range of operations to perform, and sometimes omit one or both mounting brackets.

The solution was to fool-proof the final assembly operation. An assembly jig had been needed anyhow as a holding device during final assembly. Now the jig was built, and built in such a way that the mounting brackets were the means of supporting the radios in the jig. This simplified handling the radio during final assembly and also eliminated shipment of radios with missing mounting brackets.

These two quality breakthroughs lowered the final assembly defect rate from 2.2 percent to 0.6 percent.

The trio had divided up their 15 minute presentation into three sections of five minutes each. Shoko led off, followed by Reiko and Mitsuko, respectively. In the manner of such Japanese conferences, the visual aids were large painted sheets of paper hung from a long, horizontal, wooden two-by-four, like wash on the line. These sheets showed sketches of the parts, the flow of the process, the methods of analysis, and charts of the results obtained. The trio made their presentation with a sure-footed grasp of their subject. Even to this author, whose knowledge of Japanese is minimal, the explanation was clear. The well-prepared visual aids helped quite a bit. During the seven minute question period, Mitsuko, being the final speaker, also fielded the questions from the floor. This was likewise a virtuoso performance, for Mitsuko was plenty alert, and was ready with the answers before the questions were half finished.

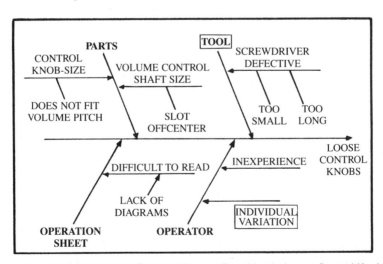

Figure 1 — Ishikawa Diagram Showing Factors Resulting in Loose Control Knobs.

4

What was remarkable about all this was the fact that the presentation of the seven reports at this conference involved not a single manager, supervisor, engineer or other management specialist; nobody from what an American calls the "exempt payroll." Instead, the speakers were mostly what we call "working foremen" or "work leaders." (The usual Japanese word is "GEMBA-CHO.") Some speakers were production operators off the assembly floor. All were either leaders or members of "QC Circles." *Shoko, Reiko and Mitsuko were girls off the assembly line.* Their full time job is to assemble car radios. Shoko and Reiko were 21 and 23 years old, respectively. *Mitsuko was 18!*

Each of these seven reports represented the work of a "QC Circle," QC meaning Quality Control. This QC Circle movement, which began in 1962, has been snowballing into something massive. As of April 1966, there were already over 10,000 such circles in Japan, and every one of them exhibited the following characteristics:

- the membership consists solely of people at the bottom of the company organization — non-supervisors and working supervisors;
- membership is voluntary;
- the work of the circles is mostly conducted outside of regular hours;
- compensation for this out-of-hours work varies from full time down to nothing.

To understand how a QC Circle, such as the three young girls off the assembly line, could take on and complete a project like improving the assembly quality of car radios, it is necessary to go back a few years, and in some respects, a few centuries. We will shortly return to this.

RESULTS TO DATE

There is a good measure of results achieved by the QC Circle movement because a measuring stick has been built in. Each Circle is required, as part of each project undertaken, to evaluate the results. From these evaluations, the editors of GEMBA TO QC (Quality Control for the Foreman) have determined that:

- the Circles have averaged savings of about $3000 each;
- the 10,000 Circles have collectively achieved $30 million in improvements.

This is astounding for a movement which is still only a few years old. No less significant is the fact that this has been done without pre-empting the time of the managers and engineers, who remain free to devote themselves to inter-departmental and upper level projects. The idea that these Japanese companies have found a way of going through all operations with a fine tooth comb, and without adding to the burdens of the managers and engineers is something to ponder on.

The main effect has been in control, this being inherently the basic role which can be played by the QC Circle. There has been much analysis of sporadic troubles, and much done to reduce variation and to prevent recurrence. More and sharper control tools have been made available to the factory floor: clearer interpretation of standards; more complete instrumentation; better data feedback; control charts.

Part of the improvement in control has been an increased awareness of the sequence of steps in the control cycle. As quality improvements are worked out, action is taken to incorporate the improvement into revised, standardized methods. Further steps are then taken to set up the fool-proofing, the feedback and the alarms which will hold the gains.

Beyond improvement of control, a gratifying proportion of the projects are of a breakthrough nature — by systematic study they take the department to better levels of performance, levels not previously attained.

The intangible by-products of the foregoing results are evident but not measurable:

- the foreman's ability to control and lead his department is increased. His job of promulgating instructions is noticeably eased.
- the operators have greater interest in their job, and a higher morale. This extends to people formerly indifferent, and to the older age group as well.
- the relationship between the staff people and the line workers has improved noticeably.
- there is being developed, on the factory floor, a generation of workers with successful experience in use of what have to date been regarded as management tools. The potential of these workers to become the managers of tomorrow is simply breathtaking.

HOW THE QC CIRCLES STARTED

The QC Circles are not some isolated invention; they are a very logical outcome of the Japanese drive for training and accomplishment in quality control. It is easy to trace this evolution.

The authoritative Japanese narratives (by Koyanagi, Ishikawa and others) all trace formal training in modern quality control methods to the early 1950's. The seed courses were Deming's lectures in statistical methodology (1950) and Juran's courses on Management of Quality Control (1954). The Japanese zeal for learning and for self-sufficiency brought out a follow-up of numerous courses, by local experts, for engineers and managers at all levels.

The Japanese were not content to conduct this training for engineers and the supervisory levels. Japanese concepts of organizing work do not follow the strict Taylor concept of division of work, i.e., planning to be done by the engineers, and execution to be done by the foremen and workers. Instead, the Japanese leave a good deal of planning and creativity to be carried out by the production force.

These same concepts of organizing work have carried over into the quality function. The broad based Quality Control Department, with its arrays of Quality Control Engineers, Reliability Engineers and still other specialist categories, so commonly found in America, is a minority organization form in Japan. The Japanese approach has been to teach quality control methodology to managers in *all* functions — Research, Development, Design, Production, Purchasing, Sales, Accounting, etc. With such a broad base of training, the need for a broadly-based

Quality Control Department is diminished, as is the need for specialist engineers. (Japanese engineers are seldom specialized as Quality Control Engineers.) As a consequence, the Quality Control Department in Japan has mainly an advisory, consulting and promotional role. A minority of these departments do conduct quality planning. More usually, the various line departments have the responsibility for achieving quality by utilizing modern quality control methods, while the quality audit is done by a specialized staff department.

Under this Japanese system of organizing work, it became logical to extend training in quality control to the category of "Gemba-cho." The Gemba-cho is a sort of "working foreman," i.e., he is partly a work leader and teacher, and sometimes a production worker. Since this category of Gemba-cho consists of many thousands of people, it was necessary to resort to mass media of training. Japanese ingenuity rose to the occasion by creating new training forms as well as by adapting conventional forms.

The conventional forms consisted of textbooks and manuals such as Professor Ishikawa's textbook, *Introduction to Quality Control*. First published in 1952, the third edition (1964 and 1966) has grown to 350 pages and to two volumes, and now includes much on management of quality control. The more recent (1959-1960) *Quality Control Text Book for Foremen* runs to 234 pages and provides cook-book information on quality improvement as well as quality control. This manual is edited by Professor Ishikawa's group of consultants in the Japanese Union of Scientists and Engineers (JUSE) and is published by JUSE Press Co.

Turning now to the unconventional training forms, the first of these was the radio broadcast courses in quality control. The pioneering course was a series of 91 lessons of 15 minutes each, broadcast daily from June through September 1956, and repeated later in the year. This course was repeated annually through 1962. The radio text for these courses sold over 100,000 copies!

A television lecture series was next. The first of these ran from April 1960 to March 1961 and consisted of a series of weekly lectures, each 30 minutes long.

The journal "Quality Control for the Foreman" (GEMBA TO QC) was launched in 1962 on a quarterly basis. Now on a monthly basis, it has a lively, practical content, and a circulation of over 28,000 copies.

Annual Foremen's QC Conferences started in November 1962. (November is designated as Quality month in all of Japan, and the Q flags really fly all over.) These conferences are staged in various industrial cities, with a burgeoning attendance.

With such a background, the logic of extending training to the rank and file becomes more evident. Given an extensive training of the Gemba-cho, his ability to put this training to use is in proportion to the use he can make of the resources around him, and especially the human resources. It remained to find a mechanism for using these human resources, and this mechanism turned out to be the QC Circle.

Evidently the initiative for the QC Circle concept came from the editors of GEMBA TO QC, who saw in the non-supervisors an immense potential for contribution through training and motivation. The QC Circle idea was born in about 1962. By August 1966, there were about 8,000 *registered* circles, with a membership of over 120,000 employees. The unregistered circles probably involve an even greater number of employees.

The regional and national organization for QC Circles followed as a matter of course. The journal GEMBA TO QC became, naturally, a national journal for the QC Circles as well. The first regional conference was held in May 1963. A little over three years later, the 20th conference was in session.

HOW THE QC CIRCLE MOVEMENT SPREADS

Now that these circles already number in the thousands, the pattern for creating new ones has become well established.

The concept makes its way into a company through awareness of successful results in other companies. This awareness comes from the numerous success stories in GEMBA TO QC; from attendance at the annual foremen's QC conferences; from attendance at QC Circle conferences; from visiting companies which have active programs going. Further stimulus comes from the internal QC staff people or from the external consultants who are on the staff of GEMBA TO QC, or of the Japanese Union of Scientists and Engineers.

As the gathering awareness creates a favorable atmosphere, various Gemba encourage the formation of QC Circles in their departments. Each circle is trained, mainly off the job, by a combinaiton of three training methods.

1. Training by the book. This is a course, of 10 to 20 hours duration, in specific techniques, mainly:

— The Pareto analysis to find the ''vital few'' problems
— The Cause and Effect Diagram (The Ishikawa diagram)
— Histograms
— Graphs
— Control charts
— Stratification
— Binomial probability paper

2. Discussion of cases worked out in other companies, as reported in GEMBA TO QC.

3. Discussion of internal quality problems, solved and unsolved.

With the training behind them, the Circle identifies a problem to be solved, tackles it and solves it. It then tackles another, and another. (Some have solved over 60 problems.) The record of successful internal solutions breeds other QC Circles within the same company, and the movement spreads. As the number of Circles in one company grows, there arise new opportunities for stimulating interest and action. Companies organize in-house conferences of their QC Circles, providing opportunity for publicizing results and for giving recognition to the Circles who achieved the results.

At the Matsushita Training Center near Osaka, I saw a large training facility devoted to QC Circle activities. The walls of this large room were literally pa-

pered with the record of projects successfully carried out at various plants —
projects on transformers, tuners, speakers, resistors, etc. An example is shown
in Fig. 2. In addition to the reports, there were pictures of the members of the
Circles which had achieved the results, along with other forms of recognition.

In the Toyota Motor Company plant in Nagoya, I saw use made of a most
interesting information center in each shop department. The information center
consists mainly of a large bulletin board, plus satellite boards for exhibiting samples of defects and such. The bulletin boards commonly exhibit:

— a diagram of the flow of the process, including location of control stations
  as well as control points and control levels at each station;
— the Pareto analysis for key defects;
— the Ishikawa cause and effect diagram for these key defects;
— data on current quality performance, usually in the form of control charts.
  (The bulletin boards also carry some non-quality information such as departmental cost trends, the safety record, etc.)

An interesting diagram on one board was a matrix listing on one axis the operations performed in the department, and on the other axis the names of the
operators. The chart showed which operators had qualified to perform which operations, and was displayed for information and motivation.

Figure 2 — A Display of the Records of Successfully Completed Projects.

EXAMPLE OF CIRCLE ACTIVITIES FOR TQC

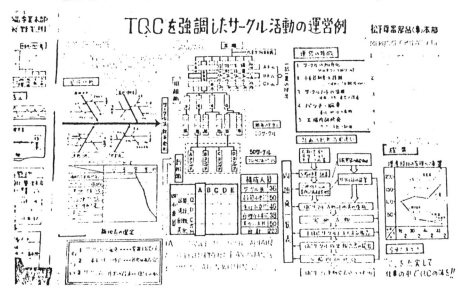

The most successful QC Circles have the opportunity to get their projects published in GEMBA TO QC, and to attend the QC Circle conferences. These are important forms of recognition to the foremen and workers involved, many of whom are astonishingly young. One of the interesting projects reported on the walls of the Matsushita Training Center was by a QC Circle of four men and three girls whose ages ranged from 16 to 23, with an average of 20.3 (Matsushita's car radio assembly line has several QC Circles in addition to that of Shoko, Reiko and Mitsuko. The ages of these circle members range from 15 to 26, the average being 19.)

The published reports of projects completed are remarkably well documented. The typical report relies heavily on graphic presentation to tell the story. It is the rule, not the exception, for these reports to show:

— Sketches of the product under study.
— The flow diagram of the process.
— The Pareto analysis identifying the vital few troubles.
— The Ishikawa Cause and Effect Diagram mapping out the variables which might be causing the trouble.
— Histograms, frequency tables, control charts and other statistical analyses of data.
— Charts showing the reductions in defects resulting from the project.
— A computation of the Yen of cost improvement.

In companies with a firm history of use of QC Circles, the collective results have begun to show up in the company planning and budgeting as something substantial and predictable — a form of budgeted cost reduction.

THE ROLE OF THE HIERARCHY

While participation in the QC Circles is voluntary, the existence of such Circles raises practical questions of how to coordinate the work of the Circles with that of the hierarchy. When the company is large, and the QC Circles number in the hundreds, this coordination can become complex, since the grain of the two structures runs in different directions. To date, the experience gained has already identified some helpful principles of coordination. One of these is a dual approach to selection of projects. Projects for the QC Circles are proposed in two ways:

1. By the Circle itself, based on its job knowledge plus the collective creativity of the members.
2. By the management hierarchy. For example, the company goal may be to cut rejects from 5 percent to 2 percent. Breaking this goal down into sub-objectives can result in projects for QC Circles.

From the nature of things, the first projects taken on by a QC Circle are those of control — improved control of the local process, reduction of operator-controllable defects. As a firmer grip is secured on these control problems, more elaborate projects are chosen, involving breakthrough into new levels of performance. Here the Circle finds itself conducting more sophisticated analyses, setting up experiments and otherwise walking boldly into the unknown.

As these more elaborate projects are tackled, the QC Circle may find itself faced with causes and influences which are outside of its own department. Commonly such matters are beyond the scope of the Circle, which is necessarily limited to intra-departmental problems. Except for the Gemba-cho, the members of the Circle are limited in their knowledge of, and access to, the happenings in other departments. For example, Kanto Auto-Works Company has found it useful to set up a two-way feedback of findings of the QC Circles and of the field service mechanics, to promote the Circle leader's quality and cost consciousness, and to provide special guidance in pre-delivery inspection and maintenance work. Such communications can be made only through the hierarchy.

When problems of a inter-departmental nature are encountered, the approach is to broaden the communication through a QC Circle leaders' meeting or a QC Circle joint meeting. If a project of an interdepartmental nature needs to be taken on, it is assigned to a QC *Team*. The QC Team is quite different from the QC Circle as is seen in the following comparison:

Aspect	The QC Circle	The QC Team
Creation	Voluntary	By management order; hierarchical
Identification of projects	Mostly by the Circle	Mostly through management planning
Scope of activities	Intra-departmental	Inter-departmental
Membership	Gemba-cho and his non-supervisors	Gemba-cho and supervisors and engineers
Life	Can be continuous, for project after project	For this project only

An added problem facing the hierarchy is that of providing the training facilities, the budgets, the support for aiding the Circles in their work, the follow through to make remedies effective, and the means for giving recognition. In a large company like Nippon Kokan K.K., or Kobe Steel (which has about 1000 QC Circles), this requires positive organization machinery. To date, the companies have gladly paid the price, since the return on investment has been eminently satisfactory.

There is also evidence to suggest that the QC Circle concept may be broadened considerably, in two respects.

1. To deal with non-quality problems as well as with quality problems, i.e., a universal way of using non-supervisors for projects of all sorts — for improvements in cost, safety, productivity, etc. Some of this has happened. Matsushita's "QC" Circles are in fact involved with some non-QC matters. Even the company chauffeurs have a QC Circle. However, for the QC Circle movement to broaden out into an all-purpose movement will require, as a pre-requisite, that additional tool kits be developed, one for each area of subject matter. The success of the Circle movement as applied to quality control has, to an important degree, been due to the existence of a kit of tools which simplify greatly the attack on quality

problems. Some of the tools in this kit, e.g., the Pareto principle, are universals — they are helpful in solving *any* problem. However, as applied to other subject matter, the kit is incomplete, and would need to be supplemented.

2. As a leading device for strengthening relations between the company and the employee body. During my April 1966 seminars in Japan, several company directors made this point. In Nippon Kayaku K.K., the managers stimulated a QC Circle movement as part of a defensive program to prevent leadership of the work force from being taken over by radical agitators. The resulting QC Circles played a significant role as part of a total program of "turning around" the performance of a sick plant.

THE MOTIVATIONAL BASE

To a Westerner, the most astonishing aspect of the QC Circles has nothing to do with quality control. What is astonishing is the degree to which the Japanese have succeeded in harnessing the energy, ingenuity and enthusiasm of the work force to the unsolved problems of the company. In the West, (on both sides of Churchill's "Iron Curtain") it is difficult enough to do this during working hours. The Japanese have gone beyond this — they have done it outside of working hours as well. It is of the utmost importance to understand how it is that the Japanese have been able to bring this off.

First of all, it must be recognized that the Japanese manager has, for the most part, retained the leadership of the work force, and has not lost it to the Union, the politician, or the intellectual. In Japan, the usual, traditional relationship of companies to employees has been one of lifelong employment, with the company voluntarily assuming important social responsibilities: sick benefits, unemployment benefits, old age benefits, etc. In the non-Communist West, the tradition has been otherwise. Companies generally did not voluntarily provide these benefits. (Even those which did usually did it badly — they were guilty of "paternalism.") In consequence, the work force was driven to find elsewhere the solutions to the problems of unemployment, sickness, old age. New leadership sprang up to propose collective solutions, and the political power of the many made these proposals effective over the resistance of the managers. In the process, the leadership of the men passed from the managers to someone else, and still rests there. The Western manager may look askance at the high fringe benefit percentages of Japanese companies (as do some Japanese managers). But the Western company has paid the price both ways — it is taxed to pay the benefits, and has lost the leadership to boot. To regain this leadership is a long journey, and the present generation of managers will not make it (in my opinion).

Secondly, the Japanese concept of organization of work differs markedly from that followed in the West, especially that followed in the United States. American companies, under the Taylor influence, have gone far down the road of separating manufacturing planning from execution. The engineers play the dominant, if not the exclusive, role in planning, leaving to the production supervision the execution of the plan. The Western European countries tend to give the top managers the main role in the planning, really a dual role of directing and engineering.

However, the Japanese evolution resulted in less formal planning, either by the engineers or the top managers. There remained a considerable residue of planning to be done by someone else, i.e., the production supervision. This evolution has, of course, enlarged the responsibility of the Gemba-cho. In turn, the carrying out of these broader responsibilities has broadened the skills and effectiveness of the Gemba-cho. (We have some of this in America, in some job shops and in some service departments, where there has been no tradition of extensive use of engineers for planning.)

Finally, the priority of industrial motivational incentives in the Japanese culture is quite different from that prevailing in the West. However illogical this priority may seem to the Westerner, it is very logical to the Japanese. As well as I was able to determine, here is the order of importance:

1. *Improving the company's performance*. Under a tradition of lifetime association with one company, and enlightened company practices as to employee welfare problems, the employee has a stake in the company's health, and responds to opportunities to do something about it. This loyalty to the company is evidently not limited to the company as an abstraction. There are loyalties to the particular shop and to the local work group which can contribute further to the overall relationship between the company and the work force.

2. *Self-improvement*. The Japanese zeal for learning and for doing attaches itself to opportunities for training and for creativity. This self-improvement is also one of the tools for by-passing seniority as the basis for promotion.

3. *Recognition*. The QC Circle movement has enlarged the social standing of the Gemba-cho, who previously had not participated fully in social recognition. Opportunities now exist for the Gemba-cho to get out to conferences, to visit other companies, and even to become a member of a team to go abroad to study foreign practice. The journal GEMBA TO QC is itself a recognition of a status of importance. Collectively it all adds up to quite a rise in social stature.

4. *Creativity amid boredom*. Particularly among non-supervisors, and to a degree among all who work on the factory floor, the day-to-day job can be monotonous and boresome to an oppressive degree. If essential human needs (ego needs, social needs, creativity, self-fulfillment) are not met on the job, the employee must find them elsewhere — in his hobbies, in sports, in non-company associations. By providing a group opportunity for creativity with respect to the job (though out of regular hours) the company has provided a new opportunity to neutralize the problems of boredom and monotony.

5. *Money incentives*. it may come as a surprise to a Westerner that this incentive (for joining a QC Circle) has the lowest priority. Yet such seems to be the case. There is wide variation in practice so far as paying for time spent is concerned. Some companies make no payment at all. At Kobe Steel Company, one hour a month is paid for; the rest is not. The Matsushita girls were paid at rates equal to half of their regular pay (not time and one-half) plus tea and cake. Some companies pay at full time rates for the out-of-hours work of the QC Circles. The above relates to payment for *time* spent out-of-hours. In the case of *results* achieved, there is no payment as a direct consequence of such results. There is,

however, an indirect effect. The results of a successful project improve the company's profit, and thereby the employee bonuses which are commonly geared to company profits by one formula for all employees.

As it happens, Matsushita has recently conducted a morale survey among QC Circle members. All workers mentioned the benefit of learning through the studies. In addition, they pointed out the following advantages:

1. By attending the QC Circle meetings, they acquired the ability to speak in public.
2. They made more friends and this contributed to a more cheerful atmosphere in the workshop.
3. They became more conscious of the importance of their jobs and their responsibility, and through the awareness of this importance, now have more pride in their jobs.
4. They improved their personality and acquired the ability to concentrate on solution of problems. These experiences with the QC Circle they apply in their home life.

COMPARISON WITH OTHER MOTIVATIONAL PROGRAMS

Inevitably the QC Circle concept must be compared with other motivational forms. What is different about it? In what respects is it limited in application to the Japanese culture, and in what respects is it based on universals?

To make this comparison, we might look at a wide assortment of motivational schemes as practiced in the West: the long-standing systems of piece work; the familiar suggestion systems in force in many companies; the system of Stakhanovism and its derivatives as practiced in Eastern Europe; the Scanlon plan of joint committees for improving productivity; and, because of current interest, the Zero Defects (ZD) family of programs.

We may look at these various plans from a number of standpoints:

1. *Voluntary or compulsory?* Joining the QC Circle is voluntary, and this characterizes most motivational schemes. Piece work is an exception. So also is the ''voluntary'' signing of ZD pledge cards which can hardly be considered voluntary, though most of the rest of the ZD activity is left to voluntary action.

2. *Out-of-hours or on the job.* Here the out-of-hours QC Circle is virtually unique. This feature may be unique to Japan as well. In Western countries it is common for employees to take training courses on ''their own time.'' However, in no Western country known to me would there be any significant response by the work force to studying projects on their own time, unless this were negotiated through the Unions, and paid for at acceptable rates of pay. In the Eastern European countries there may be some of this, but I am not clear on this aspect of their practice.

3. *Premises as to need for analysis.* The QC Circle concept starts with the assumption that the causes of poor quality performance are not known, and that there is need for analysis to discover what actually causes the poor performance.

Except for the Scanlon plan, the other programs largely assume, as an axiomatic belief, that the work force could do better but is holding back for no good reason. While in all companies there are instances which can support this assumption, on a broad basis, the assumption is defective, and is misleading to many, many managers and companies all over the world.

4. *Need for prior training in use of the tools of analysis.* The QC Circle concept is unique in accepting this need. This is, of course, consistent with the belief that the causes of poor performance are not really known. Other motivational systems, founded mainly on the prior assumption that the work force "can but won't," see no need for training in how to analyze, i.e., what is there to analyze if we know the causes at the outset? It is a tribute to the Japanese that they have recognized this need for prior training.

Elements of the Plan	As Practiced In	
	Conventional Motivational Plans	QC Circles
Choice of projects	Left up to employee to identify his own project	Some projects identified by management; others identified by the QC Circle
Training in how to analyze a project	None provided	Formal training program provided. Out-of-hours; voluntary
Analysis of the project	By employee himself or with such aid as he can muster; otherwise, by formal suggestion which is analyzed by someone else	Analysis is by the QC Circle, out-of-hours, using training tools previously provided
Payment for time spent	None	Varies from no pay to full pay for hours spent
Payment for successful idea	Definite payment varying with value of idea	No payment. Indirect effect on company profit and resulting bonus which uses one formula for all employees
Non-financial incentives	Opportunity for creativity and recognition; pride of workmanship	Opportunity for training; opportunity for creativity and recognition; membership in a group response to company leadership

5. *Group or individual analysis?* The QC Circle is designed for group study. Except for the Scanlon plan, the rest all look to individuals for contribution.

6. *Identification of projects.* The QC Circle concept provides for projects to be proposed by the company hierarchy as well as by the QC Circle itself. Again except for the Scanlon plan, other motivational plans look mainly to the individual to identify "his own" project.

7. *Conduct of the analysis.* The QC Circle conducts its own analysis, though with access to the hierarchy if needed. To a degree, all systems provide for self-analysis, but for the most part the analysis, if any, is left for someone else, e.g., a suggestion blank is filled out and dropped into a box. Here again, the prior training has served a vital purpose, by making the QC Circle largely self-sufficient as to analysis.

8. *The reward.* The QC Circle emphasis is mostly on non-financial rewards, featuring improvement (company improvement, self-improvement) as a goal in

its own right. The system of Stakhanovism also has this feature, though emphasizing the abstraction of Communism, or its derivative of "building a better Socialist world." The ZD schemes stress pride of workmanship. The piece work and the suggestion systems rely on money incentives, the amount being related to the value of the work or the suggestion.

9. *Follow through to make changes effective and set up controls* Here the QC Circles play a larger role than is found in other motivational systems, again because of being trained in how to play this role.

It is evident that the QC Circle is different enough to be regarded as a new industrial form. The Scanlon plans have some of the features, but are not really based on the work force — they involve joint committees of managers, Union officials and the work force. (Union officials are debarred from membership in the QC Circles.)

The table above summarizes the foregoing comparison as applied to creative projects.

MORE THAN MOTIVATION

Of the utmost importance is the fact that, through the QC Circles, the Japanese have made a clean bread with a tired, outworn theory which plagues the West. This is the theory that the company's quality troubles are due to operator indifference, blunder and even sabotage. Under this theory, the operators could solve the company's quality problems if only the right motivational lever could be found and thrown.

The QC Circle concept starts with a different set of beliefs:

• we don't really know the cause of our quality troubles; we don't even know which are the main troubles. Hence,
• we must teach people how to analyze the trouble pattern to identify the main troubles. Also,
• we must teach people how to list the suspected causes of the main troubles, and how to discover which are the real causes. Then
• we must help people to secure remedies for these real causes. Finally,
• we must teach people how to hold the gains through modern control methods.

All this is in refreshing contrast to the painted, noisy spectacles which characterize all too many of our motivational programs.[3] The speeches are made, the posters go up, the pledge cards are signed, the hot potato is thrown into the lap of the operators. Yet, except as a show for customer relations, what good is it if the basic assumptions are defective? Have these assumptions been checked? Are the main troubles really operator-controllable? Can the operators, by themselves, discover what to do differently from what they have been doing? If these assumptions are not sound, the structure built on them cannot be sound either.

CONCLUSION

The QC Circle movement, standing by itself, must be characterized as a brilliant achievement — a *tour de force* in management leadership. Nowhere else have I seen industrial companies succeed in so constructively harnessing the interest, the time and the ingenuity of the work force to the myriads of intradepartmental problems — not only problems of control, but problems of breakthrough as well.

Whether the QC Circle concept can be adapted to other cultures is at present open to serious doubt. At the June 1966 Conference of the European Organization for Quality Control (in Stockholm, Sweden), I related the QC Circle story from the lecture platform. It turned out to be the high point of the conference. The questions from the audience required that a special, added session be set up, devoted solely to the QC Circle story. At this special session, and in the corridor discussions thereafter, it became evident that no one envisioned readily how to make the QC Circle concept effective in any other culture. It is amazing that such should be the universal reaction.

Finally, it is well to note the broader setting of which the QC Circles are a part. That broader setting is the revolution which the Japanese have created in their approach to quality. Here I venture to publish, for the first time, the prediction I have made in my 1966 lectures (in America, Japan, Sweden and Yugoslavia).

This prediction is based on seeing, at first hand, the trend of events in Japan and in a good many other countries over the last two decades. During those decades the Japanese, through a revolution in quality control practices, have already attained a world competitive position, though starting with the worst quality reputation among the industrial nations. Now there is evidence that the energy which created this revolution, far from being spent, is still in full vigor.

In my observation, no other nation is so completely unified on the importance of good quality achievement, so eager to discover and adopt the best practices being followed in other countries, so avid in training all company levels and functions in modern methods of controlling quality, so vigilant in regulating the quality of exported goods. To be sure, there is progress along these fronts in all countries, but nowhere else is there the broad-based sense of devotion and especially, the *sense of urgency* which is so evident among the Japanese. Witnessing their accelerated pace, and comparing this with the pedestrian progress of other countries, the conclusion is inescapable:

The Japanese are headed for world quality leadership, and will attain it in the next two decades, because no one else is moving there at the same pace.

REFERENCES

1. Juran, J.M., *Managerial Breakthrough,* McGraw-Hill Book Co., Inc., New York, 1964, Chap. 4, "The Pareto Principle."
2. Juran, J. M. Ed., *Quality Control Handbook,* 2nd ed., McGraw-Hill Book Co., Inc., 1962, pp. 11-13.
3. Juran, J. M., "Quality Problems, Remedies and Nostrums," *Ind. Qual. Control,* 22, 647-653 (June 1966).

WHAT HAPPENED IN JAPAN?
W. Edwards Deming

INTRODUCTION AND PURPOSE OF THIS ARTICLE

The competitive position of many Japanese products, according to the testimony of their own manufacturers, has been achieved largely through understanding and use of the statistical control of quality in the broad sense (*vide infra*). Statistical techniques were not wholly responsible for what happened, as deeper perspective of later paragraphs will bring forth, but statistical techniques certainly played an important role in the miracle. The first step was to fire up desire on the part of management to improve quality and to impart confidence that improvement was possible; that utilization of statistical techniques would help.

The purpose of this article is to offer some observations on the causes of success in Japan, from the viewpoint of the statistical control of quality, with the thought that energetic application of statistical techniques in other parts of the world, including the United States, might have healthy impact. Appreciation of what happened in Japan might also be taken seriously on programs of scientific and professional societies that are interested in statistical methods applied to production.

NINE FEATURES OF THE STATISTICAL CONTROL OF QUALITY IN JAPAN

As I see it, there are nine main reasons for the success and speed of application of the statistical control of quality by Japanese manufacturers:

1. Genuine and resolute determination on the part of management to improve quality.

2. Confidence in their ability to lead Japanese industry forth from the bad reputation that Japanese products had built up in the past, confidence in Japanese scientific ability, and confidence in Japanese skills. Confidence also, I might add, in statistical methods.

3. They were Japanese, with industrial experience, and with an inbred pride of workmanship.

4. Japanese top management, statisticians, and engineers, learned the statistical control of quality in the broad sense of Shewhart, as defined further on.

5. Management took immediate interest and learned something about the techniques of the statistical control of quality as well as about the possible results, and still more about what their own responsibilities would be. Proper arrangements for contact with top management, at the outset, was one of the fortunate features of statistical education in Japan.

6. Statistical education became a continuing process. Statistical methods can-

This article is based in part on an article published in SANKHYA (Calcutta), series B, vol. 28: 1966.

not be installed once for all and left to run, like a new carpet or a new dean. They require constant adaptation, revision, extension, new theory, and new knowledge of the statistical properties of materials. Perhaps the main accomplishment in the eight-day courses that began in 1950 was to impart inspiration to learn more about statistical methods.

7. The Japanese learned the difference between a statistical problem and one in engineering, chemistry, management, or marketing. They learned that statistical knowledge is not a substitute for knowledge of engineering or of other subject-matter, and that knowledge of engineering does not solve statistical problems.

8. Japanese manufacturers took on the job themselves. They did not look to their government nor to ours for help. When they arranged for consultation, they sent a ticket and a cheque. They gave financial and moral support to statistical education, mainly through the Union of Japanese Scientists and Engineers.

9. Suggestions and technical information have a fairly clear channel from lower to higher levels of supervision and management. A Japanese executive is never too old or too successful to listen to the possibility of doing it a better way.

One ought also to mention the stimulus of a prize offered annually in the name of an American statistician* to the Japanese manufacturer who, in the opinion of the Committee on Awards, has made the greatest advance in quality of his product during the past calendar-year. Many companies compete for the prize, often laying plans years in advance. Although only one company, or at most two, can receive the prize, the continual competition of many companies has had an important leavening effect in quality.

LECTURES TO TOP MANAGEMENT

Lectures to management, beginning in 1950, brought up a few simple questions to think about. I am not an economist, nor a business-man, only a statistician, but some conclusions seemed inescapable. Why was it necessary to improve quality of Japanese products? Because Japanese products must now become competitive: the market in Asia was lost. The market for poor quality in the western world is a losing game.

It is not necessary to raise all your own food, it seemed to me. Chicago doesn't. Switzerland doesn't. It may be smarter for Japan to import food and pay for it with exports. There is a market for quality. How do you build quality, and a reputation for quality?

No country is so able as Japan, I pointed out, with its vast pool of skilled and educated industrial manpower, and with so many highly proficient engineers, mathematicians, and statisticians, to improve quality. Statistical methods could help: in fact, realization of any goal to raise quality to a sufficiently high level would be impossible without statistical methods on a broad scale. Seeing their serious determination, predicted at an assembly of Japanese manufacturers in Tokyo in July 1950 that in five years, manufacturers in other industrial nations would be on the defensive and that in ten years the reputation for top quality in Japanese products would be firmly established the world over.

*Editor's Note: The American statistician is W. Edwards Deming.

Statistical techniques became a living, vital, and essential force in all stages of Japanese industry. The whole world knows how well Japanese manufacturers met the predicted time-table.

Management must assume the responsibility to optimize the use of statistical methods in all stages of manufacture, and to understand the statistical control of quality as a never-ending cycle of improved methods of manufacture, test, consumer research, and re-design of product. Lectures described in simple terms management's responsibility to understand the capability of the process, management's responsibility for common causes (*vide infra*) and the economic loss from failure to accept these responsibilities.

Japanese manufacturers took these arguments seriously to the point of doing something about them with concerted effort. A little fire here, and a little there, would be too slow. Concerted effort meant cooperation amongst competitors, assistance to vendors, and — probably for the first time in Japan — immediate attention to the demands of the consumer, and need for consumer research on a continuing basis, with feed-back for re-design.

Results were spectacular, even after only one year, especially in productivity per man-hour, with little new machinery. One steel company saved 28 percent on consumption of coal per ton of steel. A huge pharmaceutical company put out three times as much finished product per unit of input of raw material. A big cable company reduced greatly the amount of paper and re-work on insulated wire and cable. Many companies reduced accidents to a permanent low level. Improvement in quality and dependability came in due course, and in five years, as predicted, many Japanese products had earned respect to the point of fear in markets the world over.

DEFINITION OF THE STATISTICAL CONTROL OF QUALITY

The Japanese never knew the statistical control of quality in any way but in the broad sense introduced by Shewhart.* The statistical control of quality was defined in plain English in 1950 and ever after in big letters like this:

THE STATISTICAL CONTROL OF QUALITY IS THE APPLICATION OF STATISTICAL PRINCIPLES AND TECHNIQUES IN ALL STAGES OF PRODUCTION, DIRECTED TOWARD THE ECONOMIC MANUFACTURE OF A PRODUCT THAT IS MAXIMALLY USEFUL AND HAS A MARKET.

Translated into action, this definition of the statistical control of quality means:

1. Use of statistical methods to construct meaningful specifications of raw materials, piece-parts, assemblies, and performance of finished product, by appropriate statistical design.

2. Assistance to suppliers. Any raw material or piece-part is someone's finished product. Improvement of quality of incoming materials from vendors or

---

*W. A. Shewhart, *The Economic Control of Quality of Manufactured Product* (Van Nostrand, 1931); *Statistical Method from the Viewpoint of Quality Control* (The Graduate School, Department of Agriculture, Washington 1939). "Nature and Origin of Standards of Quality," *Bell System Technical Journal,* xxxvii, 1958: pp. 1-22. No attempt is made here to give a full list of Dr. Shewhart's papers.

from a previous operation is one of the most important requirements in a program of quality.

3. Control of process. Detection of special causes by statistical methods ($\overline{X}$- and R-charts, run-charts, design of experiment, and other techniques). Distinction between special causes and common causes, with examples. Separation of responsibility for finding and removing:

    a. Special causes of variability (local).
    b. Common or general causes of variability (upper management).
4. Use of acceptance sampling where appropriate.
5. Consumer research. Test of product in service.
6. Re-design of product.
7. Tests of new product, in the laboratory and in service.
8. Use of proper theory for finding optimum levels of inventory, and for economy in distribution.

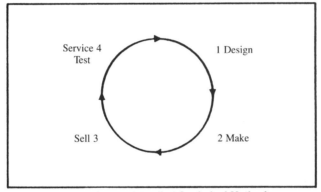

Figure 1. Cycle of Applied Statistical Methods.

The statistical method shown in Fig. 1 was taught as a continuing process, in a never-ending cycle:

1. Design a product
2. Make it
3. Try to sell it
4. Test it in service
5. Repeat Step 1. Re-design the product on the basis of tests in service.
6. Repeat Step 2.
7. Repeat Step 3, etc.

SPECIAL (ASSIGNABLE) CONTRASTED WITH COMMON (GENERAL) CAUSES OF VARIATION OR OF WRONG LEVEL

One of the important uses of statistical techniques is to help an engineer or scientist to distinguish between two types of cause, and hence to fix (with adjustable risk of being wrong) the responsibility for correction of undesired variability or of undesired level.

21

Confusion between common causes and special causes is one of the most serious mistakes of administration in industry, and in public administration as well. Unaided by statistical techniques, man's natural reaction to trouble of any kind, such as an accident, high rejection-rate, stoppage of production (of shoes, for example, because of breakage of thread), is to blame a specific operator or machine. Anything bad that happens, it might seem, is somebody's fault, and it wouldn't have happened if he had done his job right.

Actually, however, the cause of trouble may be common to all machines, e.g., poor thread, the fault of management, whose policy may be to buy thread locally or from a subsidiary. Demoralization, frustration, and economic loss are inevitable results of attributing trouble to some specific operator, foreman, machine, or other local condition, when the trouble is actually a common cause, affecting all operators and machines, and correctible only at a higher level of management.

The specific local operator is powerless to act on a common cause. He cannot change specifications of raw materials. He cannot alter the policy of purchase of materials. He cannot change the lighting system. He might as well try to change the speed of rotation of the earth.

A mistake common amongst workers in the statistical control of quality, and amongst writers of textbooks on the subject, is to assume that they have solved all the problems once they have weeded out most of the special causes. The fact is, instead, that they are at that point just ready to tackle the most important problems of variation, namely, the common causes.

SPECIAL CAUSES OF VARIATION

Variation of any quality-characteristic is to be expected. The question is whether the variation arises from a special cause, or from common causes. A point outside limits on a control chart indicates the existence of a special cause. Special causes are what Shewhart called assignable causes. The name is not important: the concept is.

Statistical techniques, based as they are on the theory of probability, enable us to govern the risk of being wrong in the interpretation of a test. Statistical techniques defend us, almost unerringly, against the costly and demoralizing practice of blaming variability and rejections on to the wrong person or machine. At the same time, they detect almost unerringly the existence of a special cause when it is worth searching for.

What statistical tests do, in effect, is not just to detect the existence of a special cause, or the absence of special causes: they do more: they indicate the level of responsibility for finding the cause and from removing it. The contribution that statistical methods make in placing responsibility squarely where it belongs (at the local operator, at the foreman, or at the door of higher management) can hardly be over-estimated.

This aspect of the statistical control of quality was not appreciated, I believe, in the earlier history of statistical methods in American industry, and is even now neglected. The Japanese had the benefit of advanced thinking on the matter.

COMMON CAUSES OF VARIATION AND
OF WRONG SPREAD, WRONG LEVEL

If we succeed in removing all special causes worth removing, then henceforth (until another special cause appears), variations in quality behave as if they came from common causes. That is, they have the same random scatter as if the units of product were being drawn by random numbers from a common supply. The remaining causes of variability are then common to all treatments, to all operators, to all machines, etc.

Some common causes are in the following list. The reader may supply others, appropriate to his own plant and conditions.

• Poor light
• Humidity not suited to the process
• Vibration
• Poor instruction and poor supervision
• Lack of interest of management in a program for quality
• Poor food in the cafeteria
• Inept management
• Raw materials not suited to the requirements
• Procedures not suited to the requirements
• Machines not suited to the requirements
• Mixing product from streams of production, each having small variability, but a different level

Common causes are usually much more difficult to identify than specific causes, and more difficult to correct. In the first place, carefully designed tests may be required to identify a common cause. Then problems really commence. Would it be economically feasible to change the specifications for incoming material; to change the design of the product; to install new machinery? to change the lighting? to put in air-conditioning? Only management can take action on these things. If the trouble lies in management itself, who is going to make the correction?

Although the detection and removal of special causes are important, it is a fact that some of the finest examples of improvement of quality have come from effort directed at common causes of variation and at causes of wrong level. One example, interesting because it is outside the usual sphere of industrial production, is the improvement of quality and decrease in the cost of statistical data put out by the Census in Washington. For many years, effort has been directed at common causes of the system that lead to error and to high cost, as well as elimination of special causes. The result today is quality, reliability, and speed of current statistical series that are the envy of other statistical organizations in the U.S. and abroad, and at costs that are about a third of what private industry in this country pays out for similar surveys in consumer research.

OTHER STATISTICAL TECHNIQUES

Consumer research was taught as an integral part of the statistical control of quality. In fact, small surveys of household inventories and requirements of pharmaceuticals, sewing machines, bicycles, and the like, constituted part of the course in sampling the summer of 1951. These have been designated by the Japanese as the first studies in consumer research to be carried out by Japanese companies with the aid of modern methods of sampling.

Shewhart charts were taught in Japan as statistical tools for the economic detection of the existence of special causes of variation, not as tools that actually find the cause. However, emphasis was on action to find the cause and remove it, once a point goes outside limits. Once statistical control is established, then do something about common causes.

Acceptance sampling was taught as a scheme of protection (provided one will really reject and screen a lot when the sample contains more than the allowable number of defects). The specification of unit of product is of course vital. However important it be, a vendor does not know how to predict the cost of making a product unless he has in hand, in addition, the plan by which his lots will be sampled by the purchaser and accepted or rejected. How big is a lot? What is to be done with pieces found to be defective? Answers to these questions are a necessary part of any plan of acceptance, if vendor and purchaser understand each other. The plan of acceptance sampling is a specification of a contract for lot.

Acceptance sampling was frequently at first confused in America with process-control. Some people looked upon it as a detector of special causes. Other people supposed that acceptance sampling furnished estimates of the quality of lots. Still others supposed that it separates good lots from bad.

Problems in statistical estimation are very important in industrial production, as in decisions of whether one type of machine is sufficiently better than another to warrant the cost of replacement, or to warrant the higher cost of purchase of a better machine. Consumer research presents hosts of problems in estimation. Determination of the iron-content of a shipload of ore is a common problem in estimation.

In a problem of estimation, one is not seeking to detect the existence of a special cause. He is not trying to discover whether there is a difference such as $p_1 - p_2$ or $x_1 - x_2$ between two processes, or between two machines, standard and proposed. One knows in advance, without spending a nickel on a test, that there is a difference; the only question is how big is the difference?

Statistical calculations using data from two samples (coming from two treatments, two operators, two machines, two processes) provide a basis on which to decide, with a prescribed risk of being wrong, (a) whether it would be economical to proceed as if the two samples came from a common source, or (b) whether it would be more economical to assume the converse, and to proceed as if the difference has its origin in a special cause, not common to the samples, which makes one of the treatments, operators, machines, or processes different from the other. Essential considerations in fixing the probability of being wrong lie in the economic losses to be expected (a) from the failure of being too cautious — failure to make a change that would turn out to be profitable, or (b) from making a change that turns out to be costly and unwarranted.

The teaching of statistical methods in Japan did not confuse statistical estimation, nor Shewhart charts, with statistical test of hypotheses.

The effectiveness of mass education in statistical methods in Japan was more pronounced and more rapid than results observed in the U.S. In the first place, Japan was in 1950 in desperate circumstances. Every minute must count. Second, management was more responsive. Third, practically everyone in attendance at technical sessions in Japan had studied calculus.

A vigorous system of courses for continuation and advancement in theory was instituted by the Union of Japanese Scientists and Engineers. The levels are varied. The duration, days, and hours meet the requirements of engineers who must come from distant points, as well as for those that live in or near Tokyo. Some idea of the thoroughness of the courses for continuation and advancement may be gained by perusal of bulletins from the Union of Japanese Scientists and Engineers.*

An additional point of strength came from the formation of committees to work on new theory, and to investigate various areas of application, such as the sampling of bulk materials (mainly ores), design of experiment, queueing theory, and other problems. The impact of the work of these committees has substantially changed much industrial practice in Japan.

Publication of a journal *Statistical Quality Control* (in Japanese) was started by the Union of Japanese Scientists and Engineers; the journal is now in its 18th year. *Research Reports*, a journal now in its 17th year, has a high reputation amongst mathematical statisticians the world over. A journal specifically for foremen has been started, and one for engineers.

Some idea of the importance of these Japanese publications may be had by noting that in the *International Journal of Abstracts*, a third of the citations refer to Japanese journals.

Many people, in America as elsewhere, in a burst of enthusiasm, confused statistical methods with engineering or with other subject-matter. They would substitute statistical calculations for knowledge of engineering, and then try to solve statistical problems by consulting their own knowledge of engineering.

The Japanese were spared some of these miscalculations.

POWER AND LIMITATION OF
STATISTICAL TECHNIQUES

Advances in uses of statistical techniques would come, the Japanese learned, not by searching a manufacturing plant for a chance to apply this or that tech-

*Kenrchi Koyanagi, ''Statistical Quality Control in Japanese Industry,'' a paper delivered at the national convention of the American Society for Quality Control in Syracuse, 1952. Also, his paper, ''Some Case Histories of Increased Production and Improved Quality Through Simple Techniques in Japanese Industry'' and another paper, ''Education Activities for Industrial Statistics in Japan,'' both presented at the 29th Congress of the International Statistical Institute, Rio De Janeiro, 1955.

nique, but to search the plant for problems, and then to enquire what statistical techniques might be helpful.

No amount of statistical theory will generate a problem. To find problems is the responsibility of management or of the expert in subject-matter (engineering, production, consumer research, medicine). A problem in industry might be simply to enquire whether it would be possible to decrease the variability of some quality-characteristic, and if so, how? The problem might be more complex, such as to question the basic design of a product. It might be comparison of two or more processes or machines. It might be a new idea in a chemical process.

Which quality-characteristic to test and to use in a Shewhart chart, or what questions to ask in a comparison of products in a study of consumer research, is fundamentally a problem in subject-matter. No statistical theory will tell anyone which quality-characteristic to test, although it is necessary to use statistical theory for reliability and economy in the design and interpretation of tests.

Statistical teaching in Japan put emphasis on the responsibility of management and of the engineer to foresee problems and to state them explicitly. Statistical techniques were taught, not as a kit of tools to try out here or there, but as an aid to solution of problems, aids to knowledge and creativity.

The Japanese learned something about what statistical techniques can do, and what they can't do.

Statistical theory, like any other theory, is transferable. The symbols don't care what the problem is, nor what the material is. Therein lies the power of theory: the solution to one problem may aid in the solution of many other problems. Our words *theory* and *theatre* come from the Greek $\theta\epsilon\alpha$ to see, to understand.

There is not one distinct theory of probability for process-control, another theory for acceptance sampling, another for reliability, another for problems of estimation, another for design of experiment, another for testing materials, another for design of studies in for statistics, another for engineering. Instead, there is statistical theory.

Statistical work, in the hands of a statistician, means optimum allocation of human skills and of machines to provide and interpret with speed and reliability as aid to administration, management, and research, the results of tests and of other observations. Other professions (e.g. management, administration) have the same goal, but the statistician is the one that has the skills and tools for accomplishment of the goal.

An essential requirement of the statistician working in industry is to know statistical theory, and to continue to learn more. He must learn something about the subject-matter, of course, in order to work in it, but his contribution will be more successful if he will enhance day by day his knowledge of statistical theory, instead of trying to become expert in the subject-matter. Thus, the statistician need not be an expert in a production process in order to make a contribution to production. He works with people that know production; what the statistician needs to know and do is his own job, statistics, not someone else's job.

On this principle, the efforts of many of Japan's greatest statisticians (which is to say, some of the greatest in the world) found their place in industry.

26

Of course, in a small plant, the same man must sometimes work both as statistician and as engineer. He must nevertheless observe the same rules. He should, to be effective, use only the statistical theory that he understands, and he should use it for the statistical aspects of problems. He should not try to substitute statistical techniques for the basic input of engineering that must go into a problem.

Such principles were woven into the teaching in Japan.

LEARNING FROM THE JAPANESE:
PROSPECT AND PITFALLS
Robert E. Cole

It has become extraordinarily fashionable in recent years for leading management experts to trumpet the potential for learning from the Japanese. Particular
attention has been called to the advantages of Japanese management style and
techniques, especially as they relate to the organization and training of the labor
force.

What accounts for this surge of interest? The enormity of Japan's economic
success as it moved to the second largest economy outside of the communist bloc
and its successful penetration of Western markets are clearly the major factors.
When you are getting hurt at the marketplace, you are inclined to sit up and listen.

Yet, there are still many American managers who would dismiss the Japanese
experience as one that grew out of Japan's unique cultural heritage and therefore
could not have much applicability for U.S. firms. The ranks of this core group,
while still strong, have been thinned by the recent invasion of Japanese-operated
subsidiaries in the United States. The bulk of the reports on this ''invasion'' have
reported the activities of Japanese companies quite favorably. They emphasize
their ability to import Japanese management techniques and philosophy and apply
them successfully to their management of American workers.

This turn of events has made it more difficult for the doubters to claim these
approaches will work only in the rarified atmosphere of Japanese cultural conditions. Above all, the Japanese are now seen as having a winning package that has
catapulted them to success. That American managers are beginning to study carefully and apply Japanese practices in this environment is not surprising. Yet, they
often make such decisions in the absence of very hard data showing the applicability of these practices. For example, the literature on the practices of Japanese
subsidiaries in the United States is very impressionistic and lacks systematic comparisons, not to speak of control groups. Yet, as Herbert Simon (Carnegie Mellon
University's Nobel laureate in economics) has shown us in his observations on
the adoption of computers in the 1960's, management decisions are often based
on the fads of the moment rather than some carefully calculated economic ration-
ality.

In one sense, then, these developments must be reckoned as quite positive. In
the area of worker-manager relationships, American managers have historically
kept themselves unusually insulated from the experiences of other industrial nations; one need only contrast U.S. practices with those in Western Europe where
large amounts of information and learning experiences are exchanged. No doubt
this is a function of the unique relationship worked out in the course of our history
between human and national resources in a relatively isolated geographical setting.

What, then, are the prospects of learning from the Japanese in the area of worker-manager relationships? To answer this question, two approaches are useful:

1. Consider the obverse case — that is, what has been the experience with the Japanese in borrowing from the Americans in this area.

2. Consider the concrete example of Japanese quality control circles (QC Circles).

THE PATTERN OF JAPANESE BORROWING

When the United States was unquestionably the most advanced industrial nation in the early postwar period, in addition to being the conqueror and occupying power of Japan, it was not surprising that the Japanese were willing and eager to learn from American management techniques. Generally, the Japanese were willing to make the assumption that American management techniques must be the most advanced, independent of any objective confirmation. These developments were part of a "management boom," as it was called in Japan, during which American management formulas and techniques were introduced into all spheres of business administration from the 1950's, particularly personnel administration.

How QC Circles Work

A QC circle is a relatively autonomous unit composed of a small group of workers (ideally about ten), usually led by a foreman or senior worker and organized in each work unit. Participants are taught elementary techniques of problem solving including statistical methods. It is in principle a voluntary study group that concentrates on solving job-related quality problems. These problems are broadly conceived as improving methods of production as part of company-wide efforts. Some typical efforts include reducing defects, scrap, rework, and down-time. These activities in turn are expected to lead to cost-reduction and increased productivity. At the same time, the circles focus on improving working conditions and the self-development of workers. The latter includes: development of leadership abilities of foreman and workers, skill development among workers, improvement of worker morale and motivation, the stimulation of teamwork within the work groups, and recognition of worker achievements. Above all, the circles involve recognition that hourly workers have an important contribution to make to the organization.

The attention the Japanese pay to Western developments in management theory and practice is still astonishing. A significant component of the large literature on management and work in the Japanese language consists of translations and analyses of the work of Western scholars. One estimate puts translations alone at 9 percent of the some 1,000 books published a year. The research and proposals of American organizational specialists such as Rensis Likert, Peter Drucker, Chris Argyris, Douglas McGregor, and Frederick Herzberg are widely known, and the use of their ideas is commonplace in large Japanese firms. Indeed, Japanese managers are often surprised when they visit the United States to find such hostility to their ideas on the part of many American managers.

We can get a sense of the Japanese capacity to borrow and adapt Western organizational technology to their own needs through a brief tracing of the introduction of QC circles. QC circles may represent the most innovative process of bor-

29

rowing and adaptation in the personnel policies of large Japanese companies in the postwar period.

Before 1945, Japan had only moderate experience with modern methods of statistical quality control. An early postwar effort was organized by U.S. occupation officials to have American statisticians go to Japan and teach American wartime industrial standards to Japanese engineers and statisticians. Prominent in this early effort was a series of postwar lectures beginning in 1950 undertaken by Dr. William Deming to teach statistical quality control practices. Indeed, the Deming Prize was established to commemorate Dr. Deming's contribution to the diffusion of quality control ideas in Japan; an annual competition by major firms for the award serves further to promote the spread of these ideas. These various efforts were a major factor contributing to the formal adoption of Japanese Engineering Standards (JES) provided for by legislation in 1949. The Korean War had a further impact on the acceptance of these standards. In order to win military procurement orders from the American military between 1954 and 1961, the quality standards defined by the U.S. Defense Department had to be met.

In 1954 Dr. J. Juran, the noted quality control expert, arrived in Japan for a series of lectures. He emphasized a newer orientation to quality control, stating that it must be an integral part of the management function and practiced throughout the firm. In practice, this meant teaching quality control to middle management.

From 1955 through 1960 these ideas spread rapidly in major firms. But there was a critical innovation on the part of the Japanese. In the Japanese reinterpretation, each and every person in the organizational hierarchy from top management to rank-and-file employees received exposure to statistical quality control knowledge and techniques. Workers began to participate in study groups to upgrade quality control practices. This practice gave both a simple and most profound twist to the original ideas propagated by the Western experts. Quality control shifted from being the prerogative of a minority of engineers with limited shop experience (''outsiders'') to being the responsibility of each employee. Instead of adding additional layers of inspectors, reliability assurance and rework personnel when quality problems arise, as is customary in many U.S. firms, each worker, in concert with his or her workmates, is expected to take responsibility for solving quality problems.

This pattern of taking ideas developed in America for management employees and applying them to hourly personnel is not unique to QC circles. Rather, it is a distinctive approach adopted by the Japanese manager. For example, the American ideas on career development that have so much currency today in the personnel administration field were developed and are being applied to management personnel in the United States. The Japanese, however, have taken these same ideas and applied them to their hourly-rated personnel.

To fully understand the process of borrowing and adaptation, it is important to understand why these transformations of American ideas take place. What is it about the Japanese environment of the firm in Japan that makes their response so different from American firms in this regard? We can offer three levels of explanation: cultural, sociological, and economic.

In the cultural arena, the Confucianist doctrine of perfectability of man harmonizes nicely with a belief in the educability and the potential of even blue collar workers to contribute to the firm. The Japanese manager tends to view his employees as having sociopsychological needs, which, if nurtured, will yield economic returns to the firm. They see all regular male employees as resources with substantial potentialities for human growth. This contrasts sharply with the doctrine of original sin that characterizes our Judeo-Christian heritage. Here the emphasis is on the fundamental weaknesses and limitations of man.

While it is appealing to lay the difference in willingness to invest in training and responsibility at the feet of Confucianism versus Christianity, this explanation is much too simplistic. In constructing a value-added explanation, we can add first a set of sociological factors. A matter of particular relevance here is the impact of racial, ethnic, and religious differences between the managerial and worker classes. Japan is a remarkably homogenous country in race, ethnicity, religion, and culture. To be sure, there is a significant Korean and Eta minority, but they are by-and-large excluded from the large-scale manufacturing sector and relegated to various retail and wholesale trades. For all practical purposes this means that the Japanese manager can accept the proposition that the average worker is really not so very different from them and that "there for the grace of God go I." I maintain that this is a profound point critical to understanding the willingness of Japanese employers to invest in the training of and provide responsibility for blue collar employees.

There is a fundamental egalitarianism in Japanese industry that is quite impressive and is apparent to most careful observers: *Japanese managers believe in their labor force*. They believe that given the opportunity, their labor force can and wants to contribute to organizational goals.

Compare this approach to the situation in American industry. We have a management that is largely white Anglo-Saxon Protestant and a labor force that often comprises diverse racial, religious, and ethnic groups. Cultural gaps reflecting the failures of our public school education system are also wider in the United States. These differences make it much more difficult for management to put itself in the role of the ordinary production worker. Rather, this bifurcation of functions by race, religion, and ethnicity makes it much easier for American managers to see themselves as an elite whose superior education entitles them to make all the important decisions. It makes it easier to dismiss the idea that investment in education and training of ordinary blue collar workers or the sharing of decision making with them would make a significant contribution to the firm.

The final factor is this value-added explanation is an economic one. You can believe all you want in Confucianism and egalitarianism, but if your firm is not growing, you are not likely to make major investments in employee training and education, particularly if you have high rates of employee turnover.

The difference between the U.S. and Japanese economies is obvious in this respect. For the better part of the postwar period, Japanese managers have operated in the context of a high growth-rate economy and, until the early 1970s, a labor surplus economy. Investments in education and training that would enable workers to better participate in organizational decisions could be recouped. Promotion opportunities for talented and even not-so-talented workers were quite large. Moreover, the system of lifetime employment, especially in large Japanese firms, meant that the probability of employees staying on at the same firm was much higher in Japanese that in U.S. firms. Under these conditions, it was not unreasonable for Japanese employers to make large investments in employee training and education. It was easier for them to treat all employees as important resources. In the United States, high turnover and sluggish growth rates in many industries made such investment less likely. Employers were more likely to see hourly rate employees as interchangeable parts, particularly in the context of a large army of reserved unemployed.

EFFECTS OF QC CIRCLE PRACTICES

The QC circle movement in Japan has grown explosively. The number of QC circles registered with the Union of Japanese Scientists and Engineers (JUSE) increased from 1,000 in 1964 to some 87,000 by 1978. With an average of almost ten members a circle, the membership totalled 840,000. Unregistered QC circles are estimated conservatively to total an additional five times the number of registered circles, with a membership of some four million. With a total Japanese labor force of some 37 million in 1978, this means that approximately one out of every eight Japanese employees was involved in QC circle activity. The movement has drawn most of its members from hourly employees in the manufacturing sector. These summary figures are inflated because the data do not strictly discriminate between QC circles and some other forms of small group activity such as zero-defect programs, industrial engineering teams, improvement groups, and so on. Nonetheless, we are dealing with a movement that has had a significant impact on managerial practices and the degree of employee participation in the workplace.

Three characteristics of the QC circles as they have evolved in Japan are particularly significant.

- The QC circle is not a response to specific problems. Rather, it is a continuous study process operative in the workshop. This is, it functions as monitoring behavior that scans the environment for opportunities, does not wait to be activated by a problem, and does not stop its activities when a problem has been found and solved. This is a rare quality and constitutes an enormous asset where operative.
- Most U.S. motivational schemes assume that workers know how to raise productivity and improve quality but that they are holding back for no justifiable reason. Operator indifference or even sabotage are assumed to be the normal problems which management must combat. Under these assumptions, close supervision and/or financial incentives is the common response. The QC circle, to the contrary, starts with the assumption that the causes of poor quality performance are not known by either management or workers and that analysis is needed to discover and remedy these causes. A corollary of this assumption is that you must provide participants with the tools and the training necessary to discover causes and remedy them.

• Even if the solutions arrived at by workers are no better than those arrived at by technical personnel, we can anticipate that workers will more enthusiastically carry out solutions to problems that they have solved. You tend to carry out with enthusiasm policies where you have been part of the problem-solving process. This is one of the most fundamental of motivational principles.

It should be noted that the QC circles do not always perform in Japanese companies as they do on paper. Because of Japan's remarkable economic success, we have a tendency to see the Japanese as miracle men who never make mistakes. Some of their common problems are:

— For all the emphasis on voluntarism in QC circle activity, there is a great deal of top-down control in many companies. A significant minority of workers see the circles as a burden imposed on them by management rather than their own program. Thus, the circles often take on somewhat of a coercive aspect that is not the best incentive for motivating workers to produce innovative behavior.

— While in theory there is equal emphasis on the development of worker potential and productivity, in practice the emphasis on productivity has played a more prominent role. This leads workers to often question the benefits that the circles have for them.

— As the QC circle movement has developed, there is a tendency toward the routinization of that original spontaneity. This leads to workers going through the motions and turns their participation into ritualistic behavior.

THE PATTERN OF U.S. BORROWING

We are now in the remarkable situation in which the transmission of information on quality control practices is coming, full circle, back to the United States. Over 100 American firms have now adopted or are in the process of adopting some version of the QC circles. They include firms of different sizes, industries and technologies. Some of the early innovators are: American Airlines, Babcock & Wilcox, Champion Spark Plugs, Honeywell Corporation, Cordis-Dow, Federal Products, Ford Motor Company, General Motors Corporation, Huges Aircraft, J. B. Lansing, Lockheed Missile and Space Company, Mercury Marine, Pentel of America, Rockwell International, Solar Turbines, Verbatim Corporation, Waters Associates, and Westinghouse Defense and Electronics Center. In truly American fashion, a variety of consultants have sprung up to implement the QC circles, and the circles are now a regular feature in seminars offered by leading management organizations. The American Society for Quality Control is also providing more publicity and information on the subject. Two former employees of Lockheed Missile and Space Company who were involved with the QC circle program have not only set up their own consultant firm but have also established the International Association of Quality Circles (IAQC). In short, a broadly based publicity campaign designed to diffuse the QC circle practice is beginning to develop and accumulate momentum.

Conversations with officials in various companies suggest a variety of incentives, often multiple, responsible for their decision to introduce QC circles. Some

33

of these more commonly mentioned include: need to maintain or improve quality, search for new ways to raise productivity, fear of a plant closing or shutting down of a product line unless more productive methods are found, worry about a direct Japanese threat to one's market position, desire to reduce the likelihood of unionization, desire to improve relations with existing unions, and a concern with reducing the adversary relation between management and workers. In a very real sense, we have a case of solutions chasing problems. The packaged solution, wrapped in the winning colors of Japan, is being exhibited and marketed for all potential buyers. Management, the consumer, is carefully examining the wares and asking if this solution might not speak to some of its problems. Despite the variety of explanations company officials give for their interest, the desire to raise productivity and improve quality seem paramount, often in the face of increasing competition from the Japanese. With these concerns goes the recognition that perhaps they have underutilized the worker as an organizational resource.

If one examines the industry composition of the early innovators, one finds further confirmation of this position. They tend to be characterized by firms in which quality has long been an unusually important consideration such as aerospace, pharmaceuticals, and high technology companies, as well as those firms in which a stronger concern for quality has recently come to the fore (often through the vehicle of increasing numbers of product liability suits) as in the case of the automobile. The auto industry receptivity involves a case in which producers are being increasingly criticized for the quality of their product at the same time that the Japanese are making sharp inroads on their markets backed by substantial evidence for the claim that the Japanese are both more responsive to the consumer as well as producing a high-quality product.

The reaction of Japanese firms operating in the United States is interesting. Pentel of America is one Japanese subsidiary that has a QC circle program here. Its parent firm in Japan is a leading maker of pens and won the 1978 Deming Prize for the most successful QC circle program. Pentel has nonetheless had some difficult start-up problems with its circle program in the United States, as has another major Japanese firm in California, whose efforts to establish a circle program have been resisted by its American managers.

What is perhaps most curious is that a number of Japanese firms with established and successful QC circle programs in Japan have not pushed for their adoption in their U.S. subsidiaries. Matsushita Electric, a pioneer in the Japanese QC circle effort, does not have QC circles in its Chicago Quasar plant. One of the American managers explained to me that they were proceeding very cautiously. (See Cole, "Will QC Circles Work in the U.S.?" *Quality Progress*, July 1980.) By this he seemed to mean that he doubted whether American employees had sufficient organizational commitment to make the QC concept work in America. Many Japanese subsidiaries in the United States seem to be adopting a wait-and-see attitude. For all the ballyhoo about their success in the U.S., Japanese managers in this country feel quite unsure of their ability to understand and master the intricacies of American labor-management relations.

Most of the experiences with QC circles have been quite shallow; few companies have had the circles in operation more than two years. Thus, it would be premature to make assessments as to their suitability to the American environment.

There are those who would argue that workers are the same everywhere and that few adaptations will have to be made to fit the circle concept to the needs of American managers and workers. Experience thus far suggests this is a fallacious view and that unless the circles are adapted to U.S. conditions, they will fail here. Just as the Japanese adapted Western ideas on quality control to develop the QC circle, so will the Americans have to adapt QC circles to fit the needs of American management and labor. This has been most vividly demonstrated in the very use of the term *quality control circles*. Many companies have found that this name itself does not sit well with workers and unions; in particular the word "control" has coercive tones that many firms would prefer to avoid. Consequently, they have chosen other names such as *Employee Participation Circles* and *Quality Circles*. Some companies, however, have stuck with the name Quality Control Circles.

A second area in which adaptation is taking place concerns the role of the union. In Japan, the unions have usually been consulted by management at the time of the introduction of circles but have had relatively little to do with circles operations once they were established other than to monitor excessive demands on workers. In heavily unionized industries in America, this does not seem to be a suitable strategy. It was a strategy that was tried in Lockheed Missile and Space Company, which seemingly had the most successful program in the U.S. But when a strike occurred and the workers and union did not receive what they felt was their due at the end of the strike, they responded by reducing their participation in the circles. To be sure, there were other important factors involved. But loss of key personnel and failure to institutionalize QC circles were extremely significant in contributing to the decline of circle activity at Lockheed.

In a number of other firms, management has simply installed the circles with only minimum consultation with the unions. The consequences were predictable; the unions saw the circles as just one more attempt to extract increased productivity from the workers without sharing the rewards and/or as an attempt to win the loyalty of workers away from the union. Union leaders put pressure on workers not to cooperate, and the circles either never got off the ground or collapsed soon after they were started.

In one company, a poor choice of circle leader in the trial program nearly wrecked the initiative with circles. A worker hostile to the local union committeeman was appointed as QC circle leader. The union committeeman did everything in his power to sabotage the program and reduce worker participation in the circles. Failure was narrowly avoided by bringing in a national headquarters union official, who was sympathetic to the program. He smoothed the ruffled feathers of the local committeeman and explained the rationale for the program from a union perspective.

If the circles are to be introduced in a union situation, they need to be part of the program. The union needs to have a "piece of the action" so that success

35

rubs off on them as well. Otherwise they will see QC activity as an attempt to weaken the union, as indeed it is in some companies. If management tries to go it alone, the union will find a thousand ways to sabotage the program. In a number of firms, I asked managers responsible for initiating the QC circle program how they would do it if they could start all over. Again and again, the answer came back that "I would design it together with the union so that they felt they had a stake in its success." One strategy for involving the union is to create a steering committee for the circles with local union leaders as members.

A third area in which adaptation is occurring concerns the voluntary character of participation. We have seen how the Japanese approach often takes on coercive tones through pressures from either management or peer groups. In the United States the voluntaristic principle will have to be maintained more firmly to fit with the expectations of American workers and unions. Should this not be the case, workers will in all likelihood reject the QC circles; the experiences with the zero defect movement are suggestive in this regard. Adherence to the voluntaristic principle may make getting the circles started more difficult in the beginning. On the other hand, there are far greater rewards associated with the operation of the circles if you stick to a voluntary approach for workers. Genuine enthusiasm for developing innovative suggestions is more likely to emerge.

A related problem of adapting the circles to the United States environment concerns the nature of peer pressure. In large-scale Japanese organizations, for a variety of reasons management has been able to mobilize a good deal of peer pressure on behalf of organizational goals. This was not always the case, but it has been true to a large extent since the early 1960's. Thus, they have been able to use peer pressure on the shop floor to encourage workers to join and participate in circle activities. In the United States, given the adversary relationships that predominate between management and labor, it is difficult to mobilize such pressures. The circles are often seen as just one more in a series of management gimmicks designed to hustle the workers. When I asked one worker why he was suspicious of the circles, he replied, "I'm a union man." He reported that although 40 percent of the hourly personnel in the plant were participating in the circles, there was still a lot of resistance, especially from the older workers who didn't see any virtue in circle activity and didn't think they were likely to change the way things had always been done. In expressing their hostility, the noncircle participants referred to those in the circles as "circle jerks," and those in the circles were clearly quite defensive on the subject.

Given this often hostile atmosphere reported in both union and nonunion firms, two strategies seem relevant.

• The volunteers must struggle to develop ways to make their circle activity provide benefits for all workers as a way of providing its worth and making their participation legitimate in the eyes of their co-workers.
• The introduction of the circles must be done carefully and gradually with attention to reaching opinion leaders among the hourly-rate personnel and local union officials. Ultimately, the opponents of the circles among the shop person-

36

nel will change their minds only when they see changes on the shop floor which they believe are serving worker interests.

Still another area in which adaptation of Japanese practices is taking place is that of wage payments for circle activity. In those situations in which circle activity is conducted on overtime, which is often the case in high volume production operations, American managers will have to pay normal overtime rates. This is not always the case in Japan where sometimes nominal payments are made. Given the practice of permanent employment in Japan, circle activity can be seen as just one of a long stream of contributions that the worker makes to the organization and that will be recognized over the long haul in promotion or wage increases.

In the United States the absence of this long-term commitment means that workers expect their rewards to be more immediate. Instead of monetary incentives for circle suggestions, Japanese employers rely heavily on providing recognition to circle participation through a variety of activities. Again, this makes sense in the context of long-term employee commitment. In the absence of such commitment, U.S. managers will have to provide greater financial rewards for circle suggestions. Not all U.S. companies using circles have accepted this position, but one strategy that does seem to be emerging is that the circle suggestions are channeled into existing suggestion systems with any payments being split among circle members.

One additional point deserves mention here. The provision of recognition to circle members can be complementary to the use of financial incentives. Firms with QC circles have generally found that there is an enormous craving for recognition on the part of participating workers that can be met in a relatively cost-free fashion. Management presentations, meeting in management reserved rooms, T-shirts imprinted with the name of the company circle program have all been found to be useful approaches. The point is not that you can buy off the workers cheap through figuring out some gimmick for recognition. Rather, there is a demand on the part of workers for recognizing their dignity as individuals and their ability to make meaningful contributions to their organization. They want to be recognized both financially and otherwise.

POTENTIAL FOR EXPANSION

Potentially one of the most exciting areas for adaptation of Japanese practices lies in the scope of QC circle activity. The Japanese have concentrated almost exclusively on applying the circles to hourly-rated personnel. U.S. companies have recently made a few breakthroughs to salaried personnel, but even here success is far from assured.

This is a case in which U.S. ignorance of Japanese practices may have been an asset. Most U.S. companies adopting circles have not known that the Japanese have not applied the circles very extensively to white collar workers. Consequently, the American companies have not been subject to any restraint in this area that might otherwise have been the case. As a result, a number of U.S. firms are experimenting with QC circles for technical and staff personnel, office personnel, and even union-management circles. It is too early to evaluate such efforts, but there may be something in the U.S. environment that makes circle activity among salaried personnel more feasible than is the case in Japan. It will be an interesting area to watch.

A final area in which adaptation will have to take place and is taking place is in the treatment and behavior of middle management. While strong top-level management support is critical to the success of the QC circle program, it is the lack of middle management support in many adopting American companies that has proved to be the major obstacle to their success. This has not been a major problem in Japanese companies where traditionally a strong consensus has usually been forged between top management and middle management before innovations are introduced. Top management usually works through middle management in implementing the circles; it may be characterized as a top-to-middle-down model. In U.S. companies that have adopted the circles, more often than not, middle management has been bypassed in introducing the circles with predictable results. They came to see the circles as a threat to their own positions and not necessarily incorrectly so. Thus, insuring the cooperation of middle management in the United States requires the initiation of formal guidelines.

Middle management resistance can take many forms. At one plant, the staff person in charge of QC circles (facilitator) was astonished to find suddenly that his best circle leader was transferred into a section where there was no opportunity to lead QC circles because of a hostile supervisor in his new department. The facilitator had lost his best leader and gained nothing. When he asked the supervisor who ordered the change his reason for making the transfer, the supervisor replied that it was a normal operating decision. He said he didn't take the circles into consideration in making his decision. It was not that the supervisor was hostile to the circles as much as that he did not see any connections between his responsibilities and circle activity. Consequently the circles had a low priority vis á vis other demands being made upon him. While this was not a conscious attempt at sabotage, it had the same effect.

In another company the circles and the facilitator were instructed to make reports to the manufacturing manager. Middle management felt that the information contained in these reports was a way of checking up on them. They responded by refusing to cooperate with the facilitator. The facilitator, recognizing her problem, asked top management to call off the reports so that she could win the confidence of middle management.

In general, two strategies for involving middle management in QC circles seem advisable. First, a concerted training program involving all middle management supervisors should be established so that even those who do not volunteer to participate will at least understand the program's needs and operation. The emphasis should not be to pressure middle managers into involvement but to win them over gradually through an educational process. It must be made absolutely clear, however, that they will not be allowed to block the program's installation. One way of involving middle managers more fully in circle activity is to create a steering committee in which both union leaders and middle management are well represented.

A second strategy for harnessing middle management cooperation involves performance appraisal. In some companies the degree of success in circle activities is a factor in their performance ratings. When middle managers understand that top management gives the circles high priority, they will have a stronger incentive to pursue circle activity. This kind of restructuring of middle management priorities can take place only when top management is committed to circle activity. The ideal, however, is to get middle managers to see circle acitvity as a tool for better accomplishing their everyday objectives.

SUMMING UP THE BASICS

Six basic principles of QC circle activity seem operative. They are:

1. *Trust your employees.* Accept that they will work to implement organizational goals if given a chance.

2. *Build employee loyalty to the company.* It will pay off in the long run.

3. *Invest in training and treat employees as resources which, if cultivated, will yield economic returns to the firm.* This involves the development of worker skills. Implicit in this perspective is that you aim for long-term employee commitment to the firm.

4. *Recognize employee accomplishments.* Symbolic rewards are more important than you think. Show workers that you care about them as individuals.

5. *Decentralize decision making.* Put the decisions where the information is.

6. *Work should be seen as a cooperative effort with workers and managers doing the job together.* This implies some degree of consensual decision-making.

A simple examination of these principles should lead most readers to respond, "What's the big deal? — there is nothing new here." We can make two responses to that. First, as noted earlier, while the ideas may not be new with regard to managerial personnel, they are new with regard to blue collar applications. Secondly, all these six principles can be found in any good survey of behavioral science literature in the United States. What is particularly fascinating is that the Japanese have taken many of the basic ideas developed in the American behavioral sciences and acted to institutionalize them in daily practice in their firms.

In thinking about this matter further, consider the following analogy to technological hardware. The transistor was invented in the United States but was initially commercialized most successfully in Japan. Now many Americans like to emphasize that the invention is the really important thing and that took place in America. So they conclude with a sigh of relief that we still maintain our position of leadership. This interpretation totally misses the point! Much of the history of America's successful industrialization can be attributed to our ability to take inventions developed in Europe and commercialize them successfully in the United States. The jet engine, for example, was invented in England but commercialized in the United States. It is just this that the Japanese are increasingly doing to us now, and it is a terrible mistake to downplay the creativity needed to take an invention and adapt it to commercial possibilities. This applies just as much to organizational software (including techniques for organizing the labor force) as it does to technological hardware. Although the management principles operative in the QC circle may not strike an American manager as terribly original, it is the ability of the Japanese to synthesize these principles in a system and institutionalize them in daily practice that is extraordinarily original.

Simon Kuznets, in his pathbreaking study of industrialization (*Modern Economic Growth*, Yale University Press, 1966), maintains that the increase in the stock of useful knowledge and the application of this knowledge are the essence of modern economic growth. This increase, in turn, rests on some combination of the growing application of science to problems of economic production and changes in individual attitudes and institutional arrangements which allow for the release of these technological innovations. As industrialization spread through the world, technological and social innovations cropped up in various centers of development. These innovations were the outcome of a cumulative testing process by which some forms emerged superior to others; each historical period gave rise to new methods and solutions. The economic growth of a given nation came to depend upon adoption of these innovations, Kuznets concludes, by stressing the importance of the "worldwide validity and transmissibility of modern additions to knowledge, the transnational character of this stock of knowledge, and the dependence on it of any single nation in the course of its modern economic growth."

We are dealing here with the borrowing and adaptation of social innovations. Although Kuznets speaks of both technological and social knowledge, his reasoning applies most forcefully to the realm of technological choice. It is here that the selection of the most progressive technique will be made most unambiguously in terms of cost-benefit analysis. For example, the blast furnace using a hot blast and a mineral fuel adopted in nineteenth-century America was clearly superior, in terms of reducing costs and increasing productivity, to its predecessor based on charcoal technology. One can make a similar point with regard to adaptation of technology to specific environmental conditions. Thus, to pursue the steelmaking example, the basic oxygen furnace developed in Austria depended, in part, for its success on the availability of special heat-resistant brick used to line the converters that were not available outside of Austria. It was not until comparable heat resistant bricks were developed outside of Europe that the basic oxygen furnace became economically feasible in North America and Japan.

With social knowledge and institutional arrangements, the situation is more complex. To be sure, certain institutional arrangements are fairly rapidly grasped under the right conditions as being essential to economic progress. Consider the spread of the joint stock company, double-entry bookkeeping and the diffusion of multi-divisional decentralized management structure. Many other institutional innovations, however, are not easily compared and evaluated vis á vis existing arrangements. This is because social innovations often interact with a variety of other processes in a way that obscures their respective contributions to economic growth. Furthermore, the output of social innovations is often not as easily quantified as is usually the case with hard technology.

40

It is the lack of clarity in these relationships and the abundance of unwarranted inferences that lead to an element of fad in the adoption of social innovations and give free rein to arguments grounded more in ideology and power relationships than in tested generalizations. A rapid rate of diffusion of a particular social innovation may reflect these considerations more than the proven superiority of the innovation in question. Ironically, the claims to superiority of one social arrangement over another often are cloaked in the language of objective social science.

Thus, the task of evaluating the applicability of Japanese management practices in the United States and judging what are to be the needed adaptations is a herculean task. Many claims are being made and often by those with vested interests in the outcome. How is one to separate the wheat from the chaff? How are we to insure diffusion of best practice? There are no simple answers to these questions. The problem is made more difficult by our dependency on consultants for diffusing information on such innovations. Naturally, they treat such information as proprietary. Yet, consultants posses and diffuse both good and bad information in varying proportions. It is extremely difficult for the manager to separate the good consultants from the bad consultants. By the nature of their business, consultants don't like to talk about failure. Moreover, each consultant is devoted to creating a differentiated product that they can market over a broad client base. For all these as well as other reasons, the manager seeking to identify a program in work restructuring that fits his or her needs has great difficulty.

Yet, even here the Japanese case may be instructive. In the case of QC circles, a nonprofit professional association (Union of Japanese Scientists and Engineers) set up a structure that provides for a standardized collection of information (including a central repository) and a ''public testing'' of strategies and programs. This information is then fed back to individual firms in a variety of packages carefully tailored for different levels of personnel. The Union of Japanese Scientists and Engineers helps develop a consensus on what constitutes best practice and encourages the dissemination of these ideas. It may be time for organizations such as the American Society for Quality Control and the American Society for Training and Development to assume such functions. There is already some movement in this direction, and it is my hope that it will crystallize in a concrete form.

To be sure, even if successfully applied to American firms, QC circles will continue to evolve into new forms of worker participation in decision making. If one could say that their major contribution was to convince American management that hourly-rated workers do have an important contribution to make to the organization and are prepared to do so when given the opportunity, then the innovation will have had a lasting impact in America.

QUALITY CIRCLE:
A TOOL FOR THE '80s
Edwin G. Yager

One of the most fascinating movements of the past few explosive years in management/employee and organization development has been the incredible growth of the Quality Circle (although originally known as Quality Control Circles, more and more U.S. organizations are dropping the word "control," feeling a negative connotation).

The Quality Circle movement came into this country in the early '70s, having become a way of life in industrialized Japan. Nearly one-quarter of all Japanese hourly employees are members of a voluntary Quality Circle. It received particular emphasis and attention during the 1980 drop in United States automobile sales with the overwhelming growth of the Japanese competition being attributed primarily to the higher quality of the Japanese product.

Although the results are not 100 percent guaranteed, the overwhelming success of the technique must be noted. However, the successes should surprise no one familiar with behavioral science concepts. Perhaps the success of the technique can be seen in the simple fact that the process is based on sound, proven concepts. So far as the manager is concerned, a Quality Circle is just a technique for doing the job. So many agonizing years have been spent teaching managers about the behavioral sciences with so few attempts at actual application that change has been slow to come. Although it may be true all those years were schoolmaster years — preparing the industrial world for what was to come, few of us expected so simple a program to take the country so by storm. (But then — on a philosophical note quite unlikely — hasn't this been repeated over and over again throughout the history of humanity?)

The following concepts are soundly developed in a Quality Circle.

BEHAVIORAL SCIENCE CONCEPT	QUALITY CIRCLE APPLICATION
• Management must be committed to a change effort and all involved in the change must be involved in its initiation.	• A Quality circle effort is initiated only upon the decision of senior managemnent. • Initial meetings for a Quality Circle are held with all union management and supervisory personnel. • Participation in the Circle is voluntary. • The managers who decide to try a Circle then have presentations to the hourly workers and, again, participation of the hourly worker is voluntary. • Participation of management in the Circle is voluntary.

BEHAVIORAL SCIENCE CONCEPT	QUALITY CIRCLE APPLICATION
• People should have control in deciding about or changing work elements close to them.	• Circles are made up of workers with a common area of interest and intervention. Changes have to do with the work that each person does daily. • Only the most advanced Circles work on inter-departmental issues. No Circle works on management problems (this is a fault in many ''participatory'' management efforts; i.e., workers are brought up to higher levels of decision making than they are prepared or equipped to handle and problems that they must deal with on a daily basis are not resolved).
• Individuals should not be coerced to change.	• Participation in a Circle is voluntary and participants work on problems they decide need to be worked on in their own priority order.
• Work should have intrinsic motivation and be enriching.	• New skills regarding problem solving, statistics and measurement are taught to Circle members which enrich their lives and are seen as interesting.
• Any change effort should be monitored and measured for impact.	• Because a Quality Circle is primarily concerned with measurement — all change is monitored and measured constantly. The major efforts of a Circle involve measuring current performance, initiating or constructing change and measuring results.
• Workers need opportunities to meet higher motivational needs through the job.	• The intrinsic value of seeing change and improvement, coupled with the regular management presentation, gives visibility and exposure and ownership of results that few other change interventions allow. • The time off the job for the Circle to meet provides its own brand of recognition. So does the social need that members address with each other. The manager or supervisor who has long been told to develop people now has something to do to develop people (development has always been so abstract a concept when given the context of the need to get the job done).
• Managers will be more effective as they work toward developing a team or consensus style of leadership.	• Although possible, it is difficult for a manager to be domineering in a Circle because of the training that Circle members and leaders receive. There is also a greater focus on various creativity/brainstorming or measurement techniques instead of an authority-based leadership. A Circle leader is cast in a ''9/9'' role without really knowing it — or without consciously trying to alter his or her attitude or behavior.
• Jobs need feedback to be reinforcing.	• A QC Circle is a feedback device. It is built on the basis of feedback and measurement.

There are a number of questions that are commonly asked about Quality Circles when presentations are made to management to discuss the concept. These include, for example, the following:

Where are the failures?

Though infrequent and usually related to too fast or improper installation, failures do occur. This is not a program to be bought and plugged in. It is a serious intervention and needs careful and professional planning. It is not just another rehash of old participative management techniques.

How much does it cost?

Typically, the first Circle will be operating within weeks after installation begins and it will cost between $8,000 to $15,000 to launch using an outside consultant. Additional Circles are added internally with little additional cost.

What is the return?

Typically, a six to 10 divided by one return can be anticipated. Many Circles have returned thousands of dollars within the first few weeks of operation.

How soon will a Circle be contributing?

Sometime within the first few weeks. Generally, it will take six to eight weeks before the Circle is making sound recommendations.

Doesn't a Circle undermine the supervisory and staff department authority?

On the contrary. It casts the staff and the supervisor in a support and research role rather than in the historic adversary or superior role. They gain new levels of authority by virtue of their expertise rather than by virtue of edict or position.

Aren't Circles apparently limited to assembly or manufacturing operations?

Not at all — in fact, more and more banks, hospitals, retail stores and service organizations are beginning Circles. Different measurement techniques sometimes apply, and sometimes incentives need to be clarified, but the success in many ways is even more impressive than those found in many industrial units.

Circles are for big companies, aren't they?

Although many firms like Lockheed, RCA, GE, GM, Martin-Marietta, Westinghouse, AMF and others have been the first to move into the field, it is clear that even the very smallest organizations have much more to gain. A 10 percent improvement in productivity for a million-dollar company (which is barely just over the break-even), is a much more significant gain in the profit column than the activities of a single Circle might be in a very giant company. Although it may take a little longer to pay back the original investment, the long-run return will be much more impressive.

In summary, it is quite clear to us as we've had the the opportunity to meet with management and to install Quality Circles in a number of firms, that the behavioral science concepts that underlie the installation are soundly applied and it has not surprised us at all that the effect of the Quality Circle has been so great. It has been noted by some of the social scientists and behavioral scientist writers that the Japanese visited the United States during the '50s in order to study our concepts of management and quality control and, upon returning to Japan, implemented them with great success.

For some reason, U.S. managers were able to communicate to them the ideas that they had but have never fully implemented within this country due to resistance of unions, workers, and long-standing tradition. As a result, we find the concepts with regard to employee participation and quality control well developed but their application lagging two decades behind while the Japanese took the concepts and applied them immediately with resounding success. We now find ourselves looking to their successes and trying desperately to catch up with our own concepts.

WHAT IS A QUALITY CIRCLE?

A Quality Circle is a voluntary group of workers who have a shared area of responsibility. They meet together weekly to discuss, analyze and propose solutions to quality problems. They are taught group communication process, quality strategies, and measurement and problem-analysis techniques. They are encouraged to draw on the resources of the company's management and technical personnel to help them solve problems. In fact, they take over the responsibility for solving quality problems, and they generate and evaluate their own feedback. In this way, they are also responsible for the quality of communications. The supervisor becomes the leader in the circle and is trained to work as a group member and not as a "boss."

A Quality Circle is a small group of employees doing similar work who voluntarily meet for an hour each week to discuss their quality problems, investigate causes, recommend solutions and take corrective actions.

A circle is primarily a normal work crew — a group of people who work together to produce a part of a product or service.

Circle leaders go through training in leadership skills, adult learning techniques, motivation and communication techniques. The Quality Circle itself is trained in the use of various measurement techniques and quality strategies, including cause and effect diagrams, pareto diagrams, histograms and various types of check sheets and graphs. More advanced circles move on in their training to learn sampling, data collection, data arrangement, control charts, stratification, scatter diagrams and other techniques.

A typical Quality Circle includes five to 10 members. If the department requires more than one circle, then a second leader is trained, and a second circle is formed. The circles then call on technical experts to assist in solving problems.

Circle meetings are held on company time and on company premises. Where companies have unions, the union members and leaders are encouraged to take an active role in the circle, to attend leader training and to become fully aware of circle principles.

CAN WE ADOPT THE JAPANESE METHODS OF HUMAN RESOURCES MANAGEMENT?

Kae H. Chung and Margaret Ann Gray

Japan is a small island, about the size of California, with few natural resources and yet it has emerged as the third most powerful industrial nation, after the United States and the Soviet Union. Despite the oil crisis in the 1970s, which hurt the Japanese more severely than others, Japan has demonstrated remarkable economic growth. Its productivity grew an average of eight percent annually in the last decade, while that of American industries grew less than two percent. The United States is still ahead of Japan in gross national production per employed person. When the agricultural sector is excluded from the productivity index, however, the Japanese show a higher productivity than Americans. A *Fortune* magazine survey indicates that most American and Japanese executives believe that Japan is now stronger in overall industrial competitiveness than the United States and that Japan is continuously gaining an even greater edge. (*Fortune*, August 10, 1981.)

Until recently most American executives were unruffled by such an adverse development. But as American consumers turn their backs on American-manufactured products in favor of foreign-made goods, especially those of Japan, American managers become concerned. Robert B. Reich of the Federal Trade Commission indicated that, in the early part of 1980, foreign goods purchased by Americans amounted to 28 percent of new automobiles sold, 30 percent of athletic and sporting goods, 34 percent of microwave ovens, 90 percent of motorcycles and almost 100 percent of video-cassette recorders. The list grows longer as days go by, expanding into calculators, cameras, bicycles, footwear, radial tires, steel, digital watches and others.

EXPERTS CITE MANAGEMENT TECHNIQUES

American responses to the adverse development are understandably complex and confusing. Some managers may argue that the Japanese success is primarily due to the supportive government policy, low cost financing and friendly unions rather than due to any particular managerial practice. These observers blame the U.S. decline in productivity growth on excessive governmental regulations, anti-business tax laws and unfriendly unions. Many experts such as William Abernathy, Robert Hays, William Ouchi, Richard Pascale and Ezra Vogel, acknowledge the importance of these factors, yet cite the Japanese managerial practices as the key to Japan's success. Similarly, these observers imply that poor managerial practices in the United States (*e.g.*, short-term profit-orientation, market driven behavior and employee exploitation) have caused a low level of capital investment and adversary relationships with government and unions.

Granting that the Japanese managerial practices are a key to Japan's success, a lingering question still remains unanswered. Can or should Americans emulate the Japanese experience as a way of reviving the American competitiveness? A growing number of scholars and practitioners, including William Ouchi and Ezra Vogel, feel that what the Japanese are doing is "good management", meeting the needs of both the employees and their organization and consequently they assert that such good management should be used universally. Contrary to this view of management, a number of scholars and practitioners question the applicability of the Japanese practices in this country. For example, Robert Cole and Edgar Schein argue that the Japanese managerial practices are so unique that they cannot be successfully transplanted in the United States unless they are substantially modified to reflect cultural, economical, social, political reality. They maintain that such managerial practices as paternalism, seniority systems, lifetime employment, and participative management can be successfully utilized in the Japanese culture because it is characterized by racial homogeneity, uniform education, cooperation and collectivism. In contrast, American culture is characterized by heterogeneity, diverse education, individualism and competitiveness. Because of these cultural differences, the importation of Japanese managerial practices would not produce the same positive outcomes — high institutional loyalty and productivity — that the Japanese experience does. Tino Puri and Issac Shapiro further argue that we should not adopt the Japanese management systems because their emphasis on collectivism and group harmony would destroy American individualism, creativity and entrepreneurial spirit.

This article seeks to 1) understand the characteristics of Japanese human resources management and 2) see if we can adopt them in the United States. To this end, the article reviews the distinctive characteristics of the Japanese managerial practices, studies their cultural and philosophical backgrounds and discusses the adoptability of the Japanese practices in the United States.

HRM JAPANESE STYLE

What are the essential characteristics of Japanese human resources management? Are they different from that of American companies? Although not all Japanese or American companies have the same managerial characteristics, there are some practices that differentiate the Japanese from American companies. For example, William Ouchi pointed out that many Japanese companies practice lifetime employment, slow performance appraisal, nonspecialized career paths, informal controls, collective decision-making, collective responsibility and wholistic concern. American companies practice just the opposite of these.

Long-Term Employment. In Japan, this term can be transformed to "permanent employment", particularly in the large firms. These companies hire new people once a year and retain them, barring the most severe infractions, until their retirement. In times of prosperity, these firms may hire individuals who know they are temporary employees or may subcontract some work. When encountered with economic difficulties, the companies may take such steps as reducing salaries or bonuses proportionately for all employees, releasing temporary workers and reassigning the permanent ones accordingly or reducing working hours. This no layoff, no-firing policy greatly increases the loyalty between the individual and the firm. It enables the company to provide larger amounts of personal support, welfare benefits, belongingness and training which eventually yields economic returns to the business. Likewise, it allows the employees to build long-term relationships based on trust, to understand that the company's attainment of such relationships will benefit them and to readily accept such changes as new labor-saving devices which people without the benefit of permanent employment may see as a threat to their own jobs.

Slow Promotion And Evaluation. Seniority is a major factor in salary increases. There are low differentials in pay and status to workers of a given age group, particularly during the first several years of employment. This practice attaches value to the individual rather than to the job or title. Japanese employees know that they will work together for a lifetime and that the corporation will provide recognition later, hence, they learn to work together for mutual benefit. Furthermore, to accentuate awareness, there are frequent informal interactions allowing senior observations. Also evaluations rank loyalty, zeal and cooperation ahead of actual performance and knowledge; rewards make more of a psychological impact than a financial one. Because of the concept of permanent employment, Japanese workers may not anticipate immediate recognition. In addition, a bonus amounting to as much as five month's salary is tied to the performance of the entire firm at the end of the year.

Non-Specialized Careers. Permanent employment also makes it realistic for workers to rotate throughout the company. This lengthy continual training practice enables persons to learn different aspects of the business and establish a comradship with many people. When individuals are in a more permanent position, they are generalists and thus able to consider the consequences of any action in terms of how it affects the superordinate goals of the entire organization; they also have established a network of people with whom they can work to meet these goals.

Collective Decision-Making. The Japanese word *nemawaski* means root binding; it is the term used to characterize the type of decision-making that takes place in business. Everyone has a sense of running the firm because virtually nothing gets done until all the people involved agree. The Japanese assume that differences can be resolved not by adversary means or by one side achieving a final victory, but by gathering as much information as possible from as many sources as possible. As a result, all parties are well-informed, everyone has time to adjust to the emerging decision and all are committed to the determination once a consensus is reached. This can be a lengthy procedure, but because of the ultimate commitment, implementation takes relatively little time.

QUALITY CIRCLES EMERGE

An example of this type of decision-making can be shown on a smaller scale by examining the quality control circles that have grown out of Japanese management. After the war, the Japanese recognized that the quality of their products would have to increase before they became a leader in the international market. Quality is not just a function of the finished product; it also includes such factors as the time to produce, prompt delivery, billing accuracy and followup repair and maintenance. Cost reductions in any of these areas may lead to increased productivity.

With this knowledge, the Union of Japanese Scientists and Engineers invited Edwards Deming to come to Japan for a series of lectures about quality control. Deming stressed the importance of placing quality control in the hands of middle management. The Japanese adapted his ideas to their country and gave this responsibility to the people on the shop floor. The result was the QC circle.

A quality circle is a relatively autonomous unit of approximately eight workers and one senior worker. In Japan participation is voluntary, but it is estimated that one in eight workers takes part in circles. The group is trained in problem solving including elementary statistical methods. The circles are not created as a response to a specific problem. They meet regularly and are able to find answers which reduce defects and scrap, decrease rework and down time and also improve working conditions and enhance self-development. These people are a better utilized, creative resource for the organization and even if the solutions are no better than those found by technical personnel, the workers are more highly motivated to carry out the results due to their own personal involvement.

Individual Responsibility. While such concepts as consensus decision-making and quality control circles place a great deal of emphasis on group responsibility, the individual also has certain obligations. The chief responsibility is that of loyalty of the group due to the long-term commitment between the firm and the individual. Duties include continual development of skills, improvement of quality control, maintenance of social harmony, service to the firm and interaction with its members outside of the normal working day. The Japanese systems will not function without such individual commitment to their organizations.

Implicit, Informal Control. While explicit measures are often necessary in the operation of many firms, the Japanese place more emphasis on implicit and informal controls. These controls focus on long-term developmental potential of employees rather than short-term performance. Since the employees are committed to each other on a long-term basis, they are less concerned with short-term benefits. The fact that the Japanese spend a great deal of time developing relations enables group norms to become an important source of implicit control. The control is further possible because of the undifferentiated pay and status system; small differences in treatment by those in authority are greatly noticed and have great psychological significance.

Wholistic Concern For Employees. Because employees are envisioned as resources for the firm, the growth of the whole person, rather than merely his or her job skills, is emphasized. One way the company displays its concern is through its substantial benefits and programs. Long-term employment allows individuals to develop multiple bonds through play and community involvement as well as through work. The result is personal growth through intimacy, trust and understanding.

MANAGERIAL CULTURE AND PHILOSOPHY

Can we adopt the Japanese managerial systems in the United States? The answer is mixed. Experts William Ouchi, Richard Pascale and Steven Wheelwright argue that several well-managed companies such as IBM, General Electric, Hewlett-Packard, Lilly Company and Westinghouse have been using or are adopting something similar to the Japanese managerial practices of lifetime employment, participative decision-making, quality control circles and *clannish* management style. Despite this optimistic note, a prevailing feeling among some management scholars such as Cole and Schein is that the Japanese managerial practices are the outgrowth of Japan's unique cultural heritage, thus rendering these practices unadoptable in the United States.

JAPANESE MANAGERIAL PHILOSOPHIES

What are the Japanese managerial philosophies that stimulated the use of human resources management in Japan? There are three managerial philosophies that may have positively impacted the use of humanistic approach to management. The first philosophy is the Japanese perception of the role of business enterprises in their society. As Peter Drucker and Ezra Vogel explain, the Japanese tend to view a business firm as a human community which serves the needs of its members including the employees, managers and the general public. Profits are important to the Japanese managers, but the bottom line performance becomes secondary to other functions such as meeting employees' needs and providing employment opportunities. This philosophy allows the Japanese managers to be sensitive to the needs of their employees and to develop a sense of common purpose among the members regardless of their ranks. In contrast, American managers tend to view their organizations as economic entities which serve the profit motives of their stockholders. In this view, meeting the needs of the employees and the public becomes secondary to the profit motive. The resulting difference is that American managers tend to be exploitative.

The second managerial philosophy concerns the way Japanese view their employees. Ouchi argues that Japanese managers see their employees as valuable resources who can make a major difference in organizational performance. Managers view employees to be as intelligent and responsible as they are. Because of these *Theory Y* assumptions about human beings, managers rely on workers for solving organizational problems and for producing high quality products and services. This view is in contrast with *Theory X* assumptions of human nature which view employees to be lazy, irresponsible and unintelligent. This philosophy prevents many American managers from utilizing the talents of workers in solving organizational problems.

Finally, Japanese managers tend to view groups as superior to individuals in solving their operational problems. This group philosophy is that most tasks in contemporary organizations require cooperation of their members. Few decisions of any consequence arise from individual effort. Most happen as a result of collective effort. It may take time to produce cooperative effort, but it pays off in prompt implementation. In contrast, American managers tend to have faith in individual effort, creativity and initiative. Collectivism usually means to them a loss of individual freedom and motivation. American decision-makers, however, must pay the price for slow implementation since many people resist change if they have had no input in the planning stages.

JAPANESE CULTURAL BACKGROUNDS

What caused the differences in managerial philosophies between Americans and Japanese managers? Experts on Japanese management offer the following explanations. First, Cole asserts that the Confucian doctrine of human goodness, filial piety and altruism taught people to be well-educated, disciplined, committed to their organizations and compelled to help others. The pursuit of pleasure is viewed as moral decay and a person seeking this pleasure is considered to be a public enemy. This doctrine encouraged businessmen to be more altruistic and thereby they gained the public's respect. According to Pascale, Zen Buddhism also may have influenced the Japanese to be more harmonious in group settings. Rather than seeking individual competition and disharmony, Zen Buddhism taught them to search for harmonious living with others. In contrast, the Western culture has its root in Judeo-Christian heritage and capitalistic doctrine. Cole points out that the Christian concept of original sin places an emphasis on the fundamental weakness of human beings and the capitalistic doctrine motivates people to pursure self-interests.

JAPANESE ARE SAVERS

Second, Peter Drucker has argued that the difference in industrial structure, especially the method by which industrial firms raise capital, has influenced a way the Japanese view the role of these organizations. The lack of individualized capital formation has caused Japanese firms to rely on banks as the primary sources of financing. The Japanese save about 20 percent of their incomes, providing a major source of capital. With less pressure from stockholders and the capital market, they are able to pursue goals other than the short-term oriented profit goal. In contrast United States managers' performance is measured by their success in generating profits.

Third, Ouchi argues that the homogeneity in Japanese society encourages managers to view their employees as not very different from themselves. This egalitarianism in Japanese industry helps managers to treat their employers in a more humanistic way. Opportunities are given to employees equal to that which they have received. In contrast, Cole states that the heterogeneity in American society serves as an impetus for differentiating largely white Anglo-Saxon Protestant managerial groups from working classes, composed of diverse religious, ethnic and other social groups. This differentiation might hinder the use of human resources management tools in the United States, since it could foster an elitist attitude on the part of managers.

Fourth, Japan is an old nation which has a long history of paternalistic arrangements between employers and employees and between superiors and subordinates. The paternalistic relations known as the *"oyabu-kobun system"* govern the relationships between superiors and subordinates in industrial organizations. Persons of authority assume the responsibility of guiding and mentoring their subordinates as if they were foster parents and conversely the subordinates behave faithfully and hold personal loyalty toward their superiors. George DeVos maintains that the feudal-familial relationships foster mentoring relationships between superiors and their subordinates. By contrast, the United States is a relatively young nation, settling in a new sparsely populated land, encouraging people to be self-reliant and individualistic. This historical circumstance reinforces the cultural values expressed in individualistic pursuits of happiness, wealth and success. Although mentoring exists in American firms, it is not as widespread as it is in Japan.

Finally, the difference in natural endowment has caused differences in managerial philosophy. As indicated earlier, Japan is a small island, with few natural resources, but with a population of more than 100 million, half that of the United States population. This limited natural endowment indirectly forces the Japanese to pursue business strategies that promise the attainment of common goals — survival, high employment and international market expansion. According to Drucker, this kind of survival mentality has been the major force behind Japan's success. In contrast, the United States has been a land of plentiful natural resources and vast frontier. Although American managers are becoming increasingly aware of the problem of limited resources, many of their decisions are still made on an assumption that resources are plentiful.

ADOPTABILITY OF JAPANESE PRACTICES

What are the implications of these cultural and philosophical differences in adopting Japanese managerial practices in the United States? One's managerial practices are the reflection of his or her managerial philosophies which in turn are the reflection of culture. If American managers want to adopt the Japanese managerial practices, they need to adopt the Japanese managerial philosophies and cultural mores. This requirement will make the adoption of Japanese practices extremely difficult. It is not likely that American firms will restructure their methods of obtaining funds; it is unlikely that lifetime employment with slow promotion will be accepted by American managers; it is unlikely that labor-management relations will see the degree of compatibility they have in Japan and it is unlikely that homogeneity in employment could be achieved or would be allowed. In fact some Japanese companies with plants in the United States (for example, Matsushita's Quasar plant in Chicago) have not adopted their managerial practices in the United States because they are aware of the cultural differences. Furthermore, those companies which have adopted the Japanese systems (*e.g.* Sanyo's San Diego plant and Honda plant in Ohio) are experiencing labor problems leading toward unionization.

Ironically, the basic ideas of the Japanese human resources management were originated by Westerners, mostly Americans. For example, the concept of stable employment was advocated by Max Weber in his famous theory of bureaucracy. The ideas of organizational family, employee participation, group management, and job enrichment were advocated by such American scholars as Chris Argyris, Peter Drucker, Fred Herzberg, Rensis Likert and Douglas McGregor. The Japanese borrowed such concepts and adapted them to their culture. Although these ideas were originated by Americans, they have not had the same impact on managerial practices in this country. Strong emphasis on individualism and competition, along with the United States history of labor-management relations, which is full of mistrust, has probably hindered a widespread use of human resources management in this country. Walter Nord and Wickham Skinner point out that the human resources management's more honored than practiced in American firms.

Does this mean that it is impossible or unadvisable to adopt the Japanese systems in this country? It all depends. The following points are germane when one considers an adoptation of the Japanese managerial systems. First, firms in relatively stable and dominant industrial positions are more likely to or may more easily adopt the Japanese managerial systems than those in weak and unstable positions. Strong companies are less vulnerable to environmental constraints and can develop an internal organizational climate compatible to the Japanese management style. They can provide their employees with lifetime employment and make major investments in employee training. It is no surprise for IBM and General Electric to adopt such a managerial philosophy. A struggling company is less likely to look beyond current operational results, let alone long-term developmental goals. The irony, of course, is that the stable and dominant firms may not see the need for change.

Second, not all Japanese managerial practices are culturally-bound and nontransferable. Many of the technically-oriented programs such as quality control and plant maintenance can be easily transferred without much resistance. This is a reason many American companies, including General Motors, Champion Spark Plugs, RCA and Westinghouse have adopted quality control programs. Even among the culturally-bound managerial practices, some are more adoptable than others. For example, American managers seem to be receptive to the idea of long-term employment but not the practice of slow promotion with an emphasis on seniority. Many managers, especially those who feel that they are capable, seem to prefer a reward system based on performance rather than seniority.

Third, the Japanese managerial practices which stress consensual decision-making and group harmony are not all that desirable for industries pursuing aggressive and risky ventures. The Japanese systems are good at managing the nuts and bolts of manufacturing activities, but the emphasis on group harmony and consensus can easily smother creative thinking and innovative behavior. When technological innovation is the key to organizational survival, the American way of managing people, stressing creative ideas and individualistic performance, can be more advantageous than the Japanese approach.

Finally, if a company chooses to adopt the Japanese managerial system, it has to prepare the foundation on which the newly adopted system can stand. It involves careful selection of people who can function effectively under the new system, major investment in employee training on a continuous basis, decentralization of operational decisions and sharing its benefits with the employees. It also requires the development of a partnership attitude between management and unions. It is indeed a time-consuming process, requiring much dedication and subtlety on the part of management. Unless one is willing to change the whole philosophy of managing people, one would be better off by not altering the existing system of management.

REFERENCES

1. Cole, Robert E., "Learning from the Japanese: prospects and pitfalls", *Management Review*, September 1980, pp. 22-42.
2. De Vos, George A., "Apprenticeship and paternalism". in E.F. Vogel (ed.), *Modern Japanese Organization and Decision Making*. Berkely, CA: University of California Press, 1975, pp. 210-227.
3. Drucker, Peter F., "Behind Japan's success", *Harvard Business Review*, January-February 1981, pp. 83-90.
4. Drucker, Peter F., "Economic realities and enterprise strategy", in E.F. Vogel, (ed.), *Modern Japanese Organization And Decision Making*. Berkely, CA: University of California Press, 1975, pp. 228-250.
5. Hatvany, Nina, and Pucik, Vladimir, "Japanese management practices and productivity", *Organizational Dynamics*, Spring 1981, pp. 5-21.
6. Hayes, Robert H., "Why Japanese factories work", *Harvard Business Review*, July-August 1981, pp. 57-66.
7. Juran, J.M., "International significance of the QC circle movement", *Quality Progress*, November 1980, pp. 18-22.
8. Nord, Walter, and Durand, Douglas, "What is wrong with the human resources approach to management?" *Organizational Dynamics*, Winter 1978, pp. 13-25.
9. Ouchi, William, *Theory Z*, Reading, MA: Addison-Wesley Publishing Company, 1981.
10. Puri, Tino, and Bhide, Amar, "Crucial weakness of Japan, Inc.", *Wall Street Journal*, June 8, 1981, p. 18.
11. Schein, Edgar H., "Does Japanese management style have a message for American managers?" *Sloan Management Review*, Fall 1981, pp. 55-68.
12. Shapiro, Isaac, "Second thoughts about Japan", *The Wall Street Journal*, June 5, 1981.
13. Skinner, Wickham, "Big hat, no cattle: managing human resources", *Harvard Business Review*, September-October 1981, pp. 106-114.
14. Vogel, Ezra F., *Japan as Number One*, Cambridge, MA: Harvard University Press, 1979.
15. Wheelwright, Steven C., "Japan — where operations really are strategic", *Harvard Business Review*, July-August 1981, pp. 67-74.

A HISTORICAL PERSPECTIVE:
JAPAN AND THE UNITED STATES
David L. Shores and Mary C. Thompson

THE BEGINNING OF
QUALITY CIRCLES IN JAPAN

The end of World War II brought many changes to Japan, effecting politics, culture, and industrial production. The revered Emperor was removed from power. Occupation troops were stationed throughout the country. The industrial facilities were destroyed. Only the Japanese reputation for cheaply made products remained intact.

The newly formed Japanese government, with the aid of the U.S. government, directed its efforts towards rebuilding its devastated industry. In response to a request from General Douglas MacArthur, two U.S. statisticians, Drs. W. Edwards Deming and Walter Shewhart, offered their services to assist with the massive task of rebuilding and reestablishing Japanese industry.

Deming began his work with the Japanese in 1946 by teaching statistical quality control methods to Japanese industrial middle managers. Through his lectures and the Japanese desire to compete in the world marketplace, Deming's statistical quality control techniques became a living, vital, and essential force in all stages of Japanese industry.

Closely following Deming's lecture series were quality control talks for employees at all levels of an organization by Dr. J. M. Juran, a management consultant. His emphasis to the Japanese audience was a new orientation to quality control, insistance that it must be an integral part of the management function and practiced throughout the organization.

So effective were the teachings of Deming and Juran that from the mid-fifties through 1960, the concept that quality control was the responsibility of every employee spread rapidly throughout the country. The government response was a National Productivity Council, and the Japanese Union of Scientists and Engineers (JUSE) was formed. The Japanese news media prepared and aired a series of 90 fifteen-minute radio broadcast courses on statistical process control.

A significant interest in the writings of U.S. organizational theorists and social scientists developed, adding to the strong feelings that quality control could change the future of industrial production in Japan. Avidly read were Peter Drucker, Rensis Likert, Chris Argyris, Douglas McGregor, and Fredrick Herzberg. Their ideas were freely adopted in many Japanese management circles.

The first formal Quality Control Circle (QCC) was formed in 1962 by Dr. Kaoru Ishikawa in cooperation with JUSE. Known today as the Father of Quality Control Circles, he initiated, in 1962, Quality Control Circle activities for the purposes of educating foremen and workers in quality control and in the improvement of their work through the concept of quality control.

By 1975, JUSE had officially registered 70,000 Quality Control Circles, and in 1983, JUSE estimated that over 8 million employees were involved in Quality Control Circles.

QUALITY CIRCLES IMPORTED
TO THE UNITED STATES

The Japanese results and success of quality circle techniques attracted the attention of a Lockheed Space and Missile management study team in 1973 and the group toured Japanese industries. Their purpose was to observe Japanese quality control procedures, more specifically Quality Control Circles, in operation. Just one year later, in November 1974, Lockheed introduced the first Quality Control Circle in the U.S. Quality Circles, as they are also referred to in America, caused little reaction during their early years. By 1977, only five companies were actively involved with Quality Circles.

In the last six years, however, there has been a surge of popularity for the Quality Circles. Companies implementing circles began to grow at an exponential rate. In 1981, the projections for the number of organizations initiating quality circle programs had reached as high as 1500, and the companies ranged in size from 19 to tens of thousands employees. A 1982 survey of 713 companies identified 12,424 active Circles and the respondents estimated that the number of Quality Circle programs could be implemented in as many as 6,288 locations throughout the U.S.

QUALITY CIRCLES IN PERSPECTIVE

The idea of employee involvement and participation in achieving organizational goals is neither new nor revolutionary. Social scientists, managers, and administrators have studied the effects of participative management styles upon productivity and worker attitudes for decades. The studies repeatedly conclude that increased job responsibilities, allowing workers to make decisions that affect their job, and creating an environment of trust all tend to improve organizationl effectiveness, increase worker productivity, and improve employee morale.

As early as 1924, the Western Electric Company conducted a series of experiments related to worker productivity known as the Hawthorne Experiments. Covering a nine-year period, researchers designed and conducted studies to establish relationships between working conditions and hourly output. The researchers manipulated lighting, length of rest periods, and length of working day. The conclusions puzzled the scientists because they could discover no single correlation that would account for steadily increasing output despite the numerous changes among the workers involved in the study.

Another study, conducted at the Harwood Manufacturing Company's pajama factory in Marion, Virginia by social scientists from the Survey Research Center of the Institute for Social Research at the University of Michigan, spanned nearly 20 years. The researchers redesigned the jobs of the the work groups and then measured the effect of different degrees of worker participation. The conclusions supported strongly the success of worker participation in management decision making affecting employee tasks. Many subsequent studies have resulted in similar conclusions. Feelings of cohesiveness, greater productivity, job satisfaction, and morale were reported by involved workers.

A highly publicized program directed toward improving the total organizational climate and productivity emerged within a plant of the country's largest auto manufacturer in the late 1960's. Known as Quality of Work Life, the term was defined as covering a worker's feelings about every dimension of work including economic rewards and benefits, security, working conditions, organizational and interpersonal relationships, and its intrinsic meaning in a person's life. The early results at General Motors were impressive, and Quality of Work Life (QWL) began to receive national attention. Between 1975 and 1979, more than 450 articles and books were written on the Quality of Work Life and at least four national and international studies were conducted.

The basis of the QWL programs at the GM car plant, located in Tarrytown, New York, was to involve the employees, the union, and management in joint problem solving sessions. The plant had acquired the reputation of having one of the poorest labor relations and production records within the GM Corporation. Started in 1974, after several years in preparation, the QWL program initially involved only a few selected work groups. Three years later, the program was expanded to plant-wide participation. The conclusions were not clearcut. The union claimed that the facility went from one of the poorest plants in quality performance based on inspection counts or dealer complaints to one of the best among the 18 plants in the division. The union further reported that absenteeism went from over 7% to below 3%. And in December 1978, at the end of the training sessions, the union said there were only 32 grievances on the docket where seven years earlier the number reached nearly 2,000 filings.

When the General Foods Company established a new plant in 1971, they initiated a total reorientation of plant management philosophy. Using the new facility and situation, the managers installed a participative management program.

To involve all workers in the decision-making processes of the organization, self-managed teams were organized to bring people from separate units into production teams where each team's job was designed to be equally challenging. The activities of producing a product blended maintenance, quality control, and custodianship, etc. into the responsibilities of each team.

Long before QWL programs at General Motors and General Foods began, the concept known as Organizational Development (OD) emerged in management literature. This concept is a holistic approach to managing an organization. It may be defined as a strategy initiated to increase organizational effectiveness and health through implementation of a complex educational design.

Organizational Development is based on the ideas that people and organizations must be motivated to change and ready to work together. Changes in the individual must be followed by changes in the organizational structure, practice, leadership, and reward systems. Change comes from the opportunity to experiment with new ways of doing things because people learn best from their own experiences and become committed to the things they help create. People can learn to take responsibility for change and become self-directed. The quality of the solution to problems improves when people who are part of the problem participate in shaping the final solution. Trust, collaboration, and open confrontation of conflict are required for organizations to continue to adapt.

Many management studies support and call for more participative management techniques. As society changes so must organizations and organizational behaviors. Whether the solution is quality circles or another form of participative management remains to be seen; however, behavioral changes in both labor and management practices will always require dynamic leadership and adaptive leadership techniques.

INTRODUCTION: CHAPTER TWO
IMPLEMENTING QUALITY CIRCLES

Seven articles in this chapter describe the "how to" of establishing quality circles within an organization. They cover the steps involved, with emphasis on approval, support by senior managers, and intense preparation to gain acceptance for the program at the middle management level. Preliminary planning, these authors say must include keeping all middle managers well informed because they will ultimately be responsible for the success of the project.

Interested employees should be included in establishing the objectives for the group — goals may be stated as simply as "enhance the quality of the product, service, and working life." Creation and commitment of all levels of management can be accomplished by education — by talking about the concept, its success in competitive industries, by providing literature describing the techniques. The approval for quality circle groups should be made at a top level. There will be corporate costs involved due to hiring consultants, release time from jobs, perhaps overtime pay to cover meeting beyond the workday hours, and training classes.

Leadership for the group cannot be dictated. After approval for the group is given, a steering committee is appointed, a leader/facilitator is selected, and the goals of the group are finalized. Union leaders and management briefings must be included in the process because they are critical to the success of quality circle activities.

Training sessions are viewed, by experts, as mandatory to achieve quality circle success. Most groups receive day-long sessions in statistical methods, presentation of data, graphing, problem solving, and other orientation to organizational work groups. The group members are encouraged to meet with and consult with experts within the organization regarding the areas under investigation.

Participants report that the activities of the quality circles can be exciting and rewarding. They also report that there are many frustrations, but that the rewards outweigh the disappointments. All writers stress that success is dependent upon support and approval at the introductory phase and that employers and employees in the U.S. must adapt the quality circle concepts to fit their particular organizations.

IMPLEMENTING QUALITY CIRCLES
IN YOUR ORGANIZATION

Donald L. Dewar

ABSTRACT

Quality circles do not just happen. It is not something done with a snap of the corporate fingers. Rather, it comes as a result of a well thought out and carefully executed plan. It may take time — perhaps more than you prefer, but in the long run that is more likely to be to your benefit.

There are a number of steps to be followed. Ultimately, sooner or later, you will — or should — touch all of them. Some companies have installed Quality Circles, haphazardly jumping back and forth between the necessary steps. This often results in a needless wake of strewn wreckage which builds doubts and creates obstacles in the minds of management and workers alike. It is much better to have a course charted that will steer clear of potential trouble to inspire confidence and lay the groundwork for continued growth and progress.

WHAT STEPS ARE INVOLVED?

Figure 1, "Steps In Implementing Quality Circles," describes the steps that should be followed.

A. The Discovery

Someone in the organization discovers Quality Circles. From a probability point of view, that person is most likely to be from the Quality Control department. However, increasingly, Quality Circles are being discovered by people in the manufacturing or industrial relations areas.

Immediately upon discovery, there is a search for articles and books to gain further knowledge of the concept of Quality Circles. It is wise, at this time, to pass along any of the more pertinent materials that are uncovered so that others in the organization can become familiar with it.

Attendance at a seminar can be helpful to clarify and reinforce what has been learned from the written material.

Information available from the International Association of Quality Circles (IAQC) may also supplement what has been discovered.

Conferences offered by a number of professional societies, in addition to the IAQC, have enriched their proceedings by including papers on the subject of Quality Circles. Most notable is the American Society for Quality Control (ASQC).

60

STEPS IN IMPLEMENTING QUALITY CIRCLES

A. The Discovery:
   Collect information:
   - Research of literature
   - Attend seminar
   - Information from IAQC
   - Conferences

B. Set preliminary objectives

C. Build management support

D. Decision to start

E. Select a consultant

F. Organize the Steering Committee

G. Facilitator selected by Steering Committee

H. Finalization of objectives by Steering Committee

I. Develop the implementation plan:
   - Develop alternative courses of action
   - Identify the negative consequences of each course of action
   - Finalize the implementation plan
   - Develop sequence and timing of major steps

J. Collect pre-implementation measurement data

K. Conduct briefings for management and union

L. Select pilot program circle leaders

M. Develop individual leader performance goals that are mutually agreeable to the leader and his/her manager

N. Issue pre-publicity to inform all employees

O. Conduct training classes:
   - Facilitator
   - Leader

P. Initiate Circles

Q. Member training by leaders

R. Periodic review by Steering Committee

Figure 1

B. Set Preliminary Objectives

Early in the game, define what the objectives of your Quality Circle program will be. The author has seen it stated as simply as: "Enhance the quality of the product, service, and working life."

Or, it may be stated in considerably more detail such as was done by a leading manufacturer in the State of Iowa:

1. Reduce errors and enhance quality
2. Inspire more effective teamwork
3. Provide job involvement
4. Increase employee motivation
5. Create problem solving capabilities
6. Build an attitude of "Problem Prevention"
7. Improve company communications
8. Develop harmonious manager/worker relationships
9. Promote personal and leadership development
10. Develop a greater safety awareness

This could be expanded even further. Examples are:

11. Develop cost consciousness
12. Promote greater productivity without speedup
13. Build increased energy awareness and conservation
14. Improve employee morale
15. Develop a reputation for quality so as to be competitive and improve job security
16. Provide for personal growth through training
17. Provide opportunities for recognition

Again, let it be emphasized that the list does not have to include all of the items listed above. Give your people an opportunity to participate in selecting those that have personal appeal to them. There are many reasons why people at all levels in your company will support Quality Circles. In developing your primary list of objectives, keep this in mind and you will better assure their enthusiasm and support.

C. Build Management Support

This is the crucial area that must happen if one is to expect the Quality Circle program to be successfully initiated and succeed.

There are three main factors in developing management support:

1. *High as possible in the organization.* Strive to get support for Quality Circles at the highest level in your organization. This may be a vice president, president, or even the Chairman of the Board. It is desirable to have the blessing of the chief executive officer. Managers at lower levels have often expressed their concern, "I support the concept wholeheartedly, but I am reluctant to stick my neck out until I find out whether it has support at a higher level. I have been burned too many times in the past." This concern is set to rest when someone at a high level is supportive.

What is the lowest level of management support? It should have at least the endorsement of the Quality Control Manager and the Manufacturing Manager. It would also be helpful if the individual in charge of Industrial Relations was supportive.

2. *Management support in the organizations that have Circle members.* If we are talking about a manufacturing organization, it is mandatory that the director of manufacturing be supportive.

3. *Depth of management support.* You want as many people in the management structure as possible to be supporters of the program. Those who are on your level, those who you report to, as well as those who report to you.

A frequently asked question is, "How do we go about building depth of management support?" This is done by talking about it. It is as simple as that. Use every opportunity to express your enthusiasm for this concept of worker participation. At times this may seem a discouraging process as your words appear to fall upon deaf ears. Wrong! Many people have to have time to ponder such innovative concepts. Time is on your side. Talk to these people on a continuing basis. Provide them with literature that you feel would be useful. The response time will vary. Some will become equally enthusiastic as yourself on the first contact . . . others will take longer.

Above all, do not expect that the process of building management support will be easy. Neither should you expect it to happen immediately. Rome was not built in a day, nor should you expect that Quality Circles will have the required management support in a day.

D. Decision to Start

Finally, the decision to start will be made. This should be at as high a level as possible. It should not be, "OK, we will let you do it." Rather, it must be, "We are ready to move ahead and will provide the kind of support necessary to make it a company commitment."

E. Select a Consultant

Before proceeding further, select a consultant. It costs money but experience has shown that it is an investment which, in the long run, saves money and results in a better program. The cost of a consultant will run in the neighborhood of $500 a day. The consultant will be engaged for a minimum of one day and perhaps as much as a week or more.

Your consultant should be able to furnish a list of satisfied clients specifically in the field of Quality Circles. That may appear as a needless word of caution, but, there are consultants willing to offer services in almost any field regardless of whether they have the expertise and experience to back it up. Further, select a consulting firm that will stand behind its services.

A consultant should be able to do much more than simply make presentations to management, teach facilitators, and instruct Circle leaders. He should have the necessary training materials and aids. Further, he should be able to furnish Circle facilitators, leaders, and members with training materials that they can use to study during the training phase.

One of the surest ways to select a competent consultant is to rely on recommendations of satisfied clients. Check with them.

Your consultant should work with you to assure that the resulting Quality Circle program belongs to your organization. It should be *your* program, not the consultant's.

F. Organize the Steering Committee

The Steering Committee is the group that provides overall guidance and direction for your Quality Circle activities. The various features that describe this function include:

- Quality Circle Board of Directors
- Members from various organizations
- One man — one vote
- Selects the Facilitator
- Prepares implementation plans
- Establishes guidelines

The Steering Committee consists of management level or staff personnel who have an interest in the Quality Circle activities. Committee members should represent various major functions of the organization such as manufacturing, quality control, education and training, personnel, finance, engineering, and marketing. In many companies, the union is invited to participate in the Steering Committee.

The levels represented by Steering Committee members will vary from middle management to as high as top level executive personnel. In several companies, the chief executive officer is a member of the Steering Committee. This includes the company presidents and in two instances that I am aware of, the Chairman of the Board of the corporation.

G. Facilitator Selected by Steering Committee

One of the key initial steps to be followed by the Steering Committee is the selection of the facilitator. It is recommended that the facilitator not be picked or appointed by some key figure involved in the Quality Circle activities. The facilitator selection has worked best where the individual is selected on the basis of competition. Recently, one company advertised the facilitator position internally. The pay level was to be the equivalent or slightly better than a supervisory position. They were amazed that 48 people applied! Several supervisors were included in those seeking the position.

H. Finalization of Objectives by Steering Committee

The preliminary objectives have already been established, but these need to be finalized. By this time you will be far enough into your Circle activities to have much clearer ideas about what to select as final objectives. The all important implementation plan is prepared by the Steering Committee. This is really a combination of two or more documents. One document is the Quality Circle procedure which defines the way Quality Circles will interact with the other organizations. An important part of the procedure is the objectives which have already been established. The procedure also defines those items that should *not* be addressed by Quality Circles. The other document is the implementation time table and denotes all of the various activities that must occur and when they should happen.

I. Develop the Implementation Plan

The implementation plan is a vital document and it takes time and care to develop. The way it should not be done is to have the Steering Committee ask the facilitator to "put something together and we'll take a look at it." Rather, it should be done by various members of the Steering Committee talking to members of management at all levels. They should explain the Quality Circle concept and ask for suggestions on how it can best be implemented. They *will* get excellent suggestions that will help to customize the Quality Circle activities so that they fit in best for your company. You can also count on the fact that many of the suggestions you will receive will be repeats of what somebody else has said. You may even hear the same ideas repeated several times. Even that is okay, because after the plan is finalized and presented back to management, they will take a look at it and say, "By Golly, they actually used some of my ideas!" Not only will everyone have pride of authorship in the implementation plan, but it will work better because everyone will have a greater commitment toward the success.

The consultant will guide the Steering Committee to assure a "company program" and to enhance the likelihood of success. It also helps to avoid the likelihood of alternatives that could result in disastrous consequences.

The involvement of all members of the Steering Committee is important. It should be their program. Their egos must be involved in guiding the program to a successful operation.

The facilitator is a member of the Steering Committee and, generally, serves as one of the hardest working members. However, the other Steering Committee members should not abrogate their responsibilities to the facilitator just because he is more intimately involved in the day to day operations of Circle activities.

J. Collect Pre-implementation Data

You can depend on it — you will ultimately be asked the question, "What kind of results is Quality Circles producing? To answer that query it is necessary to have before and after data. Before starting Quality Circles, certain baseline information should be gathered for future reference. This information should be in the areas of quality, cost, absenteeism, turnover, attitudes, safety performance, schedule adherence, cost of rework, scrap, labor costs per unit of product and volume of units produced.

Be in a position to respond to questions regarding the effectiveness of Quality Circles. There will be times when the only way to convince individuals is with concrete numbers.

After Quality Circles have been in operation for some time, additional data can be gathered and compared to the baseline measurements. This will give you the evidence you need to convince management and to serve as a valuable feedback to Circle members who are also highly interested in what they are accomplishing.

Certain kinds of baseline data can be determined afterwards by examining records. However, occasionally it must be done ahead of time or it can't be done at all. One example is in the case of attitudes surveys. There is no way that employees can "remember" how they felt about their company, their job, their supervision, and communications.

K. Conduct Briefings for Management and Union

There will be a number of people in management who were not directly involved in Quality Circle activities up to this time. It may be in the interest of Circle activities that these individuals be advised on what is occurring and the plans for the future. There will be other management personnel who will simply be interested in knowing what is happening. There is always the possibility that they may wish to include Quality Circle activities in their own organizations at a later date. There will also be staff organizations who may have varying degrees of interface with the Quality Circles. Therefore, it is in the best interests of everyone that a full awareness of Quality Circles be established. You want to alleviate the fears of those who feel that Quality Circles represents some kind of competition to them. As ridiculous as it may seem, it can occur and needs to be dealt with. Everyone has to understand that they can help Quality Circles do a better job, and in turn, Quality Circles can help them do their job better. It gets back to striving for a win-win philosophy on the part of all participants.

The union officials certainly should be briefed on what is occurring so that they can respond to questions from their membership. It would be unfortunate to put union officers in the undesirable position of not understanding what was occurring to the people in their bargaining unit. The union officials, all the way from president to union stewards, are normally amongst the most responsive and receptive to this kind of activity. In fact, often they have been arguing for this kind of worker participation for years. Further, union stewards normally are members of the Quality Circles in their areas and are typically very enthusiastic.

L. Select Pilot Program Circle Leaders

Now comes the difficult task of selecting which leaders will participate in the Quality Circle pilot program. The pilot program usually runs for five months or so and usually consists of five Circles. Who will these leaders be? By the time the word has circulated about the upcoming Quality Circle activities, often several supervisors have stepped forward and volunteered to be part of it. It may not bet a case of recruiting who will be leaders of the pilot Circles — rather, it may be, "How will we select from those that want to do it?"

The selection process is enhanced when the Steering Committee sets aside the time to interview candidates for Circle leader positions. Another excellent alternative is for the Steering Committee, when interviewing candidates for the position of Facilitator, to ask those supervisors who are in the runner-up position if they would like to start Quality Circles during the pilot program. Think of it! These supervisors are already excited enough about the concept that they are interested in doing it on a full time basis. Why not take the extra step and get them as leaders of the pilot Circles?

M. Develop Individual Leader Performance Goals That Are Mutually Agreeable to the Leader and his/her Manager

After the Circle leaders have been chosen, it is important that the Facilitator sit down with each and discuss performance criteria and goals. What is expected? What does each leader plan as far as their own activities are concerned? There will be questions in the minds of the leaders as to how much time will be utilized in the pursuit of these performance objectives and how well equipped they are to achieve them. Also, they will want to know what resources they can draw on to assure attainment. These performance goals must be acceptable to each leader. They must also be acceptable to the manager they report to. Each performance goal should be written in such a way that it is measurable. There must be provisions made for feedback so that it will be clear to both the leader and the manager as to how successfully each goal is being met.

N. Issue Pre-publicity to Inform All Employees

There will be curiosity as to what is going on. If the company does not act to fill this gap, the grapevine will. The kind of publicity is important. You simply want to inform. If the publicity comes on too strong and is too enticing, you may expect a deluge of requests on the part of the employees to become involved in Quality Circles. Requests that you may not be prepared to handle. Information is all that is required at this time. Simply state that the company is conducting Quality Circle activity on a pilot basis. After a pre-established number of months, the pilot activities will be completed and the gradual expansion will occur. Make certain that employees understand that they are not being excluded on a permanent basis. Their turn will come as soon as conditions permit.

The publicity can be issued in one of several ways:
• Letters to the employees' homes
• Company newspaper
• Mass gathering in the auditorium
• Numerous small group sessions
• One-on-one

Obviously, of the several methods listed above, the last one is the most time consuming and costly. No one can dispute its effectiveness. But, because of its higher cost, it is rarely used.

O. Conduct Training Classes

Facilitator. Training classes for the Facilitator are usually conducted by the consultant at the company location. These may be done on site or at a nearby location, such as a motel. Occasionally, a company elects to send their Facilitator to an outside training course such as is provided by the (IAQC) International Association of Quality Circles on a periodic basis.

Leader. The original set of leaders for the pilot program activities are normally trained at the same time the facilitator is trained by the consultant. This is not necessary, but it is nearly always done. After all, the consultant is already there and might as well be utilized as fully as possible during the kick-off phase.

Typically, the facilitator/leader training classes are attended in part or in full by other members of management who have an interest in Quality Circle activities. Sometimes these are members of the Steering Committee. In one instance that the author is aware of, it was the Chairman of the Board who participated fully during the entire training period.

P. Initiate Circles

The leader, freshly trained in Quality Circle techniques, finalizes the membership in his or her Circle. This, in itself, may be no easy task. Take, for instance, the supervisor who had 37 people reporting to him. Thirty-two wanted to be members of the one Quality Circle he was going to operate during the pilot phase. He solved the problem by simply putting 37 names into a hat and drawing out 8 of them. Other times the selection can be done on a job classification or some other basis. Agree on a meeting schedule and you're ready to go!

Q. Member Training By Leaders

The first several weeks will be devoted to training Circle members in the techniques of problem solving. Quality Circle members receive instructions from their Circle leader. The facilitator is encouraged to attend these training sessions to provide back up for the leader as necessary. It is important that the leader carry the ball, at this time. The facilitator works behind the scenes, assisting the leader when necessary. There will be opportunities to apply some of the training techniques to actual problems during the training process.

R. Periodic Review By Steering Committee

Quality Circles is no different than any other kind of activity — it requires managing. It is vital that goals be established. It is also important that measurable milestones be put in place towards the achievement of these goals. That is the purpose of the implementation plan that the Steering Committee establishes at an earlier phase. Now, we have moved ahead to a point where the progress must be checked against the plan.

The success that the Steering Committee will have in performing this valuable function is contingent, in part, on the care with which the original implementation plan was drawn up. The milestones must be measurable, otherwise they cannot be evaluated with any degree of success. The results of the review of the Steering Committee should be conveyed to all of the people directly affected.

This periodic review does something else. It provides information necessary to make modifications and corrections in your Circle activities. And, thereby lays the foundation for increased opportunities for success.

ESTABLISHING THE TIME TABLE

There is an endless variety to the timing of the events enumerated on the above list of steps in implementing Quality Circles in your organization. Figure 2 represents a typical time table that will serve as a guide for what you might expect. The completion of each step is indicated by the letter that corresponds to that step in the implementation process.

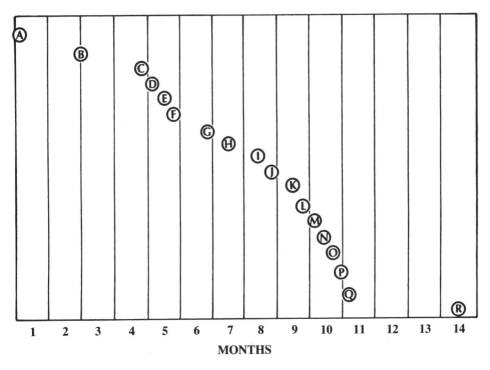

FIGURE 2

A TYPICAL TIME TABLE
FOR
IMPLEMENTING QUALITY CIRCLES

The most difficult part of the process is in the earlier months. A lot of seeds must be planted and a lot of questions answered. There will be doubters who will frustrate you and slow down the process. However, keep persisting and things will eventually come together and start moving quickly as the chart indicates.

CONCLUSION

Implementing Quality Circles in your organization can be an exciting and rewarding activity. It will have its frustrations, to be sure, but the rewards will more than compensate. There are certain steps that should be followed. Do not try to by-pass or circumvent these steps.

It is equally important to remember that the steps indicated will help you to establish Quality Circles in your organization. The process does not end when these steps have been fulfilled. Remember, Quality Circles is an on-going activity and it is an activity that must be managed.

PREDICTABLE DEVELOPMENTAL STAGES IN THE EVOLUTION OF A QUALITY CIRCLE

Vivian C. Comstock
Gerald E. Swartz

ABSTRACT

Most groups, be they social or work related, pass through a series of predictable developmental stages. The purpose of this paper is to describe these stages as experience has shown they apply to Quality Circles. Facilitators and leaders alike should be aware of this cycle in order to best meet the operational needs of their circles.

INTRODUCTION

Bringing people together in a group and calling the group a Quality Circle by no means guarantees that the group will achieve positive results. A circle's productivity will depend directly upon the degree to which it becomes an effectively operating team.

Moreover, even an effectively operating team cannot be expected to be without problems throughout its existence. It is normal for a Quality Circle to go through predictable stages during its operational life, and during stages of lowered effectiveness, it will take the cooperative efforts of the Circle leader and the Facilitator to revitalize the circle and bring it back to its highest potential for productivity.

It is the purpose of this paper to provide an understanding of the developmental stages that can be anticipated during the existence of a Quality Circle, and to indicate when revitalizing action by the Leader and the Facilitator is required. Examples are given of regenerating actions, but revitalization will best be achieved by specific ''on-the-scene'' observations and the creativity of both the Leader and Facilitator.

STAGE 1 — INTRODUCTION

The first stage is an introductory phase during which the Quality Circle is initially formed. The workers will have received an indoctrination to Quality Circles by the Facilitator and will have voluntarily agreed to start a circle in their particular work area. All that can be said at this point is that each new Quality Circle formed constitutes the beginning of a prospectively dynamic problem solving team. To a great extent much of what the circle becomes will depend upon the guidance and support they receive from the Leader and Facilitator. These key people have a great responsibility for tapping the human resources existing in each circle and developing it to the fullest.

STAGE 2 — DEPENDENCE

The second stage — the period during which members are instructed in Quality Circle techniques and policies — is one of dependence. Circle members do not know what is expected of them and they are dependent on their Leader and Facilitator for training and direction. The members possess no real authority during this stage. It is crucial that during this training stage the members receive a solid schooling in the problem solving techniques which will become the backbone of their Quality Circle.

STAGE 3 — COUNTER DEPENDENCE

Following this period of almost total dependence there can come a stage of counter-dependence during which authority issues begin to emerge, and conflicts arise. Circle members now have a better grasp of the program, and may feel moved to challenge program policies and techniques. For example, it is not uncommon for members to object to the length of the training phase. Impatience develops and members want to rush into problem solving before they understand the fundamental techniques. Rebellion against the Leader, and management in general, may also emerge at this time. In spite of the Leader's instructions that they concentrate, initially, on the problems in their own area, circles often want to place blame on other departments or upon a management policy. It is imperative at this point for the Circle Leader and Facilitator to be assertive in adhering to the guidelines of the Quality Circle program.

STAGE 4 — RESOLUTION OF AUTHORITY

For a successful circle there will be an amiable resolution of the authority issue, and the circle will enter into a stage where members understand that they must work as a disciplined team in conjunction with the Leader. Traditionally defined roles such as "supervisor" versus "employee" are minimized, and an equality of status emerges as Leader and members work together as teammates.

STAGE 5 — ENCHANTMENT

A stage of excitement and enchantment will normally occur at this point. Training has been completed and energies run high. Members delight in their new voice in decision making. They are proud of their contributions and the opportunity to demonstrate their abilities. Ideas flow freely and a feeling that no problem will be left unresolved prevails. Improved rapport among circle members is characteristic of this stage, and increased productivity can be expected.

STAGE 6 — DISENCHANTMENT

A natural succession to the stage of enchantment is a stage of disenchantment. Members discover that not all problems can be resolved, and for those that can, implementing change can be a frustrating and difficult task. In addition, suggested solutions may be rejected or modified by management causing members to become discouraged that their efforts were in vain. In time, the novelty of problem solving wears off and what once was a challenge now becomes a chore. Individual members in this stage tend to leave the circle or engage in nonproductive behavior which negatively affects the group. Circles in this stage may unnecessarily choose to disband. It is during this stage the Facilitators and Leaders must exert extra efforts and exercise creativity to successfully guide the circle through this difficult period. It is recommended that workshops in team building and/or effective communication skills be offered to the circle at this time so members can become aware of their own contributions to their current situation. Efforts must be exerted to direct the circle towards achieving a small success so members can once again feel encouraged to go on with their problem solving. It may be appropriate, or necessary, to invite a member of upper management to visit a circle meeting to demonstrate support of the Quality Circle concept and to show appreciation for the contributions the circle has made. Providing a measure of recognition to circle members is another suggestion. Pictures can be taken and posted on bulletin boards, or in-house newsletters published focusing on circle activities.

There is no one right answer for circles in this stage. Each situation will be unique and the corrective action will have to be hand tailored to suit each particular circle and situation.

STAGE 7 — INTERDEPENDENCE

If disenchantment can be worked through, a new phase of interdependence emerges. Members now view the program more realistically and accept the fact that some of their solutions may not be accepted. They are still faced with problems in their work area which need attention and they are willing to direct their energies towards solving them. In this stage the circle redefines its approach and attitudes and decides to carry on despite the occasional roadblocks and disappointments. This is a more stabilized period than the enchantment phase, and members will begin to engage in prime functioning during their approach to problem solving.

STAGE 8 — CLOSURE

Ultimately, all circles must prepare for closure, either because most area problems have been addressed or the circle has simply failed to jell as an effective team. At this point interest wanes, attendance falls off, and realistically everyone recognizes that the circle has served its purpose or has reached a non-productive state. It is important that the Leader and Facilitator sense this eventuality in its initial stages and begin to prepare for the dissolution of the circle. Another measure, short of final closure, which might be tried here, is placing the circle in a holding or maintenance mode; scheduling meetings monthly rather than weekly until it is finally determined whether or not a circle can become productive. But once it is obvious that the circle is not productive, closure should be performed decisively and in a timely fashion.

STAGE 9 — DISCORPORATION

Thus, the final stage in the life cycle of a circle is its official discorporation. It is recommended that management attend to express appreciation to the circle for their involvement and assistance. Recognition should be given to every circle member during this meeting.

CONCLUSION

It should be noted that while these stages are normal behavior for all circles, the sequential pattern may vary from circle to circle, with any given circle fluctuating from one phase to another at any time. In addition, an individual member may be in a different phase than the circle as a whole. It is felt, however, that an understanding of the normal stages and probable progression can be helpful to leaders and members alike to enable them to realize what is happening to them as a circle, and to best determine what has to be done to enable the circle to operate with maximum effectiveness.

In summary, it should be noted that the long term success of a Quality Circles Program is dependent upon two important factors: the dedication of the Leaders and Facilitators to the concept of participative programs; and their mutual ability to meet the operational needs of each circle as it progresses through its evolutionary stages.

QC CIRCLES' SUCCESS DEPENDS ON MANAGEMENT READINESS TO SUPPORT WORKERS' INVOLVEMENT

Keith A. Brooke

Quality control or QC Circles are often presented as a new approach to involving the work force in solving problems related to product quality. Reputed to have been developed in this country, QC Circles met with relatively limited acceptance here until the Japanese became interested and, almost universally, adopted the concept in most of their key manufacturing companies.

In Japan, small, intact work groups generally assume the QC Circle mantle. These small work groups are encouraged to meet and develop suggestions for solving quality problems and improving product quality. As these groups successfully implement their suggestions, they are sometimes rewarded monetarily on the basis of the estimated value of the suggestion.

In 1978, while on a trip to Japan, I learned first-hand that Japanese managers consider the QC Circle concept fundamental to their remarkable advancements in product quality. These sentiments were expressed by officials at Toyota, Nissan, Isuzu, Mitsubishi and Nippon Denso. In fact, a production superintendent at Mitsubishi expressed his thanks to the U.S. for developing and providing his organization with the QC Circle concept. He added that prior to the company's QC Circle involvement, product quality and employee morale were low, but installing QC Circles had caused major ongoing improvements in these areas.

In the U.S., QC Circles are generally implemented to solve a specific problem, usually one related to product quality. The circle is then disbanded when the employees submit a suggested solution to the problem. However, ongoing circles such as those used in Japan are gaining popularity here. And this gain in popularity is creating a problem for a number of U.S. companies.

Circles Extolled

It is virtually impossible today to pick up a professional journal that doesn't make some mention of QC Circles. These articles generally conclude that the installation of circles in an organization leads to improved product quality, productivity and overall employee performance. Armed with this information, more and more managers are now advocating and initiating QC Circles in their organizations. And, as one might expect, these managers are meeting with varying degrees of success. Why?

A key element in the long-term success or failure of QC Circles is the philosophical readiness of the organization. In short, does management philosophy support, in theory and practice, an intervention in the form of employee involvement? And is management willing and able to assess some of the potential effects of QC Circles on organizational roles, structure, technology and the like?

If these assessments have been made and management, employees and union agree that the organization is indeed ready, chances for success are greatly improved.

Unfortunately, it has often been our practice in this country to discover a "people program" that has been used successfully in another company and, much as with a piece of equipment, lift that program into our company and expect the same results. We have even become adept at rationalizing this phenomenon by openly agreeing that organizations are different and then, having taken comfort in this admission, proceeding as if all organizations were identical.

Intervention Implications

Finally, and of greatest concern, is the almost whimsical acceptance of the QC Circle concept by managers who seemingly have given little forethought to the potential long-term implications of this intervention within the organization.

Certainly, enough data are available to support the value of the QC Circle approach to problem solving. However, as we have learned at General Motors, installing a circle in an organization without attention to readiness can lead to failure. The very nature of the concept, which entrusts the employee with problem-solving responsibility, presumes an organizational philosophy of employee involvement and participation.

At one GM location, the plant manager and his staff spend an entire week together deciding and coming to agreement on the management philosophy that would form the basis of the management employee relationship. By the end of the week this group had decided on the following statement:

The plant organization is dedicated to the principle that our accomplishments are dependent on developing the potential of our human resources. By establishing a work climate that promotes the worth and dignity of people the plant's success is assured.

In addition, the group evaluated the long-term effects this philosophy might have on company structure, technology, training, management-employee relationships and so on. Clearly, the QC Circles concept has a greater opportunity to flourish in this kind of a management environment.

However, there are other organizations whose management has no apparent concern regarding the prevalent management philosophy and whether that philosophy supports the intervention of a QC Circle.

For example, contrast the following philosophy with the previous philosophy and consider the merits of installing a QC Circle in this organization:

We believe that applying coercion, intimidation, pressure and threats will make people perform in an efficient manner. Moreover, by pitting people and departments against each other, the organization's objectives will be secured.

Obviously, the QC Circle concept will have major difficulty surviving in an organization with a philosophy of coercion and intimidation.

Assessing Organizational Readiness For QC Circles

Fundamental to the success of QC Circles is the readiness of the key people — management and union — to sanction and support this kind of process. By using various techniques of observation, interviewing and surveying, the level of readiness can be assessed.

For the most part, this is a data collection task that should be carried out by a person or persons who can be objective and who have some measure of credibility with most of the people in the organization.

At a minimum, the following areas should be explored:

• *Organizational structure* — Through interviews, discussions, observations and so on, it should be determined to what extent people feel compelled to protect and maintain their functional "turf." For example, if the quality reliability people resent "interference" or feel threatened by ideas coming from people outside their department, the QC Circle concept is in jeopardy.

• *Management philosophy* — Top management may have one perception of the prevalent management philosophy while the rest of the organization has a totally different one. Through interviews, surveys and observation it can be determined whether the perceived management philosophy is indeed compatible with the participation and involvement necessary for QC Circles to succeed.

• *Overall knowledge of concept* — Another sign of organizational readiness is general knowledge and understanding of the QC Circle process. On the other hand, if some of the key people in the organization are questioning the use of QC Circles, readiness is questionable. In short, there should be a general acceptance that this process is an essential ingredient for improving the organization.

• *Implementation plans* — A plan developed and sanctioned by the key people, complete with contingencies and detailing the installation process for QC Circles, is a sure sign that the organization is ready to proceed.

If there are any major problems or concerns in these four areas, a "fall back and regroup" strategy is advisable.

Organizational Readiness

If the organization is not ready, starting QC Circle may have long-term negative consequences. People generally enjoy participating in meaningful problem solving processes, and when these are begun and subsequently terminated, reactions of anger and indifference can be expected. Restarting a QC Circle in this kind of situation is extremely difficult.

Bill Voll, president of Sibley's Machine and Foundry, a family-owned business, became interested in some form of employee involvement because of his belief that employees' contributions of ideas and solutions to problems could provide the company with a competitive edge.

Working with his staff, it is Voll's intention to launch a "Sibleyized" QC Circle process. However, before such a change will be undertaken, he is determined that his organization will be ready. That means:

- All management and union officials understand the QC Circle concept.
- A management philosophy is in place that supports employee involvement.
- Training needs have been identified and appropriate programs developed and administered.
- Union officials have been involved in developing and administering the concept.

Clearly, meeting these conditions prior to launch will greatly improve the chances that QC Circles will be successful at Sibley's.

At General Motors, a standardized approach has been developed that is aimed at maximizing the chances for success. Specifically, General Motors Education and Training has developed a training package tailored to the needs of the corporation. Member locations desirous of launching a QC Circle process will generally send both management and union representatives to the week-long training classes.

At the end of the week these representatives are prepared to return to their locations and assist in starting up what are called employee participation groups (EPG). Because GM's approach to QC Circles is substantively different from others, the title "employee participation group" was adopted.

Along with the training materials, an organizational readiness questionnaire was developed. This questionnaire is used as a self-assessment tool by the GM member location to determine whether it is actually ready to launch participation groups. If there is some question regarding its readiness, the location generally contacts its divisional office or the Corporate Organizational Research and Development staff for consultative support.

Directional Concerns

Assuming your organization has a compatible management philosophy, top level support and sanction and, in organizations with represented employees, a union leadership anxious to participate in the growth and development of the membership, what's next?

The statement, "If you don't know where you're going, any road will get you there," has meaning for those contemplating the next step. That step should be assessing how QC Circles will contribute to the overall direction of the organization. For example, they should be compatible with the existing or planned technology, and they will require an overall organizational structure that will support the concept.

For example, as people become more and more technically knowledgeable, they run the risk of interfering with those who have functional responsibilities in such areas as quality control, industrial engineering and so on. Key people in the organization need to think through and carefully anticipate the changes in traditional roles that will evolve out of an employee involvement process. The industrial engineering role in a QC Circle organization might change from a more traditional role of dictating job standards, methods, etc., to that of expert resource, trainer and consultant.

QC Circles have the potential to cause people to positively reexamine and rethink their commitment to an organization. However, if they are treated as an "add on" or something that might be "sort of nice" to do, the potential long-term value will probably be lost.

In Japan, QC Circles are not an add on, but an essential ingredient in the overall fabric of organizational life. In every company I visited, management universally agreed that QC Circles were essential to the continued excellent quality of company products.

Beyond QC Circles

A personnel specialist from one Japanese company suggests that we in the U.S. need to learn how to manage *groups of individuals* and that when we do, we will be optimally effective as managers. Furthermore, he observed that the QC Circle approach — with some modifications to account for cultural differences — would be a good place to start but not to finish. QC Circles should be a step in an evolutionary process and not an objective or end in themselves.

For the most part, GM management would concur with these observations. Local managers are encouraged to adopt strategies for change aimed at developing a trained, involved work force beyond the mere implementation of QC Circles. Already at various GM locations, workers have responsibility for establishing and maintaining quality and cost goals as well as maintaining various operating budgets. Generally, these employees have organized themselves into work teams.

As these changes are planned, it becomes obvious that the employees and the supervisors require different skills. For example, as the employees assume team responsibility for more and more of the daily production requirements, the supervisor becomes more of a resource available to the team in virtually a consultative capacity. The supervisor is also more readily available for planning, coordinating and developing with regard to product, method and people.

Additionally, the work group benefits from training in problem-solving techniques as well as team development methods. In these examples the organization is going beyond the traditional QC Circle concept. However, it is also true that these steps seem to be logical extensions of a QC Circle.

We are in the process of evolving into an organization in which commitment is not the exclusive ownership of the top, but is shared by all; ideas and problem solving are part of everyone's job; and people work cohesively and collaborate in a unified effort to help the organization achieve its purpose. Certainly one of the main vehicles for achieving this ideal is the QC Circle concept.

DIAGNOSING READINESS
Edmund J. Metz

"Quality circles will work in any type of organization and every organization should have the program." These words were spoken by one of the presenters in a workshop at the Third Annual International Association of Quality Circles Conference in Louisville, March, 1981. I wrote the words down because I had heard similar words before and I think they represent some sort of "belief" or "accepted mythology" about quality circles.

Briefly, the mythology implies that all one needs to do is to start a quality circle program and the whole organization will become more participative and better. "Success" appears to be assumed.

Success can *not* be assumed; too many circle programs are being started without recognition of or sensitivity to the organizational impact of quality circles. This factor is one reason why a number of circle programs will eventually fail.[1]

Although "diagnosing organization readiness" for circles is often spoken about as a necessary step in the implementation process, the sad reality is that in most cases it is not done at all or is done in only a very superficial way. If a pre-implementation diagnosis is important, then why isn't it being done as a standard implementation practice? There are two reasons:

1. **Lack of Skill**

   The driving force behind the quality circle movement in the United States (industrial engineers, quality engineers, process and product line managers, etc.) does not generally have a background in formal organizational diagnostic skills ("how to").

2. **Lack of Knowledge**

   Most managers don't know "what to" diagnose. Specialized education and experience in working with organizational systems is needed. Typically, managers don't have time to learn.

My purpose is to present what "diagnosis" is, why it is important, the intervention implications of quality circles into an organization system, and to list some readiness factors existing within a systems model.

WHAT IS DIAGNOSIS?

A definition of "diagnosis" is offered by Harry Levinson: "it is a method to fully describe an organization's concept, objectives, plans, its view of itself as well as its relationship with others, and its leadership. It must enable the consultant to understand systems of communication, coordination, guidance, control, and support. It must help him to delineate relevant environments and behavior settings. It must be a guide to unfolding the rationale of the organization, explaining its activities, and critically evaluating the organization's adaptive adequacy, followed by a reasoned series of recommendations."[2]

"Diagnosis" is, then, the drawing of conclusions about what collected data means. The collection of "data" is the assembly process which precedes the diagnosis. "Diagnosis" means assigning meaning, weight, priority, and relationship to the data. For quality circles, diagnosis is done to identify organizational "gaps" between what is and what ought to be. What is, for example, the present "acceptance of the participative style" by middle managers and what "ought it to be for circle success?" This question can be asked to identify a number of other key organizational readiness elements.

WHY IS DIAGNOSIS IMPORTANT?

Organizations, like people, are complex systems of interrelated subsystems. Each system within an organization affects and is affected by other systems. An organization is an "open system" in that it strives to maintain some equilibrium among its internal subsystems, between itself and other internal systems, and between itself and larger systems of external society. This means that it must continually adapt in order to survive. Sometimes internal subsystems do not function well together: some subsystems change faster than others; some are more highly defined and goal driven than others; some are more autonomous than others; and some have different norms, beliefs, and values than others.

To attempt to prescribe and install quality circles in an organization without a knowledge of, or sensitivity to how circles will impact both the total organizational system and the different subsystems is to flirt with program failure. There are at least three reasons why diagnosis is needed:

1. Introducing quality circles represents an "intervention" into the total system of an organization. Diagnosis helps determine which subsystems will be supportive of circle success, which subsystems will not be affected, and which subsystems contain weaknesses which could undermine the circle endeavor.

2. Quality circles represent a "prescription" for some organizational gap between what is and what ought to be. Diagnosis helps determine whether quality circles are really the appropriate program and acitvity for the organization. Diagnosis also helps to identify what other types of programs or activities (i.e., team building, operations research, M.B.O., strategic planning, etc.) might be needed in combination with quality circles to maintain some relative organizational equilibrium.

3. Diagnosis can help identify the best "time" for the intervention. Should the program be started now or be delayed until a later time i.e., pending planned involvement in key support subsystems?

Behind such a major intervention as quality circles a diagnosis needs to be done. No *one* program such as quality circles can, by itself, improve everything. "Improving an organization means diagnosing and intervening in ways and places that increase productivity *and* enhance people's self-esteem."[3] The appropriateness of quality circles for an organization at any point in time should not be assumed.

READINESS FACTORS WITHIN
A SYSTEMS MODEL

The desire by management for improvements in quality, productivity, morale and attitudes are the primary driving forces behind implementing quality circles. Quality circles represent an intervention into these subsystems, the purpose being to generate some prescribed influence or actions that will yield desired results (i.e., quality and productivity gains). A systems model which I like for both its completeness yet its relative simplicity was designed by William G. Dyer, Dean of the Graduate School of Business, Brigham Young University. This model contains the three key organizational systems which interact to produce organization outputs: The Social System, Operation System, and Administrative System. (See Figure 1 — Organization Systems/Outputs.)[4]

The Social System contains those dynamic conditions resulting from people in all different organizational positions who constantly interact by talking, deciding, solving problems, etc., for the dual purposes of achieving organizational goals and satisfying personal needs.

The Operation System is the special arrangement of material, equipment, processes, and people used to accomplish work. This system can be altered readily by changing to different materials, rearranging or changing equipment, and changing staffing or work assignments. The Social System is closely connected to and influenced by the Operation System. For example, changing the equipment arrangement and work flow has an influence on people's ability to interact, the patterns of supervision, and perhaps the planning and decision process.

The Administrative System represents the skeletal frame of policies, procedures, control mechanisms, and reporting systems that help the Operational and Social Systems to function. Some major elements within this Administrative System are the wage and salary system, the hiring and promotion process, financial reporting and auditing system, and the total package of fringe benefits.

A model of this system's structure is shown in Figure 2.[5] The model demonstrates that a number of different interventions are possible at the different levels of human involvement. Quality circles represent an intervention within the Social

Organization Systems/Outputs[4]

Social System	Operation System	Administrative System	Organization Outputs
Climate	Work Flow	Policy – Wage & Salary	Profit / Loss
Status Role	Equipment	Promotions	Production
Decision Making	Location	Fringe Benefits	Costs
Management Style	Physical Environment	Hiring – Firing	Absenteesim
Values	Material	Raises	Turnover
Communication	Work Arrangements	Budgets	Commitment
Goals	Schedules	Reporting System	Involvement
Problem Solving		Auditing	Apathy
			Quality

Figure 1.

A Matrix of Interventions

	Social System	Operation System	Administrative System
Individual	management training counseling coaching	technical training job enrichment	incentives/promotions m.b.o. – individual
Team/Unit	team building process consultation QUALITY CIRCLES	work re-design job enrichment	wage review unit goal-setting
Inter/Group	confrontation conference inter-group building	work-team formation work-flow analysis	strategic planning scheduling review
Total Organization	survey/feedback organization diagnosis	system re-design capital projects	forecasting long-range planning analysis of information system

Figure 2.

System at the team or unit level. In fact, most Organizational Development interventions occur within the social system. Many O.D. efforts have experienced more failure than success (O.D. is sometimes called "organized disappointment"). Quality circles will also be in for its share of difficulties. According to Robert E. Cole, professor of sociology and the director of the center for Japanese Studies at the University of Michigan, only about one-third of the circles established in Japan are doing well.[6] Clearly, some unidentified factors are involved.

Within the total systems model there are some key readiness elements which need to be diagnosed. These are:

Social System
Top management understanding and motivation for the program
Management practices
Middle management support
Management training and development
Organization climate
Interface/support groups

Operation System
Physical organization climate
Work flow and arrangements
Facility location
Size — numbers

Administrative System
Funding and facilities support
Availability of effective facilitator candidates

Organizational time commitments
Union acceptance/contract limitations
Reporting and control systems
History of "programs"
Health/stability of overall business

A comprehensive presentation of all of the specifics to be diagnosed under each of these elements is beyond the scope of this article. A few examples may be helpful.

SOCIAL SYSTEM

Top management understanding and motivation for the program.

Consider:

How did the top manager hear of quality circles?

What specifically about quality circles interested him/her?

What are the main reasons why he or she would like to have quality circles in the organization?

What does the top manager already know about the program?

Does the top manager appear to practice and model to some degree the basic principles of participative management?

If not, how large is the gap of management practice?

Organization climate (a result of management practices, it is the prevailing emotional state shared by members in the system; this may be formal, relaxed, defensive, cautious, accepting, trusting, etc.).

Consider:

What is the dominant emotional theme you see and feel?

What are the variances in emotional tone within/between key groups?

What is the level of intensity of the prevailing emotions?

How free or constricted are people to say what they feel?

Does the "joking" you see serve as the basis for relationships or is it suggestive of something else?

How long do the emotional expressions last?

Do feelings and attitudes differ by organization level?

How?

Are there signs of inter-group/departmental hostility or conflict?

OPERATION SYSTEM

Physical organization climate (plant and equipment, and how they affect people who must work in and with them).

Consider:

Do seasonal cycles cause periodic peaks and valleys of energy expenditure?

Are there daily peaks of activity?

What are the time units used to plan the future? (6 mos., 1 yr., 5 yrs.)

How much are people's daily activities regulated by time?

What are organizational norms and rules on punctuality?

How much pressure is there to meet deadlines?

What happens when deadlines are missed?

ADMINISTRATIVE SYSTEM

Organizational time commitments (is the organization time-bound by season, by inventory, by book-balancing tasks, by fiscal, or product, or by manufacturing processes?).

Consider:

Do seasonal cycles cause periodic peaks and valleys of energy expenditure?

Are there daily peaks of activity?

What are the time units used to plan the future? (6 mos., 1-yr., 5-yrs.)

How much are people's daily activities regulated by time?

What are organizational norms and rules on punctuality?

How much pressure is there to meed deadlines?

What happens when deadlines are missed?

CONCLUSION

Quality circles are a major intervention into an organizational system. This program should not be introduced until after a period of data gathering and analysis has been done. While the long range success of a circle program in any company can never be absolutely guaranteed a good diagnosis will go far in helping to establish successful implementation and in generating overall organizational improvement.

NOTES

[1]Edmund J. Metz, "Caution: Quality Circles Ahead," *Training and Development Journal* (August 1981).

[2]Harry Levinson, *Organizational Diagnosis* (Cambridge: Harvard University Press, 1972). p. 6.

[3]Marvin R. Weisbord, *Organizational Diagnosis*, (Reading, Mass: Addison-Wesley Publishing Company, 1978), p. 52.

[4]Public Seminar, *Team Building*, (presented by William G. Dyer, Snowbird, Utah, June 1979).

[5]William G. Dyer, "Selecting an Intervention for Organizational Change," *Training and Development Journal* (April 1981).

[6]Robert E. Cole, "Japan Can But We Can't," (IAQC Conference Presentation, Louisville, Ky., March 1981).

AVOIDING PROBLEMS IN
DEVELOPING QUALITY CIRCLES
Roger W. Berger

Quality Circles can enhance the quality of working life, reduce the cost of producing goods and services, and improve the quality of workers' output. However, there are five main ways in which Quality Circle programs fail to develop into successful organization-wide processes. This article will examine each of these five problems in more detail and suggest appropriate responses.

The five problem areas are:

1) Lack of middle management support.
2) Poor communications.
3) Unrealistic expectations.
4) Conflict with other programs.
5) Transfers and excessive turnover.

LACK OF MIDDLE MANAGEMENT SUPPORT

This is probably the greatest of all pitfalls in an evolving Quality Circle program. Typically, at the outset, there are a *few* middle managers who, along with a dedicated top manager and the enthusiastic pilot Circles, get the program started. A large number of middle managers often remain either indifferent or hostile.

A key objective for the pilot program is to change hostile managers to neutral status, and to convert the indifferent managers to enthusiastic support. Only if this is done can Circles ever become an integral part of organizational culture.

An initial lack of wholehearted enthusiasm is not a sufficient reason to postpone or cancel the pilot group. Many people have had ample reasons to be suspicious of new "programs" that promise great gains and threaten to change established ways of doing things. However, if there is not a shift away from hostility and indifference towards acceptance and support the program will obviously wither in time. An extremely important goal, once the initial Circles are started, is to actively promote this shift.

DEVELOPING MIDDLE MANAGEMENT SUPPORT

Here are some ideas for the facilitator:

1. Get top management to include support for Circles in the evaluation process for middle managers. This is a tangible way for top management to include in the review (for promotions and raises) a part on cooperating and supporting circles, then that manager will make a more serious personal effort to understand the good features, the favorable potentials, of Circles. Everybody would rather get a good review than a poor one!

2. Provide periodic training/orientation for the uninvolved managers and their key assistants. This could be in the form of occasional luncheon meetings, or special presentations to regular staff meetings. At such meetings, there will normally be both supportive and rejective managers. You should see that the supportive managers are prepared to speak up in a constructive fashion at such a meeting. A shortened version of a successful management presentation by a live-wire Circle can do wonders to help open people's eyes about the program.

You might even consider a really solid "Management Workshop" that would encompass a series of up to eight one-hour sessions. Bring the advocates and critics together in a spirit of friendly discussion. Start off with a lighthearted quiz about Circles and related topics. Plan for formal and informal presentations about aspects that are concerning people in the organization. You might even consider a debate between the two opposed factions. This should occur well before the end of the workshop so that people have a chance to react informally to ideas presented during the debate. Do not ask people to commit themselves, but give them information and viewpoints which may help turn their attitudes around.

PLAN OCCASIONAL PRESENTATIONS

3. Schedule an occasional presentation by an outside consultant or facilitator. Every organization depends on getting some new ideas from the outside. The Quality Circles process in particular, being an open-systems form of activity, thrives on free and open communication patterns. What better way to promote Circles than for successful outsiders to share their favorable experiences and impressions? You would be surprised how many proponents of Circles are happy to share in this way! Such a presentation might be in connection with your management club, or a local professional society such as Society for Advancement of Management, American Institute of Industrial Engineers. American Society for Training and Development, and American Society for Personnel Administration.

4. Provide some financial incentive. This is very dangerous ground, and should be approached only with caution. Circles historically have been relatively free of financial rewards. However, if you have top management that strongly believes in the use of money payments as immediate reward, then it does make sense to use this form of expression to move the Circles process along. It is probably best to use indirect financial methods rather than straight dollar payments to the new converts. One attractive way to do this is to provide a special budget allowance to departments that establish successful Circle activities. (You will have to think carefully about how to define "success.") With a financial incentive in view, which can be realized if Manager X helps get a Circle operating and producing cost saving ideas, that manager will have a rather compelling reason to get involved. This should be a one-shot deal, and the use of the funds might be limited to providing training or work-place en-

hancement — a special luncheon, a picnic, support for sending a Circle to a nearby conference — things like this that do not put money directly into anyone's pockets.

DEVELOP A DIAGNOSTIC APPROACH

5. Be willing to ask questions and listen patiently to the answers. It is not always easy for people who object to a new program to tell their reasons why. Yet, if you know the specific reason, you may be able to resolve it with common sense. Thus, you should learn to ask constructive questions and to be a good listener. Often you will find that ignorance or misconceptions are the basis for serious resistance. Objective discussion of the facts in a nonthreatening manner can alleviate such concerns.

6. Look at your steering committee. Is it doing the job of informing and coordinating? Maybe a key resistor should be made a member of the committee. This has two salutory effects. It gives the other members of the committee a chance to respond to his/her objections. More importantly, perhaps, it gives the objector an opportunity to influence the committee in a constructive fashion. Like monetary rewards, this technique should be approached with great caution. Be sure, before suggesting such an appointment, that the objector is both sincere and open-minded. Otherwise, you may be letting a bull into a china shop.

POOR COMMUNICATIONS

One of the objectives of Quality Circles is to improve communications. But, of course, saying so doesn't make it so! Using the diagnostic approach mentioned in the previous section, you should carefully investigate any indication that the word is not getting out to the necessary people. A good facilitator uses informal conversations, occasional memos, questionnaires, and third parties to find out how people feel about things pertaining to Circles.

Many resentments are based on incorrect or incomplete information. Check your firm's memos to employees, news releases, and newsletters. Do they have good, accurate reports of what the Circles have done? Are they giving recognition to achievers? Is credit being given to non-Circle members who assist the Circles in problem solving? (This is a must!)

Check to see if achieving Circles are getting recognition through other channels. The Quality Circle concept depends heavily on open and consistent recognition of achievement. But people sometimes forget. They need to be reminded. For example, one Circle program suffered a severe setback after the following sequence: When the pilot Circles were first formed, the general manager was totally enthusiastic. He treated all members to a lavish luncheon in the executive dining room. The program got off to a very optimistic start! The Circles had not even done anything yet, and already top management was lavishing recognition.

Later, after one of the Circles had solved a really significant problem and given a first-class presentation to management, the general manager was preoccupied with an unrelated problem. He thanked the Circle for its work and that was that! All through the pilot phase, the members of all the Circles eagerly anticipated management's reaction to their first big breakthrough. When management showed indifference, the Circle members went flat as a punctured balloon. In this case, the program survived the setback, because an alert facilitator sensed what was happening. A less sensitive or forceful facilitator might have failed to take any corrective action, and progressive disillusionment might have set in.

UNREALISTIC EXPECTATIONS

American managers are highly attuned to short-run results. A program like Quality Circles, whose best results often show up only after years of concentrated effort, may seem strange to such managers. The facilitator and other proponents should not oversell the promise of the program at any time — it is not a panacea. If management expectations become too high, it is up to the facilitator to bite the bullet, to explain that quick dramatic results were not promised and should not be demanded.

This admonition to promote subdued expectations may seem like a paradox, in view of the exciting results that have been reported in the media. An analogy may be in order. Periodically, a news release comes out from Las Vegas, Nevada, that S. R. Anybody has struck it rich with a $300,000 jackpot. News like this lures many people to Las Vegas to try their luck, and most of them lose most of their gambling stake. Any rational person knows that, on the average, the gambling houses must pay all their regular expenses, plus the occasional big jackpot, out of the losses of the great majority of their clients.

Now, by analogy, the vast majority of Quality Circle successes are of the modest variety. A few hundred dollars are saved here, a few thousand there. Improved work attitudes, occasional improvement in work flow and work environment result. Perhaps, over a year's time, a measurable decrease is reported in the defect rate — nothing dramatic.

Occasionally a Circle scores a really big success, and the news spreads like wildfire. It appears in the local newspapers, and perhaps on the evening television news. If we step back and look at this phenomenon rationally, we know that a very small percentage of the Circles are going to have really spectacular success — if everybody did it, it wouldn't be spectacular any more! But, human nature being what it is, we should not be surprised when people's expectations become unrealistic.

CONFLICT WITH OTHER PROGRAMS

Some firms just have "programitis." This is a manifestation of the fad phenomenon. An executive reads about a hot new trend in the business press, or hears about a big breakthrough from a friend at the country club. First thing you know, one of his/her staff has been assigned to "get that program going here as soon as possible." Some of these crash programs work out fine, most just sputter along; a few are outright disasters. Suggestion systems, computerized incentive programs, short-interval scheduling, management by objectives, job enrichment, zero defects, work simplification — these are just a few of the many "programs" a given company may have in various stages of development or disillusion at any given time.

Quality Circles depend, at rock bottom, on measured, voluntary cooperation and long-term trust. Sometimes it is tough competition against flashier programs, such as suggestion systems with hefty cash awards. Further, there may be inherent conflicts among the motivational base of some of these programs. The facilitator may find him/herself in a very difficult position in trying to maintain enthusiasm and positive effort in the face of such conflict. This is a subject that must be addressed by the Circle's steering committee, and ultimately, top management. The best advice is to carefully collect factual data. Do not jump to hasty, unsupportable, conclusions. When the facts are in and clear, prepare a definite recommendation to resolve the conflict.

TRANSFER AND EXCESSIVE TURNOVER

One difference between American and Japanese industry is in employment patterns. In Japan, lifelong employment is the norm, and promotions occur only at intervals of several years. The effect of this is that people working in one area become very well acquainted with each other for a long period of time. On the other hand, U.S. industry, for the most part, experiences intermittent layoffs in consonance with the business cycle. This usually means quite a bit of job turnover, which can in turn play havoc with Circle activities.

Industrial planners who wish to build strong organizations soon realize that layoffs, followed (especially in manufacturing plants with union contracts) by a series of job "bumps" are quite counterproductive to effective group interactions. So long as the worker only had to interact with his/her supervisor and a machine or two, it may not have mattered much. With Circles, sometimes a key member or even a leader will change jobs. This poses an immediate challenge to the facilitator and the remaining Circle members. The replacement will need special training and coaching, as well as sympathetic understanding, before getting up to speed.

If a key Circle leader is transferred, it may stunt the growth of Circles for a while. If a key top manager is transferred, it may kill the Circles dead on the spot. This is especially true if the successor to the top job was opposed from the outset, for whatever political or philosophical reason. There is really no solid defense against this pitfall, but the alert facilitator can establish links between the Circles and as many of the key managers as possible. There is some safety in numbers.

QUALITY CIRCLES AND CORPORATE CULTURE
William B. Werther, Jr.

Quality circles rest on several key assumptions:

- Employees want to participate in the decisions that affect them.
- Employees have valuable insights that can improve productivity.
- Employees express higher job satisfaction when they participate in job-related decisions.
- Employee expertise should be tapped by management to improve productivity and quality of work life.

Few managers would reject these assumptions. In fact, their truth seems self-evident, and the results obtained by many U.S. companies further validate them. Such companies as IBM, Hughes, Lockheed, Northrop, RCA, Union Carbide, Tektronics, Control Data, and scores of others have all reported considerable success with quality circles. (For an in-depth look at the Hughes program, see the following article in *National Productivity Review*.)

Quality circles are groups of workers and their supervisor voluntarily meeting to identify, analyze, and solve work-place problems. They are based on a concept for a highly specific type of team building that uses problems within the group's influence as a focal point for action. Although the concept has proven successful in many companies and is anchored firmly in the bedrock of behavioral science, any executive who cares to try this tool must make some specific adjustments.

The four areas of concern most frequently encountered by companies that have implemented circles are:

- Establishing the organizational commitment and culture.
- Creating an organizational capability to support circle activities.
- Overcoming barriers to implementation.
- Reducing resistance to circle ideas.

This article — which is the result of over thirty interviews with executives and quality circle facilitators in companies with active productivity programs — examines the benefits of and obstacles to the establishment of quality circles.

ESTABLISHING COMMITMENT AND CULTURE

Most organizations in the United States tend to be top-down oriented. Decisions and communications originate within middle and top management and flow downward to supervisors and employees. Classical management theory gave leaders the authority and responsibility to make decisions. As organizations have grown, some of this authority and responsibility has been shared with middle managers. But the prevailing organizational culture still perceives workers as existing primarily (if not exclusively) to follow orders.

This "efficiency-oriented" organizational culture allows little room for employee involvement in decision making. Moreover, this culture so thoroughly permeates most organizations that its alteration requires considerable commitment on the part of top management. Permission is not sufficient. If the top manager at a plant site or the head of a functional department is not actively committed to creating an environment in which participation takes place, it will not happen. Unlike many organizational changes that merely need permission from top management, a change in an organization's culture cannot be delegated. Instead, the top manager must lead the change by his or her behavior. That manager's style needs to become more participative; examples of participative employee involvement throughout the organization must be encouraged. Successes that result from employee involvement must be recognized.

The Japanese Setting

The emergence of quality circles in Japan during the 1960s was aided by the attitudes of that country's managers, who view their jobs differently than their U.S. counterparts. Japanese managers more commonly saw themselves as facilitators of their subordinates' ideas. They worked to encourage and refine employee suggestions. Not only was participation expected, but the expectation was reinforced by the managers' actions up and down the chain of command.

Furthermore, the economic problems facing Japan required radical solutions. A nation with half the population of the U.S. was crowded on a land mass about the size of Montana. Economic survival rested upon the ability of Japanese firms to import raw materials, add value, and export finished goods. To do this successfully, they had to produce quality products. To produce quality goods at low cost meant that Japanese firms had to find new, better, and lower-cost methods to produce exportable goods.

One part of their strategy was to tap the creativity of their workers through involvement in work-place decisions. Thus, quality circles were begun in organizations that had cultures receptive to a bottom-up flow of ideas.

It would be an exaggeration to suggest that quality circles were the only innovation undertaken by Japanese managers. However, quality control circles, as they were originally named, were one of the most noteworthy of the changes that affected workers directly. Today, the Japanese Union of Scientists and Engineers estimates that 8 million workers in Japan participate in quality circles. Other estimates place the figure at 25 million employees.

Toward a New Culture

Perhaps the major roadblock to moving U.S. firms toward a more participative culture is time. U.S. managers look for quick results, but effective quality circles require considerable time to establish. Successful quality circle efforts at companies such as Solar Turbines, Northrop Aircraft, RCA, Reynolds Metals, Control Data, and others have proceeded at a deliberately slow pace. The organization culture cannot be changed by fiat, regardless of top management's commitment. At Solar Turbines (now a subsidiary of Caterpillar Tractor Company), a total of a dozen circles were operating more than a year after management committed itself to quality circles. With only 120 or so employees involved in a company with more than 3,000 employees, many managers would regard progress as slow. However, this rate of development has been common in many organizations with successful quality circle undertakings.

The reason for what appears to be slow progress in moving the organization toward a new culture has to do with creating a support capability, overcoming barriers, and reducing resistance to circle ideas.

CREATING SUPPORT CAPABILITY

A receptive climate for quality circles depends on effective organizational support and training. Outside the circle meetings, there is a need for direction and assistance to facilitate the circle process. Within the circle meetings, success depends on effective training of circle leaders and members.

A typical quality circle effort involves the use of a steering committee, facilitator(s) or coordinator(s), circle leaders (supervisors), and circle members (employees). The roles and training of these groups merit careful consideration.

Steering Committee

The steering or coordinating committee generally consists of the top manager and those who report directly to him or her. If circles are to begin at the division or plant level, then the division or plant manager and staff form the committee. Its purpose is to set goals for the circle effort. These goals often include the number of circles to be started, the timing and growth rate for circles, and other policy matters. One purpose of the committee is to develop commitment and support among these key managers. By participating in the decisions that are necessary to start and maintain circles, understanding is facilitated.

Although these managers do not need to have a detailed training program for every facet of quality circles, they do need to understand the circle process diagrammed in Figure 1. In that process, problems that affect the work group are identified. These problems may sometimes be detected by management, but most of them are identified by the circle members through brainstorming. Regardless of how problems are identified, the circle members voluntarily select the ones they wish to solve. If there is a pressing problem of concern to management, the circle may select it. But since the circle is based on voluntarism, its members may reject management's request. Management must then solve the problem as it would have done before the circle existed.

Once identified and selected, the problem is subjected to analysis by the circle members. Additional data or technical assistance may be needed from others in the organization. The steering committee, which includes the managers of the departments that provide the technical aid, can affect the success of the circles significantly by encouraging prompt assistance from those outside the circle.

The circle's solution is then presented to the steering committee or to those in management who have the authority to decide on the circle's recommendation. The decision is then communicated to the circle, sometimes after further study by management.

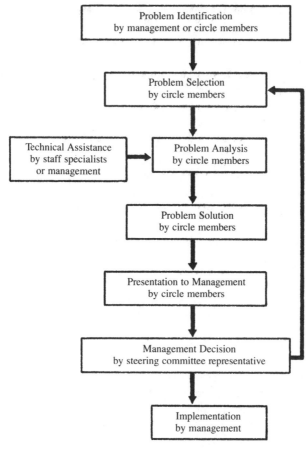

Figure 1.
Quality Circle Process

This explanation of the circle process and the roles of facilitators, supervisors, and members is usually provided to the steering committee through seminars or outside consultants before a circle effort is launched.

Facilitators

The facilitator is the key individual involved in the operation and training of circles. Circle plans begin with the hiring of a facilitator. This person normally is the only addition to the staff required to begin the process.

The facilitator often is an in-house employee who was asked to study the feasibility of beginning quality circles. After several months of study, attending seminars, and planning activities, this key individual brings a recommendation to management about a circle effort. Assuming the decision is favorable, this person often is appointed as a facilitator. Otherwise, an outsider is recruited.

A facilitator is responsible for designing the training materials, conducting orientation seminars for management, initiating interest among supervisors, and training circle leaders and members. Once circles start, the facilitator (or coordinator, as he or she is also called) aids circle leaders by coaching them, maintaining records for them, and securing the technical assistance requested by the circles.

The work histories of facilitators tend to be varied. Some have industrial engineering backgrounds, while others may have experience in training, organizational development, personnel, or general management. At a minimum, facilitators need to have training in the quality circle process, decision making, group dynamics, committee leadership, and consulting skills. Many facilitators begin with a five-day training program provided by the American Productivity Center or the International Association of Quality Circles.

Once the number of circles grows to 10 or 20, a second facilitator is needed. Even when circles are highly experienced, a facilitator can seldom assist more than 20 of them. The need for additional facilitators — and the time it takes for them to "apprentice" to an experienced one or to acquire the needed training and experience — often serves as a brake on the rate at which circles can be started in an organization.

Circle Leaders

Once the steering committee and facilitator are ready to begin, several supervisors judged to have good interpersonal skills are invited to a presentation about quality circles. The facilitator provides an overview that explains the circle concept. Supervisors are told about the training they and their subordinates will receive; the quality circle process is explained; and questions are answered. At the end of the presentation, volunteers are sought.

When a supervisor volunteers, the overview presentation is made to his or her employees. If five to twelve of the employees volunteer, a circle is begun.

The next step in creating a circle is the training of the supervisor, usually by the facilitator. This training lasts two or three days. Its content includes such topics as committee leadership, group dynamics, and problem-solving techniques. The training focuses on teaching the supervisor to conduct a circle meeting more like the chair of a committee than a "boss." He or she is trained to run the circle meetings by seeking consensus at each stage of the circle's deliberations. The supervisor is expected to lead the circle meetings, not direct them. Aside from building consensus, the role entails attending to such logistical details as the time and place of the meeting. The leader also communicates with the facilitator concerning any unique needs or any assistance the circle may require for a particular meeting.

Circle Members

Following the supervisor's training, those employees who volunteered for membership are trained. Their training usually lasts eight hours and focuses on decision-making techniques such as brainstorming, Pareto analysis, fish-bone or cause-and-effect diagrams, and data-gathering techniques. Members also are trained in making presentations.

The training enables workers to attack problems systematically by gathering and analyzing data. They are encouraged to "learn and talk" management's language by justifying their recommendations in cost/benefit terms. This not only leads to a high rate of accepted ideas — 75% or more in most cases — but causes employees to screen out frivolous suggestions.

The Circle Support Network

With a commitment from top management, an active steering committee, and competent facilitators, a network exists to support the ongoing change in the corporate culture that is needed to move away from classical top-down orientation.

Then, the success of circles in solving problems creates a climate of change. The employee and management grapevines report the benefits of circle activities. Employees tell co-workers about the process and stimulate grass-roots interest. Their discussions reflect the positive feelings that come from a sense of making a more meaningful contribution, of being a part of the organization and its decision-making apparatus. A feeling of teamwork and a "can-do" attitude slowly replace the feeling of helplessness employees often have about the ongoing process of change.

Supervisor-employee relations improve because communications are on a more adult-to-adult level. The supervisor is seen more as a coach or leader and less as the "boss." As employee morale and commitment improve, peer pressure becomes more congruent with work-related goals. Often these developments are first noticed when production improves despite the one work hour a week devoted to the circle meeting. In fact, in cases where jobs are not machine-paced, many supervisors report that their department output does not drop even on the day when the circle meets.

As cost-saving/productivity-enhancing ideas are implemented, supervisors or middle managers who are not directly involved with circles learn of the advantages. In short, the circle process feeds on its own success.

Admittedly, some workers and supervisors do not want to participate in the process. Some simply fear the change; supervisors in particular may fear the loss of authority that consensus problem solving implies for them. However, since circles are voluntary for supervisors and employees alike, both are free to continue as in the past, especially since the growth rate of most circle programs would make it impossible to bring everyone into the process for years anyhow. Admittedly, peer pressure often exists, which encourages supervisors to start circles and employees to join them.

OVERCOMING BARRIERS TO IMPLEMENTATION

The support network and the circle process do not remove every barrier to a successful quality circle effort. Other barriers have hindered the development of quality circles. These barriers do not arise in every company's attempt to implement circles, but when present they can materially affect the usefulness of and receptivity to quality circles.

Middle Management's Support

Once the decision to begin circles is made, most training activity centers around first-level supervisors and employees. Middle managers are sometimes overlooked. They may not even be formally notified of the forthcoming quality circles. When supervisors and employees are off the job for training or in weekly meetings, middle managers may feel threatened. They may reasonably ask, "What is going on in those meetings? How are those meetings going to help me meet my objectives?" Pronouncements by top management of its support for circles may even keep these questions from being asked openly.

One step in overcoming this barrier is to provide an overview of quality circles followed by a question-and-answer session exclusively for middle managers. Such companies as American Express and AmHoist have used this strategy. Other companies offer the supervisory training to the middle managers to ensure their understanding and support. Still other companies ask the affected middle managers to sit in on circle presentations to the steering committee.

Regardless of the strategy used, middle management support is crucial. It is these managers who will encourage or discourage interested supervisors. And it is the middle managers who are often responsible for overseeing the implementation of circle suggestions. Unless the steering committee and facilitators take action to create a sense of "ownership" among middle managers, the results of the circle effort will be diminished.

Purpose And Name

What is the purpose of installing quality circles? Is it to improve productivity? Product quality? Quality of work life? The answers to these questions materially affect the character of quality circles. Different companies seek different objectives. Solar Turbine sought to maintain and improve its product quality image. The company called its effort "Quality Circles." Union Carbide called its program "PRIDE circles," an acronym for Productivity through Recognition, Involvement, and Development of Employees. This theme was selected to emphasize the importance of developing productivity and pride among employees through recognition and involvement. Control Data called its approach "Involvement Teams," even though the result was traditional quality circles. To emphasize the quality-of-work-life benefits it sought from circles and to avoid making these teams appear to be just another cost-cutting approach, Control Data initially did not even measure the dollar savings from circle ideas.

The purpose and name, therefore, affects the philosophy and approach the company uses. Interestingly, however, regardless of the theme, successful circle efforts yield improvement in quality of work life, attitudes, productivity, and cost savings. In fact, most facilitators refer to the documented savings from circles by rounding the return on investment to the nearest 100%, with 300 and 400% returns mentioned most commonly. For example, Solar Turbine consistently has averaged a 300% rate of return once its program got past the eighteen-month start-up period.

Outside Consultants

Many quality circle efforts begin by tapping the skills of outside consultants. They are often used to present an overview of the productivity crisis and the role quality circles can play in solving this corporate dilemma. Inland Steel, Philadelphia Electric, and Ohio Blue Cross/Blue Shield are among the companies that brought in consultants. Reynolds Metals and other companies speeded up the planning process by buying the training materials offered by an outside consultant, although these were eventually modified for internal use.

However, the use of outside consultants can be a significant barrier if the company relies on the consultant to make the program work. Internal responsibility for the results of quality circles was recognized at every company studied that had a successful program. Operational responsibility for success rests with the facilitator or, when more than one facilitator exists, with the administrator of the quality circle effort. Ultimate responsibility resides in the steering committee. To use an outside consultant beyond the planning and introductory phases may result in a perception that responsibility for success or failure does not rest with management. The resultant lack of ownership would probably doom to failure even the most carefully planned circle effort.

One other major barrier merits special attention: How can management help modify the organizational culture sufficiently to reduce resistance to circle ideas?

REDUCING RESISTANCE TO CIRCLE IDEAS

A high proportion of quality circle suggestions are accepted by management. This is not surprising, because the quality circles offer data-based — rather than opinion-based — recommendations. Also, the extensive planning and training efforts needed to start circles predispose management to expect a return on its ''investment'' in the form of usable employee ideas. Lastly, if the acceptance rate were low, circles would likely disband because of their limited success and voluntary nature.

However, resistance to circle suggestions does (and sometimes should) occur. Poorly thought through recommendations may be rejected because the circles did not adequately justify their case. Or, their ideas may conflict with well-reasoned policies, budget limitations, union contracts, or laws. When fully explained to circle members, these reasons for rejection cause few if any problems.

The growing concern among some facilitators and circle members is the rejection of ideas that are considered marginal or even trifling by management. But although these suggestions may have little immediate economic impact on the organization, this limited economic significance may mask a more serious effect on quality of work life and the long-term success of the quality circle effort.

Reality vs. Perceptions

When dealing with economically marginal ideas, managers often see a reality that differs from their employees' perceptions. Since such ideas would have a limited economic impact, steering committee members may think that cost/benefit ratio does not justify the effort of implementation. But when rejection of marginal suggestions occurs, it may raise serious doubts among circle members about management's sincerity — especially if the circle is new.

Problems may arise because the steering committee assumes that circle members know their idea is a minor issue. This assumption, when made, seems reasonable at first when the idea is, in fact, of minor importance. However, a second look at the circumstances reveals some underlying dynamics worthy of note. The group presumably selected the problem by consensus. So regardless of how trivial it may seem to the steering committee, the circle deemed the issue important enough to select it.

Even in the unlikely event that the topic was initially raised on a lark, after several meetings circle members will have infused the issue with a high degree of importance. It is not likely that they will see the topic as trivial after all their efforts, because the importance given to an issue usually correlates with the amount of time and effort devoted to it. To work for several weeks on a problem and then agree with management that it is trivial leaves participants with the unresolved dissonance caused by the question, "Why did we work on a problem we now view as trivial?" More likely, members will see the problem as important and thus congruent with their behavior. What will seem incongruent is management's rejection of a suggestion that circle members viewed as significant to the workers.

The irony in this situation is that both circle and steering committee members believe they are correct. And, from their respective perspectives, they are correct. Reality for both groups is what they perceive it to be. To argue that one group must be right and the other wrong is futile, if not counterproductive.

In Search of Common Ground

What is needed is a perspective that provides maximum benefit for all parties. For management, the overall goals of the circles are to improve productivity and quality of work life. Circle members have, as their goal, the removal of problems that obstruct their satisfaction. Two vantage points offer a mutually satisfactory perspective: the no harm/implement philosophy and the retail philosophy.

No harm/implement. Through business schools, management development programs, and experience, managers learn to apply a cost/benefit approach to decision making. In most instances, this philosophical standard is fine. Where it fails is in the case of ideas whose benefits are not verifiable or are roughly balanced by the costs. Since this viewpoint demands that benefits exceed costs, rejection often results when the balance does not favor the benefit side of the equation. In other words, the burden of proof falls on the employees' ideas, not on management.

The inverse of the cost/benefit view is the no harm/implement philosophy. This approach puts the burden of proof on management to argue that costs outweigh benefits. The circle is still expected to justify its suggestion. However, when a marginal idea emerges from the circle, management is required to demonstrate that some harm will be caused. If such is the case, employees will have little problem accepting management's refusal to implement on the grounds that costs would clearly outweigh benefits. But where the steering committee cannot point to a harm, the benefit of the doubt should fall in favor of the circle's idea. That is, if there is no harm, implementation should proceed.

This distinction is not merely one of semantics. With a no harm/implement philosophy, management will be seen as even more supportive of circle activities. The change in behavior that emerges from a shift in management's cost/benefit attitude toward a no harm/implement one powerfully encourages circle members to tackle a wide variety of job-related issues. Workers are assured that management is supportive of their ideas. Yet management is still free to reject those ideas whose costs significantly exceed benefits.

Retail philosophy. The problem with the no harm/implement approach is training managers to adopt this attitude, which is contrary to what they have been taught. Perhaps the most effective parallel to the no harm/implement viewpoint is the retail store philosophy that "the customer is always right." Managers instantly understand the value of a customer-salesclerk relationship that holds the customer in high regard. Too often, managers do not give their subordinates that kind of respect. If one turns the organization chart upside down, it becomes more obvious that management exists to facilitate the work of those who actually create the firm's goods or services: the circle members. When management accepts the philosophical approach that the employees' ideas are all good, the prevailing presumption becomes "all employee suggestions have worth." In those rare cases when the idea is not justified or the circle members have overlooked a salient point, management can identify the specific cause of the rejection. When such a cause is lacking, implementation proceeds.

What makes the no harm/implement and retail philosophies useful is their potential to increase the already high proportion of circle ideas that are implemented. It is the implementation of employee ideas that serves as the primary reinforcement for the employees' circle activities. Efforts by management to increase the percentage of implemented ideas are the most important actions it can take to foster the success of an ongoing circle.

Feedback

Another action that encourages successful circles is supervisory feedback that recognizes good performance. If employees sense a positive climate, cooperation in and out of circle meetings is enhanced. The use of positive reinforcement often is limited. What often is not limited is criticism of performance.

When the organizational culture is characterized by the use of criticism more than praise, circles function against a negative backdrop. In such a setting, circles may be little more than a quick fix that is incompatible with the organization's culture. Once the novelty (or Hawthorne effect) wears off, the viability of circle activities may fade. Their epitaph will be that they were a fad. In reality, whether they are a fad or a long-term element of well-managed organizations depends on the fit between the circle concept and the organizational culture. If supervisory feedback is not an appropriate blend of positive and negative comments, circles will be an adjunct to the organization, not an integral part of it.

Ideas represent change. Change is generally resisted by most organizational members. To encourage the changes needed for an organization to prosper, the work environment must be supportive. Management can create a more supportive environment by recognizing that employees' ideas are important and worthy of implementation. It follows, therefore, that managers need to respect even marginal ideas and apply a no harm/implement philosophy. Beyond this philosophical viewpoint, it is also crucial for management to ensure that good performance outside the circle is met with positive reinforcement. Only in a positive work environment are circles likely to be a useful, long-term management approach.

CONCLUSION

Each organization encounters unique obstacles in a quality circle undertaking. It is impossible to identify each of these barriers before the implementation of quality circles. However, the common factor that facilitates or hinders — and usually hinders — quality circles is the organization's culture.

Like the personality of an individual, an organization's culture permeates the entire organism. Difficult to define, it is nevertheless real. But changing that culture is an elusive goal.

Quality circles offer a proven strategy for changing a corporate culture slowly by tapping employees' ideas and thereby making the employees part of the decision-making process. But dedication by top management to the evolving of a new culture is also required for such change to occur. Without this commitment, the network of capabilities needed to identify and solve problems at the first level of the organization is unlikely to develop. Even with top management commitment, other roadblocks will impede progress. It is probable that such barriers as middle management reservations, ill-conceived objectives, or overreliance on consultants will develop in the course of most circle undertakings. In addition to these roadblocks, other impediments are likely to emerge that are unique to the organization. Also, in virtually all organizations, varying degrees of resistance can be expected to employee ideas.

After decades of evolution, a corporate culture is unlikely to change quickly. But if top executives believe that their employees can solve job-related problems, then that assumption must be backed by a commitment. This commitment must be evidenced by the creation of a network that generates and facilitates employee ideas. For top managers to do otherwise would be to squander their organization's greatest resource, the creativity of its people.

IMPLEMENTING QUALITY CIRCLES:
A HARD LOOK AT
SOME OF THE REALITIES

Gerald D. Klein

Lament over the recent decline in the growth of U.S. productivity has led a number of U.S. firms to become interested in adopting a system that has been identified as an important contributor to Japan's current high annual rate of productivity growth — that is, quality circles (QCs). In general, QCs are teams of workers that include managers and nonmanagers who meet regularly to solve production and quality problems and to brainstorm ways to improve productivity — that is, to increase the number of units produced per unit of time and to find other ways of reducing the per unit cost of a product or service.

QC groups tackle operational problems traditionally handled by management alone. Favorable reports on Japan's QCs and on those of some U.S. companies have led U.S. executives to want to establish QCs in their own organizations on a scale comparable with that of the Japanese; quality circles are being viewed as the vehicle for tapping factory personnel for an imagined wealth of new ideas and approaches for streamlining operations, reducing costs, and boosting production. Corporate behavioral scientists and humanists have also begun to view QCs as the medium for accomplishing ends that are important to them: increased job satisfaction and worker fulfillment.

Unfortunately, in their rush to realize benefits similar to those of others, and proceeding on the basis of an after-dinner speech or the few mass media accounts of QCs, U.S. executives and behavioral scientists may not be fully aware of the realities and resistances that must be addressed if such programs are to meet their high expectations. For example, there is the need for a program rationale that is compelling not only to management, but also to the nonmanagerial workforce if their wholehearted participation is desired. Furthermore, U.S. executives and behavioral scientists may not realize that reports of successful QC programs can create a misleading picture of what needs to be done, the length of time it takes to launch an effective program, and the costs involved.

This article, then, will describe some of the "realities" with which U.S. firms must deal. It focuses especially on those factors that bear on the involvement of factory-level workers and their unions. It will be seen that QC programs may require certain managerial decisions that may change an organization's very character. I will also suggest several reasons why Japanese QC programs work as well as they do.

THE NEED FOR A COMPELLING RATIONALE

Common wisdom suggests that it should be easiest to get a large number of factory-level workers involved in programs geared toward improving quality and productivity when the survival of their firms, and hence their jobs, is directly at stake. In fact, there are considerable data to support this assumption.

The reader may know that the first successful Scanlon Plan, a type of plan that involves the active collaboration of management and workers in solving company problems, was instituted in a small steel fabricating plant whose closing was imminent. In the early seventies, similar collaboration and cooperation between management and labor began in various industrial plants in the Jamestown, New York area, partly because workers feared widespread plant relocation. Similar circumstances explain the recent and apparently successful involvement of some U.S. steel and auto locals and workers in QCs and other pilot cooperative efforts with management. Their involvement has been spurred by their awareness of real crisis — sometimes at the plant rather than at the industry level (for example, the Tarrytown, New York plant of General Motors).

While many cultural and social factors explain the reportedly extensive and intense involvement of the Japanese worker in QCs, one important and generally overlooked factor has been the workers' desire to secure their futures by helping their companies overcome ''underdog'' and initially uncertain market positions. Until comparatively recently, Japanese companies have been underdogs in their markets, and their survival and success has been by no means assured.

Even in the absence of an immediate crisis of the kind that now plague steel and autos, most U.S. organizations can accurately argue that their long-term survival requires close attention to product costs and quality. However, when there is no immediate crisis or threat to the organization (and, possibly, confirmation of the ''crisis'' by some independent and respected source), most arguments that dwell on the need to increase quality and productivity will lack the credibility and impact on workers and their unions that is needed to gain their widespread involvement in and support for QCs. Unions, in particular, will be cautious about endorsing the plan because, historically, a company concerned with increasing productivity has sometimes translated into speedups or layoffs.

Furthermore, companies that don't enjoy a reputation for candor among employees or that are perceived as manipulative will find that the argument for long-term results may fall on deaf ears. Such a company might find itself dealing with the residue of past labor-management dealings and collective bargaining encounters. In collective bargaining, for example, it is widely perceived by workers that management usually overstates or exaggerates the degree of current crisis to extract contractual concessions from labor. This alleged practice and similar ones contribute over time to worker skepticism about both management pronouncements and management-initiated programs. In such an atmosphere, written and oral statements from management presenting a rationale for quality circles — no matter how objectively correct and honest — are likely to be viewed with skepticism. Workers generally see appeals to their long-term self-interests as attempts by management to play on their fears simply to increase productivity and short-term profits — that is, a management attempt to get ''something for nothing.''

The implementation of quality circles may also prove difficult when it is obvious that a plant's management traditionally has little say in plant staffing levels, or even about plant survival. When higher management makes the decisions about staffing levels and survival and when such decisions do not necessarily depend on a plant's objective performance, local management cannot guarantee that worker contributions to improving quality or reducing costs will result in long-term benefits such as greater job security, reduced layoffs, and higher wages. With no such incentives, employees may reason that the risk of receiving no payoff from participating in a QC program is too great to be worth becoming involved or expending much effort.

THE VALUE OF FINANCIAL INCENTIVES . . .

There is a tendency to believe that the increased psychological satisfaction workers derive from greater participation in decision making and peer recognition are in themselves sufficient incentive or reward to induce and maintain participation in QCs. In this view, financial incentives are not necessary, are redundant, or are even harmful. Of course, such a view favors the least expensive approach for an organization. However, it is my view that companies can reduce, although not necessarily eliminate, rank-and-file skepticism, fears of exploitation, and consequent resistance to QC programs by offering to share with workers a healthy part of the annual cost savings and productivity gains created by these programs. While the importance of the monetary incentives may diminish as certain intrinsic rewards from the process are realized, offering such incentives is certainly a potentially powerful tool to generate initial employee interest and involvement.

Financial incentives enable managers to talk easily and comfortably with workers about the program. Other appeals and rationales — for example, improving the company's long-run position or seeing one's ideas influence operations — are more likely to be met with skepticism or to be perceived as too psychological. Even the Japanese provide monetary incentives to QC workers, although this, in itself, probably doesn't explain the high level of participation in their programs. The more publicized U.S. quality circle programs also offer financial incentives.

Several sources also suggest that, for maximum effectiveness, at least some part of the savings or increased productivity generated by the workers should be returned to them as soon after their suggestions are accepted as possible.

It is also obvious that retaining a suggestion system that rewards employees on an individual basis can undermine a QC program and create tensions whether or not such a program includes financial incentives.

Financial incentives of the kind suggested may run counter to management's attitudes and historical practices. The attitude toward such incentives among the top managers of one organization — which probably reflects a general attitude — is: "We are already paying these people enough, possibly too much, as it is. Therefore, they should feel some obligation to offer their ideas for improving the productivity and competitive position of the company without further reward." "Shoulds" aside, jobs at the factory level are typically designed in such a way that the worker has difficulty identifying with either the product or the company. Traditionally, jobs at these levels have been designed so as to involve techniques and goals that are distinct from those of the organization as a whole.

Another source of management resistance to financial incentives is the fear that offering such incentives at one site will create pressure from those at other company sites for similar programs. What should be kept in mind, however, is that the installation of such incentives (and maintaining over time a management climate that's receptive to new ideas) can lead to the generation of suggestions and ideas that would not be forthcoming otherwise.

. . . AND THEIR LIMITATION

Even where financial incentives are offered to workers to induce them to participate in QC programs, however, obtaining their wholehearted support is more certain in nonrecessionary periods and in noncontracting industries. It is also easier in cultures like that of Japan, where workers in most of the large companies are, in effect, guaranteed lifetime employment. Generally speaking, in this country during a recessionary period or in a contracting industry when manufacturing orders decrease, methods that are found to increase output per labor hour many eventually, if not invariably, result in the furloughing of workers who are no longer needed. It is both predictable and understandable, therefore, that most unions and some rank-and-file employees will, in the absence of either a crisis situation such as a possible shutdown of operations or some assurances from management, have little interest in participating in quality circles and other programs that are likely to lead to layoffs. Observers have noticed that some rank-and-file employees in contracting industries are opposed to these programs for this reason. Using financial incentives to gain the widespread involvement and support of unions and factory personnel for QC programs under such circumstances may prove difficult unless management also assures workers that the program won't lead to a net reduction in employment. Without such assurances, employee involvement can be expected to be both partial and controversial.

THE PROBLEM OF MISCONCEPTIONS CREATED BY SUCCESSFUL EXAMPLES

Some current optimistic beliefs and perceptions about QC programs in general and the rank-and-file can actually be harmful and, ironically, work against establishing successful QC programs. These perceptions have been strongly influenced by recent successful projects in this country and abroad that have involved lower-level employees in decision making. Because it is the successful rather than the unsuccessful cases of employee participation that tend to be publicized and then only to a limited extent, assumptions that are drawn from these cases about QC programs and workers in general are probably distorted.

It has already been suggested that successful cases tend to overestimate the importance of intrinsic rewards in QC programs and to underestimate the importance of extrinsic rewards. Reports of successful cases also tend to ignore industry differences that may lead to different reactions to QC programs by workers.

Also, it is possible, in reading about these cases, to overestimate the ease and speed with which a quality circle program can be initiated and installed. There is the need, for instance, to secure the support and involvement of workers and their unions, who may have some tough questions about and preferences concerning the structure and outcomes of the program. Unions, for example, might look for assurances that the QC program will not result in the loss of jobs, that it will return to workers a substantial portion of savings that are generated, and that it will be entirely voluntary. In exchange for their support, they might also want the right to withdraw their support at any time. More typically, however, unions will not have had many experiences that are especially relevant to a QC program, and will adopt a go-slow attitude until all the implications of the proposed program are clear. In either case, to clarify these issues, a formal written agreement of understanding between the company and its unions may be required.

A company may also overlook or underestimate the need to prepare their supervisors for participation in the program. Because supervisors are usually responsible for leading QC sessions, their adequate preparation for this task may well determine the success of the program. QCs need active yet open and flexible leadership to work well; where supervisors don't have the relevant group leadership skills, they will need to be developed.

Focusing only on successful cases can also lead to overestimating the readiness of the workforce itself for participation and possibly to overstating the contributions that lower-level employees can initially make. The publicity attending successful cases can easily lead one to assume that all a company need do is to bring workers together, make a case for the need for improvement, and then turn them loose. Indeed, given the current climate generated by this publicity it seems somewhat heretical to suggest otherwise.

In addition to the previously mentioned factors that may make workers skeptical and/or hesitant about participating in QCs, factory-level workers are generally engaged in mind-numbing routines, and they often deliberately try not to think about the work they are doing. Such workers will probably have to be prepared intellectually and emotionally to participate in and contribute to workplace problem solving. Employees of whom not much has been asked over the years may feel they have little to offer. Even if the other obstacles can be overcome, a company may need to invest more time and money than it expects in preparing workers.

The Costs and Company Responsibilities

Case histories of successful programs may lead us to forget that there are costs as well as benefits associated with such programs. A company must anticipate in some detail the costs that will be incurred, and it must be willing to incur these costs. Organizational proponents of QC programs may be so excited about and preoccupied with the possible benefits that they neglect to look at the real costs and possible initial and long-term productivity losses. The failure to anticipate and project the downtime and other costs can lead to the withholding of support by a crucial organizational group, component, or system. Failing to inform top management at an early stage of the costs as well as the potential benefits of such a program can result in their withholding support and approval or to their abrupt withdrawal of support at a crucial stage.

Obvious, but not necessarily apparent in the reports of successful cases, is the need for an organization to formulate in advance some notion of the desired scope of the work that will be tackled by the group. Knowledge of the scope of the program will be especially important to first-line supervisors, who are frequently responsible for actually carrying out the program. I think that companies will find that a typical group of workers, when brought together, will run through their own ideas for area and organizational change rather quickly. If these constitute the group's formal agenda, the group will soon lose its sense of purpose. In the long run, the maximum organizational contribution of these groups can be obtained by preparing them to take on an ongoing problem solving, investigative, and fact-finding role in the organization, and by using them on an ongoing basis to review others' ideas and plans that pertain to their operation area.

A commitment to use factory-level personnel in this way, of course, can impinge upon and affect existing collective bargaining agreements, can threaten the existing prerogatives of various persons and groups in the organization, and can actually change the very character of the organization — for example, from a "top-down" system to one that accepts greater input from lower-level personnel.

Furthermore, it is very possible that workers in a QC program will use the group meetings as a forum, will more actively question existing and new company policies and practices, and will propose substitutes of their own design. While such activity is healthy and can actually lead to reducing tensions and improving working relationships, management should anticipate that a QC program may lead to a greater investment of time and energy in responding to the questions and reactions of workers than in the past.

Finally, focusing on the successful cases, especially the Japanese experience, can lead to overestimating the number of factory-level people in the United States who can eventually be encouraged to become involved in a QC program. The U.S. factory workforce is more mobile than its Japanese counterpart. Japanese workers see themselves as remaining with their employers for a lifetime; therefore it is in a worker's self-interest to work at making one's company more successfull and to use QCs to showcase one's aptitudes and worthiness for promotion. However, some members of the U.S. workforce — notably but not exclusively the younger ones — are interested less in making their jobs more secure and their companies more competitive than in escaping their jobs and their companies at the first opportunity. To some of these workers, factory work, no matter how "enriched" through QC work, offers little in the way of a career. Even economic incentives may not mean much to these individuals.

FROM A MANAGEMENT FAD TO AN
ONGOING ORGANIZATION PROGRAM

Most current QC programs in this country have been modest efforts involving relatively few workers and groups and small bonuses. While what we are seeing may merely be the initial phase of an evolving and growing organizational movement — and some users suggest this is so — the euphoria over fairly modest gains and the eagerness with which programs have been declared a success indicates that some managers view short-term success as indicating or promising long-term success. Their small size and informal nature, however, while inevitable and advantageous for the most part in innovative organizational projects, make most QC programs seem especially vulnerable to the normal movement of personnel in an organization and to shifts in individual and group interests and priorities. Those companies that see quality and productivity improvement as serious concerns now and over the long-term need to take steps to ensure that these concerns are regularly dealt with by the workforce at large.

The Scanlon Plan as a Model

One organizational model that seems capable of being modified to fit a variety of organizational situations, including QCs, is the structure used for information exchange and decision making by many firms with Scanlon Plans. Under a Scanlon Plan, as in an ideal QC program, management and workers collaborate to reduce costs and solve company problems, and all employees — managerial and nonmanagerial — share in any cost savings and productivity improvements over prespecified and agreed-upon base levels. A pervasive operating structure for Scanlon Plans is recommended; in practice it is capable of enlisting regular and widespread workforce participation. The structure consists of departmental or area committees with an overall screening committee if the organization is large enough, or just one overall company screening committee if it is not.

The primary purpose of the area committees is to process suggestions for operating changes and improvements that are placed before it by management and nonmanagement personnel. These committees are composed of management and nonmanagement (employee) members; management members are appointed by the company and the employee members are usually elected by department or area employees or appointed by the union leadership. To indicate the importance of the committee's work, the committee chairperson is frequently the department or area head. (To build a sense of responsibility and to increase involvement, some companies with QC programs have experimented with rotating the chairperson's position among a group's members.)

Scanlon Plan area committees meet regularly — at least once a month — to process all the suggestions submitted to committee members, to attend to previous suggestions on which action has not been completed, and to discuss any issues that are relevant to the department's or area's performance. In practice, management often brings up for discussion at the meeting matters that it wants to communicate to all employees. This last function is extremely important. The area committees are more than groups who screen suggestions for workplace improvement; they are communication conduits. Management needs to use them to familiarize workers with the problems and successes of the department, area, or the firm as a whole, and to increase employees' involvement in the organization's operation. Fred G. Lesieur and Elbridge S. Puckett, experts on Scanlon Plans, have written:

If the (area) committee has been functioning properly during the month and is doing its job thoroughly, the meetings described may take approximately one hour or slightly longer. If the (area) meeting is over in 15 minutes, it is clear that the committee is functioning strictly as a suggestion committee and probably is not getting sufficient management leadership and direction.

Typically, an area committee cannot get into traditional labor-management issues — for example, grievances, wages, and standards — although it may certainly indicate to the appropriate parties the desirability of temporarily suspending or modifying the collective bargaining agreement when this is in the interest of both employees and the company.

In a traditional Scanlon Plan, management reserves the right to accept or reject ideas that are presented at the department or area level. However, requiring decision making by consensus, or essential agreement by all, achieves the same end while permitting all committee members to participate as full equals in the problem solving process.

The overall screening committee serves as: (1) a forum for consideration of operating improvements that are likely to affect more than one department or area, or the company as a whole, and that may involve plant or capital expenditures of more than a marginal amount; (2) a court of appeal for ideas that are not accepted at the departmental or area level; and (3) a forum in which management can raise issues and matters of interest it wants to communicate to all employees. Time is also set aside at the regular, usually monthly, meetings to go over the organization's performance for the previous month — especially that portion of the organization's performance that bears directly on the calculation of the monthly bonus under the Scanlon Plan — and to analyze why it was favorable or unfavorable. It is important that all committee members understand the variables that affect the bonus so that they can share this information with other employees.

This committee, which should be kept to a workable size, usually includes a top executive, who serves as chairperson, top executives from various departments or areas, the president, a steward or other officer of the local union or unions, and employee members who represent various departments or areas and, sometimes, an employee representative from each department or area committee.

CONCLUSION

This article has described some of the issues involved in establishing QC programs and in maintaining them over time. It has indicated the need for a compelling program rationale to gain the participation and support of a firm's workforce and unions. The usefulness and limits of financial incentives in achieving this end have been considered. Various obstacles to establishing a successful program have been identified, including management's philosophy and attitudes, current organizational practices (for example, suggestion systems that reward individual employees), the quality of past and present management-labor relations, and general economic and industry conditions. The ability of a QC program to surreptitiously change or create pressure for changing an organization's basic character has also been noted.

This article also suggest that a QC program requires management to work closely with the unions who represent its workforce, adequately prepare supervisors and workers to take part in the program, acknowledge and be willing to accept the real costs involved in program implementation, and determine in at least some preliminary way the organizational role and responsibilities of individual area groups. If QC programs are not to go the way of traditional cost-reduction, productivity-improvement programs — which often "run out of gas" after a few months — organizations need to establish ongoing structures whereby discussion about costs and operational problems are carried on a regular and widespread basis. If companies are truly concerned about improving quality and productivity, they must find ways of keeping these issues alive and the subject of ongoing assessment and discussion by their workforces.

INTRODUCTION: CHAPTER THREE
TRAINING AND TOOLS

There are horror stories and war stories about successful quality circles. Seven articles in this chapter point out pros and cons about why enthusiasm for the technique is high and the success rate is difficult to measure. They cover training programs and describe specific techniques.

Measuring success is a particular concern to management. In Japan, the results are often measured in direct dollar savings, but you must not lose sight of the fact that quality circles have been an integral part of their management style since the mid-fifties. Quality of work life, staying with a company until retirement, and learning a variety of jobs within the organization are part of the Japanese work life in many industries.

In comparison, in the U.S. and due in large part to the work of the industrial engineering sciences, work has become more and more specialized with the emphasis upon learning a skill and performing a single task using minimum motion. Efficiency has been the goal of the production supervisor. The union's function has been to protect the workers' rights as set out in binding contracts. Employee input in contract negotiations are carried to management meetings by elected union stewards. Quality of work life and feelings of importance in the company's success are often included (nonverbally) in salary demands negotiated for by the union.

Overcoming the adversarial attitude and achieving cooperation between management, workers, and union officials are included in the concerns of the authors writing about gaining acceptance for quality circles in American industry.

QUALITY CONTROL CIRCLE PROGRAMS — WHAT WORKS AND WHAT DOESN'T

Matthew Goodfellow

There has been a growing interest in quality control circles (QCC) and the wonders they perform. It may be of some value, therefore, to look at some of these programs and determine what makes some of them successful — and many of them unsuccessful. After studying 29 American companies with such programs, we found that most were unsuccessful. Only 8 of the 29 produced satisfactory results. What explained their success?

QCC involve small groups of workers who meet in groups of up to a dozen under the direction of their foreman and his manager. Their task is to analyze and resolve problems which directly affect their work, problems which may have gone unresolved for a long time, but for which they are able to develop solutions because of their "closeness" to the work involved. This may involve productivity, or waste and spoilage, or absenteeism, or quality rejects, or excessive inventory, or poor work flow — or anything else.

Impressive achievements have been recorded. One steel company revealed that by implementing a simple modification suggested by a circle, it had managed to save $48,000 a year by reducing the number of damaged wire rod coils. In the Missiles System Division of Lockheed Corporation, an investment of about $700,000 to establish a QCC program produced savings of more than $5 million over a four-year period. Johnson and Johnson tackled the issue of reducing the 16 days taken from arrival of materials at the plant to their eventual use. Through the mechanism of a QCC program, that was cut to six days and led to a savings of $480,000. In Japan, the achievements of QCC programs are considerable. Nippon Steel, the largest steelmaker in the world, estimates that 25% of its profits result from circles' activities of its shopfloor personnel.

While success has a thousand fathers, failure is an orphan. Nobody boasts of a Quality Control Circles program that failed to achieve its objective. In studying 29 companies with Circles programs, we found only eight that were unquestionably successful. All had a common element which many companies overlook.

The basic element that crowned eight companies with success in their programs was the nature of their supervisory training. Since a great deal of the effectiveness of the programs depends on the foremen and managers, it is no surprise to find supervisory training to be a key element in the successful programs. Perhaps the best way of illustrating what made eight supervisory training programs so effective is to describe our findings in a question-and-answer form.

DIFFERENT COURSES

Q.: *In preparation for our QCC program, we gave our supervisors courses in "Human Relations," "Leadership Principles," "How to Write Effective Reports," "Cost Analysis," "How to Manage," and so on. Was this right or wrong?*

A.: We studied the foremen training procedures which were preliminary to the QCC programs in all 29 companies. Most companies emphasized the courses mentioned. The eight companies (out of the 29) which achieved success and were paid off in "measurable improvements" flowing from their QCC programs had a different training procedure.

Q.: *In the eight successful cases, what was the purpose of foreman training?*

A.: The purpose of such training was to provide the foremen with the proper understanding and supervisory tools that they may use to *motivate their employees* to do their best for the QCC program. That should be the real object of supervisory training. If a foreman's employees can be motivated to produce improvements in quantity or quality or on-time shipments within cost estimates safely and willingly, that is as much as any management can expect from any QCC program. Whether a training course helps the foreman bring about such improvements should be provable *by results* in the QCC program.

Q.: *Our QCC foreman training course seemed to be a standard course. Is there anything wrong with that?*

A.: Many top executives believe that there is a standard brand of foreman training. They believe, further, that this brand should be as successful with foremen in chemical plants as it is in TV manufacturing plants; in electric utilities as in textile plants; in paint factories, or camera plants as in plastics molding plants, banks and insurance companies. The same brand of training can't work in all these situations because different industries require different kinds of supervisory techniques.

DIFFERENT SITUATIONS

Q:. *How do supervisory situations differ from industry to industry?*

A:. Most managements assume that the good foreman will have the same abilities and skills regardless of differences in the manufacturing technology of the different factory operations. Nothing can be further from the truth, mainly because situations differ according to the industry, the materials, the department, the degree of skill among the workers, the sex, racial variety, and so on.

For example, many foremen in assembly line situations (automotives, shoes, food, furniture, wearing apparel, radio and TV, aerosol packaging) have large numbers of very brief conversations with individual workers, *one at a time*. These foremen go up and down the line, and their conversation with any one worker is usually brief and work-oriented. By contrast, the foreman in a processing industry, such as a steel fabricating plant, foundry, paper mill, insurance company, or textile plant, has *extended* conversations with several individuals and more often with *groups* of employees.

These distinctions seem trivial, yet they merit some thought, because if a supervisor wishes to motivate his QCC to perform on more than the minimal level, he must persuade them by his leadership role that he (and the company) are worthy of such effort. To carry on a leadership role successfully, a certain mode of operation is required of an assembly line supervisor who deals briefly with his workers, *one at a time*. A *different* mode of operation is required in a steel mill, foundry, utility, or bank, where supervisors deal with *crews* or *groups* of employees as units. Sometimes these interactions are lengthy.

In short, there is enough of a difference here to indicate that one must look at the foreman's job in terms of what his situation is, whom he has to motivate and what opportunities he has to do so — before deciding what sort of supervisory training is best for him. There is no simple description of *the* foreman or *the* foreman's job, and hence, there can't be a simple, "canned," foreman's training course.

Two earlier studies published by Universtiy Research Center throw additional light on this point: "Those New Young Employees — Are They Lemons or Lemonade?" and "Why Are Spanish-Speaking Employees So Militant?" Both are available free by request to the University Research Center at 121 W. Adams Street, Chicago, IL 60603.

TRAINING NEEDS

Q.: *What did the eight successful companies do with regard to foremen training needs?*

A.: *First*, all foremen training was designed to achieve certain measurable goals. These can involve absenteeism and turnover, waste, spoilage, customer returns, accidents, productivity, or anything else. *Good foremen training should result in before-and-after differences, measured in achievement toward pre set goals.* Foremen training that has no specific goals is about as reliable as dreams of love.

Second, the training was "adjusted" to the kinds of employees that forement supervise. Obtaining and gaining the cooperation of employees in a grey-iron foundry is vastly different from influencing employees in a cotton textile mill or the mail room of a bank.

Third, the training took into consideration the working environment of the plant (or store or office). Here, the degree of "closeness" of supervision and the amount of responsibility the individual worker had are important. A foreman in a blast furnace has different problems than a foreman in an air-conditioned drug manufacturing plant, or a steamy meat packing plant, or a suburban department store, or a hosiery mill.

Fourth, the training was of a particular kind — viz., *not* how to do scheduling, work planning, cost analysis, write effective reports or any of these standard topics, because a man has no business being a foreman if he doesn't have a modicum of knowledge about these things. The training was devoted to helping the foreman understand how he can *motivate his employees* to do their best for the company. That was the *real* object of QCC supervisory training in these eight companies. The rest is technical and should be part of a foreman's preparation or on going indoctrination by the company. If the training on how to motivate employees is effectively done, it should lead to certain measurable improvements, part of company goals.

Q.: *What kind of training enables a foreman to motivate his employees so that they will work diligently?*

A.: Our findings in these 29 companies indicate that the best kind of training to achieve those ends is training the foremen *how to listen*. That was the secret of the foremen's success in the eight successful plants. Obviously, listening is not a substitute for a foreman knowing how to plan and schedule the work flow, or how to operate the machinery. It is no substitute for technical job knowledge. How to listen is the key to human motivation, and without it, the cooperation of hourly labor is minimal.

FURNITURE EXAMPLE

In a furniture company QCC program, for example, we found the foremen were rotated among the seven assembly lines (each a QCC), in order to determine the influence of the supervision on QCC productivity. Before-and-after questionnaires and interviews with the hourly employees established the fact that the foreman's "personality" (pleasant-unpleasant) was the outstanding difference between the "most successful" and "least successful" foremen.

Q.: *What qualities characterized the foreman who could command the utmost in employees' cooperation in a QCC?*

A.: First, he was not "critical," nor was he "bossy," nor "hard to talk to." He was a "good listener." Second, he could handle "emergencies and problems." A foreman with these traits was "most preferred" by the hourly workers. With him, they would cooperate wholeheartedly — and did.

Q.: *Where did "listening" fit into the worker-foreman relationship?*

A.: Employees in every plant or office have work-related problems from time to time. Either the machine is not adjusted correctly, or the tool breaks easily, or the lighting over the typewriter is faulty, or the calibration on the titrator seems wrong, or the thread keeps snapping, or the file referral system is cumbersome, or the gage is stuck, or the fork lift gears are shot, or the candy sticks to the conveyor belt, or the electric ovens overheat, or the paint fumes are irritating, or the copying machine needs overhauling, or the cloth is not dyed evenly, or whatever.

If the employee can turn to a foreman who is not "critical," who is not "hard to talk to," and who can help with "problems" — if, in short, the foreman is a good listener and *tries to do something* in response to a production problem, he will receive excellent cooperation from his work force on their QCC goals.

Q.: *Is that all there is to listening?*

A.: Being a "good listener" was only one-half of the desirable features of "most preferred" foremen in the successful QCC programs. The other half was the foreman's ability to get things for his men from "higher management." A preferred foreman was a good listener; he offered helpful, non critical advice, and took whatever action was necessary to help. But, if that action necessitated the approval of the foreman's superior, the preferred foreman was judged on his willingness to talk to "higher management" on behalf of his men.

SOME DEMANDS

Examples are common. The department needs some newer equipment in one area, or the cement floor needs repair, or the poor ventilation requires larger exhaust fans, or the parking lot needs attention, or the food in the vending machine is tasteless, or new trays are needed for the ceramic ovens, and so on. Employees know that certain matters lie outside their foreman's authority. So they expect the foreman to carry the problems to higher management. Where he listens and helps, or where he listens and then goes "upstairs" for help, he is a "preferred foreman," and his department's performance or his QCC performance is often outstanding because he not only elicits employee cooperation, *he can command it*.

Q.: *Doesn't every foreman listen?*

A.: At least 30% of the foremen we discovered never listened at all. Normally, such foremen regard their sole duty as to issue orders to employees on jobs to be done.

Another 40% listen imperfectly. When the employees complain about a problem, the foreman will limit his comments to "tsk, tsk," suggest something, and then usually returns to his own business of planning, scheduling, or stock ordering.

Only the remaining 30% listen carefully, make notes of the problems or complaints, follow-up with suggestions and check back regularly to see if the problem is cleared up. This ensures that the foreman will win the gratitude and cooperation of his subordinates in making the QCC program work well.

Q.: *Can foremen be taught to listen?*

A:. The role of listening, the manner of acting during the listening role, the mode of questioning to derive information about the problem, the technique of acting in response, the importance of reporting back to employees, the use of the listening technique and how it fits with foreman goals and corporate objectives — all this can be taught.

TWO ELEMENTS

Sound techniques have been developed by a few companies and a few consultants in this new field. Two things are involved. First, you must have many examples of *typical employee problems* in a particular plant or department or office. These examples are normally derived from skilled interviews with employees throughout the facility in which the foreman training takes place. An experienced interviewer might be brought into the plant and go through a few days of employee interviews. (It is almost mandatory that he be from outside the company; otherwise employees may be reluctant to talk frankly.) These interviews are bland, open-end, non directive interviews which elicit employee comments of all sorts. Some of these comments are quite silly, but many are constructive and enlightening to higher management. Most of these comments are then rewritten into a case material to illustrate the typical problems of employees in that facility. This pinpointing of material to a particular plant illustrates common problems *in the foreman's own plant*, not in some other company.

Using such material, the second element comes into the training: case studies, role playing, programmed instruction, comment analysis, examination of human motivations in the comments, and so on. No short cuts can serve. The value and role of listening are emphasized.

In one QCC program aimed at cutting turnover in a major hotel, the results were summarized by management thus: "Within 18 months after the beginning of the project, turnover kept dropping from over 20% per month to 6%. Other hotels in the city continued on the 20% or higher turnover level. . . ."

Training used the case method, but (as to the company reported) the cases did not come out of canned material, but "grew out of continuing interviews we had all along with hotel employees."

Union and Nonunion

Q.: *How does all this apply to union and nonunion plants?*

A.: One of the most important reasons why employees seek out union organizers and sign union cards is the abusive, tyrannical foreman — the man who won't listen. If a plant is nonunion and management would like to keep it that way, perhaps the *first* important step is to teach foremen how to listen, and to teach the higher-ups how to listen to the foremen. Union organizers always listen.

In many unionized plants, foremen do not usually bother to listen because management has permitted the personnel function to be taken over by union stewards in effect, and the rules-of-the-road are laid out in the union contract. Most managements of union plants are concerned mainly with scheduling production, while wrestling over grievance disputes and hoping for acceptance of the next union contract without a strike. Regretably, listening is almost forgotten in many union plants, even though it is the most effective way of curtailing grievances, preventing strikes and improving employee performance.

To gain employee acceptance of corporate goals today, management must listen. This is perhaps the most effective method of keeping a nonunion facility out of the hands of union organizers, and of keeping a unionized work force from ever seriously considering a strike. In both cases, training the foremen to listen is the key to better company performance and profitability.

A TREND IN THE WRONG DIRECTION
Jeff Dewar

"A ton of enthusiasm is worthless unless backed by an ounce of scientific knowledge." Dr. Kaora Ishikawa, Quality Circle Headquarters, Union of Japanese Scientists and Engineers.

A trend is forming in the U.S. that greatly disturbs many practitioners of the Quality Circles concept — a trend that, if continued, may erode the sweeping wave that has been dramatically altering the way companies view and involve their employees. While we are devotedly sending our future engineers, doctors, lawyers, business leaders and others, through years of study, building their skills and knowledge through a variety of exotic training techniques, we are at the same time observing the first sprouting of neglect in recognizing the crucial importance of educating our Quality Circle members in the the techniques of problem analysis. The question arises, "What is the difference in the *need* for tools for the engineer and the Quality Circle member?" Let's take a look.

To begin with, there are a number of companies, even a few well-known ones, that have implemented, to one degree or another, Quality Circles with apparently *no* training in Quality Circles techniques. The author has spoken with Quality Circle members and leaders from companies who were reasonably enthusiastic about the Quality Circles idea, but had not received any training. These individuals are always surprised to hear that leader and member training is routinely provided by most companies. One foreman said, "Somebody handed me a book on Circles techniques and told me "Go do it." Another supervisor, without even textbook training remarked, "My people and I have a meeting once in a while just to keep the ivory tower happy."

Why is this happening? Why do we hear more and more of this? If we can make the assumption (and a reasonable one, too) that increasing numbers of companies that get involved in Quality Circles will follow this pattern, let's examine the pros and cons that provide the motives.

One can list several reasons why training is not feasible. Probably the most often stated is "Why bother to train? Our people know what the problems are already!" Of course, if this is the reason, then it indicates a misunderstanding of one of the key elements of the Quality Circles process. As any properly trained and active Circle member knows, the *identification* of various problems is only the *first* step in the total process. Selection of that one particular problem which best suits the Circle is next. From this point on, training is imperative. First, the Circle arms itself for its attack by gathering data and documentation, just as any pragmatic problem solver would, so as to evaluate the situation. The data collection step requires a certain amount of technical knowledge so that time is utilized efficiently. But even more importantly, when a member is questioned as to why data was collected over a certain time period, why a certain line was sampled, why the data was recorded, or a drawing was used instead of a tally sheet, etc., a Circle member can respond in an educated way that demonstrates credibility.

This can only be brought about by exposure to these data collection techniques.

As a second reason for the absence of training, one often hears that the cost is too great, either in terms of lost production time, the cost of materials, or instruction expenses. In cold hard business terms this comes down to a return on investment (ROI). The only data available that even remotely gives any indication as to the "value" of training was a survey taken by an organization that included a portion on Circle members' attitudes. In response to the question as to what degree did members find training helpful, approximately three-fourths said "very helpful." Of course, this does not give a comparison of results between two similar Circles in similar environments — one with training exposure, the other without. But it is interesting that a solid majority of members feel this strongly toward training in problem analysis.

A third often-stated excuse for not training is the assumption that Circle members, by and large, do not have sufficient technical background to be able to comprehend the Quality Circles techniques. This attitude in general is not held by professionals involved in education and training — teachers, instructors, and, of course, facilitators. They all recognize that the complexity or simplicity of any training course, whether university physics or Quality Circles techniques, rest in a large part on the shoulders of the instructor. For example, the Pareto principle in relatively complex terms is the "graphic representation of a quantifying prioritization in descending progression coupled with a cumulative tracking device." What a mouthful! Simply stated, the Pareto tool is simply a chart that displays the most severe problem or highest costing item, etc., by using a special type of bar graph. The columns read from left to right, with the largest column on the left and the smallest on the right. Often a line is used that keeps a running total of the column amounts. The general purpose of Pareto is to simply separate the few important items from the many trivial items.

To put the Quality Circles techniques and their use into perspective, let us ask, "Do we find it necessary to fully understand the electrical and mechanical workings of our automobiles to be safe and effective drivers?" Of course not. What we must comprehend is the functional and practical use of our vehicles — when to turn, brake, accelerate, etc. The same applies to Quality Circles techniques. One does not have to be a mathematician to *utilize* a histogram with its standard deviations and other features. Leave the concepts to the theoreticians; but give us the practical hardware to use.

The last often stated objection to training is the fear that once Quality Circle members receive it, comprehend it, and demonstrate its usefulness, they will gradually stop applying it. Obviously, even the most disciplined of us can, and do, slip into bad working habits when we have no incentive to maintain high levels of performance. A reasonably skilled facilitator or coordinator can help to make the incentive strong and clear: justification and documentation that demand credibility of a circle's problem analysis. However, it is, of course, justified to view training costs as unnecessary start-up costs if a Circle does not continually apply techniques. The author has two such circles in mind. While monitoring their performance, it was clear that they had degenerated from a top notch problem-solving team, to a third rate coffee-break club. They had originally been very diligent at applying their newly learned skills; but because of a poor program manager (facilitator) they began slipping into sloppy habits of guessing instead of analyzing, proposing solutions without verifying true causes, and stating goals with no plan drawn up to attain them.

Those involved in the day-to-day function of Quality Circles must always remember that those Circles that consistently use the classic techniques will have decisively stacked the deck of success in their favor.

When we examine the role of management, the facilitator, and the leader in training, we find a specific place for each. Management, first and foremost, must recognize the value of the previously stated comments for training, and then place a high priority on it. For example, a number of companies have expressed their strong commitment to this new management style, and have emphasized that training in problem analysis techniques is "forever" a part of the Quality Circles program. With such strong emphasis, and the action that must follow the words, it certainly gives Circle members more than just a minor indication of how a Quality Circle should operate. In a broad sense, this is the way the Japanese Quality Control Circle is viewed. Even after years of working together, and mastering the application of the more basic problem analysis techniques, the Circle members are continually upgrading their knowledge of statistical problem analysis tools. This upgrading and continual training is very clearly supported and nurtured by the Japanese management. At Kobe Steel Co., for example, workers are encouraged to work on their projects at the training center building. Meals are provided and cots are available for overnight use!

The role of the facilitator is many-fold. At or near the top of the list, we find training of the Circle leaders usually amounts to a three-day course. In that time the facilitator must convey the importance of training and must, also, act as a role model, displaying methods of teaching for the leaders to imitate. The facilitator must, of course, insure that all the techniques are fully understood, and will be applied by the leader during Circle activities. Naturally, feedback to the steering committee on the progress of training must be included.

The leader is the person who carries the torch of knowledge back to the Circle. If there is to be difficulty in the transference of knowledge, it usually occurs here. The risk of members not understanding the techniques is greatly minimized by having the facilitator attend Circle meetings, especially during training. He or she is then able to provide that vital back-up or support for the leader as needed to insure member understanding. For example, a leader may fully understand what a Pareto chart's purpose is, but be unable to relate it to something the members work with. A skilled facilitator can ask a few key thought-provoking questions to "facilitate" everyone's understanding. However, it is crucial for the leader to be the instructor during training for his or her own self-esteem and feeling of control and ownership; but even more importantly, for the purpose of building a team. A team is more than just a group of people thrown together, but a number of individuals who enhance each other's performance; and this is something that can occur only if the leader trains the members.

Finally, let us realize that there is a definite place for training Circle members in problem analysis techniques, within the framework that classical Quality Circles exists. This training is one of the distinguishing elements of Quality Circles — and as history continues to bear out, one of the most likely reasons for the tremendous success of Quality Circles we have seen so far. There are definite roles, with specific purposes garnished with significant responsibility, within the context of training for those of us involved in this exciting concept.

It is becoming more and more apparent that the justifications for not training must be met with strong and documented opposition, so as to preserve a healthy, effective and classically successful Quality Circles movement.

The following is an example of an agenda for a leader training course that is relatively simple and inexpensive to provide; and the effects can make the difference between success and failure of the Circle activity.

1st Day Selected management and staff personnel should be invited to morning session.

8:00 AM	Kickoff by key company executive.
8:15	Facilitator provides status of Quality Circle activities.
8:30	What is it? Objectives. How does it operate?
9:30	BREAK
9:45	Elements of successful Quality Circle activities.
10:30	Roles of the steering committee, facilitator, and leader.
11:00	Training preview.
11:30	Students prepare for their upcoming Quality Circle presentations.
12:00	LUNCH
1:00 PM	Facilitator presents Quality Circle (Q-C) technique, "Case Study and Problem Prevention Techniques."
2:00	BREAK
2:15	Motivation.
3:00	Question & answer session with one or more experienced Quality Circle leaders, if available.
4:00	ADJOURN

2nd Day

8:00 AM	Questions & answers.
8:30	Q-C Technique, "Brainstorming." (Include a practical example.)
9:30	BREAK
9:45	Q-C Technique, "Data Collection Techniques."
10:30	Communications.
11:00	Q-C Technique, "Data Collection Formats, Plus Graphs."
11:45	Questions & answers.
12:00	LUNCH
1:00 PM	Using schedules and/or action logs to maximize results.
1:30	Q-C Technique, "Decision Analysis Using Pareto."
2:15	BREAK
2:30	Group Dynamics.
3:00	Q-C Technique, "Basic C-&-E Problem Analysis." (Include a practical example.)
4:00	ADJOURN

3rd Day

8:00 AM	Q-C Technique, "Process C-&-E Problem Analysis." (Include a practical example.)
9:00	Q-C Technique, "The Management Presentation."
9:45	BREAK
10:00	Q-C Themes — examples.
10:30	Potential problems.
11:00	Records to be maintained.
11:15	Measurement techniques.
12:00	LUNCH
1:00 PM	Discussion: "Starting your Circle."
1:30	Leader examination.
2:15	BREAK
2:30	Critique of leader examination.
4:00	ADJOURN

WHAT ARE THE TOOLS OF THE QC CIRCLE?
Virgil Rehg

INTRODUCTION

The purpose of this paper is to describe the tools and techniques that are normally used by QC Circles teams to solve problems. These tools are not revolutionary in their own right. Most of them have been applied by problem solvers for a long time. So you may wonder, what's new about a QC Circles' application of them. Nothing, except they are being applied by *the workers* in a *prescribed order* and with *management support*.

The tools to be presented are:

Histograms	Cause and Effect Diagrams
Graphs	Scatter Diagrams
Check Sheets	Multi-vari Charts
Pareto Diagrams	Control Charts

THE TOOLS

This presentation shall begin with the histogram and proceed in the order listed above.

HISTOGRAMS. To discuss and illustrate a histogram we must collect data or presuppose that data has been collected for some justifiable purpose. For this discussion, let us assume that data has been collected and we wish to present it in an orderly manner so that certain characteristics can be determined.

Raw Distribution. In many instances the data is in "raw" form in which case much valuable information is hidden.

To illustrate, suppose that 30 observations are taken from a process and we would like to determine how close the process is to the specification. In "raw" form the data might appear as follows:

Table I — Raw Data

.228	.226	.230	.229	.229	.228	.231	.230	.227	.228
.230	.226	.231	.227	.228	.228	.227	.230	.229	.229
.229	.230	.228	.228	.227	.230	.228	.231	.229	.228

At a glance, is the average dimension obvious? Can you tell what are the high and low observations? Can you accurately estimate the range between the high and the low values? If the specification is .225 ± .005, is the process capable of meeting its specification and is it doing so? Most people cannot answer those three questions very quickly but if you give them sufficient time to "study" the data for awhile these questions could be answered.

Ordered Data. If the observations were placed in a sequence from low to high the problem of estimating the average, the range (a measure of dispersion), and the high and low readings would be simplified. But some "study" time would still be required. To illustrate, the *ordered* observations are as follows:

Table II — Ordered Data

.226	.226	.227	.227	.227	.227	.228	.228	.228	.228
.228	.228	.228	.228	.228	.229	.229	.229	.229	.229
.229	.230	.230	.230	.230	.230	.230	.231	.231	.231

After a brief study it is apparent that the low value is .226 and the high value is .231. That's a range of .005 (i.e., .231 - .226). The average? Probably around .228 or .229, and the process is not meeting the specification because three observations are larger than .230, the upper specification.

The *tally sheet* and *frequency distribution* are more descriptive ways of presenting the data.

Tally Sheet. To construct a tally sheet, data in either raw or ordered form can be used. A scale over the range of observed values is established and a mark is placed opposite the corresponding value on the scale for each observation.

Frequency Distribution. The frequency distribution differs from the tally sheet in the way the number of occurrences of an observation is presented. The tally sheet shows the tally marks and the frequency distribution shows the tally as a number (representing the number of times an observation occurs). A tally sheet and frequency distribution for the data in Table II are illustrated in Figure 1.

Tally Sheet

Observation	Tally
.226	11
.227	⊬⊬
.228	⊬⊬ 1111
.229	⊬⊬ 1
.230	⊬⊬ 1
.231	111

Figure 1. Tally Sheet

Frequency Distribution

Observation	Frequency
.226	2
.227	4
.228	9
.229	6
.230	6
.231	3
Sum	30

Figure 2. Frequency Distribution

All four methods used thus far to present the data collected from the process contain the same amount of information. The latter two provide a more descriptive picture of where the average is located (centering), the dispersion and the range. Do you agree?

125

Histogram. The histogram is closely related to the tally sheet. It is usually constructed with the observation side on the horizontal axis and a frequency side on the vertical axis. Above each observation a rectangle is drawn with a height equal to the frequency of the observation. The area of the rectangle is in proportion to the frequency of the observation. For example, if one-fourth of all the observations were the same value, then one-fourth of the total area would be contained in the rectangle above that value.

For the example presented above the histogram would appear as shown in Figure 3.

Of the thirty observations, nine are observations of .228. This is 9/30 or .3 or 30% of the total. Hence, 30% of the area of the histogram is contained in the rectangle above .228.

The value of the histogram when compared to raw data is that we can easily see that the lowest value of the 30 observations is .226 and the highest value is .231, and that the range is .005 (i.e., .231 - .226). Also the process appears to be centered between .228 and .229 and is not meeting the specifications which are .220 to .230 but appears to be capable since the specification range is .010 (i.e., .230 - .220) as compared to a sample range of .005. Perhaps this idea of capability may be more apparent if you visualize moving the histogram to the left so that the centering would be near .224. In practice some process adjustments would have to be made but the observation would all be within the specification limits with room to spare.

Some other examples of histogram are illustrated in Figure 4 thru 7.

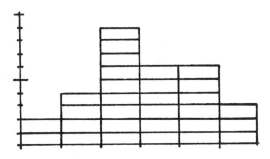

Figure 3. Histogram

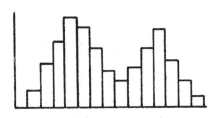

Figure 4. Two-peaked Histogram

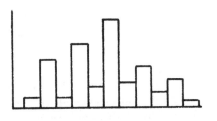

Figure 5. Incomplete Histogram

126

Figure 6. Truncated Histogram

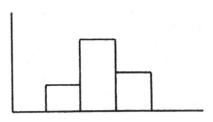

Figure 7. Condensed Histogram

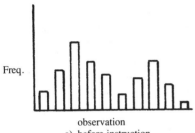

Freq.

observation
a) before instruction

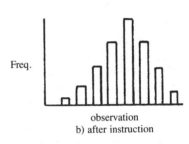

Freq.

observation
b) after instruction

Figure 8.

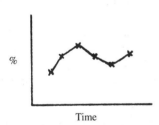

%

Time

Figure 9. Unemployment Rate

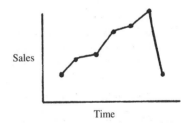

Sales

Time

Figure 10. Stock Market Volume

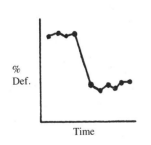

%
Def.

Time

Figure 11.

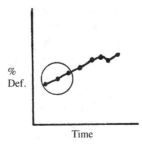

%
Def.

Time

Figure 12.

Prob.
of
Accp.

% Defective

Figure 13. O.C. Curve

127

Figure 4 is an example of mixed data. It could be due to the products of two operators, or two shifts, or two gauges being mixed together. Figure 5 is the pattern that results when an operator is rounding the results of a measuring operation toward a certain value, or it could be the result when there is a tendency to record data in even numbers rather than odd numbers. Figure 6 shows the results that occur when a batch of parts are sorted but a few still get through. Figure 7 shows how the histogram may look when the scale of the measuring device is too large.

There may be other explanations for these examples, and there are many other examples possible. The point is histograms provide the user with a great deal of information (process centering and dispersion) easily communicated (visually) and inexpensively displayed.

GRAPHS. The second tool to be discussed is graphs. Unlike the histogram which has one general shape, a graph can be drawn in many ways. The histogram for example, is one type of graph, a bar graph. Graphs can also be pie charts, line graphs or pictorial graphs. In any case, like histograms they can tell us a lot about a process, a product, a working environment, company sales, employment, and many other aspects of our society.

Bar Graphs. We have seen applications of histograms in the preceding section, and we will see more of them when we discuss the Pareto diagram. Bar charts can be used for other applications, be drawn horizontally, and can be a line rather than a bar. In Figure 8 we are using a bar chart to illustrate the difference in a process before and after an operator was trained on the correct procedure to use on a milling machine.

In Figure 8a the operator was not following the process correctly and a distribution with two peaks resulted. When the operator was trained in the correct procedure the pattern of observation changed to that of Figure 8b. *Notice how evident the difference is when presented graphically.* Other applications of the bar chart will be used in the section on multi-vari charts.

Line Graphs. Line graphs are constructed by drawing a line to represent the data collected from a process or other operation. For example, the unemployment rate is illustrated in Figure 9 and the stock market volume in Figure 10.

A line graph can show changes in a process over time. We can judge the effects of a new policy, employe, gage or other factors in a process on the process itself. (Figure 11.) We can develop patterns and detect trends. (Figure 12.) In a later section we will use the line graph to display control charts.

Sampling risks can also be analyzed using line graphs by examining the operating characteristic curves of a sampling plan. (Figure 13.) Line graphs can be deceiving. The user is cautioned not to mislead the reader. For example, change between point #1 and point #2 in Figure 12 does not appear to be large. Let us define the difference as .001. (That is, point #1 is .251 and point #2 is .252.) If the vertical scale of Figure 12 ranged from a low of .250 to a high of .350 then .001 would appear as a relatively small change. Suppose we decide to show only the first three points of Figure 12 on a line graph but reduce the range of the vertical scale so that the low value of the scale is .250 and the high value of the scale is .253 using the same size graph paper. The first three points of Figure 12 would then appear as illustrated in Figure 14. The difference between them appears relatively larger now because we have increased the space on paper between the plotted points. The values have not changed but they appear to be farther apart. Therefore in presenting data the user must be careful so as not to mislead the reader.

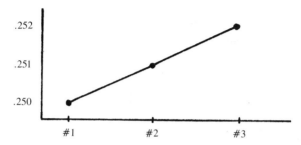

Figure 14. Points #1, #2, and #3 from Figure 13

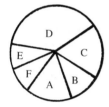

**Figure 15.
Pie Chart of Defects**

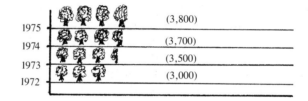

Figure 16. Trees Planted in a Forest

Pie Charts. Another type of graph is the pie chart. It has the advantage that a lot of information can be illustrated in a relatively small area. Figure 15 illustrates an application of a pie chart in which the types of defects are illustrated. From this graph it appears that defect D is the largest contributor. Pie charts have applications similar to histograms because the pie is proportioned in the same way that a histogram is proportioned.

Pictorial Graph. A pictorial graph probably catches the eye of the reader because pictures of the item are shown on the graph. If it is a bar type graph, then the pictures replace the bars and occur at fixed intervals. Usually the picture represents a certain quantity so that less than that quantity is shown as a partial picture. Figure 16 shows the number of trees planted in the forest during the past five years.

In the first two sections we discussed graphical ways of presenting data. In the sections that follow application will be made of these techniques to help solve problems. The user is encouraged to use graphs whenever possible because their value as a communicative technique is very good.

CHECK SHEETS. Many of us are guilty of being disorganized when trying to collect data to solve a problem. The check sheet is designed to help individuals overcome this deficiency. The check sheet has other purposes but its chief application in problem solving is as an aid in assembling and compiling data.

Using this definition, the tally sheet illustrated in Figure 1 is a check sheet. By setting up the frequency scale the collection of data has been simplified and the data can be more easily analyzed.

In his text,[1] Dr. Ishikawa defines the functions of a factory check sheet as:

1) Production process distribution checks.
2) Defective item checks.
3) Defect location checks.
4) Defective cause checks.
5) Check-up confirmation checks.
6) Others.

The production process check sheet is used to collect data on a process to see if any unusual or unwanted elements are present in the process. If tally sheets had been used to collect the original data in Figures 4 thru 7 then those tally sheets would have fit the definition of a check sheet.

With the data in this form the relationship between the specification limits and the process can also be observed. For example, Figure 17 is the tally sheet for Figure 3. It is apparent that the process is running too high because part of the pattern is above the upper specification. It also appears that the process is capable of meeting the specifications because it is much narrower than the specifications.

Corrective action is not always this easy. In most cases further analysis must be made of the defective items.

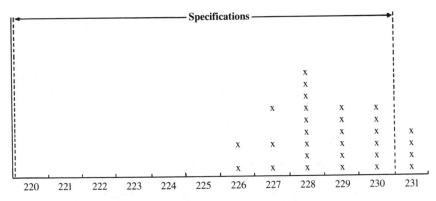

Figure 17. Tally Sheet for 30 Observations

Defective Item Checks. A defective item check sheet contains a list of the types of the defects and their frequency. This is important as we shall see when the Pareto diagram is discussed. An example of a defective item check sheet for a painting process is illustrated in Figure 18.

130

Part: Cover Model: 45AP-9	Date: 8-20-76 Inspector: Jan	Lot #: 3A Quantity: 3,000	
Defect	Frequency		Total
Scratches	⊔⊔⊤ ⊔⊤⊤		10
Dirt	⊔⊔⊤ ⊔⊔⊤ ⊔⊔⊤ 11		17
Thin	111		3
Thick	⊔⊔⊤ 11		7
Other	111		3
		Sum	40

Figure 18. Defective Item Check Sheet for a Painting Process

The biggest problem appears to be dirt since dirt was the highest frequency. The next step in solving the problem would be to locate the source of the dirt and implement the corrective action. The defective item check sheet provides input to the Cause and Effect Diagram that will be discussed in a later section.

Defective item check sheets can be developed for individual parts, subassemblies or a complete item. In all cases they provide the user with a tally of the type of defects and their frequency.

Defective Location Check Sheet. This check sheet is also an important tool for analyzing a process. It is a pictorial way of indicating the location of defects on a product. An oversimplified example would be the location of rust spots in certain model years of passenger cars. One of our leading auto manufacturers produced a car that had a serious rust problem on the lower left door post panel. If you were to stand on a busy street with a picture of that car in hand and place a mark on the picture where the rust was observed when that model car passed, your picture would contain a concentration of marks on the lower left front door post panel. This is an indication of a design and/or quality problem. Now visualize your doing the same thing for an item produced by some process. The concentration of marks on the picture would indicate the location of the defect. With this knowledge you could then investigate the process and consider why it was occurring in a certain location. Thus the defect location check sheet can be a valuable aid in problem solving.

In addition to its application to parts it would also be applied to defects where the location in the production process could be valuable information. Then the picture would not be a part but the production process. Marks would be placed on the picture where defects occurred. For example, if the seventeen dirt defects observed in Figure 18 were analyzed as to the location of their source the results could appear as indicated in Figure 19.

Production Process   Defect Location Check Sheet

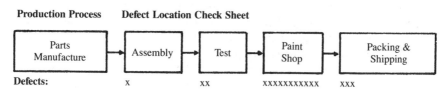

Figure 19. Distribution of 17 Dirt Defects on Cover for Model 45AP-9

131

Defective Cause Check Sheet. This type of check sheet is used when the user is trying to determine the cause of a defect. It is similar to a cause and effect diagram in terms of its results but it is mainly applied to simple cases.

To illustrate its application let us examine the 11 defects that were traced to the Paint Shop in Figure 19, and list them by operation and operator.

Operation	Dip	Spray	Clean-up	Touch-up	Inspection	Total
Operator						
Jan		XX XXXX		X		7
Lynn	X	XX				3
Mary		X				1
Total	1	9	0	1	0	11

Figure 20. Paint Shop: Defective Cause Check Sheet

From the check sheet in Figure 20 it looks like Jan is the major source of the problem and merits further investigation. Another Defective Cause Check Sheet could be used to isolate the when, where, and under what conditions Jan is producing defects.

The application of these check sheets is limited only by the user's imagination.

Check-up Confirmation Check Sheet. This type of check sheet is used to keep a record of operations performed to make sure that nothing is overlooked. It has application where the list of opeerations is long and/or complex. For example, when you take your car to a diagnostic center the mechanic methodically checks off each test upon its completion. This not only provides you with a record of each operation but saves him from having to go back and set up for a test he may have forgotten to do. Or, when you are getting ready for a trip you may make a list of things that must be done. Then as you do them you check them off one by one. The confirmation check sheet is that kind of a check sheet applied to a process.

Other Check Sheets. There are many other possible check sheets that may be used in problem solving. Each of us would have his own list if we kept records on how we recorded data. Again, there is no limit to the types that would be designed. The objective is that we use them to help analyze data and solve problems.

PARETO DIAGRAM. The pareto chart is a histogram that is used to identify the most costly machine, departments, tools and/or individuals contributing to a problem. If we are concerned about defects, the Pareto diagram will indicate the part that is the biggest contributor to the problem in either cost or percent defective. If we are concerned about operators then the Pareto diagram will point out the operators in need of training. The rule of thumb is that 70% of a problem is caused by 30% of the operators (or parts, departments, machines, etc.).

The steps in developing a Pareto diagram are:

1) Decide upon the item to be analyzed. Is it machines, people, parts, departments, or what?
2) Decide upon your data source. Is it historical data or must you collect current information?
3) Decide upon the sample size. How far back will you look into historical records? Or, how many current observations will you take?
4) Will you verify historical data, or check for accuracy in calculations?
5) Record the data on a suitable check sheet.
6) Order the data from lowest to highest.
7) Develop a cumulative sum beginning with the high values.
8) Divide each value in the cumulative sum column by the total to find a cumulative proportion (or percentage).
9) Construct a bar chart. Let the cumulative proportion be drawn vertically and let it correspond to the height of the bar. The items will be described along the horizontal axis and will be identified in accordance with order determined in step 6.
10) Analyze the results.

CAUSE AND EFFECT DIAGRAMS (and Brainstorming). The reason for having brainstorming sessions is to get all the members of a team to share their knowledge and ideas of the process and problem at hand. The Cause and Effect Diagram (C & E) which is generated during the brainstorming session is designed to illustrate in a clear and precise manner how the factors affecting a problem are related. Actually the effects go much deeper than that. C & Es are also educational for both the novice and the ''old pro;'' C & Es provide a basis for discussion of the factors of a problem and their relationship; and they can improve communications within the organization.

To construct a C & E the following steps are recommended:[2]

1) Identify the effect for which causes are sought in clear, concise terms. These effects to be studied could have been the high item on a Pareto chart, or it could have been assigned by management or selected by the circle team.
2) Estabalish goals for the brainstorming activities with an established time limit.
3) Construct the C & E framework by drawing an arrow horizontally with the arrow pointing to a box on the right in which the effect has been written.

Figure 21. Process line for a C & E

4) Draw two or three diagonal branches on both sides of the arrow and at the end of each branch draw a box in which the words manpower, method, material, machine are written. These are the main causes. From these branches draw other branches for sub causes that will be added.

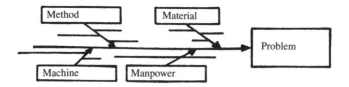

Figure 22. Branch and Sub-branches on a C & E Diagram

5) Write in the causes as suggested by the brainstorming group. Have the team members suggest causes in an orderly fashion.
6) Have everyone study the C & E. If other causes are brought up at a later time they should be added.
7) Have the group select a cause (or causes). Their selection could have resulted from another Pareto study, from their own critical analysis or be based upon expert opinion.

The team members assigned to the various causes use check sheets to help in the analysis of a "cause." More complex analytical methods are sometimes required to get at the source of a problem. This includes control charts, multi-vari charts, scatter diagrams, designed experiments, tests of significance and regression analysis. Staff assistance is usually required for the more sophisticated techniques.

If the causes selected from the C & E does not solve the problem, other causes are selected and the analysis continued until a solution is achieved.

SCATTER DIAGRAMS. Scatter diagrams are used to examine the relationship between two factors of a process to see if they are related. If they are related, then by controlling the independent factor the dependent factor will also be controlled. For example, if the temperature of a process and the quality of the yield are related, with yield depending upon temperature, then by controlling temperature the quality of the yield is determined. In Figure 23 it can be shown that when the process temperature is set at B a higher yield results than when the temperature is set at A. In Figure 24 we see that hardness reaches a maximum for a boiling time of "B" while a higher or lower boiling time will result in a lower hardness.

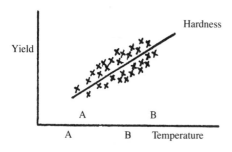

Figure 23. Scatter Diagram

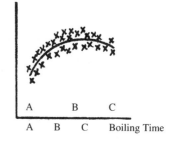

Figure 24. Scatter Diagram

134

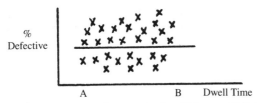

Figure 25. Scatter Diagram for Dwell Time vs % Defective

In both illustrations there appears to be a relationship between the independent factor on the horizontal axis and the dependent factor on the vertical axis. A test of hypothesis could be applied to the data to determine statistical significance of the relationship but that is beyond the scope of this paper. In some cases it appears that two factors are not related. In Figure 25 the percent defective for a process does not seem to be related to the dwell time (between the limits of A and B) on the welding fixture. The percent defective rate can be high or low when the dwell time is at A and at B.

So you ask, when does a circle team use a Scatter Diagram? They can use it when they are trying to find a solution to a problem on a C & E. After team members have selected a subcause to analyze they might find the scatter diagram useful in explaining why a process acts the way it does, and how to control it. For example, in Figure 24 if hardness was a subcause then an analysis of boiling time may explain why hardness changes; and what can be done to control it.

The steps to be followed in conducting a Scatter Diagram are:

1) Select the dependent and independent factors. The dependent factor may be a cause on a C & E, a specification, a measure of quality or some other important output, result or measurement. The independent factor is selected because of its potential relationship to the dependent factor.

2) Set up a scatter diagram check sheet. The dependent factor is plotted on the vertical axis and the independent factor on the horizontal axis.

3) Choose the values of the independent factor that you wish to observe during the analysis.

4) For the values of the independent factor selected in step 3 collect the observations for the dependent variable in a random fashion and record on the Scatter Diagram check sheet.

5) Analyze the results.

MULTI-VARI CHARTS. Multi-vari charts are graphical control charts. They show the dispersion in a process over a short span of time and over a long span of time. In the example in Figure 26 five parts were taken from a turning operation every 20 minutes. The diameter of the parts were measured and then plotted on the multi-vari chart. A straight vertical line was drawn through each set of five points.

In the analysis, the length of the line describes the dispersion over a short period of time (the time it takes to manufacture five parts). If the lines are consistent in length throughout the experiment we can conclude that the dispersion during the short time period is stable. If the location of the lines is about the same then

135

the dispersion over a long time period is stable. In Figure 26 the dispersion over the short time period is stable but dispersion over the long period looks suspicious. There appears to be a trend. To isloate the cause of the trend could be the next step.

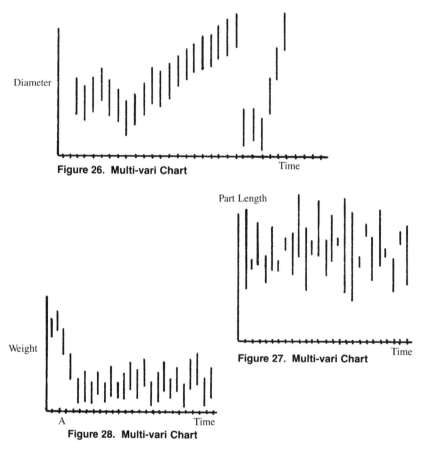

Figure 26. Multi-vari Chart

Figure 27. Multi-vari Chart

Figure 28. Multi-vari Chart

Multi-vari charts can be used during problem analysis to help isolate the cause of a problem. But their main application is to control a process. The multi-vari chart indicates when processes are stable and when there is an assignable cause that explains the behavior of an unstable process.

In Figure 27 there appears to be a significant difference between the length of the lines since some lines are long and some lines are short. This means the variation in the lengths of the parts was not consistent during the short period of time it took to produce the sample. When a process is not consistent during a short period of time it could be an indication of a serious problem with the processing equipment.

The process appears stable over the long run because the location of the vertical lines with respect to each other is consistent.

In Figure 28 the dispersion over the short time period appears to be consistent

136

but the process was not stable during the long time period because the first three lines are too far above the rest of the process. This type of pattern is usually descriptive of situations where a tool slipped sometime near point A in time; or some other cause.

The steps in constructing a multi-vari chart are:

1) Select the process and characteristics to be analyzed, and decide upon a sampling interval.
2) Develop a means of recording the sample observations.
3) Collect the samples from the process, measure the characteristics and record the values.
4) Plot each sample point on the multi-vari chart and connect the lowest point to the highest point with a straight line.
5) Analyze the results by looking to see if the vertical lines are all about the same length, and if they are in about the same vertical location.
6) If the lines are of the same length in general, and if they are in the same relative position then the process is probably stable. Otherwise there is an assignable cause that should be sought out.

CONTROL CHARTS. Control charts are similar to multi-vari charts. They provide the user with an indication of stability in a process. But instead of the analysis being done visually by comparing lines it is done on a mathematical basis.

Instead of drawing a line to illustrate dispersion the range for each sample is calculated and plotted on a range chart. An average range is calculated as are range control limits. If all the sample ranges fall within the control limits and do not show an unusual trend the process is said to be stable during the short time period. Figure 29 illustrates a range chart for the data in Figure 28.

The equations needed to develop a range chart when the sample size is five are:

$$\overline{R} = \frac{\text{Sum of sample ranges}}{\# \text{ of samples}}$$

upper limit =
lower limit = $0\overline{R} \times 2.11$

In this illustration the range chart indicates stability. Therefore we would conclude that there are no assignable causes present in the process during the short time period.

To analyze the dispersion over the long time period an average is calculated for each sample, and an overall average of the sample averages is calculated. The sample average and overall averages are plotted on a line graph similar to the range chart.

The control limits for the sample averages are calculatd using the following equations when the sample size is five:

$$\text{upper limit} = \text{overall average} + (.58 \times \overline{R})$$
$$\text{lower limit} = \text{overall average} - (.58 \times \overline{R})$$

137

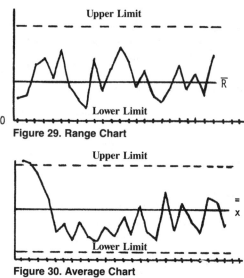

Figure 29. Range Chart

Figure 30. Average Chart

These two lines are drawn on the line graph for sample averages. If all the sample averages fall within these two lines and do not show any unusual trends the process is said to be stable over the long time period. The results of these calculations are illustrated on Figure 30. Is the process stable?

One of the advantages that the control chart has over the histogram and other methods of analysis is that the control chart considers the time at which the samples were selected enabling us to observe the effect that time has on a process. In Figure 30 for example, you can see how the process moved around as time increased.

It is unlikely that such process variation would be due to chance causes as illustrated by the fact that the chart for averages has two points above the upper control limit. Whether it was caused by the machine, the method, the material or the operator is not known but the control chart does show that unusual variation is present.

Figures 29 and 30 are examples of control charts for measurements. Control charts can also be developed for defectives (p chart) and for defects (c chart).

Summary. These eight tools that have been presented are the kinds of tools used by the QC Circle teams to help solve problems. The discussion of them has been purposely kept short to provide the reader with the purposes of each of them. If more information is required the reader is urged to consider the material in the bibliography.

REFERENCES

1. Ishikawa, Dr. Kaoru, "Guide to Quality Control," Asian Productivity Organization, 1976, p. 29.
2.   IBID, p. 19.

138

QC CIRCLE WORKSHOP: APPLICATION
Virgil Rehg

The narrative that you are about to read is presented here to serve as an example of how a QC Circle team operates from day-to-day and how they apply the basic tools commonly used by QC Circle Teams.

The circle that we shall be examining has chosen as their name, the Glamour Girls. It is one of fifty QC Circle Teams at the Soso Electric Company. The Soso Electric Company manufactures small appliances and electrical fixtures.

THE PRODUCT

The Glamour Girls consist of nine members who all work on a production-assembly line that assembles a small, two-slice toaster for noncommercial use. To assemble the toaster, seven work stations are positioned along a 40-foot table. A conveyor belt is used to move the toasters along the center of the table. The stations and the name of the team member at the station are listed in the order of assembly:

1. Assemble Heater to Frame (Ellen)
2. Elevator Assembly (Anne)
3. Bimetal Switch Assembly (Carolyn and Eileen)
4. Wiring Harness and Loading Level (Linda)
5. Functional Test (Sue and Joan)
6. Case Assembly (Nancy)
7. Final Test and Packaging (Marie)

Figure 1 illustrates the location of each worker on the assembly line. The team leader and line foreman is Bill Richard, and the subleader is Eileen.

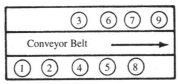

Figure 1. Two-Slice Toaster Assembly Line.

CHOOSING A PROJECT (THEME)

The Glamour Girls have been meeting for about one year. They have worked on two projects during that time. One of the projects resulted in a substantial savings in assembly time of the toaster.

The Glamour Girls meet for one hour every other Friday afternoon during company time, usually the last hour of the working day. Small groups of circle members meet informally during lunch and after working hours to discuss the progress of a project.

February 6

As we drop in on the Glamour Girls, we find that they are trying to decide on a project. Bill is leading the discussion:

BILL: *As you already know, management was very pleased with the success of our last project; so let's see if we can repeat that success. I have a suggestion I would like the group to consider as a theme. It is* safety. *We haven't had many accidents that resulted in lost time, but any lost time we experience causes a disruption on our production line and that affects the quality and output.*

In addition to safety, *management has asked us to consider working on* absenteeism. *Our absenteeism rate has been running about 7%, and they would like to see that cut in half. Now what are your suggestions?*

EILEEN: *In my opinion, the biggest problem we have is with bimetal switch assemblies. We rework a high percent of them. Why don't we choose* bimetals *as our theme?*

ELLEN: *Parts! Or lack of them when we need them. That's the problem. Why can't the stockers get the parts to us when we need them. Everyone on this line has to go looking for parts at least once a week and that costs money. I suggest that we use the* parts supply system *as our project.*

SUE: *As far as I am concerned, something better be done about those failures at the functional test. We are still running about 8% defective. I think our project should be* defective toasters.

The discussion continued in this manner, and by the end of the hour each team member had suggested at least one problem. In summary, the following suggestions were proposed: *safety, absenteeism, bimetals, parts supply system, defective toasters, location of the production line, defective heater elements, too much torque on power tools, and defective parts.* The Circle gave consideration to each of these problems, and prior to the next meeting, Circle members are going to collect information on the costs related to each of the problems suggested.

PROJECTS

1 — Defective Toasters
2 — Bi-metals
3 — Safety
4 — Absenteeism
5 — Parts Supply System
6 — Others

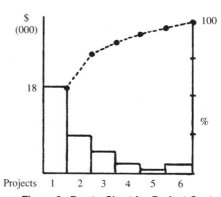

Figure 2. Pareto Chart for Project Cost.

140

February 13

At their third meeting, the Glamour Girls discussed different causes of defective toasters in more detail. Again, each team member suggested possible causes of the problem. They also defined a goal that they would try to achieve during the next six months; namely, to reduce the costs due to defectives by 80%. Since the costs of defectives were about $18,000 a year, they would need to reduce that amount by $14,400 a year.

Suggestions were made as to the cause of defects and the following comments were heard:

MARIE: *I have noticed that there are a lot of electrical shorts that arise when the wiring harness isn't attached properly.*

NANCY: *The cases aren't so hot either! They don't fit and quite a few are scratched.*

LINDA: *Yes, but the rework on defective bi-metals just about kills us.*

CAROLYN: *I'll second that!*

ELLEN: *But the heaters require even more rework when they don't work right.*

BILL: *Marie, don't you and Sue and Joan keep records on the types of defects that cause a toaster to be rejected?*

MARIE: *Sue and Joan do on the rejects they find before packaging, but I don't because Quality Control keeps track of the defects at packaging.*

BILL: *OK, let's stop guessing at what we think is the real cause of the problem. Sue, suppose you work with Anne and Carolyn; and Joan, you work with Nancy and Linda, and find out how much each of the defects reported in the last two months has cost us. And Marie, I'd like you to work with Eileen to make a Pareto analysis of these costs. Then we'll know where to concentrate our efforts.*

TOASTER DEFECTS

1 — Bi-metal Switch Assembly
2 — Scratched Case
3 — Heater Element Damaged
4 — Wiring Harness Shorts
5 — Will Not Latch
6 — Others

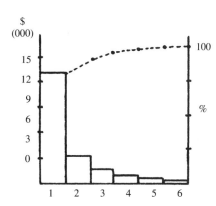

Figure 3. Pareto Chart for Toaster Defects.

141

March 12

The Pareto chart for costs of defects is illustrated in Figure 3. It is immediately apparent that the bi-metal switch assemblies are the most serious problem, since they are costing $12,600 a year, which is more than any other type defect. The Circle had previously stated that their goal was to reduce costs of defective toasters by about $14,400. To achieve the goal, the circle must reduce the bi-metal costs substantially, and also reduce the cost of scratched cases or other defect categories so that the total savings adds up to at least $14,400.

Their next step will be to locate the cause of bi-metal switch assembly defects. For this endeavor, they will construct a Cause and Effect Diagram.

CAUSE AND EFFECT DIAGRAM

BILL: *On our last project, the Circle did a very good job. As I recall, we took turns suggesting possible causes of the problem. Let's do that again. Keep in mind that we are concerned about* bi-metal defects and their causes.

CAROLYN: *Sometimes it is difficult to position the bi-metal in the fixture when we are assembling the bi-metal to the bracket. I think the* fixture *could be improved.*

LINDA: *Other times, the holes in the brackets have* burrs *on them so that it is hard to get the rivets through the holes. One of the causes is* defective brackets.

JOAN: *I've noticed that we get a lot of bi-metal assemblies that are out of line. It looks like more care should be taken when they are being positioned in the toaster. Let's improve the* assembly method.

ANNE: *The* lighting *at this end of the table isn't too good on cloudy days. Maybe if we had brighter lights, we could do better.*

SUE: *I've noticed that some of the bi-metal assemblies are so loose that the bi-metal moves at the point where it is riveted. Maybe the* striking pressure *of the coining fixture should be considered.*

LINDA: *As you know, the pre-heating coil that surrounds the bi-metal is spot-welded to the bi-metal bracket. Maybe the* welder *is inconsistent and causing the trouble.*

MARIE: *How about the electrical properties of the pre-heating coil? Couldn't that affect the operation of the bi-metal?*

The brainstorming session continued well past the usual hour set aside for the meeting, until the suggestions of the Circle members were finally exhausted. As an assignment, the Circle members were to stratify the causes by placing them in one of five categories: Material, Operator, Method, Set-up, and the Machine. The complete list of possible causes suggested by the Circle members.

March 19

The Circle met on their own time after working hours today to construct a Cause and Effect Diagram (C & E). With this technique, they could illustrate the relationship between the cause(s) of defective bi-metal assemblies. The C & E Diagram is illustrated in Figure 4.

March 26

Prior to the meeting on this date, the Circle members studied the possible cause and their relationship to each other and to the process.

At the meeting, the Circle discussed the C & E Diagram to learn as much as possible about the process so that they could isolate the cause(s) of the problem. Each Circle member was given an assignment to do more studying in regard to the possible causes before the next meeting.

Figure 4. Cause and Effect Diagrams for Defective Bi-metal Switch Assemblies.

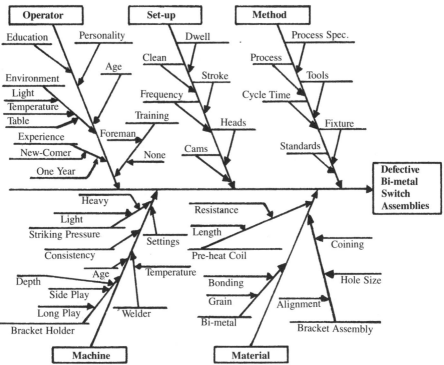

CHECK LIST

April 2

The members discussed the potential causes of the problem based upon what they had discovered since their last meeting. As a result of their findings, some of the potential causes of the problem could be eliminated. The Circle did not feel that time would permit a Pareto analysis and decided to investigate the *pre-heater coil* of the bi-metal assembly. This is a subfactor of material on the C & E Diagram.

To find out if pre-heater coils were the cause of defective bi-metal assemblies, the Circle will conduct experiments, gather data on the outcomes of the experiments, analyze the results and draw a conclusion. If necessary, staff assistance may be brought in when more technical help is required. The check list is used to organize the activities and to keep track of the progress being made while the experiments are being conducted.

For the pre-heater coil experiments, the check list contained a detailed list of experiments to be performed, instructions, procedures, responsible members, histograms, due dates and an analysis of the outcomes. For preheater coils, the results are summarized as follows:

Experiment	Actions	Responsibility	Outcome
Coil Length	Short Coils	Eileen	Negative
Coil Length	Long Coils	Anne	Negative
Electrical Properties	High-Resistance Wire	Nancy	Negative
Electrical Properties	Low-Resistance Wire	Marie	Negative

All team members are involved in the experiment and, in some instances, staff experts are consulted. Outcomes were judged to be negative when the fraction defective obtained during the experiment were compared with the results of the control groups.

April 23

BILL: *Well, we didn't solve the problem; but we did learn something about the process that will be helpful. Did you get any ideas during those experiments?*

SUE: *How about the welding machine! We bowl with those girls and they were telling us about the troubles they have been having with that machine.*

BILL: *That's a possibility. We have worked with other departments in the past when it was necessary.*

CAROLYN: *What about the brackets?*

BILL: *What about them?*

CAROLYN: *Well, if you don't get a good alignment between the bracket and the bi-metal, you are in trouble; and sometimes it is really difficult to stay within the specification.*

144

LINDA: *Carolyn's right. The size of the hole in the bracket and the adjustment we make on the bracket affect the alignment. And if it's off, the bi-metal will bind-up when it's assembled.*

After considerable debate about possible causes (from the C & E Diagram in Figure 4), the team has decided to experiment with the bracket assembly and striking pressure of the coining machine. Staff assistance was requested to help set-up a designed experiment, but the data gathering was performed by the members of the Glamour Girls Circle.

The experiments required were divided between the team members. Linda, Carolyn, Eileen and Nancy would work on the material used in bracket assembly with Eileen in charge of the experiments. The other girls and Bill would work with the coining fixture and experiment with the striking pressure and the bracket holder.

For the bracket assembly, a summary check sheet was set up to show the results obtained from the experiments.

Experiment:	Bracket Assembly		**Sample Size:**	50 Each	
Leader:	Eileen		**Due Date:**	5/21	

Alignment	Hole Size	Clearance	Bi-metal Pressure	Percent Defective	Category
Right 5°	.120E	–	Low	8.0	(1)
	.125C	+	OK	.5	(2)
	.130E	0	OK	1.0	(3)
On Center ± ½°	.120E	0	OK	2.0	(4)
	.125C	+	OK	0.0	(5)
	.130E	0	OK	1.5	(6)
Left 5°	.120E	–	Low	10.0	(7)
	.125C	+	OK	1.0	(8)
	.130E	0	OK	1.0	(9)

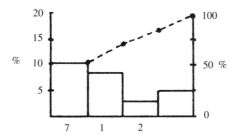

Pareto Chart for Defective Category.

Hole size and alignment cause 72% of the defective bi-metals. Alignment and hole size must be controlled if defective bi-metals are to be reduced.

For the bracket assembly, the control groups are indicated by a "C" and experimental groups by an "E." The data was collected and analyzed with the help of the staff. For each experiment, a check sheet was set up to summarize the data collected for the experiment being conducted.

The conclusions from the experiments on brackets, striking pressure and alignment were positive. Thus, hole size, alignment and striking pressure have significant effects upon the defective bi-metal assemblies.

May 21

BILL: *The reports on the experiments look very good, but now the question is how can we control these factors?*

ANNE: *Why can't the hole sizes be checked after the final forming operation, or why can't they de-burr those rivet holes?*

BILL: *That's a good point. I'll suggest that the QC Circle Team on the bracket manufacturing line study the problem. I don't think we should have to check them on the line. Engineering may have to change the hole size on the bracket specification.*

JOAN: *I think that we may need a control chart on the coining fixture to help control the striking pressure. We used one during the experiment and it worked quite well.*

NANCY: *But that may only be a temporary solution. We need better control over the factors that affect the coining pressure. I collected some data during the experiment on line voltage. Whenever the line voltage would drop, the striking pressure dropped off. In fact, I have a copy of the Scatter Diagram that we used.*

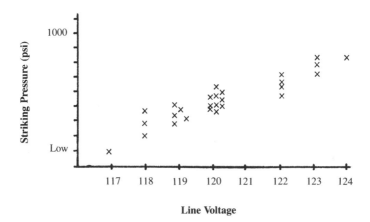

Line Voltage

146

BILL: *Hey, that's great! We can use this to convince engineering that they need to take a look at our power sources. Perhaps some sort of a regulator can be installed.*

LINDA: *OK, so we know what must be done with the holes in the brackets and the striking pressure. Now, I have a suggestion on aligning the brackets. Why don't we attach a spring-loaded plunger to the side of the fixture? Then the alignment would always be close to 0°?*

CAROLYN: *Sounds good to me.*

BILL: *I think we can get that done. I'll check with engineering. We have made a good start on reducing the cost of defective toasters, and we have done it at a relatively low cost. We still have to check out the controls we were discussing earlier, but they look very promising. At our next meeting, we'll start on the scratched cases.*

CONCLUSION

We shall leave the team at this time since the problem of defective bimetal assemblies has been solved. The team will now move on to attack the scratched cases so that they could achieve their goal of cutting annual costs by $14,400. The approach would be similar and for that reason will not be repeated.

I hope that you now have a better idea of how QC Circles operate. Please bear in mind that each Circle may operate slightly different than the Glamour Girls, but the overall approach is similar.

PROBLEM SOLVING COMPARISONS: QC CIRCLES, KT, ETC.

Robert T. Amsden

INTRODUCTION

During the past twenty years, there have grown up a number of procedures to identify and solve problems. The ones this paper specifically examines are Kepner-Tregoe Analysis (KT), Quality Control Circles (QCC), and Zero Defects (ZD). This is not to say that there are not other systems. We have chosen these three chiefly because they are fairly well known and some of you may work in firms which presently use them. The paper looks at these techniques in light of how each one works to solve problems. That is, how does each define the term problem; what kinds of problems does each attack; who solves problems; what procedures and tools does each technique use; what type of training, if any, do the problem-solvers receive; and what is the creativity-quotient of each method. It will be helpful, before we go on into the body of the paper, if first we define "problem" and "problem solving." Then it will be easier to see how well the different techniques fit the definitions. We can view the term "problem" in the following ways. A problem is a discrepancy or difference between an actual state of affairs and a desired or ideal state of affairs.[1] Another way of saying it is, that a problem is a "gap between current results (or ends) and desired results (or ends)."[2] A problem exists whenever there is an imbalance between what should be and what actually is; or whenever there is a deviation from a standard.[3] The key words in these definitions are "deviation," "gap," "imbalance," "discrepancy," "difference." Quite simply, problem solving is the means we use to reduce the gap, imbalance, or difference between what is and should be. It is how we get to where we want to go from where we are.[4]

DEFINITION OF PROBLEM

KT: The definition of "problem" contains two corollary ideas. The first says that a problem is a deviation from a standard. On the other side is the idea of problem being the imbalance between what actually happens and what should happen.[5]

QCC: The concept of problem contains the idea of deviation from a standard as well as that of gap between the actual and ideal. This view of what constitutes a problem appears to be the same as in KT, but there is a subtle difference in the two which shows up in the kinds of problems each procedure addresses.

ZD: Problem is seen in a specific, all be it limited, way, i.e., as deviation from[6] a set standard, perfection, and such deviation results in errors or defects. In other words, if every employee did his/her job right there would be no errors, no defects.[7]

KINDS OF PROBLEMS ATTACKED

KT: The type of problem KT addresses is by and large the sporadic one. This is evident in the KT definition of problem since this definition includes the concept tha the deviation or imbalance is *always* caused by an unexpected, unplanned change.[8] This view implies that something has occurred at a specific point in time.

Up until the change the process is acceptable. KT procedure is an example of end-product-well-defined because its aim is to stop the sporadic happening and to return to the predetermined standard. KT works well in the area of management-controllable problems such as in the example of the blackened filaments (chapter two of The Rational Manager).

QCC: The basic thrust of activity aims at the solution of relatively low-level problems which are chronic in nature. That is the discrepancy between actual and ideal or the deviation from standard has been happening over a period of time and may or may not have been occasioned by a marked change. The process may be operating up to standard but may not be at ideal performance. Moreover the process itself may cause the discrepancies between actual and desired and/or deviations from standard. These conceptions differ from the KT approach inasmuch as KT addresses a different sort of problem.

Generally the problems handled by the circles are operator-controllable.[9] The operator knows what he/she is to do and what he/she actually is doing and has the means to regulate the job. Consequently the circle members themselves find, analyze, and implement solutions to work-problems such as defects or scrap reduction. QC activity looks to the long-run performance. It solves the problem and initiates follow-up, guidelines and safeguards for the solutions.

ZD: This program works to reduce defects by prevention.[10] ZD theory says that defects are operator controllable. Since the operator already has all he/she needs to do the job, knowledge and tools, there will be no errors, i.e., defects, if only the employee cares enough to work accurately according to preestablished standard.[11]

However, there are certain kinds of problems workers under a ZD program cannot address. These are ones which arise from difficulties in the process itself.[12] These types of problems are routinely handled by QC Circles whereas, in the ZD process, they are handled by supervisors, ZD administrators, or production or quality engineers.[13]

WHO SOLVES PROBLEMS

KT: Essentially it is the manager who is the problem solver. He is responsible for analyzing the problem, making the decision to put to work whichever solution he has selected, and preparing preventive action.[14] From others who are involved with the area under study, the manager elicits help and information in analyzing and solving the problem.[15]

QCC: Problem solving in the circle is primarily a team effort. The circle is a small group of people who work in the same area, together with their foreman/

supervisor. They usually choose the particular problem themselves, then analyze it, find and implement solutions. Participation by each member of the circle is essential and everyone's responsibility. The circle functions as a team and "stars" are not encouraged. There may be interaction with circles in other work areas if the problem is that broad. For example, a circle in the warehouse might work with a circle in final assembly to prevent cracking of glass tanks. Personnel from quality assurance, engineering, or other areas serve as resource people.

ZD: This is a broadly based program which applies to all levels of the organization.[16] In one sense each person in the organization is a problem solver because he strives to improve his own performance, to work without error. However, in the sense that problem solving is used in this paper, the responsibility for solving problems rests with the supervisor and/or ZD administrator[17] and a team which is not directly involved with the work area. The supervisor corrects problems discovered by the workers and reported on the Error Cause Identification (ECI) form. Should the problem prove too difficult or require handling by superiors, the supervisor passes to the ZD administrator or other appropriate officials. The man on the line has no responsibility to solve problems other than to remove defects. Should he spot a problem in the process, he is encouraged to fill out an ECI form and forward it to his supervisor. If he has thought of a solution, he submits this through the suggestion system.[18]

PROBLEM SOLVING SEQUENCE

"Problem solving is a process that follows a logical sequence."[19] The process, by whatever name, contains familiar and recognizable steps: once the problem is recognized, the problem solver looks for causes. He collects information about it from what he observes. Next he speculates about the causes, analyzes them, develops solutions, chooses one, and puts it to work, always revising as necessary.[20]

KT: Messrs. Kepner and Tregoe have developed a very orderly and precise method for analysis of problems, for making decisions and obviating potential difficulties in the solution. We give here a brief summary of this procedure, based on material from *Results Planning Manual*, the KT workbook.[21] The procedure has three parts, problem analysis, decision analysis, and analysis of potential problems. Problem analysis is the systematic way of finding the real cause of the problem. First *specify* exactly what the problem is and is not, noting areas of sharp contrast. Next *develop possible causes*. *Test* each possibility to determine the probable cause. *Verify* the results.

Decision analysis is the method used to choose the best solution to the problem. First, *establish* the objectives, what are the desired results and what are the necessary resources. After the objectives are clear, *classify* as must: the critical area; and *want*: those things of relative importance. Next, find alternatives. *Compare* these to the objectives for consequences.

Potential problem analysis anticipates potential problems and devises plans to prevent their occurrence or to protect the solution from the impact of the potential problem if it should occur.

QCC: The first step in the problem solving sequence followed by the circles is to *identify goals*.[22] Usually the goals are fairly broad, such as reduction of scrap or defects in a particular department. In order to narrow the goal to a workable size, the circle breaks down the general problem area into its components. At this stage the circle *collects data* by means of check sheets, tallies, etc. The circle proceeds to analyze the data by means of Pareto analysis which sets priorities and by frequency histograms. In determining causes, the circle employs *brainstorming*, and records ideas on a Cause and Effect diagram (C & E). Incidentally, it is well to note Kepner's and Tregoe's caution about brainstorming that the technique "does not lead to an understanding of precisely what is wrong, how things got that way, and what is the most economical way of correcting the trouble."[23] When the circles brainstorm, they are looking at four precise areas where trouble can arise: men, method, material, or machine. By using the C & E diagram, the circle members can graphically see the interrelationships of different aspects of the problem under analysis.

The next step is to *experiment* to see which ideas recorded on the C & E diagram are the most likely causes. The circle analyzes these results using graphs and other statistical analysis. Once a solution is selected, the circle tests and implements it. The circle also designs and implements safeguards to make sure the solution continues to function properly.

In some respects this problem solving sequence resembles the KT approach. The circles specify the problem through statistical tools such as Pareto analysis, frequency histograms or check sheets. It is in the brainstorming phase that the circles develop possible causes. Both KT and the circles test for the probable cause and verify the results.

The KT procedure seems to follow a more definite pattern in order to determine what the solution is than do the QC Circles. The circles have selected a goal beforehand, such as reducing the percent defective parts, before analyzing the causes. Both procedures choose solutions. The circles test the solutions to find potential problems. By designing and implementing safeguards, the circles, just as KT analysis, provide for protection and contingent action.

The dissimilarities in the two approaches appear because the methods deal with different orders of problem. The QC Circle solves low level, chronic problems; KT handles sporadic serious problems.

ZD: The ZD program seeks to motivate [24] or encourage[25] people to do their job right the first time, every time.[26] Generally speaking ZD aims toward the solution of a single specific problem: reduction of defects by prevention rather than through detection.[27] The program was not designed to solve problems nor was it intended to teach techniques for solving problems.

Even so a type of problem solving procedure does take place in Error Cause Identification. The employee *recognizes that a problem exists* which either does, or has the potential to, cause errors. He fills out an ECI form which he submits to his supervisor. The main responsibility for solving the problem rests with the supervisor.[28] Then the supervisor *verifies* that a problem exists, *determines* what must be done to correct it, and then puts into operation whatever *solution* he has chosen. In some instances the quality control representative and possibly an assigned team find the solution.[29]

We would like to take a look at an instance of problem solving in the example given by J. M. Halpin in *Zero Defects*.[30] The supervisor discovered an increase of surface scratches on a product. The cause is supposed to result from careless and/or improper handling. The supervisor speaks to his workers about the scratches. When the scratches continue to occur, the supervisor calls in the ZD administrator. This person checks the end result of scratches on the finished product. He finds that this defect can cause the ruin of the finished product. The administrator demonstrates to the workers what he has found.

The manner in which the supervisor handled this particular case, as it is reported, points to a type of difficulty noted by Dr. Ishikawa,[31] and Dr. Juran.[32] The supervisor assumes that the cause of the scratches is careless handling, but it might well have come from defective tools or the process itself. No one verified the cause using standard statistical methods.

TRAINING IN PROBLEM SOLVING

KT: The manager receives training in KT analysis through study of the principles as outlined in *The Rational Manager* and through participation in a KT training session. An essential part of this training is the practice of the concepts in simulated and personal business situations. These practice sessions are critiqued by the KT instructor.[33]

QCC: The supervisor receives extensive training in group dynamics and basic statistical tools: histograms, Pareto analysis, control charts, stratification, binomial probability paper, cause and effect diagrams, graphs, etc. He, in turn, trains the people who work under him in these same techniques. Training is not limited to job training, honing of work skills or improving understanding of the process. Workers may indeed receive this sort of training if the circle finds that more job training is part of the solution to the problem it has tackled.

The skills that the worker in a QC Circle learns are practical statistical concepts. In KT the manager learns an efficient method for breaking down a problem and deciding how to solve it. He would further enhance his problem solving skills if he included some statistical analysis. KT teaches a problem solving methodology which enables an *individual* to handle problems successfully. By contrast the statistical skills allow the circle to work as a *team* with great effectiveness.

ZD: There is minimal training for problem solving for supervisors and workers, aside from instruction in the proper use of the ECI form. The expectation is that either the supervisor will correct the problem identified on an ECI form or someone else will.[34]

CREATIVITY QUOTIENT

Writers, as widely different as J. R. R. Tolkien, Francis Schaefitt, J. M. Juran, George M. Prince, and Prof. Y. Kondo recognize that creativity is a basic human right.[35] Programs and procedures which challenge people to do their job creatively and give them the methods to do it will be the most successful and will do much to improve the quality of work life. Creativity cannot perhaps be quantified, yet such things as increased employee motivation and reduction of boredom and absenteeism are the kinds of effets a program of problem solving is likely to have. People need to perceive they have some control over their work even if such control is limited.

We are outsiders: we don't manage a factory nor do we work on line. But as outsiders, we have a perspective which can focus on strengths and weaknesses of the various procedures. A program which helps to sharpen a worker's skills and teaches him how to use them will have a high creativity quotient. When a person is better prepared to handle what comes to him in life, whether at work or at leisure, he develops more self-confidence that he can participate in the control of his circumstances. KT and the QC Circle concept do these things. They recognize that people are problem solvers and that they need training to be effective. KT gives a logical, efficient method of breaking down a problem and arriving at a solution yet the procedure is flexible. KT is generally used on big, one-shot problems, but the technique can be applied in almost any situation. One strength this procedure has is that the problem solver goes to the problem and lets *it* speak. Usually it is a single individual who uses KT analysis rather than a team; but there is no reason why a team cannot use this method to solve problems.

KT is designed for managers, though if a manager is people oriented he will be concerned with those under him, that they also become strong problem solvers. Consequently he will teach the KT analysis principles to his subordinates.[36]

The QCC concept emphasizes the statistical analysis of problem solving. Because it is a team effort, each member has an opportunity to contribute, to have his ideas accepted, to be creative, and so to develop self-worth. Through the statistical analysis the team participates in the control over the work process; they are able ''to close the loop'', they can change what they *are* doing to what they are *supposed* to be doing.[37]

One of the strengths of the ZD program is that it covers the *entire* organization from management on down to the man on the line to make each person aware of his responsibility to do his job right. KT trains managers; the QC Circle trains supervisors and workers.

A caution we would post for the ZD program is one already anticipated by Dr. Juran. As long as the workers already have in their hands the proper training to do the job, knowledge of the process, and the means to change their actions or the process in order to conform to what is expected, a ZD-type program can help motivate workers.[38]

REFERENCES

1. Johnson and Johnson, *Joining Together*, quoted in paper by Laura Fasbinder, Wright State University.
2. Roger Kaufman, *Identifying and Solving Problems*, (La Jolla, California: University Associates, Inc., 1976), p. 12.

3. Charles Kepner and Benjamin Tregoe, *The Rational Manager*, (New York: McGraw-Hill, 1965),pp. 18, 4.
4. Kaufman, p. 25.
5. Kepner and Tregoe, p. 18.
6. Charles Halpin, (New York: McGraw-Hill, 1968), p. 3; American Management Association, *Zero Defects* (1965), p. 4.
7. American Management Association, p. 10.
8. Kepner and Tregoe, p. 40. See also pp. 4, 18, 50. The example of the blackened filament used in chapter two was sporadic in nature. It had never happened before, and after the corrections, would not happen again.
9. J. M. Juran, *Quality Control Handbook* (1962), pp. 4-22; "Quality Problems, Remedies and Nostrums," *Industrial Quality Control* (June 1966), p. 650.
10. Halpin, p. vii.
11. American Management Association, *Zero Defects*, p. 3. K. Ishikawa "Conclusions", p. 164, reprinted in Amsden and Amsden, *QC Circles: Applications Tools and Theory*, ASQC, 1976.
12. Ishikawa, p. 164; Juran, "Quality Problems, Remedies and Nostrums", p. 651.
13. Halpin, p. 219. See also pp. 178-180, 215-216.
14. Kepner and Tregoe, p. 53; *Results Planning Manual* introduction.
15. Kepner and Tregoe, *Rational Manager*, pp. 154-158 for example.
16. Halpin, p. 9.
17. *Ibid.*, pp. 216, 178-180.
18. *Ibid.*, pp. 216-217.
19. Kepner and Tregoe, *Rational Manager*, p. 18.
20. George M. Prince, *The Practice of Creativity*, Collier Books, New York (1972), pp. 10 & 15; Kaufman, p. 119.
21. *Results Planning Manual* (1966), R 03.002-R 03.004.
22. R. T. Amsden, See paper for this conference.
23. Kepner and Tregoe, *Rational Manager*, p. 52.
24. Lloyd A. Swanson and Darrel Corbin, "Employee Motivation Programs: A Change in Philosophy," *Personnel Journal* (November, 1969), p. 895; Halpin, pp. vii, 46.
25. Tom Finnegan, "ITT Zeros in on Zero Defects," *Purchasing Magazine* (January 21, 1971), p. 55.
26. Francis J. DeRosa, "Holding the Line on Costs," *Best's Review* (June 1972), p. 78; Halpin, p. 46. *cf* p. vii.
27. Halpin, p. vii.
28. P. J. Cathey, "Is Zero Defects Still Alive and Well?" *Iron Age* (February 25, 1971); Halpin, p. 218.
29. DeRosa, p. 78; Cathey, *op. cit.*
30. Halpin, pp. 178-9.
31. Ishikawa, p. 164.
32. Juran, "The QC Circle Phenomenon," *Industrial Quality Control* (January 1967), pp. 334-35.
33. Kepner and Tregoe, *Rational Manager*, p. 5.
34. Cathey, *op. cit.*; Halpin, p. 218.
35. Tolkein essay "On Fairy Stories," Ballantine (1966), pp. 54-5; Schaeffer, *How Shall We Then Live*, p. 133; Juran, "The QC Circle Phenomenon," p. 334; Prince, *The Practice of Creativity passim* but especially p. 3; and Kondo, "Creativity in Daily Work," ASQC Technical Transactions 1977.
36. Kepner and Tregoe, *Rational Manager*, p. 41.
37. Juran, "Quality Problems, Remedies and Nostrums," p. 650.
38. Juran, "Quality Problems, Remedies and Nostrums," pp. 650, 653; "The QC Circle Phenomenon," p. 333-35.

QC CIRCLE TRAINING PROCESS SHOULD COVER RELATING, SUPPORTING, PROBLEM-SOLVING SKILLS

Scott M. Sedam

Imagine for a moment that you are the head of an interdepartmental task force that has just installed the first quality circle (QC) in your organization. You hired a well-known consulting firm to set up the QC structure and do the required training in brainstorming, prioritizing, basic statistical methods, etc. You have asked the circle facilitator to give you a report on the activity in the first meeting.

You open the report, expecting to find some exciting details about the proposed solution to the recurrent bent flange problem on No. 2 hot bed, or perhaps some ideas on how manpower can be better allocated to keep the place running smoothly at shift change. Instead, you find a letter to your task force from the quality circle asking for answers to the following five questions.

1. Why do we have quality circles, anyway?
2. What are we supposed to accomplish in a quality circle?
3. How will we know how our circle is doing — are there ways of measuring this?
4. Being in a quality circle is extra work. What's in it for us?
5. What happens when our circle needs help in gathering information, analyzing data, implementing solutions, etc.?

Your initial reaction is probably an intense desire to hang the consultants you had thought were supposed to answer those questions. You can't, however. They are off working with someone else.

After more reflection, you begin to realize that your organization, not the consulting firm, holds the responsibility for answering those questions. You begin to understand that a quality circle or any other plan of employee involvement is not a "thing" or a "system" that can be purchased like a piece of machinery or a computer terminal. It is not a system to be installed in a firm as much as it is a process of organizational development. This fact has profound implications with regard to training for quality circles.

THE ORGANIZATIONAL PERSPECTIVE

Success with quality circles requires a fundamental change in organizational culture. This change in the organization cannot be bought, but it can be learned given the necessary time, resources, commitment and support. Training, which is best viewed as a subset of support, should be an integral part of the learning process.

To get a handle on what that training should look like, we can return to the five questions submitted by our quality circle above. When we examine them closely we see that the questions represent five very basic issues of concern to all organizations. Those issues are:

1. Mission
2. Goals
3. Feedback
4. Rewards
5. Support

ANSWERING BASIC QUESTIONS

From an organizational perspective, then, QC training must include answers to the five questions corresponding to the issues just outlined. Glitch No. 1 is that training can't begin until those answers are forthcoming. Glitch No. 2 is that the answers are often unique to each organization — they aren't available in a quality circle manual.

Those answers can be found, yet very few companies are going through the agonizing process of determining just what their position is on these issues — it is merely assumed. Such assumptions are often fatal for any long-term use of quality circles in a firm.

The good news is that a detailed description of how to approach each of these five issues is not necessary. Simply have your organization ask itself the same questions posed by our quality circle above, and the rest will follow.

WHO NEEDS WHAT TRAINING?

Assuming that the issues of mission, goals, feedback, rewards and support have been addressed, the next question is, who should be trained? The short answer is anyone who has contact with or impact on the quality circle. Breaking it down a bit reveals five distinct areas of need (although it could reasonably be argued that the areas should be broken down even further). Training must be provided for:

1. Middle and upper level management (line and staff).
2. Supervisors (line and staff).
3. Quality circle facilitators.
4. Quality circle members.
5. Staff support personnel not members of circles.

To be sure, there will be a considerable amount of commonality in the training for these five groups. By addressing the five organizational issues cited above, however, we can begin to personalize the training so that it becomes meaningful to each group. For example, the mission and general goals would normally be common to all elements of the organization, although specific objectives for each individual circle and support group might be quite different. The result should be an understanding of why the firm is involved in quality circles from both the individual and organizational points of view and, more specifically, what exactly the company is trying to accomplish.

As a general rule, people want feedback. They would like to know how they are doing if that can be presented in a constructive manner. But feedback is highly situational. It must be tailored for each element so that each support group and level of management can monitor its contribution to the quality circles' accomplishments and what this contribution means to that element's own particular segment of the company. The industrial engineering department, for example, would expect to get feedback different from that of personnel. Feedback is, of course, essential for each quality circle, and a reliable, accurate system of reporting results to the circles should be considered mandatory. QC training should have as a goal that all members of the organization understand the feedback system adopted.

The real differentiation in training each group will begin to show up in terms of rewards — the age-old (and eminently legitimate) question of "What's in it for me?" If the firm does not have some form of productivity gain sharing program — and regrettably, most do not — this will be the trickiest question of all. What will reward the director of operations is likely to be much different from what will reward the supervisor, which will be different from what rewards the process engineer, etc.

I cannot attempt to summarize the thousands of pages written on the subject of what will motivate people, but from experience I can cite one commonly used tactic that will not motivate except in the very short term. That tactic is fear, commonly presented in the guise of "motherhood" statements about the consummate greatness of American industry that is being eroded away by the menace from the East. Suffice it to say that rewards, like beauty, are judged in the eye of the beholder. When all is said and done, people will do things for their reasons — not ours — or they will not do them at all.

Finally, the most differentiation in training will be found in the area of support. On a practical basis, support for quality circles is unique to each level of management and to each support group. Here, training must address the roles and responsibilities of each of the five groups cited above. When members of the circle ask, "Where do we go when we need help?" they should not only be provided with the answer, but expect that the help will be forthcoming as well. They should not, for example, have to depend on the facilitator or supervisor to bribe the utilities department into providing electrical usage figures for the second shift. Thus the question for all those outside the circle is, "What is expected of us?"

In summary, each level of management, each support group and all facilitators must understand clearly their obligations and duties with regard to making quality circles work.

TRAINING FOR THE CIRCLE

When confronting the matter of specific training for participants in a quality circle, a firm should ask itself first just what it wants the circle to accomplish. Second, ask what skills are required to accomplish those tasks. Third, examine the alternatives for imparting the needed skill level to the group — with training being one alternative. There is a wealth of information available on specifics in regard to training for the members of quality circles.

Each company, with or without the help of a consulting firm, has established its own angle on what skills are needed, how the group should be structured and how the process should flow. It is not my purpose here to advocate any particular "brand" of skills training. There are, however, specific categories of skills that must be provided if the quality circle is to be effective. A thorough, comprehensive training program for members of quality circles must address the following four skill areas:

1. *Relating skills* — group dynamics and process.
2. *Discovery skills* — information gathering and problem analysis.
3. *Advocating skills* — decision-making and presentation.
4. *Supporting skills* — implementation and reinforcement.

This should be much more useful than providing a list of subjects and topics that other companies may have used in the past. When you examine such lists, all of the relevant topics typically fit into the four skill areas cited above. You will find, however, that the distribution of training is heavily skewed toward the problem-analysis and decision-making components of "discovery" and "advocating."

Further, within each skill area, the training tends to concentrate on the more step-by-step, procedural approach — almost technical in nature. This is as opposed to presenting the human behavior side of each part of the process. This is a serious omission in quality circle training programs. To explain further, the analogy of a bicycle is particularly useful.

Take any job — for example, that of an industrial engineer. Two sets of skills are necessary in this position, analogous to the two wheels of a bicycle. One set functions like the bicycle's back wheel, providing the driving force — the power. Those are the technical skills of the job. For an IE, one important "back-wheel" skill would be knowing how to do time and motion studies.

The other set of skills is similar to the front wheel of the bicycle, giving direction. These are the interpersonal skills needed for the job. Going back to our industrial engineer, a good front-wheel skill would be knowing how to ask a machine operator about the operator's technique without appearing threatening.

Typically, as humans we tend to operate with enormous back wheels and little or no front wheel. The result is a lot of effort being expended with little direction. And so it is in quality circle training. We provide plenty of "back-wheel" skill in the technical side of problem-analysis and decision-making while largely ignoring the crucial need to show people how to communicate and work together as a team — "front-wheel" skills.

It is important to note that neither set of skills is more important than the other. Both are needed in an effective quality circle, but the evidence shows that we tend to overlook the front wheel.

Referring back to the four quality circle skill areas of relating, discovery, advocating, and supporting, we often neglect the first category, relating, and give only cursory treatment to the final area, supporting. Why? Both are primarily front-wheel skills that American industry has traditionally placed little emphasis on.

While reviewing the brief overviews of the four skill areas that follow, keep in mind your own organization and consider whether it tends to be either back wheel or front wheel oriented. Perhaps, if you are both lucky and unusual, your company has a good balance of both.

The key word under relating is "trust." Often we expect those in the circles to dive right into task-oriented problem analysis after only a couple of meetings. Yet we have introduced a profound change into their work world and are asking them to look at their company, their work group and, most importantly, themselves in a brand new light. They are no longer just warm bodies. We have now proclaimed them genuine problem-solvers and decision-makers.

To function effectively as a group, quality circles must develop trust on all three of those levels. They must trust that quality circles are being implemented by the organization for good, legitimate reasons. They must trust the members of their work group if they are to open up and participate in the process. They must trust themselves enough to feel that participating in a quality circle is in their own best interest.

Training is at best only a partial answer to the problem of trust. Trust must come from within the organization. But if a base level of trust is established, there is a wealth of effective training available to help people understand the basics of group dynamics and how people work effectively together.

DISCOVERY SKILLS

Assuming that the quality circle members have attained a degree of trust, the next two basic skills needed are information-gathering and problem-analysis. This is called discovery — the process of gaining a thorough understanding of a problem in the work place. More training is probably available in this area than in any other.

The problem is that most discovery training falls short of the mark by its failure to acknowledge the crucial interpersonal side of the process. Even if we obtain the best problem-analysis system in the world with beautifully drawn diagrams and step-by-step instructions, three facts remain: the information needed to drive that system must be gathered *from* people; the problem must be analyzed *with* people; the solution must be implemented *through* people.

Normally, quality circle members have no authority whatsoever to force people in the organization to cooperate with them, nor would we want them to. They must use influence to accomplish their goals, and this is not a skill that comes easily. But such skills can be learned, and this is an area of high potential for training that addresses the issues of intergroup/interdepartmental conflict and how to overcome it.

ADVOCATING SKILLS

"Advocating" is the catch-all term for decision-making and presentation skills.

No one would argue that those skills are needed by the quality circle, but as with "discovery," problems arise when we treat this section as an exclusively back-wheel skill area.

Most decisions made by the circle will affect people in the work place. That effect must be taken into account, because the best decision in the world can fail if the people involved outside the circle do not support it. Similarly, a good decision may never be implemented at all if the strategy for presenting it doesn't take into account the people involved who sign off on the project. Either situation can be extremely demoralizing for members of a quality circle and can quite effectively kill their spirit.

To overcome this, we must teach members of the circle a decision-making process that considers the various people variables along with the technical ones. Further, training for presentations must cover more than how to use charts, graphs, overheads and flip charts. Of equal importance is knowing how to gear the presentation according to the personality of the audience — another "front-wheel" skill.

SUPPORTING SKILLS

Assume now that the quality circle has learned how to work together effectively (relating), has uncovered and analyzed a problem (discovery) and has formulated and proposed a solution (advocating). What now? Obviously, the plan must be implemented and maintained. This action takes a set of skills categorized as supporting. Next to relating, supporting is the area most overlooked in QC training.

Too often we assume that a great solution will, in effect, implement itself. "If it's good enough, people will buy it, right?" Not necessarily. It is likely that everyone reading this article has experienced the frustration of knowing you had the right solution at the right time, yet nobody was buying. When this happens, the barriers to implementation are most often interpersonal or intergroup, and have nothing to do with the solution itself. The tendency, however, is to question the solution and conclude that it wasn't so good, after all.

Training is available to help quality circles develop strategies for implementing their plans based on an understanding of the people and groups they are working with. Their approach to the accounting department, for example, might be quite different from their approach to safety or quality control. They will be working with different people in different ways than ever before. It makes little sense to risk losing a good decision — or a good quality circle, for that matter — because it was not given the skills to implement and reinforce the fruits of its labor.

SUMMARY

Five distinct groups need training when an organization implements a quality circle program: middle and upper level management, supervisors, QC facilitators, QC members, and staff support personnel. The training needs of those groups can be understood by asking key questions relating to organizational mission, goals, feedback, rewards, and support in regard to quality circles.

The training must be comprehensive and directed at changing the organizational culture, not merely installing a system that forces employee involvement. The training must include both technical and interpersonal skills as they pertain to quality circles. Any comprehensive training program will include both types of skills applied to four specific skill areas that must be developed in the circles. Those skill areas were relating, discovery, advocating, and supporting skills.

It should be noted that a few important matters have not been addressed due to space limitations. Although an approach to evaluating training for the four groups other than the actual quality circles was given, only the circles were covered in appropriate detail. Each group, including middle and upper level management, supervisors, QC facilitators and staff support personnel, has its own unique needs that should be addressed. These needs can be approached in much the same manner as were those of the quality circles — in short, by simply asking what are the roles and responsibilities of each group in helping the quality circle accomplish its goals and objectives, and how training can be of help.

HOW TO BE A GOOD GROUP MEMBER
Michael Doyle and David Straus

As a member of your group, you play a vital role. After all, it's your group and your meeting. You and your fellow group members are responsible for what happens; the facilitator and recorder exist only to serve you. It is you, the group members (along with the manager or chairperson), who meet, work, solve problems, and make decisions. You are the team; it's your game. It helps to have a referee and scorekeeper, but without players there is no action.

Traditionally, group leaders have been treated as an elite. They are told how important they are, how they and only they should be educated in leadership skills. They read books on leadership, they attend training programs, and like the quarterback on a football team, they get all the glory — or blame.

The Interaction Method changes that. The facilitator is not a leader in the traditional sense; the facilitator doesn't lead, but assists. He or she is more like a coach than a quarterback. It is the group collectively that must lead itself. During a meeting the group members must decide where they are going to go and how they are going to get there. So, in the last analysis, the quality of the meeting depends on the quality of the participants.

Surely you have been in enough meetings to recognize that there are effective and ineffective group members. Being an effective group member takes knowledge and skill. Almost all the techniques we described in the chapter on the role of the facilitator can be used by group members, because they can make suggestions about process as well as content. As a group member with process skills, you can be a great resource to your facilitator. Or, if the meeting is being poorly run or if there isn't any leader, you can facilitate from your seat as a participant, using most of the facilitator techniques we have already described. If you never plan to run meetings but find yourself in them anyway, we still recommend that you read this book in its entirety, because it will enable you to come up with suggestions that will make your time in meetings more enjoyable and productive.

Assuming your meetings are going to be run by the Interaction Method, the following are responsibilities you assume as a group member — and techniques you can use to improve your meetings.

HOW TO KEEP THE FACILITATOR NEUTRAL

Your first major responsibility under the Interaction Method system of checks and balances is to monitor the facilitator to make sure that he or she remains neutral and doesn't contribute ideas about content or evaluate those of any group member. As we said before, being a facilitator is hard and depends on your help.

As a watchdog, don't bark indiscriminately. Don't spend your energy lying in wait to pounce on the facilitator at the first sign of a positive or negative expression of sentiment. Be reasonable. Most of the time your facilitator won't even be aware of minor transgressions. Be pragmatic. If what the facilitator is doing

162

seems to be helping and you and your group feel good about what is happening, don't be a stickler for the rules. Rules are only helpful guidelines.

If you believe that your facilitator is consciously manipulating the group, being unfair to certain individuals, or using his or her power over a meeting's process to achieve some personal objective, by all means speak out. Try positive, non-threatening approaches first: "Facilitator, you may not be aware of this, but I think you cut off Theresa before she had a chance to finish." Or, "Facilitator, I feel you're pushing too hard. I don't think we've finished with this issue yet." Talk to your facilitator during a break. Point out what you think can be done to improve the meeting. Then, if the low-key protests don't seem to work, you and your fellow group members have a right to stop the meeting and confront the facilitator. It may be that the facilitator is too intimately involved in the issues to be unbiased, and it may be better to rotate the role or fire the facilitator and find a new one. Whatever the problem is, if the meeting isn't working, it's time to try something else.

KEEP AN EYE ON THE MEMORY

Your second major responsibility as group member is to check on the recorder to make sure that he or she is recording accurately what you and others are saying. All conditions mentioned above apply here. Recording is difficult, and an inexperienced recorder will leave out some key items or misrepresent you unintentionally. All you have to do is say, "Recorder, I said 50 percent, not 15." Or, "What George said was important, and I think you missed it." Usually your recorder will be grateful for your assistance, and a few words of encouragement and praise wouldn't hurt either.

YOU'RE FREED TO PITCH IN

Being a group member in a meeting run by the Interaction Method can be a liberating, positive experience. Other than the two monitoring responsibilities, you don't have to worry about the normal problems: being heard, being attacked, being cut off, being too talkative, etc. You can drop many of your protective guards. You know that your facilitator is watching out for these things, so you can, and should, throw yourself totally into the subject matter of the meeting.

Concentrate on the content and don't worry too much about process. Don't try to backseat-drive a meeting. Remember: There is no one right way to solve a problem or one right process to facilitate a meeting. Particularly if you're a trained group leader or facilitator, it's easy to fall into the trap of showing off your expertise and proving the facilitator wrong: "If I were you, I wouldn't have done such and such." Focus on the problem, not the facilitator, and don't kibitz unless you're asked for your advice or the facilitator clearly needs it.

LISTEN, LISTEN, LISTEN!

Respect your fellow group members. Be a good listener. When others speak, give them full attention. Don't cut them off or distract the attention of the group with unnecessary movements or snide remarks. Keep a common focus. There is nothing worse than two people whispering to each other while you explain your brilliant idea.

WHERE TO SIT

Be aware of where you sit. Don't always sit in the same place with the same people. By changing your position, you can help to shake up the seating pattern and keep a group from becoming physically polarized — cliques that favor one alternative sitting next to each other.

DON'T BE NEGATIVE

Keep an open mind. Don't evaluate an idea before it has a chance to be developed. Negativism is one of the major problems of meetings. As a group member you can help greatly to set a positive tone. Look for the worth in an idea. Don't jump on its faults. Try the little trick of saying what you like about an idea before you express your concerns: ''What I like about your suggestion is that it could solve the employment problem, but my concern is that the unions wouldn't accept it.''

DON'T BE DEFENSIVE

Conversely, don't be too defensive if your idea is criticized. Try not to take it as a personal attack. Stay open to criticism and use it to develop your ideas further, not to drive yourself into positions that may become untenable. Once your idea is recorded on the group memory, it belongs to the group. Let it survive on its own merits. What is important is that your group collectively find its own solution to its problems. The more personally you identify yourself with your idea, the harder it may be for the group to accept it.

INTRODUCTION: CHAPTER FOUR
MEASUREMENT AND EVALUATION

Evaluation is cited as one of the key elements in establishing successful quality circles. Five readings cover expectations of both participants and observers in the quality circle effort. One concern is that the visible success stories of major savings effected by Japanese industry as a result of QCCs are not nearly as common in the U.S. Reasons are presented for both sides of this concern.

Inherent in research is the need to study, analyze, evaluate, and make recommendations about subject areas. In this chapter, quality circles are subjected to scientific scrutiny, compared with control groups, measured for job satisfaction, profit and loss, and human relations success.

Draw your own conclusions about whether scientific measures are necessary or whether the improved attitudes of workers and managers outweigh the need for such measurements. Once more, the Japanese successes are compared with what is happening in the U.S. industries. Determine for yourself whether such a comparison is accurate.

QUALITY CONTROL CIRCLES:
THEY WORK AND DON'T WORK
Kenichi Ohmae

Quality Control Circles, so spectacularly successful in Japan in recent years, hold little promise of short-term gains. They take generations to bear fruit, and cannot be expected to succeed if they are ordered by edict. Moreover, the scope of their achievement, though impressive over time, is limited.

A QC Circle is a group of about ten relatively autonomous workers from the same division of a company who volunteer to meet for an hour or so once or twice a month. After work (usually they are paid overtime), they discuss ways to improve the quality of their products, the production process in their part of the plant and the working environment. Their long-term objective is to build a sense of responsibility for improving quality, but the immediate goal is to exchange ideas in a place uninhibited by barriers of age, sex, or company rank.

Japan's experience has revealed several preconditions for the success of QC Circles. Some may be indigenous.

First, the work force must be intelligent and reasonably well-educated. Members of the circles must be able to use statistical and industrial engineering analysis. They must know what it takes to make things work on a nuts and bolts level, and they must be able to brainstorm together. It is no coincidence that the Japanese companies which have been most successful with these circles and other participatory methods for improving productivity (Hitachi, Teijin, Asahi Glass and Nippon Kokan) are also well-known for their fine recruiting and internal training programs.

Second, management must be willing to trust workers with cost data and important information, and to give them the authority to implement their ideas. At Japanese companies with successful QC programs, managers have tended to work their way up through the ranks: They really believe in their work force. It is no surprise to them that groups of workers, if given information and authority to experiment by trial and error, will be able to reduce downtime, waste or reworking — the sorts of questions that the circles are most effective in addressing.

Third, workers must be willing and eager to cooperate with each other. Unlike the suggestion box and other worker incentive programs which reward individuals, QC programs reward groups. A genuine "team spirit" is therefore necessary: Workers must be willing to express themselves and find fulfillment by reaching agreement.

Moreover, if authority in production decisions is to be decentralized down to the level of these circles, then the circles have to be able to cooperate with each other lest they work at cross-purposes. Unless there is a spirit of cooperation within the work force, an attitude that talking a problem through with peers is more rewarding than taking it up to management, a company is better off using individual carrots instead of the circles. Otherwise, it may find night shifts undoing the improvements of day shifts.

166

One of the most important features of QC Circles in Japan is that they did not originate with senior management. They spring rather from a voluntary, grass-roots movement of workers and middle managers from across the nation.

The spearhead has been the Union of Japanese Scientists and Engineers, or Nika-Giren. In 1962, it began publishing a magazine, later named FQC, which called for quality control circles among factory workers and foremen and helped precipitate a change from the Western concept of quality control as the prerogative of technical experts. The magazine circulated widely among industrial workers, who bought it themselves (it cost them about the same as a pack of cigarettes) rather than receiving it through their employers, and read it together — in a circle. The magazine, together with a generation of supervisors familiar with QC concepts from the '50s, helped initiate massive training of non-supervisors.

The Nikka-Giren Union continues to have great influence. It publishes case histories of successful QC circles and sponsors regional and national conferences, where circle participants from different companies share their experiences.

Since most Japanese companies are very secretive with each other, this openness seems a paradox. But the movement was initially popular in the steel and shipbuilding industries, where there was a tradition of letting other companies freely inspect production methods and facilities. Had the movement started in the the Japanese camera or auto industry, it is doubtful whether the current openness and cross-fertilization would have developed. Today, cross-fertilization is one of the keys to the success of the circles in Japan — the exchanges not only encourage but also keep workers interested in the process.

Quality Control Circles don't run themselves. They must be revitalized. Most important is the specific set of goals they are given and a strong manager who coordiantes QCC changes with corporate objectives. In companies which use both the suggestion box and Quality Control Circle, management can gather directly from workers ideas which may require significant capital expenditures and at the same time use suggestion box successes to encourage QCC efforts.

Management spends more time today on sustaining existing circles than starting new ones, understanding that their effects are incremental and cumulative. In 1951, Toyota received 700 proposals from its new worker participation program. Today it gets 500,000 per year, which save a reported $230 million.

But there are limits to what the circles can do. The abrupt quantum leaps in cost reduction that the Japanese have achieved in industries as diverse as steel and consumer electronics do not result from QC Circles. Instead they come from major strategic decisions about new technologies and plants and entirely new ways of producing and delivering a product.

At Ricoh, for example, it wasn't a circle that figured out how to redesign the business system by changing the technology, manufacturing and marketing to completely change the game in plain paper copiers. Nor was it the circles that led to the elimination of inventory ("Kanban" system) at Toyota. QC Circles, composed of workers from a single division, can't come up with these bold strokes.

167

A SINGLE-MINDED FOCUS

Nor can they replace strategy. Indeed in many industries a single-minded focus on productivity improvements and concomitant quality control activities may be less important for success than focused R & D and targeted marketing.

Quality control circles work best when they are part of what the Japanese call total quality control, which embraces concerns about the entire spectrum of a business. And they are one of a number of productivity improvement techniques which work best when put together. As the Japanese would say, it's like collecting dust to make a mountain. But somebody has to envision the mountain, and know which way the wind is blowing.

DESIGNING QUALITY CIRCLES RESEARCH

Robert P. Steel, Russell F. Lloyd,
Nestor K. Ovalle, William H. Hendrix

The U.S. Air Force has become intrigued with the concept of quality circles as a means of better achieving its organizational mission. Popular management literature contains a large number of anecdotal reports testifying to the value of quality circles as an effective management tool. Cost reductions, increased productivity, better product quality, and improved employee morale represent only some of the purported benefits of successful quality circle programs conducted in the private sector. These often stunning accomplishments attributed to quality circle programs have caught the attention of administrators in the public sector. There is a genuine interest within the Air Force in the application of quality circle principles to the special problems encountered by public sector agencies.

The Department of Defense has recently designated the Air Force Institute of Technology (AFIT) as the principal center for overseeing education, consultation, and research on Department of Defense quality circle undertakings. If current trends are any indication, the enthusiasm generated by quality circles will soon make our task a formidable one.

Aside from our role in educating quality circle instructors and practitioners, we have also been charged with the task of researching this new management technique. It is to this latter responsibility that this paper is addressed. The purpose of this article is to describe a research design geared to evaluating the effects of quality circle participation upon the behavior of the circle participants. The objective is to show how scientifically generated data on quality circles can provide a more conclusive evaluation of their effects than can be gleaned solely from anecdotal reports.

WHAT SCIENCE CAN CONTRIBUTE

The advent of a new method of managing, such as quality circles, is often greeted with considerable enthusiasm by administrators. Managers are usually in a constant search for better ways to do their jobs. At the same time, the very newness of the technique raises many questions about what it can accomplish. We want to know if it tends to improve worker productivity, product quality, job satisfaction, or some combination of these. More often than not, when a new style of management is introduced its effects will not be felt in all these areas but will be concentrated in only a few. In many instances no improvements or changes result from a new style of management. Scientific investigation of the outcomes of quality circles can determine what benefits, if any, are realized by their application.

Research can also be used to dissect quality circle programs to determine what parts of the package should be stressed, modified, or re-evaluated. For instance, it may be revealed that Cause and Effect problem analysis is an especially effective or integral part of the process. Such an insight would tell quality circles trainers to take special care in teaching the steps involved in this skill. Research can also be employed to isolate procedural and situational factors that bear upon the success of quality circle efforts. For example, a study by Goodfellow (1981) found that organizations with successful quality circles programs reported having taken much greater pains with supervisory training than did organizations with less successful programs. Research can be used to broaden our understanding of what types of organizations, jobs, and people would be most likely to benefit from quality circles management.

SCIENTIFIC ANSWERS ARE BETTER

We could answer many of these questions by relying on anecdotal evidence, impressionistic reports, or personal testimonials. Information generated using scientific methods of data collection will allow us to draw conclusions about quality circles with more confidence than is possible with other sources of information. Research evidence is carefully collected so that the results observed may be attributed directly to the effects of the quality circles process rather than to alternative or confounding forces which occur concurrently with the study. Suppose a drop in employee satisfaction is observed after the introduction of quality circles management. An observer might conclude that the quality circles programs produced employee discontent. However, using a scientific research design employing a control or comparison group, a researcher might also observe a corresponding drop in the satisfaction of workers in the control group which did not have a quality circles program. The scientific design would permit the researcher to ascribe the drop in worker satisfaction to events occurring in both the quality circles group and the control group which were unrelated to the quality circle program, for example, a new plant-wide policy of paid parking which replaced a previous free parking policy.

AIR FORCE RESEARCH ON QUALITY CIRCLES

The authors are presently conducting a scientific study geared to answering questions like those raised above. We are attempting to determine whether a recently implemented quality circles program at an Air Force base is producing any measurable changes in the behavior and attitudes of those work groups involved. We are looking for the effects of membership in quality circles upon factors such as, work group productivity, employee turnover, grievance rate, and job satisfaction. We are attempting to employ a research design that will permit us to attribute any effects in those areas directly to the quality circle program. As that implies, a control group is being monitored along with the quality circles group in order to control for extraneous factors which might produce changes in our measures. The design we are using for this research is called a Nonequivalent Control Group Design (Campbell and Stanley, 1963). The design is diagrammed below:

Pretest Time 1		Post-test Time 2
O_1	X	O_2
--		
O_3		O_4

The 0's stand for observations (measurements) and the X indicates the introduction of quality circles management. A time continuum operates from left to right. During the initial observation period, we collected data on measures of productivity, job satisfaction, and employee morale. Groups above the dashed line were trained in quality circles skills and given time to use the technique in the solution of departmental problems. After approximately six months had elapsed, a second reading was taken on the same outcome measures. Measures were obtained for the control group concurrent with those taken on the quality circle group. After adjusting for pre-existing differences between the two groups O_1 and O_3), further group differences between O_2 and O_4 indicate a change in the quality circles group (O_2) which was not reflected in the control group's responses (O_4).

This research design is referred to as a quasi-experimental design because study participants were not randomly assigned to the quality circle or control groups. The dotted line between groups indicates this. Had we been able to use randomization, our research design would have been a true experimental design. Choice of which intact workgroups would be exposed to quality circles was beyond our control, thus channelling our efforts toward this quasi-experimental design. Since we could not assure group equivalence through randomization, we have employed the initial observations on both groups (O_1 and O_3), called pretests, to determine if experimental and control group differences existed before the quality circles program was instituted. If so, the pretest observations can be used as a correction factor in order to compensate for pre-existing group differences which might otherwise contaminate interpretation of the study's results. We have used this design during a pilot study on quality circles and have found it to be a very effective means of generating reliable and interpretable data on quality circles.

SOME EARLY RETURNS

During this pilot study we have been monitoring the progress of a quality circles program begun at a Department of Defense installation in December, 1980. A questionnaire (pretest) was administered to all members of the base civil engineering division shortly before quality circles training was provided to employees. Employees in 14 departments were trained in quality circles and had the opportunity to participate in a circle during the period of study. An additional 37 departments from the same division had no direct association with quality circles and served as the control group. Several post-test survey administrations are planned at different time intervals as the quality circle groups mature. The initial post-test measure has already been collected and analyzed. The following statistics are representative results taken from this initial post-test. These findings should be regarded as very preliminary since the groups being studied are still in the early stages of development. They are primarily intended to illustrate how the data generated by a Nonequivalent Control Group Design might be treated. A future posttest (anticipated for March 1981) should provide more conclusive results about the effects of the quality circles program within this organization.

The survey questionnaire contained 109 items (rating scales) and 24 factors. All items used seven point rating scales (e.g., one — strongly disagree to seven — strongly agree). A factor is a composite scale made up of a number of items (usually item ratings are added together). Four factors were selected for discussion in this article. They are job satisfaction (seven items), perceived work group effectiveness (five items), general organizational climate (ten items), and perceived supervisory effectiveness (eight items).

Table 1 presents the mean ($\overline{X}$) or average rating for the quality circle groups and the control groups obtained during both survey administrations.

Table 1
Quality Circle and Control Group Means
for Four Factors

| | Pretest | | |
| | Quality Circles | Control Group | |
	$\overline{X}$	$\overline{X}$	t
Job Satisfaction	4.81	5.09	1.24
Work Group Effectiveness	5.07	5.43	1.36
General Organizational Climate	4.45	4.76	1.33
Supervisory Effectiveness	4.58	4.44	.40

| | Post-test | | |
| | Quality Circles | Control Group | |
	$\overline{X}$	$\overline{X}$	t
Job Satisfaction	5.11	5.29	.80
Work Group Effectiveness	5.34	5.35	.03
General Organizational Climate	4.47	4.87	1.39
Supervisory Effectiveness	4.86	4.98	.35

*$p<.05$ (with criterion $t=2.021$)

The t statistic (Hays, 1973)[1] adjacent to each pair of means indicates whether the difference between means truly represents a significant difference between the groups or simply random score fluctuations. A criterion t statistic of 2.021 used for evaluating any tabled value would keep the probability of erroneously accepting a difference as "significant" below .05 (five times out of 100 t tests).

There are no "significant" mean differences (as revealed by the t statistics)

172

for the pretest results indicating the groups were roughly equivalent at the beginning of the study. The same is true for the post-test results suggesting that in those areas covered by the factors no gains could be attributed solely to quality circles. As already stated, these findings must be tempered by the knowledge that the results are incomplete. We are currently expanding our research effort and soon hope to follow this article with a more comprehensive and conclusive report of our research results.

A CAVEAT

The scientific method is a slow, painstaking, and arduous process. We accumulate understanding about a given subject by conducting a number of studies in that area. No individual study can reveal the entire picture about a subject such as quality circles management. Our research will provide no definite conclusions about the value of quality circles. It will only begin the process of scientific inquiry into this topic. It is as if one piece of a very complex jigsaw puzzle were put in place. It represents a starting point and may provide some directions, but the picture is far from clear. Only after many studies have been conducted on various aspects of quality circles will the complete picture begin to take a definable shape.

Footnote

[1]These results were analyzed via a t statistic because this statistic is easily computed and understood by the layman unfamiliar with more complex statistical procedures. Readers with advanced training in statistics may prefer to undertake an analysis of co-variance which more rigorously controls for pretest differences between groups while testing for significant factor differences at the post-test.

References

Campbell, D.T. and Stanley, J.C. *Experimental and Quasi-Experimental Designs for Research.* Chicago: Rand McNally, 1963.

Goodfellow, M. "Supervisors: Key to Quality Control." *Telephone Engineer and Management Magazine.* May, 1981, pp. 71-74.

Hays, W.L. *Statistics for the Social Sciences.* New York: Holt, Reinhart and Winston, 1973.

TO MEASURE OR NOT TO MEASURE
Donald L. Dewar

Anytime a group of Quality Circle facilitators assembles, and the issue of whether to measure or not comes up, a heated debate takes place.

The fact is that most facilitators will tell you that they favor maintaining good measurement of Circle activities. Those who oppose measurement are in the minority. But, the disturbing truth that emerges, if given time, is that most facilitators *do not measure at all!*

Arguments for not measuring

"Doggone it, Quality Circles is the *right* thing to do. Therefore, it just doesn't make sense to do the measurement. Besides, it has a payoff in a number of ways and that should be perfectly obvious to management."

Another argument will emerge to the effect that if management wants to measure, then it is clear that management is "using" the Circles to its own advantage. It is therefore obvious that Quality Circles is a people-using activity as opposed to a people-building activity.

Skeptics of measurement frequently contend that measurement is something done by statisticians who can make the result come out any way they want to. Thus, if it is essentially a phony exercise, then why waste time indulging in it?

An additional point is that Circle members are totally unqualified to conduct any measurement activity that would make any kind of sense anyway. "Their training just has not equipped them to do that sort of thing."

Still another argument is that managers elect to send themselves or others to seminars or conferences. Yet, there is no real way to measure the effectiveness of whether that investment ever results in a payoff. The proponents of such an argument see a direct analogy between the conference attendee and the individual who is a member of a Circle. "That, too, is an impossible area to measure. If you believe it isn't necessary to try to measure management personnel when they attend conferences and seminars, then it seems discriminatory to measure Circle members."

Others exclaim, "You want the bottom line? It costs money to measure any kind of activity, and Circle activity is no exception. We know that it pays for itself, all one has to do is to look at the data that's come out of Japan or some of the data that has been maintained by Western World countries and it's perfectly clear that it pays for itself. Therefore, it's just plain stupid to waste money reinventing the wheel!"

Obviously, many businesses do not believe in measurement. If they did, they would do such things as giving examinations at the end of company-sponsored training courses, which is rarely done in business or government. Some would say, "If it made sense to do it, it would be done." That philosophy can be extended to Circle activities. For many, the logical conclusion is, "If we don't need it for people taking company courses, then we don't need it for Circle activities.

174

After all, let's give some credit to our managers. They are well educated and wouldn't be where they are if they didn't also have a lot of good common sense."

Arguments for doing measurements

Supporters of measurement argue that reality dictates that there must be a bottom-line payoff or else Quality Circles cannot survive. As one Japanese manager told the author, "We don't do Quality Circles amongst 90% of our employees just because we think it's a good thing to do in their behalf. We do it because, rather than costing us money, it saves us precious pennies and allows us to be more competitive."

Many contend that management has an *obligation* to measure any kind of activity that affects its people resource. The union officers have the same responsibility to make sure that it is done. Why? Among other reasons, to assure no rip-off of the company, the union, or the employees. Even though it is a well-known fact that properly run Quality Circles are beneficial, one must realize that improperly operated ones may be detrimental. Measurement techniques tell us the difference.

"If someone could prove that a one-hour prayer service each week had a bottom-line payoff, then it would become part of company policy." The same person who makes such a statement says that Quality Circles is there because there is a bottom-line payoff. As far as a one-hour a week prayer service, if it was proved that a payoff existed in terms of reduced turnover, lowered absenteeism, and improved quality of workmanship, then it, too, would be implemented.

"When any presentation is made to management by any group within the organization, the dollar and cents impact is *expected* to be shown. Quality Circles is part of doing business and should be treated no differently."

The proponents of measurement are often disturbed by the charge that they lack "trust" in Circle members by their insistence on measuring the effectiveness of the activity. The following analogy is often cited: "If management proposes the development of a new line of products or services, one can be sure that it will cost a great deal of committed funds. But, there is trust that there will be a payoff." Thus, the logic goes, "Why not trust in Circles, as well?" Such an argument may sound good, but market projections are not speciously made. They do include projected costs and revenues that are based on measurements of similar previous experiences. These considerations enter and are evaluated in the process of making the decision.

Probably, the most frequently heard argument for measurement of Circle activities is that it is needed in order to sell the skeptics.

People-building versus measurement

"In the U.S., there is a tendency to describe Quality Circles as a way to increase productivity. In Japan, the tendency is to describe Quality Circles as a way to increase the skills and knowledge of the people. Therein, I see a rather significant difference." This statement was made by Mr. J. Arai, Manager, Japanese Productivity Center, Washington, D.C.

The above quote is a remarkable one, and it's at the basic essence of the Quality Circle philosophy. Others may scoff and exclaim, "Increasing the skills and knowledge of the people isn't getting at the true goals of Quality Circles such as raising the level of quality and productivity.'' The author believes they are totally wrong. It is his contention that if the skills and knowledge of the people are raised, then many other benefits flow from that as a *natural* consequence.

The author has often used the analogy about sending children to school to increase their skills and knowledge and not asking when there will be a payback, etc. It is believed, without doubt, that there will be benefits. It is not necessarily clear what those benefits will be, but most people ''trust'' that there will be positive advantages for the children, the parents, and the community. Even in school, though, the students would raise a fuss if the school authorities did not ''measure'' performance via examinations, etc., and present that information in a report card.

Look for areas of agreement. Most people concur that *feedback* is desirable. Measurement of Circle activities provides a form of feedback. When presented in a constructive manner, it provides the basis to *effect* changes that will benefit Circle members personally and in their organizational goals.

Members want to know if their Quality Circle efforts are paying off in some way. Above all, they don't want it to be treated as a joke or a meaningless charade.

Edward E. Lawler, Ph.D., from the Center for Effective Organizations, University of Southern California, stated at the 1982 Conference of the International Association of Quality Circles (IAQC) that if Circle advocates were merely trying to make people feel good, they could simply buy them hot tubs!

Management must support the measurement effort

A couple of points must be remembered: *Good* managers, at any level in the organization, *will* demand results data from Circle activities. It *will* happen sooner or later, regardless of whether the organization feels they need measurement data or not. Even the organization that specifically declared they did not feel it necessary to measure will eventually have conscientious managers who *want to* know.

The steering committee should take the lead and assure that the resources will be provided so that the facilitator can make certain that Circle activities are being properly measured. The facilitator should be able to draw on various resources within the organization — industrial engineering, finance, etc., to provide the knowledge and the assistance necessary.

Fear that management may be impatient for results

A widely-touted savings-to-cost ratio for Circle activities is 6-to-1. That ratio was reported in a survey taken by the IAQC in 1980. Some managers might say, ''Why aren't we doing that well?'' If they ask that question, at least it indicates that they have measurements in place to tell them where they are. However, they must realize that any new activity, whether it's Circles or a new line of business, takes time to gain the necessary momentum to provide the desired payoff.

In actual fact, it appears that most managements are not unnecessarily impatient for results data. In a survey taken by *Tooling and Production* magazine, February 1982, a question was posed to chief executive officers: ''If you had

Circle programs, how long could you wait to see a return on your investment?'' Sixty percent said they could wait 3 years. Twenty-seven percent said they would want to see results in less than 3 years. Thirteen percent were undecided.

The above-referenced survey counters to some degree the concern that management is too impatient. It suggests that management is quite reasonable in its expectations. It doesn't expect *immediate* results, but it does want results. Management obviously is not going to wait forever. In fact, it is very doubtful it will wait even 3 years without raising serious questions.

However, it is not necessary for management to wait 3 years. Results data can commence with the first activities of Circle operations. Results data can be provided within the first few months, and the early returns might be surprising.

Training

The main roadblock to conducting Circle measurements may be the facilitators. Many of these individuals do not have the necessary training to properly evaluate and measure what is going on in the Circles they are coordinating. It is not that these individuals do not *want* to measure, they simply do not know *how* to measure. Thus, they must be given the necessary training in order to raise their competence level in this important area.

The necessary training could come from any one of the following sources:

• Books on the subject
• One-on-one instruction from in-house experts
• Company training courses
• Outside seminars and courses

It may require more than simply providing instruction on the subject. Perhaps the facilitators must recruit the necessary skills that already exist in the organization. These are the industrial engineers, the finance people, etc., who consistently deal in cost-effectiveness studies of various sorts. One can rest assured that the ability to do cost-effective studies exists. It is simply a matter of utilizing these resources.

It would be regrettable to underestimate the ability of circle leaders and members to provide some of the measurement data on their own. Much of it is just plain common sense. An informed facilitator can provide the necessary assistance and tutelage to Circle leaders who wish to engage in measuring the success of their Circle activities.

Measurement techniques

This article was not designed to teach one how to conduct measurements. Rather, it has been offered as a forum in which the subject of measurement and its advisability are discussed. However, there are a few general considerations that should be taken into account.

Base-line measurement data should be secured prior to the startup of Quality Circles. Much of this information, particularly if it is in the area of employee attitudes, must occur prior to any knowledge of Circle startup taking place. To do otherwise would risk biasing the results with the well-known Hawthorne effect. Base-line data should be secured in all areas where Circle activities will be measured. Examples are: defect level, production levels, efficiency levels, turn-over, absenteeism, etc. Do not assume that your organization has this data on file and that you can ask for it and receive it several months later. One, they may not collect it at all, and two, they may maintain the data for a short while and then dispose of it.

To sum up, the importance of base-line data is, "If you don't know where you have been, it is difficult to know where you are, or where you are going."

Circles should not overlook the smaller activities that they engage in. It is quite easy to say, "Well, we did not spend too much time on that one, so let's not bother figuring out if we achieved anything." That is being dollar wise and penny foolish. Several small activities can and do add up and should be noted.

Any number of Circle activities, even where measurement activities take place, do not extend measurement into nonproduction items. Examples are: Turnover, absenteeism, tardiness, etc. This is an important area and *cannot* be emphasized too much. It is absolutely astounding that so little is done, measurement-wise in these areas, especially when the cost impact can be enormous. For example, the average entry-level employee who leaves the company must be replaced. That is part of the turnover picture. "So what?" one may say. "It's only one person — no big deal." It may be only one person, but that one individual can cost the organization in excess of $7,000 to replace, train, and get up to speed where they are performing as well as the individual they replaced!

In order to remain consistent with Quality Circles activities going on in thousands of Western World companies, and to be able to reference your results against others, it is important to conduct savings-to-cost ratios on the basis of a 12-month period. That often suggests a degree of conservatism that appeals to managers hearing of Circle results, especially when they are aware that the sav-ings may very well go on for a period of years. If the Circle claims savings over the life of a multi-year contract, it should always be noted that it is in excess of the standard 12-month period. But, for purposes of the saving-to-cost ratio, only 12 months of savings per project should be calculated.

Managers and others are often skeptical of results data claimed by Circles. They fear that the dollar savings may be numbers pulled out of the air. This skep-ticism can be countered if the facilitator has each Circle submit their calculations for audit by some individual who does cost-effectiveness studies and has the necessary credentials within the company. That person's sign-off provides the credibility that is necessary.

Sometimes measurement is virtually impossible. It may just be too complex to even bother with. That can very likely occur. One company reported that one-third of all Circle projects did not receive any dollar savings attached to them. Nevertheless, each project was always described. If results data had not been calculated because of reasons of difficulty, it was described and then, under the heading of "Savings," a zero amount of savings was indicated. Again, a note of conservatism was evident. That company had an overall savings-to-cost ratio of 8-to-1 over a three-period.

In conclusion

Measurement should be a required activity for Circle projects. It is not something to make management feel better and to give them bottom-line data. Of course, that is part of the reason, but it is only a small portion of the total picture. Management should not be considered as money grubbing and selfish individuals lacking in human compassion because of it. There is another segment of the Quality Circle activity in your organization that has a very strong interest in the subject of measurement, and that other segment happens to be each and every member of the total Circle activity. *They want to know* whether this Circle activity thing they have gotten so deeply involved in is really paying off, really making a difference, something that they can be proud of and hope that others will have a reason to be proud of as well.

Measuring Circle effectiveness is a way of assuring that the people-building aspects actually do occur. It is asking for and getting the true and full potential of the individual. Nobody likes to operate in a vacuum. Can you imagine what would occur if a golfer stood on a driving range in the middle of the night with no lights out on the fairway and drove a bucket of balls into the darkness? The golfer would have great difficulty in even going through the complete bucket of balls. And that would no doubt be the last time the urge would ever hit him. And yet, everything else is the same: Putting the ball on the tee, taking aim, the swing, impact, and hearing (but not seeing) the ball cut through the air. *An essential ingredient has been removed,* because *feedback* did not occur. The golfer was not able to see where each ball landed. Feedback is important to every manager worth his or her salt. If Circle members are really ''managers'' in their own area of expertise, and if that is truly believed, then they deserve feedback as well. Measurement provides that feedback.

WHAT'S GOOD FOR JAPAN MAY NOT BE BEST FOR YOU OR YOUR TRAINING DEPARTMENT

Ron Zemke

It appears that Nippo-mania hath seized the land. Personnel directors and operations vice presidents in even the most staid organizations are buying boxes of William Ouchi's book, *Theory Z*, and handing out copies with the zeal of airport religious-group converts. Every self-respecting Fortune 500 company has sent at least one senior management fact-finding delegation "Admiral Perrying" off to Japan.

Time, Business Week, Fortune, TRAINING and the *West Overshoe Chicken Pluckers Gazette,* have all investigated or at least commented knowingly and at length on the reasons Japanese industry is "so much more productive" than American industry. As Professor Harold Leavitt of Stanford University Graduate School of Business has wryly observed, "When it comes to management technique we will be facing west until further notice."

But before you begin holding your Monday briefings cross-legged and shoeless on the floor, or switch from serving coffee to tea, it would be best to consider the downside costs of "going Japanese." Kanban, Ringi, lifetime employment and other wonders of Japanese management style indeed may be the perfect cure for America's productivity blues. Then again they may not. Unexamined embrace of these techniques may compound rather than solve productivity and quality problems.

More than anything else, the vaunted Quality Control Circle (QCC) — offers a kaleidoscope through which to glimpse the polished and not-so-polished facets of Japanese management style. For it is this feature of Nippo-mania that has most affected American businesses, many of which have taken a whole-hog approach to implementing them in their organizations.

A Quality Circle is basically a small group of employees (the average number is nine) who volunteer to meet regularly in order to undertake work-related projects to improve quality. According to Junji Noguchi, general manager of the Japanese Union of Scientists and Engineers (JUSE), "QCs are based on the idea that everyone would like to use his brain in addition to his labor." Moriyuke Watanaabe, a managing director of Toyo Kogyo, maker of Mazda automobiles, says QCs work in his company because "people appreciate growth through work."

A recent report by JUSE says 100,000 QCs are registered with that organization. Toyo Kogyo alone reports 1,800 circles involving half of that company's 27,000 employees. The bulk of these circles tend to be in production departments, the study found, followed by maintenance, procurement, administration and engineering. Seventy-five percent of all QCs select their own projects; 30% of their ideas deal with quality improvement and 45% with cost reduction. JUSE also reports that 40% of the managers they polled see a relationship between improved quality and safety.

In the U.S., advocates of QCs, including such early organizational experimenters as Honeywell and General Motors, report that QCs seem to have a positive effect on employee job satisfaction, productivity, grievances and turnover. With all that apparent confirmation on both sides of the Pacific, QCs must be the best thing since sliced white bread, right? Not necessarily so.

Salvation in a Box

As with every shiny new idea, people are more likely to see, hear, and *report* the successes than the failures; the promises than the problems. And QCs, despite the great press they have received, suffer the same "salvation in a box" syndrome. Robert Hayes, professor of business administration at the Harvard Business School, recently studied six Japanese companies and found, to his surprise, that "the famed 'Quality Circles' did not appear as influential as I expected. They were not widely adopted until several years ago, after the Japanese Union of Scientists and Engineers had given them its official support in the mid-1960s."

Reporting his experiences in a recent *Harvard Business Review* article, Hayes goes on to say "Most of the plants I visited had in fact experienced problems with QCs for three or four years after their introduction. Moreover, most of the companies I talked to already had enviable reputations for high quality products by the time they adopted QCs. One company treated them as secondary, peripheral activities; another had eliminated them altogether ('temporarily' it said). But the quality levels at these plants were just as high as at others where QCs were active."

To get maximum benefit from QCs, or for that matter from *any* quality improvement program, you need commitment from the top of the organization, according to W. Edwards Deming, the namesake of JUSE's national award for innovation in quality control. "Only top management can bring about the changes required," he insists.

In addition, Deming places heavy emphasis on both a clear corporate commitment to quality and the training of all personnel, from organizational top to bottom, in the nuts and bolts of statistical quality assurance technology. Contrary to the somewhat naive American hope that quality and productivity problems can be solved "down on the floor" through QCs, Deming flatly asserts that along with our general lack of quality control savvy, another obstacle lies in the road to improvement of quality and productivity in America: "So many people in executive saddles have not the faintest idea what to do, nor any idea that there *is* anything to do."

In the U.S., and outside Japan in general, the actual *facts* of QC achievement are more limited than the consultants and corporate enthusiasts would have us believe. Take the oft-mentioned example of the Franklin, IL Quasar plant purchased from Motorola by Matsushita Electric Co. William J. Weisz, chief operating officer at Motorola challenges the pop-press assumption that Japanese management finesse was the big key in the Quasar turnabout. He argues rather persuasively that Matsushita's capital expenditures, superior market position, and sophisticated assembly technology were largely responsible.

An issue often given short shrift in the West is the issue of union relations. Non-Japanese unions have been far from open-armed toward QCs. In fact, Ford of Britain ran square into a strike threat from the Transport and General Workers Union when it tried to implement QCs in the Isles. Union officials took the position that QCs are "a matter related to working conditions" and must, therefore, be "discussed at the national level," in essence, a bargainable issue.

Back in the U.S., managers of Sharp of America, a Japanese subsidiary in Memphis, TN, are finding the International Brotherhood of Electrical Workers suspect of the avowed teamwork and quality assurance purposes of Japanese management practices. One union official has gone so far as to label management's espoused goals of trust, cooperation and teamwork "a bunch of propaganda" and suggests "that approach can't work here; Americans just don't think like Japanese."

Epic Alterations?

Professor Robert E. Cole, director of the Center for Japan Studies at the University of Michigan, and one of the country's leading experts on Japanese industrial practices, cautions against wholesale and uncritical adoption of those practices in America on the basis of how little we understand about the dependence of those techniques upon Japanese culture for their effectiveness.

"The task of evaluating the applicability of Japanese management practices in the United States and judging what are to be the needed adaptations is a herculean task," asserts Cole. Likewise, he cautions against copycatting the American corporations that have been reporting great results through their media connections. "Most of the experiences of these companies with QCs have been quite shallow; few companies have had the circles in operation more than five years," he reminds.

A number of management consultants are voicing concern over the uncritical, wildfire spread of QCs and QC-like systems. Edwin G. Yager, president of Consulting Associates Inc. in Novi, MI, is well practiced at implementing QCs, but he is concerned over the naive acceptance of QCs as a magic cure-all for organizational problems. "To use a Quality Circle as an intervention is like choosing to use team building or survey feedback," he emphasizes. "It is a specific technique. Other techniques may be used instead or concurrently. But other techniques should not be called Quality Circles.

"One of our concerns," he continues, "is the extensive Quality Circle promotion by industrial engineers who are not trained in organizational behavior and by behaviorists who know nothing of industrial engineering. Many of them promise to change any organization for $4,700, including slides and tapes. The dangers this thinking presents to the serious HRD practitioners are overwhelming — but that is another whole question, and a harder one to answer. I hope the American entrepreneurial spirit does not destroy a promising concept for those seriously concerned about meaningful organization change."

For others, the destruction has already occurred. John D. Christesen, director of the Westchester Community College Management Institute in Valhalla, NY, is emphatically skeptical of the motivation to rush toward Japanese management practices. "Someone has to say it!" he asserts. "Quality Circles *might* be just another faddish attempt to manipulate workers."

Are we suggesting there is little or nothing to be learned from studying the way Japanese managers conduct their day-to-day affairs? Just the opposite. We suggest that there *is* a lot to be learned from a concerted, reasoned consideration of what the Japanese do to promote quality and productivity. There is, however, little to gain from wishing/hoping for nice-and-easy, rice-paper-wrapped solutions to productivity problems.

Careful examination and consideration *can* produce meaningful results. Harvard's Hayes' determination to look beyond simple formulas has allowed him to see at least one unifying principle to Japanese management practice — the single-minded tenacity with which managers are able, and encouraged, to pursue quality goals. Likewise, he has uncovered one of those subtle workstyle/cultural/temperament problems Cole has warned must be puzzled through. "American managers enjoy crises," asserts Hayes. "They often get their greatest personal satisfaction, the most recognition, and their biggest rewards from solving crises. Crisis is part of what makes work fun.

"To Japanese managers, however, a crisis is evidence of failure," he notes. "Their objective is disruption-free, error-free operation that doesn't require dramatic fixes." Rumors that American middle managers often subtly — perhaps unconsciously — sabotage Quality Circle efforts may indeed have a comprehensible cause: QCs take the fun out of being boss.

EVALUATION OF
QUALITY CIRCLE EFFECTIVENESS
David L. Shores and Mary C. Thompson

Systematic measurement and evaluation are basic requirements when considering whether or not to implement quality circles. Data are required to justify the existence of any program to financial managers and to prospective participants.

Quality circles have only recently been widely accepted in the U.S., and management professionals are seeking information about how and why they work. They are concerned about the required modifications and variations for successful implementation and the effects on workers who have supported and trusted managers in the groups should the program prove inadequate. They are searching for information that will describe procedures and provide historical patterns that might be stressed or modified.

Systematic research reveals issues that must be considered and produces data from which conclusions can be drawn. It increases awareness of the elements that must be accounted for when different methods are used, of the elements that must be considered, and what kinds of data must be gathered to prove program effectiveness. Effective evaluation rests on statistical methods and requires careful planning and definition.

Evaluation can be formative or summative: data can be gathered and analyzed during ongoing program development (formative) or evaluated after the program is fully implemented (summative). Formative data can be used to make modifications as the program progresses in order to achieve specified goals. Summative data compares final results with intended goals, allowing managers to decide on the quality and type of resources to commit to further the program.

Program evaluation and measurements are most acceptable to managers and observers when they are made by individuals other than the group leader. The leader's success is too closely aligned with the results; the leader's performance is evaluated as part of the program. The selection criteria for an evaluator should include prior experience in measurement responsibilities — the individual might be an auditor, human resource specialist, or quality control manager.

EXPERIMENTAL DESIGN

Before measurement can occur, an experimental design must be drawn up. The design, a detailed plan, establishes rigorous tests for one or more questions. Two research designs are experimental and quasi experimental. Experimental design requires randomization. It allows each subject or group of subjects to have equal statistical probability of being assigned to an experimental group and spreads inherent variations across all groups throughout the course of the experiment.

Randomization allows inferences to be drawn from data collected on a segment or group within the total population. Quality circles occur in a dynamic setting that is not always readily adaptable to experimental design and randomization. The results, however, are more meaningful than those of the quasi-experimental design.

Quasi-experimental designs ignore the requirement for randomization. Inferences about the group cannot be drawn from the data; the investigator can only make statements about possible relationships between variables.

Experimental and quasi-experimental designs are similar in that they allow for replication and control of extraneous variables. In both, the researcher seeks to control all, or as many as possible, of the factors affecting the dependent variable.

To focus information gathering, researchers isolate a problem and identify possible solutions. Information is then collected to see which, if any, solution is correct. These ''educated guesses'' define the perceived relationship between the solutions and the problem. For example, the question might be whether quality circle participation improves job satisfaction.

Researchers evaluate the sensitivity, reliability, and practicality of all possible situations to determine the selection of dependent and independent variables. Practicality, environmental setting, time constraints, and material resources such as money, often take precedence over other considerations. Also considered are other studies and prior experience in identifying suitable variables. Because there is little previous research available about quality circles, a pilot study may be the best way to choose appropriate variables and simultaneously save time and money during the trial program.

The researcher is responsible for eliminating the effects of extraneous variables from the analysis of the data because they may bias the experimental results. Extraneous considerations may be historical, occurring over a period of time and affecting employees' attitudes toward the organization; or they may result from maturation, as workers mature psychologically or biologically. Testing, pre- and posttests for example, and the test questionnaire itself can create extraneous considerations. The very selection process used to select groups can result in extraneous variables due to inherent differences, such as seniority and training, between one group and another. Personnel changes may impact on group size as a result of turnover, layoff, or other factors. Controls for these variables may be randomization in the selection process or the groups can be carefully matched for job, sex, education, or other variables.

Most research books describe different techniques for designing and conducting experiments. Several options seem particularly well suited for developing and evaluating quality circles.

Pretest/posttest control group design is commonly used in field tests. The key to this design is the random assignment of subjects to experimental and control groups. The control group allows the researcher to measure extraneous variable effects upon the treatment group. If extraneous vaiables do affect the results, they will appear in the pretest/posttest score differences in the control group.

The pretest/posttest control group design is not always feasible in field studies because the design is dependent upon randomization. Instead, quasi experiments are often considered.

Quasi experiments are widely used by social science researchers in field work settings. It allows the use of subjects in different geographic locations, different work groups, multiple work groups, and control groups.

Example: A company selects two divisions for the experiment and randomly assigns all employees to six work groups, three at each location. Each worker is pretested before assignment to an experimental group or a control group. After the program has been carried out, each worker is posttested.

The difficulties with the quasi-experimental design in our example above is that the experimental and control groups may have some different characteristics. The differences may be a result of geographic location — small town versus large suburb — or based on environmental differences that affect the workers' reaction to the variable being tested. Shift work, time of year, weather, and length of the experiment can be extraneous variables.

The interrupted time series is another type of quasi-experimental design. This method utilizes a single group of subjects; no control group is used. Measuring devices are used at periodic intervals throughout the duration of the experiment with the trial program administered between measurements. The effects of the program are then indicated by the differences in the measurement results before and after the trial.

A concern in quasi-experimental designs is the extraneous variable of history. Changes in measurements could be attributed to any factor that might affect workers' responses to the survey. The researcher should attempt to introduce the new program when no other event is scheduled that would affect worker attitudes, for example, union contract negotiations or a major layoff.

HOW QUALITY CIRCLES ARE MEASURED

The effectiveness of quality circles is generally measured through quality control, cost reduction, and attitude improvement. Program outcomes, personal outcomes, and organizational outcomes are also measurable.

The growth and efficiency of quality circles are program outcomes. Outcomes to consider:

• *Participant training*.

  Total number of supervisors or leaders who have successfully completed training.

  Total number of employees who have successfully completed training.
• *Circles and Membership*.

  Total number of circles formed.

  Average size of circle.

  Ratio of employees joining circles after the introductory presentation.

- *Success.*
  Ratio of active circles to original number formed.
  Number of management presentations given.
  Presentation acceptance rate.
  Yearly number of presentations by each circle.
- *Problems encountered.*
  What types.
  Where procedural problems occurred.

Quality circle participants often spend a substantial portion of their time on quality improvement, an area that can readily be measured. Evaluation can be based on yield rate, defects, scrap levels, and customer feedback. Most organizations routinely collect this data as part of normal operating procedures.

Quality circle programs are expected to improve employee attitudes toward the organization. Measuring attitudes is not simple, but there are methods to determine attitude change. Behaviors can be measured — absenteeism, tardiness, grievances, and turnover are examples. These behaviors are assumed to reflect employee attitude.

Attitudes can also be measured by a survey; however, developing a survey is a difficult task. Writing statements and questions for employee response requires great care if the survey is to accurately assess worker perceptions. The validity of attitude studies is higher when methods that control extraneous variables, pretest/posttest group designs, or nonequivalent control group designs are utilized.

When considering the implementation of any new program, managers demand facts about the costs and savings that will result. Savings include everything that reduces costs. Costs can be calculated quantitatively; they are the dollar charges against a quality circle program. There are some obvious costs in initiating and implementing quality circles.

- Training facilitators, leaders, and circle members.
- Employing external consultants or purchasing prepackaged materials.
- Employee time spent in circle meetings.
- Facilitator time spent to coordinate circle activities.

The savings-to-cost ratio for circles has been calculated by organizations initiating them. Generally, the ratio for circles ranges between two-to-one and ten-to-one.

PROS AND CONS OF EVALUATION

Wayne Rieker, credited as an individual more responsible than any other for the widespread application of quality circles in the U.S., stated that organizations do not attempt to compute a return on investment for managerial training because of intangibles; therefore, why measure the results of quality circles. Rieker believes workers are considered to be extensions of machines and subject to the same mechanical computations applied to machines.

The concepts inherent in the initiation of quality circles are trust and faith in the employee but managers may be reluctant to trust their intuition. Some of the best managers rely strongly on intuition and information collected through informal channels to make important decisions. Is the quality circle process one that can be measured with hard numbers or is it a subjective human resource process where measurements are subject to dispute and distortion?

There are other arguments against measuring the results of quality circles. Time and energy required to design a research program, collect data, and analyze the results are costly. Time spent on these activities takes away from time available for production. Perhaps most importantly, if everyone believes in quality circles, why bother to measure outcomes. Many companies have already put programs in place that affect training, communication, and recognition. When quality circles are introduced, they interact with ongoing programs; the integration makes measurements more complex.

Research is considered the realm of academicians and scientists. Accurate assessment of the effectiveness of quality circles can be both complex and costly. But other factors must be considered. Research costs may be minor compared to ineffective company organization. Ineffective management causes high turnover, absenteeism, and lower product quality. If quality circles can improve absenteeism, raise product quality, lower turnover, are measurement costs too high?

Most large firms routinely collect data on quality and cost. For the skeptical manager, accountant, or vice-president of operations, adequate investigation and reporting on a worthwhile program are essential to prevent the program from being buried beneath more important company priorities.

Important to the success of any quality circle program is the evaluation of the people responsible for the circles. The evaluation must focus on those directly accountable for the program's success or failure. The steering committee and facilitator are the individuals responsible for the program design. The circle leader is charged with carrying out the design. If problems appear with the program, the leaders must reassess their positions and determine how they can solve the problems.

The steering committee should examine whether: Objectives have been identified for circle activities; funding arrangements for circle activities have been clearly established; base line measurements have been taken prior to implementation of circles; the steering committee itself will operate democratically as a circle; participants choose to continue involvement in circles. The facilitator should question and examine: Whether new circles are consistently being formed; the dropout rate for circle participants; the activity or inactivity rate for circles; participation/teaching involvement in leader-training classes; the facilitator role, consistently giving credit to the circles for achievements; the perception of management through at least weekly meetings. Circle leaders should evaluate: their volunteer involvement; their ''bookkeeping'' on circle projects; their membership records of attendance, training, and contributions; their success in involving all circle members in activities.

Quality circles are one part of a larger management picture. They will not cure all the ailments of U.S. business and industry; they must be kept in perspective. However, still quite new to the American management scene, quality circles have been welcomed and caused some managers to reevaluate their practices.

Quality circles in the U.S. have not been subjected to rigorous statistical testing. In spite of the difficulty of conducting experiments, in-depth research in the areas of program outcomes, quality improvement, and attitude improvement will occur. To implement a quality circle program and disregard its findings or fail to monitor its progress is fatal. Organizations and people require revitalization and periodic checks ensure proper functioning and success. The results of these studies will determine the effectiveness of quality circles.

INTRODUCTION: CHAPTER FIVE
CASE STUDIES

Nine readings in this chapter describe quality circles and other participative programs in action. The authors analyze the successes and weaknesses of these techniques.

The GM story includes the definition of quality of work life as established in the company's large Tarrytown, N.Y., plant where the union and management jointly sought to change the meaning of work itself. Their "QWL" group was born out of frustration and desperation, but with a mutual commitment by management and union to change old ways of dealing with the workers on the shop floor. It included every dimension of work and, says the author, Robert H. Guest (professor of organizational behavior at the Amos Tuck School of Business Administration at Dartmouth College), it has the earmarks of success. It also illustrates some underlying principles of successful organizational change that can be applied in a variety of work environments.

The Gaines plant in Topeka, Kansas established autonomous work teams in an entirely new factory. That story is chronicled over a seven-year period. The two-part article describes the phases, both good and bad, that the work teams have gone through in their efforts to practice participative management. The conclusions are provocative.

The Ford Motor Company uses employee problem-solving teams to solve problems at the Dearborn Engine Plant. The program encourages every interested employee to participate in decisions that affect his or her job. Called Employee Involvement (EI) Programs, Ford views the process as a long-range concept based on problem-solving groups, quality circle groups, and team-building groups. Managers and employees describe it as a totally new and different way of managing and doing business — working together, and practicing listening skills. It is very interesting reading.

Motorola reports that their people-oriented management style is "soft" management; it is demanding and results oriented. And the results prove that the hard work involved in making such a program "go" is worth it. The author cites employee attitude changes, less tolerance of dictatorial authority and rising expectations. Employee surveys indicate that most employees are eager to function effectively and productively. They want to be proud of the quality of goods and services they produce. *And*, they want to participate in the decisions that affect their work. The article's conclusion describes both results and problem areas.

Hewlett-Packard uses a combination quality team program, their interpretation of the QWL, participative management, and Japanese QCC philosophies. Using the "HP Way", they have two basic assumptions: people take more pride and interest in work when allowed to make contributions which influence decisions about their work, and the people closest to the problem are in the best position to make decisions about that problem and to take the necessary action. They see a nationwide growing emphasis on quality and have moved within their company to be competitive in that area. They see their QT concept as somewhat different than most companies and still evolving. The article describes how their quality teams function within the company and emphasize that this concept is only one thread in the fabric of participative management.

Another article describes quality circles established in Missouri hospitals. Enthusiasm for the circles runs high and the author reports that members who may not be scheduled for work on meeting day attend meetings on their own. The biggest problem, reported by one group, is providing time for people to engage in quality circle activities, particularly in the nursing areas. Hospitals have some unique concerns and possible solutions are suggested.

The Continental Illinois National Bank and Trust Company in Chicago is the basis for an article on quality control in banking. As banks expand into diverse markets, they must contend with widening geographic markets, adding large numbers of new customers and broadening the line of services. As a result, Continental established as a first major objective, in their quality assurance unit, assistance for management in updating service quality performance standards and developing monitoring and feedback systems. The methods they used to establish a successful achievement of their goals is described.

Hughes Aircraft has an extensive quality circle program. The authors of *Quality Circles at Hughes Aircraft* describe the experience within the Radar Systems Group. They say that high technology companies need a blend of skill and perspectives and therefore, many have established "involvement" types of management programs to achieve their goals. The article describes the philosophy of the Hughes' circles, the development, training, structure, measurement, process, and some case studies, along with observable results.

QUALITY OF WORK LIFE —
LEARNING FROM TARRYTOWN
Robert H. Guest

Imagine that an executive of one of our largest corporations is told that one of his plant managers wants to spend over $1.6 million on a program that has no guarantee of any return in greater efficiency, higher productivity, or lower costs. Then imagine how he would react if he were told that the union is in on the program up to its ears and that the purpose of the program is referred to as "improving the quality of work life."

If the reader imagines that the average top corporate manager would say the plant manager had lost his senses and ought to be fired, the reader is probably in the majority. The striking fact, however, is that one particular executive, the head of what is probably the largest division of any manufacturing company in the world (18 plants and almost 100,000 employees) knew just what was going on and approved the idea enthusiastically.

This is the story of the General Motors car assembly plant at Tarrytown, New York. In 1970, the plant was known as having one of the poorest labor relations and production records in GM. In seven years, the plant turned around to become one of the company's better run sites.

Born out of frustration and desperation, but with a mutual commitment by management and the union to change old ways of dealing with the workers on the shop floor, a quality of work life (QWL) program developed at Tarrytown. "Quality of work life" is a generic phrase that covers a person's feelings about every dimension of work including economic rewards and benefits, security, working conditions, organizational and interpersonal relationships, and its intrinsic meaning in a person's life.

For the moment, I will define QWL more specifically as a *process* by which an organization attempts to unlock the creative potential of its people by involving them in decisions affecting their work lives. A distinguishing characteristic of the process is that its goals are not simply extrinsic, focusing on the improvement of productivity and efficiency per se; they are also intrinsic, regarding what the worker sees as self-fulfilling and self-enhancing ends in themselves.

In recent years, the QWL movement has generated wide-scale interest. Just since 1975, more than 450 articles and books have been written on the subject, and there are at least four national and international study and research centers focusing on quality of work life as such. Scores of industrial enterprises throughout the United States are conducting experiments, usually on a small scale; and in an eight-month world study tour a few years back of more than 50 industrial plants in Japan, Australia, and Europe, I found great interest in "industrial democracy."

So what is special about the Tarrytown story? First, it has the earmarks of success. Second, it illustrates some underlying principles of successful organizational change that can be applied in a variety of work environments. Third, although a number of promising experiments are going on in many General Motors plants and in other companies, this QWL program has involved more human beings — more than 3,800 — than any other I know of. Finally, and this is speculative, I believe that Tarrytown represents in microcosm the beginnings of what may become commonplace in the future — a new collaborative approach on the part of management, unions, and workers to improve the quality of life at work in its broadest sense.

TARRYTOWN — THE BAD OLD DAYS

In the late 1960s and early 1970s, the Tarrytown plant suffered from much absenteeism and labor turnover. Operating costs were high. Frustration, fear, and mistrust characterized the relationship between management and labor. At certain times, as many as 2,000 labor grievances were on the docket. As one manager puts it, "Management was always in a defensive posture. We were instructed to go by the book, and we played by the book. The way we solved problems was to use our authority and impose discipline." The plant general superintendent acknowledges in retrospect, "For reasons we thought valid, we were very secretive in letting the union and the workers know about changes to be introduced or new programs coming down the pike."

Union officers and committeemen battled constantly with management. As one union officer describes it, "We were always trying to solve yesterday's problems. There was no trust and everybody was putting out fires. The company's attitude was to employ a stupid robot with hands and no face." The union committee chairman describes the situation the way he saw it: "When I walked in each morning I was out to get the personnel director, the committeeman was shooting for the foreman, and the zone committeeman was shooting for the general foreman. Every time a foreman notified a worker that there would be a job change, it resulted in an instant '78 (work standards grievance). It was not unusual to have a hundred 78s hanging fire, more than 300 discipline cases, and many others."

Another committeeman adds, "My job was purely political. It was to respond instantly to any complaint or grievance regardless of merits, and just fight the company. I was expected to jump up and down and scream. Every time a grievance came up, it lit a spark, and the spark brought instant combustion."

Workers were mad at everyone. They disliked the job itself and the inexorable movement of the highspeed line — 56 cars per hour, a minute and a half per operation per defined space. One worker remembers it well, "Finish one job, and you always had another stare you in the face." Conditions were dirty, crowded, and often noisy. Employees saw their foremen as insensitive dictators, whose operating principle was "If you can't do the job like I tell you, get out."

Warnings, disciplinary layoffs, and firings were commonplace. Not only did the workers view the company as an impersonal bureaucratic machine, "They number the parts and they number you," but also they saw the union itself as a source of frustration, "The committeeman often wrote up a grievance but, because he was so busy putting out fires, he didn't tell the worker how or whether the grievance was settled. In his frustration, the worker would take it out on the foreman, the committeeman, and the job itself."

In the words of both union and management representatives, during this period "Tarrytown was a mess."

BEGINNINGS OF CHANGE

What turned Tarrytown around? How did it start? Who started it and why?

Because of the high labor turnover, the plant was hiring a large number of young people. The late 1960s was the time of the youth counterculture revolution. It was a time when respect for authority was being questioned. According to the plant manager, "It was during this time that the young people in the plant were demanding some kind of change. They didn't want to work in this kind of environment. The union didn't have much control over them, and they certainly were not interested in taking orders from a dictatorial management."

In April 1971, Tarrytown faced a serious threat. The plant manager saw the need for change, and also an opportunity. He approached some of the key union officers who, though traditionally suspicious of management overtures, listened to him. The union officers remember liking what they heard, "This manager indicated that he wanted to create a philosophy of management different from what had gone on before. He felt there was a better way of doing things."

The plant manager suggested that if the union was willing to do its part, he would put pressure on his own management people to change their ways. The tough chairman of the grievance committee observed later that "this guy showed right off he had a quality of work life attitude — we didn't call it that at that time — inside him. He was determined that this attitude should carry right down to the foremen, and allow the men on the line to be men."

The company decided to stop assembling trucks at Tarrytown and to shuffle the entire layout around. Two departments, Hard Trim and Soft Trim, were to be moved to a renovated area of the former truck line.

At first, the changes were introduced in the usual way. Manufacturing and industrial engineers and technical specialists designed the new layout, developed the charts and blueprints, and planned every move. They then presented their proposals to the supervisors. Two of the production supervisors in Hard Trim, sensing that top plant management was looking for new approaches, asked a question that was to have a profound effect on events to follow: "Why not ask the workers themselves to get involved in the move? They are experts in their own right. They know as much about trim operations as anyone else."

The consensus of the Hard Trim management group was that they would involve the workers. The Soft Trim Department followed suit. The union was brought in on the planning and told that management wanted to ask the workers' advice. Old timers in the union report "wondering about management's motives. We could remember the times management came up with programs only to find there was an ulterior motive and that in the long run the men could get screwed." Many supervisors in other departments also doubted the wisdom of fully disclosing the plans.

195

Nevertheless, the supervisors of the two trim departments insisted not only that plans *not* be hidden from the workers but also that the latter would have a say in the setup of jobs. Charts and diagrams of the facilities, conveyors, benches, and materials storage areas were drawn up for the workers to look at. Lists were made of the work stations and the personnel to man them. The supervisors were impressed by the outpouring of ideas: "We found they did know a lot about their own operations. They made hundreds of suggestions and we adopted many of them."

Here was a new concept. The training director observes, "Although it affected only one area of the plant, this was the first time management was communicating with the union and the workers on a challenge for solving *future* problems and not the usual situation of doing something, waiting for a reaction, then putting out the fires later." The union echoes the same point. "This demonstrated how important it is to solve problems before they explode. If not solved, then you get the men riled up against everything and everybody."

Moving the two departments was carried out successfully with remarkably few grievances. The plant easily made its production schedule deadlines. The next year saw the involvement of employees in the complete rearrangement of another major area of the plant, the Chassis Department. The following year a new car model was introduced at Tarrytown.

LABOR-MANAGEMENT AGREEMENT

In 1972, Irving Bluestone, the vice president for the General Motors Department of the United Automobile Workers Union (UAW), made what many consider to be the kick-off speech for the future of the Quality of Work Life movement. Repeated later in different forms, he declared:

"Traditionally management has called upon labor to cooperate in increasing productivity and improving the quality of the product. My view of the other side of the coin is more appropriate; namely, that management should cooperate with the worker to find ways to enhance the dignity of labor and to tap the creative resources in each human being in developing a more satisfying work life, with emphasis on worker participation in the decision-making process."[1]

In 1973, the UAW and GM negotiated a national agreement. In the contract was a brief "letter of agreement" signed by Bluestone and George Morris, head of industrial relations for GM. Both parties committed themselves to establishing formal mechanisms, at least at top levels, for exploring new ways of dealing with the quality of work life. *This was the first time QWL was explicitly addressed in any major U.S. labor-management contract.*

The Tarrytown union and management were aware of this new agreement. They had previously established close connections with William Horner of Bluestone's staff and with James Rae, the top corporate representative in the Organization Development Department. It was only natural that Tarrytown extend its ongoing efforts within the framework of the new agreement. Furthermore, Charles Katko, vice president and general manager of the GM Assembly Division, gave his enthusiastic endorsement to these efforts.

Local issues and grievances, however, faced both parties. In the past, it had not been uncommon for strike action to be taken during contract negotiations. The manager and the union representatives asked themselves, "Isn't there a better way to do this, to open up some two-way communication, gain some trust?" The union president was quick to recognize "that it was no good to have a 'love-in' at the top between the union and management, especially the Personnel Department. We had to stick with our job as union officers. But things were so bad we figured, 'What the hell, we have nothing to lose!'"

The union president's observation about that period is extremely significant in explaining the process of change that followed:

"We as a union knew that our primary job was to protect the worker and improve his economic life. But times had changed and we began to realize we had a broader obligation, which was to help the workers become more involved in decisions affecting their own jobs, to get their ideas, and to help them to improve the whole quality of life at work beyond the paycheck."

The negotiations were carried out in the background of another effort on management's part. Delmar Landon, director of organizational research and development at General Motors, had been independently promoting an organizational development effort for a number of years. These efforts were being carried out in many plants. Professionally trained communication facilitators had been meeting with supervisors and even some work groups to solve problems of interpersonal communication.

What General Motors was attempting to do was like the OD programs that were being started up in many industries and businesses in the United States. But, as with many such programs, there was virtually no union involvement. As the training director put it, "Under the influence of our plant manager, the OD program was having some influence among our managers and supervisors, but still this OD stuff was looked upon by many as a gimmick. It was called the 'happy people' program by those who did not understand it." And, of course, because it was not involved, the union was suspicious.

Nevertheless, a new atmosphere of trust between the union and the plant manager was beginning to emerge. Local negotiations were settled without a strike. There was at least a spark of hope that the Tarrytown mess could be cleaned up. Thus the informal efforts at Tarrytown to improve union-management relations and to seek greater involvement of workers in problem solving became "legitimatized" through the national agreement and top-level support. Other plants would follow.

THE TESTING PERIOD

In April 1974, a professional consultant was brought in to involve supervisors and workers in joint training programs for problem solving. Management paid his fees. He talked at length with most of the union officers and committeemen, who report that, "We were skeptical at first but we came to trust him. We realized that if we were going to break through the communications barrier on a large scale, we needed a third party."

The local union officials were somewhat suspicious about "another management trick." But after talking with Solidarity House (UAW's headquarters), they agreed to go along. Both parties at the local level discussed what should be done. Both knew it would be a critical test of the previous year's preliminary attempts to communicate with one another on a different plane. Also, as one union person says, "We came to realize the experiment would not happen overnight."

Management and the union each selected a coordinator to work with the consultant and with the supervisors, the union, and the workers. The consultant, with the union and the management coordinators, proposed a series of problem-solving training sessions to be held on Saturdays, for eight hours each day. Two supervisors and the committeemen in the Soft Trim Department talked it over with the workers, of whom 34 from two shifts volunteered for the training sessions that were to begin in late September 1974. Management agreed to pay for six hours of the training, and the men volunteered their own time for the remaining two hours.

Top management was very impressed by the ideas being generated from the sessions and by the cooperation from the union. The regular repairmen were especially helpful. Not long after the program began, the workers began developing solutions to problems of water leaks, glass breakage, and molding damage.

LAYOFF CRISIS

In November 1974, at the height of the OPEC oil crisis, disaster struck. General Motors shut down Tarrytown's second shift, and laid off half the work force — 2,000 workers. Men on the second shift with high seniority "bumped" hundreds of workers on the first shift. To accommodate the new schedule, management had to rearrange jobs and work loads the entire length of the two miles of main conveyors, feeder conveyors, and work stations. A shock wave reverberated throughout the plant, not just among workers but supervisors as well. Some feared the convulsion would bring on an avalanche of '78s — work standards grievances — and all feared that the cutback was an early signal that Tarrytown was being targeted for permanent shutdown. After all, it was one of the oldest plants in General Motors and its past record of performance was not good.

However, the newly developing trust between management and the union had its effects. As the union president puts it, "Everyone got a decent transfer and there were surprisingly few grievances. We didn't get behind. We didn't have to catch up on a huge backlog."

What did suffer was the modest and fragile QWL experiment. It was all but abandoned. Many workers who had been part of it were laid off, and new workers "bumping in" had not been exposed to it. Also, a number of persons in the plant were not too disappointed to see it go. Some supervisors, seeing worker participation as a threat to their authority, made wisecracks such as "All they are doing is turning these jobs over to the union." Some committeemen felt threatened because the workers were going outside the regular political system and joining with representatives of management in solving problems.

In spite of the disruption of plant operations, the Quality of Work Life team, the plant manager, and the union officials were determined not to give up. Reduced to a small group of 12 people during 1975, the team continued to work on water leaks and glass breakage problems. This group's success as well as that of some others convinced both parties that Quality of Work Life had to continue despite a September 1975 deadline, after which management would no longer foot the bill on overtime.

During this period all parties had time to reflect on past successes as well as failures. The coordinators (one from the union and one from management) had learned a lesson. They had expected too much too soon: "We were frustrated at not seeing things move fast enough. We got in the trap of expecting 'instant QWL.' We thought that all you had to do was to design a package and sell it as you would sell a product."

Also, during this period, the grapevine was carrying a powerful message around the plant that something unusual was going on. The idea of involving workers in decisions spread and by midyear the molding groups were redesigning and setting up their own jobs. Other departments followed later.

At this time everyone agreed that if this program were to be expanded on a larger scale, it would require more careful planning. In 1975, a policy group made up of the plant manager, the production manager, the personnel manager, the union's top officers, and the two QWL coordinators was formed. The program was structured so that both the union and management could have an advisory group to administer the system and to evaluate the ideas coming up from the problem-solving teams. Everyone agreed that participation was to be entirely voluntary. No one was to be ordered or assigned to any group. Coordinators and others talked with all of the workers in the two departments.

A survey of interest was taken among the 600 workers in the two volunteering departments; 95% of these workers said they wanted in. Because of the large number that wanted to attend, pairs of volunteers from the ranks of the union and management had to be trained as trainers. Toward the middle of the year, a modified program was set up involving 27 off-time hours of instructional work for the 570 people. Four trainers were selected and trained to conduct this program, two from the union and two from management.

A second crisis occurred when the production schedule was increased to a line speed of 60 cars per hour. Total daily output would not be enough to require a second shift to bring back all the laid-off workers. Instead, the company asked that 300 laid-off workers be brought in and that the plant operate on an overtime schedule. Ordinarily the union would object strongly to working overtime when there were still well over 1,000 members out on the street. "But," as the union president puts it, "we sold the membership on the idea of agreeing to overtime and the criticism was minimal. We told them the survival of the plant was at stake."

FULL CAPACITY

Despite the upheavals at the plant, it seemed that the Quality of Work Life program would survive. Then, a third blow was delivered. Just as 60 workers were completing their sessions, the company announced that Tarrytown was to return to a two-shift operation. For hundreds of those recalled to work, this was good news. Internally, however, it meant the line would have to go through the same musical chair game it had experienced 14 months earlier when the second shift was dropped.

Workers were shuffled around according to seniority and job classification. Shift preferences were granted according to length of service. With a faster line speed than before, the average worker had fewer operations to perform but those he did perform he had to do at a faster pace. In short, because of possible inequities in work loads, conditions were ripe for another wave of work standards grievances. Happily, the union and management were able to work out the workload problems with a minimum of formal grievances.

But again the small, partially developed QWL program had to be put on ice. The number of recalled workers and newly hired employees was too great, and turnover was too high among the latter for the program to continue as it had been. Capitalizing on the mutual trust that had been slowly building up between them, management and the union agreed to set up an orientation program for newly hired employees — and there were hundreds of them. Such a program was seen as an opportunity to expose new workers to some of the information about plant operations, management functions, the union's role, and so forth. At one point, the union even suggested that the orientation be done at the union hall, but the idea was dropped.

The orientation program was successful. Some reduction in the ratio of "quits" among the "new hires" was observed. The union president did feel that "we had set a new tone for the new employee and created a better atmosphere in the plant."

BRAVE NEW WORLD

Early the next year, 1977, Tarrytown made the "big commitment." The QWL effort was to be launched on a plant-wide scale involving approximately 3,800 workers and supervisors. Charles Katko, vice president for the division and UAW's top official, Irving Bluestone, gave strong signals of support. The plant manager retired in April and was replaced by the production manager. The transition was an easy one because the new manager not only knew every dimension of the program but also had become convinced of its importance.

The policy committee and the Quality of Work Life coordinators went to work. In the spring of 1977, all the top staff personnel, department heads, and production superintendents went through a series of orientation sessions with the coordinators. By June, all middle managers and first-line supervisors (general foremen and foremen) were involved. Thus by the summer of 1977 more than 300 members of Tarrytown management knew about the QWL approach and about the plans for including 3,500 hourly employees. All union committeemen also went through the orientation sessions.

Also, during mid-1977, plans were underway to select and train those people who would eventually conduct the training sessions for the hourly employees.

More than 250 workers expressed an interest in becoming trainers. After careful screening and interviewing, 11 were chosen. A similar process was carried out for supervisors, 11 of whom were subsequently selected as trainers, mostly from among foremen.

The two coordinators brought the 22 designated trainers together and exposed them to a variety of materials they would use in the training itself. The trainers conducted mock practice sessions which were videotaped so they could discuss their performance. The trainers also shared ideas on how to present information to the workers and on how to get workers to open up with their own ideas for changing their work environment. The latter is at the heart of the Quality of Work Life concept.

The trainers themselves found excitement and challenge in the experience. People from the shop floor worked side by side with members of supervision as equals. At the end of the sessions, the trainers were brought together in the executive dining room for a wrap-up session. The coordinators report that "they were so charged up they were ready to conquer the world!"

PLANT-WIDE PROGRAM

On September 13, 1977 the program was launched. Each week, 25 different workers (or 50 in all from both shifts) reported to the training rooms on Tuesdays, Wednesdays, and Thursdays, for nine hours a day. Those taking the sessions had to be replaced at their work stations by substitutes. Given an average hourly wage rate of more than $7 per attendee and per replacement (for over 3,000 persons), one can begin to get an idea of the magnitude of the costs. Also, for the extra hour above eight hours, the trainees were paid overtime wages.

What was the substance of the sessions themselves? The trainee's time was allocated to learning three things: first, about the concept of QWL; second, about the plant and the functions of management and the union; third, about problem-solving skills important in effective involvement.

At the outset, the trainers made it clear that the employees were not to use the sessions to solve grievances or to take up labor-management issues covered by the contract itself. The presentation covered a variety of subjects presented in many forms with a heavy stress on participation by the class from the start. The work groups were given a general statement of what quality of work life was all about. The union trainer presented materials illustrating UAW Vice President Bluestone's famous speech, and the management trainer presented a speech by GM's Landen stressing that hourly workers were the experts about their own jobs and had much to contribute.

The trainers used printed materials, diagrams, charts, and slides to describe products and model changes, how the plant was laid out, how the production system worked, and what the organizational structures of management and the union are. Time was spent covering safety matters, methods used to measure quality performance, efficiency, and so forth. The work groups were shown how and where they could get any information they wanted about their plant. Special films showed all parts of the plant with a particular worker "conducting the tour" for his part of the operation.

To develop effective problem-solving skills, the trainers presented simulated problems and then asked employees to go through a variety of some experiential exercises. The training content enabled the workers to diagnose themselves, their own behavior, how they appeared in competitive situations, how they handled two-way communications, and how they solved problems. By the final day "the groups themselves are carrying the ball," as the trainers put it, "with a minimum of guidance and direction from the two trainers."

Trainers took notes on the ideas generated in the sessions and at the end handed out a questionnaire to each participant. The notes and questionnaires were systematically fed back to the union and management coordinators, who in turn brought the recommendations to the policy committee. The primary mode of feedback to their foremen and fellow workers was by the workers themselves out on the shop floor.

CONTINUING EFFORT

Seven weeks after the program began in September 1977, just over 350 workers (or 10% of the work force) had been through the training sessions. The program continued through 1978, and by mid-December more than 3,300 workers had taken part.

When all the employees had completed their sessions, the union and management immediately agreed to keep the system on a continuing basis. From late December 1978 through early February 1979, production operations at Tarrytown were closed down to prepare for the introduction of the all-new 1980 X model. During the shutdown, a large number of workers were kept on to continue the process.

In preparation for the shift, managers and hourly personnel together evaluated hundreds of anticipated assembly processes. Workers made use of the enthusiasm and skills developed in the earlier problem sessions and talked directly with supervisors and technical people about the best ways of setting up various jobs on the line. What had been stimulated through a formal organized system of training and communication (for workers and supervisors alike) was now being "folded in" to the ongoing planning and implementation process on the floor itself.

In evaluating the formal program, the trainers repeatedly emphasized the difficulties they faced as well as the rewards. Many of the men and women from the shop floor were highly suspicious at the start of the sessions. Some old-timers harbored grudges against management going back for years. Young workers were skeptical. Some of the participants were confused at seeing a union trainer in front of the class with someone from management.

In the early period, the trainers were also nervous in their new roles. Few of them had ever had such an experience before. Many agreed that their impulse was to throw a lot of information at the worker trainee. The trainers found, however, that once the participants opened up, they "threw a lot at us." Although they understood intellectually that participation is the basic purpose of the QWL program, the trainers had to experience directly the outpouring of ideas, perceptions, and feelings of the participants to comprehend emotionally the dynamics of the involvement process.

202

But the trainers felt rewarded too. They describe example after example of the workers' reactions once they let down their guard. One skeptical worker, for example, burst out after the second day, "Jesus Christ! You mean all this information about what's going on in the plant was available to us? Well, I'm going to use it." Another worker who had been scrapping with his foreman for years went directly to him after the sessions and said, "Listen, you and I have been butting our heads together for a long time. From now on I just want to be able to talk to you and have you talk to me." Another worker used his free relief time to drop in on new class sessions.

Other regular activities to keep management and the union informed about new developments parallel the training sessions. Currently, following the plant manager's regular staff meetings, the personnel director passes on critical information to the shop committee. The safety director meets weekly with each zone committeeman. Top union officials have monthly "rap sessions" with top management staff to discuss future developments, facility alterations, schedule changes, model changes, and other matters requiring advance planning. The chairman of Local 664 and his zone committeemen check in with the personnel director each morning at 7:00 A.M. and go over current or anticipated problems.

AFTER THE DUST SETTLES

What are the measurable results of Quality of Work Life at Tarrytown? Neither the managers nor union representatives want to say much. They argue that to focus on production records or grievance counts "gets to be a numbers game" and is contrary to the original purpose or philosophy of the Quality of Work Life efforts. After all, in launching the program, the Tarrytown plant made no firm promises of "bottom-line" results to division executives or anyone else. *Getting the process of worker involvement going was a primary goal with its own intrinsic rewards. The organizational benefits followed.*

There are, however, some substantial results from the $1.6 million QWL program. The production manager says, for example, "From a strictly production point of view — efficiency and costs — this entire experience has been absolutely positive, and we can't begin to measure the savings that have taken place because of the hundreds of small problems that were solved on the shop floor before they accumulated into big problems."

Although not confirmed by management, the union claims that Tarrytown went from one of the poorest plants in its quality performance (inspection counts or dealer complaints) to one of the best among the 18 plants in the division. It reports that absenteeism went from 7¼% to between 2% and 3%. In December 1978, at the end of the training sessions, there were only 32 grievances on the docket. Seven years earlier there had been upward of 2,000 grievances filed. Such substantial changes can hardly be explained by chance.

Does this report on Tarrytown sound unreal or euphoric? Here are the comments of the most powerful union officer in the plant, the chairman of Local 664.

"I'm still skeptical of the whole thing but at least I no longer believe that what's going on is a 'love-in' at Tarrytown. It's not a fancy gimmick to make people happy. And even though we have barely scratched the surface, I'm absolutely convinced we are on to something. We have a real and very different future. Those guys in the plant are beginning to participate and I mean really participate!''

By May 1979 the Tarrytown plant, with the production of a radically new line of cars, had come through one of the most difficult times in its history. Considering all the complex technical difficulties, the changeover was successful. Production was up to projected line speed. The relationship among management, union, and the workers remained positive in spite of unusual stress conditions generated by such a change.

As the production manager puts it, ''Under these conditions, we used to fight the union, the worker, and the car itself. Now we've all joined together to fight the car.'' Not only were the hourly employees substantially involved in working out thousands of ''bugs'' in the operations, but plans were already under way to start up QWL orientation sessions with more than 400 new workers hired to meet increased production requirements.

Tarrytown, in short, has proved to itself, at least, that QWL works.

LEARNING FROM TARRYTOWN

Although the Tarrytown story is, of course, unique, persons responsible for bringing about change in an organization might derive some useful generalizations and important messages from it.

Bringing about change — any kind of change — is extraordinarily difficult in our modern organizations. It is challenge enough to introduce new machines, computers, management information systems, new organizational structures, and all the bureaucratic paraphernalia required to support our complex production systems. It is even more difficult to organize and stimulate people to accept innovations directed at greater efficiency. Perhaps most difficult of all, as one looks at the Quality of Work Life process and Tarrytown as an example, is for managers, union officials, and even workers themselves to adjust to the idea that certain kinds of changes should be directed toward making life at work more meaningful and not necessarily toward some immediate objective measures of results.

Even when people become committed to this idea, starting the process is not easy. Witness, for example, how long it took to turn the Tarrytown ship around. Look at the roadblocks its people had to overcome; deep-seated antagonisms between management and labor and the impact of changes beyond the control of the organization itself — new facilities, new products, and personnel changes at all levels, especially among hourly workers. Just when the Quality of Work Life efforts gained some momentum, an unanticipated event intervened and the program was stopped dead in its tracks — almost. Indeed, one gets the impression that the only constant was change itself.

Some observations are in order. Developing this climate for change takes extraordinary patience. It takes time. It calls for sustained commitment at all levels. In most of the efforts to change human behavior that I have observed directly, these characteristics are lacking. Managers and leaders are under pressure to change things overnight. They draw up a program, package it, press the authority button, set deadlines, then move. It all sounds so easy, so efficient, so American.

In changing the way Americans work, we have, as the chairman of Local 644 said, "barely scratched the surfce." What went on at Tarrytown was only a beginning. The intrinsic nature of repetitive conveyor-paced jobs has not substantially changed. The commitment to quality of work life is strong at the local level and among some people at division and corporate levels, but it is not universal. Changes in management or new crises could threaten further developments. Nevertheless, a new atmosphere about change and the worker's role in it is clearly emerging. People feel they have some "say," some control over their work environment now and in the future.

The Tarrytown story may, however, reflect something important about Quality of Work Life efforts springing up in many other places in the U.S. Studies are showing that workers in our large, rationalized industries and businesses are seeking more control over and involvement in the forces affecting their work lives. Due in part to the rising levels of education, changing aspirations, and shifts in values, especially among young people, I believe we are witnessing a quiet revolution in what people expect from work, an expectation that goes beyond the economic and job security issues that led to labor unrest in an earlier day.[2]

In parts of Europe, the response to this quiet revolution is manifest in broadscale political efforts on the part of labor and government to gain greater control over the management of the enterprise itself. In the U.S., the response is different.[3] Workers or their unions have given no indications that they wish to take over basic management prerogatives. As the Tarrytown story illustrates, what they want is more pragmatic, more immediate, more localized — but no less important.

The challenge to those in positions of power is to become aware of the quiet revolution at the workplace and to find the means to respond intelligently to these forces for change. What management did at Tarrytown is but one example of the beginnings of an intelligent response.

NOTES

1. **Irving Bluestone, "A Changing View of Union-Management Relationships,"** *Vital Speeches,* December 11, 1976.

2. For recent confirmation based on survey data over a period of 25 years, see M.R. Cooper, B.S. Morgan, P.M. Foley, and L.B. Kaplan, "Changing Employee Values: Deepening Discontent," Harvard Business Review January-February 1979, p. 117.

3. For a fuller discussion of the differences between American and European responses to labor today, see Ted Mills' "Europe's Industrial Democracy: An American Response," Harvard Business Review November-December 1978, p. 143.

THE TOPEKA STORY:
TEACHING AN OLD DOG FOOD NEW TRICKS
Richard E. Walton

This two-part article reports in detail on a pioneering manufacturing plant which employs an innovative and potentially influential new work structure. Important as this plant's success is for the people who work in it and manage it, the experience is equally important as an illustration of what is taking place in a small but increasing number of work organizations in the United States.

The plant produces pet foods for General Foods and is located in Topeka, Kansas. Its seven-year history is part of a quiet transformation which may alter the standard practices in design, management, and operation of not only factories, but all kinds of work places. This report deals with successes and failures, enthusiasm and frustration, fantasy and reality. It is not the story of an ideal situation; it is the story of men and an idea.

Beginning with the Industrial Revolution managers sought to increase productivity by rationalizing the production processes. Progressively, jobs were fragmented and deskilled, planning and implementing were separated, and management controls were substituted for craft pride and self-discipline. In our time, these entrenched approaches to management increasingly produce worker disaffection, and as a result they may no longer serve the goal of productivity or they may do so only at a high human cost.

Companies in a variety of industries in many countries have found that they can create a more satisfied, committed, and capable work force and can obtain equal or better quality and quantity of output, by restructuring work along different lines: by combining jobs to create whole tasks; by assigning these tasks to teams with responsibilities, for example, for inspection, maintenance, planning, scheduling, and work assignment; by cross-training workers for broader flexibility; by adopting more participative management patterns; and by designing pay schemes to reward individual learning and group productivity, not solely individual performance.

Several comtemporary attitudes are promoting this reversal of long-established trends. One is rising expectations on the part of employees, an awareness that their labors can bring them a better life than in previous generations. Another is greater public consciousness about the quality of work life — life can be better in the office and on the shop floor. Most important of all is a growing recognition among managers and unions that restructuring work can lead to improvements in both the quality of work life and in productivity.

One of the reasons why employee expectations in the work place have increased is that the educational level has risen. Another is that levels of income and security have also risen from decade to decade, so that pay and security are taken more for granted than they used to be. Still another factor is the decreased emphasis given by churches, schools, and families to obedience to authority. Instead, they have promoted individual initiative, self-responsibility and self-control, and other social patterns that make subordination in a traditional organizational structure increasingly difficult to accept for each successive wave of entrants into the work force.

Part One provides an account of the innovations and the issues they raised at the Gaines pet food plant in Topeka. A number of innovative plants in several parts of the world have been reported upon after an initial period of success (Volvo and Saab in Sweden, for example), but no detailed accounts cover the successes and failures over a period as long as seven years. Part Two will examine the broader applicability of the Topeka work innovations. This account is based on the author's observations of the life history of the plant as a consultant during the planning stages and as an interested observer since.

Part One: Seven Years of Work Innovations at Topeka

General Food's radically innovative dry dog food plant in Topeka was conceived in 1968 and started up in January 1971. In designing the new plant, the original project team, led by GF managers Lyman Ketchum and Ed Dulworth, was determined to avoid the negative worker attitudes in the existing pet food facilities in Illinois. They were inspired by the possibility of engaging unusual human involvement in the new plant.

Self-managing teams assumed responsibility for large segments of the production process. The teams were composed of from 7 to 14 members, large enough to embrace a set of interrelated tasks and small enough to permit face-to-face meetings for making decisions and for coordination. Activities usually performed by separate units — maintenance, quality control, custodianship, industrial engineering, and personnel — were built into the responsibilities of each team. For example, team members screened job applicants for replacements on their own team.

An attempt was made to design every set of team tasks to include both manual skills and mental functions such as diagnosing mechanical problems and planning. The aim was to make all sets of team tasks equally challenging, although each set would require unique demands.

Consistent with this aim was a *single job classification* for all operators. Pay increases depended on the mastery of an increasing number of jobs. Since there were no limits on how many members of a team could qualify for higher pay brackets, employees were encouraged to teach each other their skills.

In lieu of the "foreman," a "team leader" position was created. Operators were provided with the data and guidelines that enabled them to make production decisions ordinarily made by higher level supervisors. The team leader had the responsibility for facilitating the team's decision making. As for plant rules, management refrained from specifying any in advance. Rules evolved over time from collective experience.

The technology and architecture were designed to facilitate rather than discourage informal gatherings of team members during working hours. Status symbols were minimized — for example, a single entrance leads into both the administrative office and the plant.

The new work system achieved highly positive results in both human and economic terms. A study by Robert Schrank of the Ford Foundation conducted in 1973 found high levels of worker participation in decisions, freedom to communicate, expressions of warmth amongst the workers, a minimum of status distinction, a strong sense of human dignity, commitment to the job, and individual self-esteem. Schrank gave less credit for this to certain new design features than I do, arguing, for example, that the self-managing team structure, the challenging job contrast, and the skill-based pay system were much less important than the fact that employees had the freedom to move around and socialize during working hours.

Another study of the plant was conducted in June 1974. It used the survey methodology of the University of Michigan and confirmed the Topeka work force's positive attitudes. According to Edward Lawler, of the Institute for Social Research, "Our data . . . show high levels of satisfaction and involvement in all parts of the organization. In fact they show the highest levels we have found in any organization we have sampled. I specifically compared it with other small organizations and still found it superior."

Furthermore, there is no doubt about the ecomonic superiority of the plant. Recent studies by corporate analysts outside Topeka have indicated that the savings attributable to the work innovations in the dog food plant were in the neighborhood of a million dollars annually, a significant figure in a plant with about 100 personnel and involving a capital investment in the range of $10-15 million.

Other pertinent statistics: the plant started up and went three years and eight months (1.3 million manhours) without a lost-time accident. Absenteeism ranged from .8% to 1.4% during 1971-74. Turnover was reported at 10% per year; both the rate and nature of the turnover is regarded by Topeka employees as healthy. The impressive benefits led to a corporate policy favoring similar innovative approaches in other plants where conditions were suitable. The actual diffusion of these ideas to other General Foods plants has been slow, but for reasons other than doubt about their efficacy in Topeka. Ironically, Topeka's dramatic success and its attendant publicity created a sense of rivalry and some resentment among other GF plant managers and discouraged rather than encouraged them from taking a similar approach in their own plant.

In order to understand some of the innovations at Topeka, here is a chronology of key developments.

Phase I (1968-1970) — Pre-start Up

Long before startup, team leaders were hired and included in the planning, training, and team building. Lead time was allowed for new concepts to be articulated, debated, and translated into work procedures and structures. Managers had time to develop insights into human behavior and to coalesce as a group. Team leaders screened operators drawing 63 from more than 600 applicants to form a relatively talented and receptive work force.

Certain events helped establish the new work culture. The screening process used to select team leaders included role playing and group discussion — providing a unique, involving, and even anxiety provoking initiation. According to one observer, this initial experience created a sense of hardiness, uniqueness, and elitism. The team leaders in turn, utilized similar methods in screening workers thereby transmitting these same feelings to the work force.

While healthy skepticism about the project existed within the new workforce, these initial experiences created a readiness to give the innovations a fair trial.

Phase II (1971) — Technical and Social Start Up

The first year of operation was marked by a variety of minor "tests" of the system; and by the development of potent group phenomena. In the first few weeks some cash was taken from an open change box. The universal response by workers and managers was to dig into their own pockets to replace the missing cash and continue the open cash box which was used for vending machines in the cafeteria. These gentures were symbolically important in confirming support for a system that could be built on the premise of trustworthiness.

After a number of weeks, the operators felt they were ready for their first pay increase, based on mastery of their first job. Management, however, did not anticipate this event. Their initial disagreement both reinforced the doubt of the skeptics and weakened the confidence of the believers. When management ultimately agreed to review the qualifications of operators for increases, they also reaffirmed the responsiveness of the system.

Soon after, a railroad strike tested the teams' capacities to solve new work problems, which the teams did effectively. Also, by interrupting regular production, the strike tested management's commitment to provide secure employment. Plant management tried to prevent corporate pressures from forcing them to make layoffs. The occasion once again crystallized fears and hopes about the system. As it happened, the strike ended before a definitive answer to the question.

Developments within each of the six work teams largely determined how a person viewed the work system. At times team leaders provided too much structure, seeming to contradict the stated philosophy. At other times, they provided too little structure and seemed to dramatize the impracticality of worker participation. Nevertheless, sooner or later the groups coalesced. They became the most potent factor in forming and enforcing the system's norms about cooperation, openness, involvement, and responsibility.

In brief, 1971 was a period of building technical and social skills and of testing the credibility of the system. Those who were initially receptive had their commitment strengthened and, except for a small minority, many of those who were negative or skeptical decided to "buy in."

Phase III (1972) — Pushing the Technology

In 1972, the *social capital* (skills, knowledge, attitudes, and relationships) was put to work in a demanding way. Demand for production volume, resisted during 1971, now had to be met.

The maximum production effort had several important side effects: first, quality sometimes suffered, undermining one source of pride. Second, with the plant now "humming" there was less immediate need for group problem solving and less opportunity for meetings. This reduced the amount of ongoing social maintenance within groups. Third, teams often yielded to the temptation to improve their own performance at the expense of the next shift.

A management change at a higher level also troubled Topeka managers. The man who had initiated the innovations and who had held an umbrella over the fledgling system during the past year, was replaced by a person who was seen as philosophically unsympathetic to Topeka. This change raised doubts about the General Foods hierarchy's understanding or commitment to the Topeka innovation.

Still, the plant was performing well, reaching capacity output with about 70 people (compared with the 110 originally estimated on the basis of standard industrial engineering principles). Substantial savings from lower overhead, fewer quality rejects, and other factors were attributed to the innovative human organization. Participants were proud.

The plant had become perhaps the most publicized U.S. example of a solution to what the media called the "blue collar blues." A journalist's account of his visit to the plant had been featured on the front page of the *New York Times*. Along with work innovations at Volvo and ATT, it was the subject of NBC's "First Tuesday" program — 60 minutes of prime TV time. An article analyzing this "prototype" plant and its initial successes reached over 100,000 readers of the *Harvard Business Review*.

All things considered, I judge this was a period of leveling off. Comparing the production year of 1972 with the start up year of 1971, "participation" and "openness" generally went down. However, the impressive production results increased "optimism" that the system would survive.

Phase IV (1973) — Turmoil, Decline, and Reversal

During my visit in October 1973, I found a consensus that a trough had been reached during the summer in various indexes of the system's health. This trough was followed by a steady improvement during the fall.

During the first half of 1973, the emphasis on production volume continued, along with long hours, few team meetings, and inter-shift rivalry. The negative effects were cumulative, depleting the social capital to a point that started to weaken basic commitments. Without meetings, trust and openness were declining.

The prolonged push for maximum production also deferred the movement of workers from one team to another, a movement which could occur after an operator had earned "team rate." This delay in opportunity to learn jobs on other teams postponed the date at which an employee could earn "plant rate." The delay tended to undermine commitment.

When interteam movement was finally okayed, a large number of transfers occurred betweeen packaging and processing. At about the same time, 13 team

210

members and two team leaders chose to form the nucleus for a newly-constructed canned food plant. The wholesale movement alleviated some problems but created others. The orginial teams often had identified closely with their team leaders, whose personal styles varied widely. Now team leaders were faced with new teams and vice versa.

Team leaders who were now trying to build a team for the second time often could not muster the same enthusiasm for the task. They felt unfairly resisted by the new teams, and often were faced with contradictory bids from two sub-groups: one asking for more direction; the other for less. Perhaps to avoid these cross currents, team leaders held fewer team meetings and became more absorbed in plant-wide projects.

The absence of team meetings now had a dramatically negative effect. Members needed to cooperate hourly in their tasks and weekly in learning exchanges, but had not developed the necessary mutual confidence. Moreover, the recently-hired employees were not learning about their rights and obligations in the system, and many were not developing commitment during the critical first few months.

Also, the new canned food plant helped generate negativism in the dry food plant. Many members felt they had been "deserted" by those who opted to go to a "more advanced rival." They also opposed the can plant's practices regarding pay and job design because a moratorium was placed on job rotation during the startup phase and pay increases were tied to more traditional criteria.

By summer of 1973, the site manager, previously preoccupied with his strained relations in the corporation, started attending to the issues that troubled the Topeka organization. People became aware that they had neglected the acculturation of new members and the development of the newly-formed teams; they resolved to rebuild the social capital. Openness, trust, and commitment were definitely trending up in the fall of 1973.

Another indication of strength was the fact that managers were working themselves out of their jobs by fostering the development of subordinates. The manufacturing manager of the dry food plant asked to be pulled out of the line, eliminating one level of the hierarchy. He became a consultant to other parts of the corporation and to the Topeka plants. Also, there was growing interest in eliminating or reducing the number of team leader positions.

Notwithstanding the restored commitment and other favorable developments reported above, I detected some weaknesses during my visit in October, 1973.

First, the system had not developed problem-solving mechanisms for the whole plant that were nearly as effective as those in the face-to-face teams. The problem was illustrated by two plant-wide issues in the fall of 1973: (1) differences of opinion about the selection criteria for a spare parts coordinator; and (2) whether or not the pay system for office employees could be revised along lines different from the factory pay schemes.

Representatives on the plant committees dealing with these issues were given only limited confidence. As a result, the committee actions were not truly accepted by the larger work force. Representatives were suspected of being co-opted by management. Moreover, committee members didn't support solutions shaped by problem-solving groups in which they had not been directly involved. This reflected a strong preference for ''participatory democracy'' over a ''representative'' form of self-government.

Second, although there was unusual frankness, there was also concern whether the openness and objectivity were adequate given the stringent requirements of the plant design. For the system to work, an individual had to be candid in contributing to problem solving, conscientious in judging an idea on its merits, not its source, and objective in evaluating the qualifications of peers for higher pay rates.

I observed a strong desire by participants to increase these attributes, especially in pay decisions. When peer evaluations are ''not honest,'' they said, there are three consequences: pay increases are given which are not justified (creating inequities); individuals are assumed to have qualifications they do not posses (forcing others to do the work); and a basic tenet of the system is violated.

Objective criticism was muted when a person feared he would be ostracized by a clique because influence is vested more in lateral than in hierarchical relations, which makes an operator more concerned about the judgment of peers than superiors. Furthermore, there is no quantifiable, stable, automatic basis for a person's security, such as seniority. One worker explained that the tenuous basis of his security makes him continuously concerned about his relations with many people who could help or hurt him in the future. Another worker said, ''The match in the gasoline is pay!'', explaining that decisions about the worth and pay of members are starkly real.

The result was a moderate tendency to ease up on standards, e.g., shrinking from hard, exacting evaluation of a worker's mastery of all tasks in the plant before awarding him the plant rate. Thus, reciprocation tended toward each giving the other the benefit of the doubt.

More impressive to me than the moderate gap between ideal and actual behavior were the high ideals themselves. The system had idealized influence based on *expertise* (information and skills), rather than either *positional power* (based on formal authority, rules and procedures) or *political power* (e.g., cliques). The managers and workers felt guilty whenever they did not live up to the ideals of openness and objectivity. I found myself wondering at the time: were these people expecting too much of themselves?

Third, among the team leaders there was a striking gap between ideals of high mutual support and trust and their actual behavior. Also, team leaders had a norm of self-sacrifice — most would concern themselves with improving work life for team members but not seek needed changes in their own situations. As one team leader said, ''I never did think the 'Topeka system' applied to team leaders themselves.'' Team leaders were expected to engage in dialogue with operators and some were frequently exhausted. It had not been made legitimate for team leaders to put limits on their own accessibility.

Phase V (1974-1976) — Steady State with Traces of Erosion

When I returned in November, 1976, after three years, a number of elements in the positive work culture had declined. Not a steep decline, rather a moderate erosion.

By general agreement it was still a very productive plant and a superior place to work, but the "quality of work life" had slipped. And while the majority still supported — by their own behavior — the unique strengths of the "Topeka work system," an increasing minority did not. Slippage occurred across a broad front of attributes: openness and candor; helping among team members; identification with plant management; confidence in General Foods; perceived upward influence; effective leadership within teams; and cooperation between shifts. In addition, there continued to be serious doubt about the ability of teams to make objective judgments about members' qualifications for pay increases.

Two major changes since 1973 had occurred: team members now accepted the fact-of-life of subjectivity and other imperfections, and the clique behavior was more pronounced.

Following my visit in 1973 a concerted effort had been made to improve relations among team leaders and to increase their influence over matters affecting them. Also their number was reduced from six to three. However, by 1976, the team leader position was again ambiguous and nonsatisfying. They were discouraged about their prospects for advancement, a feeling sharpened by two facts: their plant-wide project assignments had broadened their abilities and raised their aspirations; and team members provided them with more grief than satisfaction. Team leaders, not unlike foremen in other plants, felt neither a part of the work force nor of management. They complained that they were not backed by management. As a result, the position failed to attract the most talented team members.

Three factors had had depressing effects on the dry plant work system during this period.

First, during 1973-1976, three of the four managers most responsible for the Topeka system had left General Foods and the fourth had moved from the dry food plant to the can plant. Many perceived that the managers who left GF had been treated unfairly by the company; indeed, the managers themselves considered their pioneering work a loss rather than a gain in their General Foods careers. These original managers had a commitment to the philosophy and a will to "go to bat" to protect the system; but the workers could not assume that their successors would develop the same commitment. Also, one of the earlier managers had played an especially strong role in the organization's development. His contribution was missed.

Some people, however, held a contrasting view. They believed the departing managers had been too aggressive vis-á-vis the corporate hierachy, thereby contributing to the strained external relations, isolating the Topeka innovation, and hurting their own General Foods careers and the career opportunities of other Topeka managers.

Second, the neighboring can plant had lived under a cloud of uncertainty for three years — it would gear up for a national launching of a new dog food product only to have the plan cancelled when the product did not prove out in market tests. Two layoffs had occurred in the can plant in 1975. However, beginning in the summer of 1976 the product took off in the market and the plant began a highly accelerated start up, moving quickly to three shifts, and six-day schedules. In order to get the plant on stream in the shortest possible time, management deferred the introduction of many aspects of the new work structure from the dry plant. This was interpreted by dry plant members as weakened management commitment to the new philosophy.

Third, there were no new challenges of significance in the dry plant during 1973-76. A major expansion had been planned but did not occur. New products requiring significant process changes were contemplated but had not yet been introduced. So some complacency developed.

These three factors help explain the negative drift of the work culture. However, more significant for me was the absence of potent corrective devices, of a capacity for self-renewal.

As noted earlier, the work system has not dealt effectively with plant-wide issues. Committees that cut across units and levels of the plant have treated a few specific issues, but seldom, if ever, have they gained the full confidence of the employees. Moreover, there have been no regular plant-wide forums in which issues can be discussed.

In the absence of a plant-wide mechanism to which management could respond, management would have had to take the initiative to assess the health of the system, to diagnose problems, to identify opportunities, to review the adequacy of existing procedures and roles, to set goals for organization development, to propose innovative solutions. They have done little of this since 1973 except in relation to a proposed bonus scheme.

Equally important, though, the plant community sometimes lost its appreciation of the idea that the work system would need to evolve continually. Such evolution could only be derived from experience, with a widely-shared responsibility for promoting this evolution. Within the work force there is a widely shared and deeply felt responsibility to *protect,* to preserve the work system. While this is an enormous asset, it could be an even greater asset if the commitment were less defensively oriented and initiatives were taken.

One major possibility for evolving the system — establishing a plant-wide productivity bonus — has been under consideration for several years but could not be acted on in the absence of corporate level approval. This would be an appropriate development in many respects: equity would be served by further sharing the fruits of this productive human system: the total plant community could be drawn together as it never has before; individuals who are topping out in the pay scheme would have another way to increase their income. In the most general sense, the plant-wide bonus could provide the work system with a timely "second wind."

The bonus has been delayed by other corporate considerations: there is no immediate motivational or productivity problem to solve by such a measure; some people question whether sufficient potential remains in the system for productivity increases to make significant bonuses possible; a bonus would create a complicating precedent for other GF plants; and, finally, the bonus design at Topeka itself becomes more complex with the addition of the can plant.

Perhaps the inability to implement this particular change, despite the attention it has been given, may inadvertently have taught the workers that they cannot innovate further.

Why Is the Work Culture So Robust?

Despite the slippage, the very positive culture has proven to be extremely robust. Earlier, there was a distinct pattern marking development/depletion/redevelopment and in recent years a pattern of moderate decline. But never has the climate truly soured or even become neutral and indifferent, although in my opinion this will happen unless concerted effort is made to evolve the organization further. It is amazing to me how much momentum has been sustained, given the modest level of social maintenance and renewal activities over the past three years.

The following explanations of the plant's robustness are offered tentatively and without any pretense of being exhaustive.

☐ First, the original design concepts have proven sound in this situation. None have been abandoned, although, of course, some design ideals have been achieved only in relative terms.

☐ Second, the implementation of the pre-start up and the start up stages was handled especially skillfully, a judgment I can now make after observing the start-ups of several similar work innovations.

☐ Third, the system was enduring because the underlying philosophy itself was more important than personalities. Although each manager in the dry plant was respected, none aspired to become a charismatic leader. The commitment to certain philosophical principles was reinforced by the publicity given the "Topeka system." I found that many workers wanted to live up to their external image.

☐ Fourth, pay clearly has been a pivotal element of the work system. One important factor is that it pays for skills acquired and there are no quotas to limit an individual's advancement.

Another important factor is the heavy role that peer evaluation plays in the administration of pay. On the one hand, this participative feature enhances commitment: workers feel a serious responsibility to make both the pay scheme and the larger organization succeed; workers are keenly aware of their additional interdependence with each other; self-management of the formal reward scheme symbolizes their relatively low dependence on hierarchical authority, which is a source of pride.

On the other hand, peer evaluation assumes that people can maintain high standards and levels of objectivity and, therefore, equity among people. These assumptions can only be valid by degree. The gap between an ideal and the actual can be demoralizing.

After assessing the plusses and minuses of this feature, I tend to believe there has been a net gain in Topeka. Still, I remain very cautious in recommending peer evaluation as an initial feature of the pay scheme in other plants.

Since my last visit to the plant a year ago, Topeka management has been addressing many of these issues and concerns. Bill Bevans, the GF organization development consultant who has been working there, reports that the new can plant is under control and operating well. Self-confidence has been enhanced at all levels of the plant community and management is able to attend to longer term issues. The dry plant has a new manager and there has been positive response to a few issues initiated by the employees. Finally, the success and visibility within GF of similar projects in a few other plants has taken the "limelight" pressure off Topeka, freeing management from the caution that tended to immobilize it and prevent it from planning change or renewal. Although, to my knowledge, these developments have not changed anything at the shop floor level, I find them encouraging.

The Topeka organization has produced gains in the quality of work life and productivity and has remained viable over an extended period. How applicable is its general approach? How applicable are certain of its design features, such as teams with significant self-managing responsibilities and pay systems based on skill evaluation versus job evaluation? Are there additional features, not incorporated in the Topeka organization, that should be considered? These questions will be considered in Part II: "Generalizations Beyond Topeka."

This article is adapted from a recent article by Richard Walton in the Journal of Applied Behavioral Science, *Vol. 13, No. 3, ©1977, NTL Institute of Applied Behavioral Science, Rosslyn. Va.*

Suggested Reading

PEHR G. GYLLENHAMMER, People at Work.
Addison-Wesley Publishing Company, 1977. A clearly written account of the many varied work innovations at Volvo, together with business man's strategic materials for Volvo's efforts in this field.

THE TOPEKA STORY: PART TWO
WHAT'S THE BOTTOM LINE?
Richard E. Walton

The Topeka organization has produced gains in the quality of work life and productivity and has remained viable over an extended period. How applicable is its general approach? How applicable are certain of its design features, such as teams with significant self-managing responsibilities and pay systems based on skill evaluation versus job evaluation? Are there additional features, not incorporated in the Topeka organization, that should be considered?

Four conditions are frequently cited as keys to the applicability of an organization innovation: 1) the primacy of goals to be served by the innovation; 2) the unionized status of a work organization; 3) the type of technology employed; and 4) the size of the facility. Let's consider each in turn.

Goals. The Topeka design was explicitly developed for both productivity and the quality of work life. In contrast, many managers wish to find ways to reap the productivity gains and treat improvements in the quality of work life, if any, as a by-product. Some people in what is called the quality of work life "movement" are impatient with planners who insist on explicit attention to productivity. For example, Robert Schrank of the Ford Foundation, who has written insightfully about the Topeka plant, expressed disapproval of "an underlying assumption of many people concerned with improving life at the work place . . . that any change or improvement must also be reflected in an increase in production." He argues that "such an assumption tends to make workers and union people suspicious that it may be just another scheme to get more production out of them. . . ."

I appreciate the logic of that argument, but paradoxically the effect is just the opposite. Particularly in the U.S., I have observed greater suspicion by union leaders and workers when management has initiated quality of work life projects *without* a parallel goal of improving production. (The idea of "productivity" is used here in a broad sense to include reduced waste, improved quality and delivery, and other indices of the organization's ability to achieve its formal goals.) The fact is that management's interest in innovation is more credible when managerial self-interest is apparent!

I have three additional reasons for urging that we adhere to a duality of goals — quality of work life *and* productivity.

First, both goals are urgent ones nationally. In both the private and public sectors we urgently need to improve our ability to deliver more goods and services at lower costs; hence the importance of the productivity goal. The social and psychological costs of work borne by those who produce these goods and services do not show up in our accounting schemes. But they are nevertheless significant and can be ameliorated; hence the quality of work life goal.

Second, only with progress along both dimensions can we expect the sustained commitment required to ensure the success of significant innovations. Such an

217

operation will not be sustained by management unless there is reinforcement in terms of productivity and it will not be sustained by workers and unions unless there is reinforcement in terms of work satisfaction.

Third, the necessity for improvements on both counts will stimulate more inventiveness. The criteria of simultaneously enhancing the human experience at work *and* the effectiveness of work provide a challenge that will lead to more radical inventions in work organization.

Unionized status. I accept neither the idea that Topeka-type systems eliminate the need for unions nor that the present programs of unions embrace the full range of possibilities to enhance the quality of work life. The efforts to restructure work need to be pursued more vigorously in union-management contexts!

Although most projects in the U.S. have been in nonunionized plants, several joint union-management efforts have occurred, including those at Harman Industries in Bolivar, Tennessee, and the Rushton Mines in Pennsylvania. Another significant project is an International Rockwell plant in Battle Creek, Michigan, where management and the United Auto Workers jointly designed an innovative work structure comparable in spirit to the Topeka plant. General Motors and the UAW are engaged in projects in a large number of locations.

One large diversified firm is developing a strategy for change in unionized plants that often utilizes a plant-wide productivity bonus as the first step in the work restructuring process. The advantage of such an early step is that it makes credible to both workers and their union representatives the intent to achieve genuine change in the work culture and, in particular, to share productivity gains.

I do not see any major insurmountable problem in integrating the institution of collective bargaining and the principles of work restructuring which were developed earlier in non-union plants. Once a union and management sit down and sort out their common interests in both quality of work life and productivity, they will recognize that common interests require new collaborative processes as well as the continuation of certain adversary processes.

Type of technology. The complex interdependence of tasks in a continuous flow process such as at Topeka makes the close teamwork especially meaningful to participants and important for production. Moreover, due to the high amount of monitoring, planning, and coordinating — as contrasted with direct physical work — operators are not continuously tied to their work stations and have contact with other team members. Also, the high costs of capital and raw materials relative to labor costs make it economically feasible to pay the higher average rates under a skill-based compensation scheme.

The amount of planning and decision making required in a continuous flow technology usually increases the significant mental content of the work. This justifies more ''managerial'' information and more training investment per employee; both are seen as signals of positive regard for employees.

Other types of technology do not appear to have the same potential for improvement — either in terms of enhancing the quality of work life or of improving productivity through the better use of human capacities. A case in point is the second half of the work flow at Topeka, the packaging line, where some operating tasks are simple and repetitive. If automating the routine work is not possible, then redesign often includes making a team responsible for the less-routine operations such as set-up, machine maintenance, scheduling, methods, inspection, and screening prospective employees. We attempted this in the package department at Topeka — but we could not make the packaging work equally challenging with the processing work. But that did not keep us from doing as much as possible within the inherent limits of the basic task.

What is possible — and is not possible — cannot be asserted in advance or on the basis of a cursory examination. It is not inherent in mass production technology that work procedures must be minutely prescribed and then strictly adhered to. Volvo has demonstrated that even the automobile assembly line can be modified to give workers additional latitude in terms of work rhythm, methods, and organization of the tasks. The important point is to have an *aspiration level* appropriate to the task involved. For example, in the case of auto assembly work it may be possible only to decrease the undesirability or coerciveness of the task, but in the case of tending a large paper machine it may be possible to make the task absolutely exciting.

The principles employed at Topeka have been effectively applied in many different continuous processing technologies, including paper making, oil, food, and cold rolling aluminum plants; in various batch processing tasks such as machining plants and coal mines; in assembly tasks ranging from automobiles to microwave components; in large warehousing and shipping operations; and in a wide range of other work situations including tankers at sea and phone installation and repair.

Plant size. How much does plant size influence the feasibility of innovative work structure? Related to this general question are a number of more partiuclar ones. How many people can one know, at least by name? With how many people can one meet and actually discuss issues in open forum? With how large a human system can one have a strong sense of identification and see oneself as an important part of the whole?

Many observers have argued that what was done at Topeka is possible only in plants of that general size. The Topeka plant employed roughly 100 people including management and office personnel. I am certain that small plants up to a few hundred employees lend themselves to the Topeka type of work structure more readily than do larger plants. But I also know that the same general principles have been successfully employed in a number of plants with a thousand workers or more. I am well acquainted with the experience of two of these larger plants where the work culture is marked by openness, concern for human dignity, sense of personal worth, commonality of goals, and high motivation.

In one of these 1,000-employee plants there was an effective attempt to maintain a strong sense of one large community. It included a highly visible plant manager whose values and charisma made him a symbol of trust for the workforce. He stayed in contact with the workers both on a formal level and through informal encounters in the cafeteria. The cafeteria itself became the "common watering hole" for the plant community. One problem was that this positive plant culture became too dependent on a single leader who might someday leave. So the organization was taking steps to spread the bases of trust.

In the second plant the problems of size had been handled by an opposite strategy. Rather than emphasize the total community, the emphasis was on divisional units (five in number, ranging in size from 100 to 300 employees) and face-to-face work teams. Considerable diversity in policies and practices existed among the divisional units, each having a different technology and its own start-up history. Their products also were in different competitive positions in the market.

The problem with this strategy for promoting a positive culture in a large facility was that it required unusually high tolerance for diversity among adjacent units. This tolerance would be severely tested if more personnel movement between units ever became necessary.

I am now involved in the design and start-up of a Cummins Engine Company plant in which a number of diesel engine components will be machined and complete engines assembled. The whole plant has almost one million square feet and will eventually employ more than 2,000 workers. In order to achieve worker involvement and openness, the plans are to divide the large number of separate machining lines into five "businesses," each with its own part of the plant, entrance, office area, and eating facilities. Each "business" will be as self-sufficient as possible in terms of staff services.

Volvo's efforts to restructure work within the context of large facilities are also instructive. In the conventional assembly plants, Volvo modified the long continuous lines, breaking them into shorter lines separated by buffers composed of parts. In the radically innovative assembly plant built at Kalmar, Sweden, which began operations in 1974, the building layout reinforces the atmosphere of small workshops for each assembly team. In planning the Volvo plant for the United States a decision was made to create several shorter parallel assembly lines, rather than one longer line, in order to keep down the number of workers responsible for the assembly of an automobile.

While I have argued that the broad principles underlying the Topeka work structure are widely applicable, I do not claim the converse — that *all* of the principles that have wide applicability are incorporated in the Topeka design.

Due process. In a Ford Foundation report, Robert Schrank pointed out that the Topeka plant had no "procedure for redress outside the existing institutional structure." He noted that an individual may be mistreated by the capricious behavior of a supervisor or suffer at the hands of a group that gangs up on him. I agree that the absence of due process is a deficiency in the quality of work life, even if the relevance of redress procedures is potential rather than actual. Unions can provide due process; indeed that is one of their major functions. In non-unionized situations, some procedure must be developed to ensure due process.

Employment security. In my opinion, Schrank makes an important point when he asks, "What happens in an existing plant when production is increased with the support and help of workers and some of them become superfluous?" He notes that the planners of Topeka had little to say about this question.

From the viewpoint of a work force, the increased productivity of their plant may decrease the number of jobs, but may make the remaining jobs more secure. For example, I recently became involved in restructuring an older New England plant employing 600 people which is no longer competitive. The union president stated, ''I want to save jobs for this region. In order to make any of the jobs in this plant secure, I recognize that we will have to figure out how to operate this plant with 500 or even 400 employees.''

The next question is whether it is economically feasible to give certain assurances. ''We will reduce the size of the work force by normal attrition and by making early retirement attractive. No current employee will go onto the street because of productivity increases generated via new work structures.'' If economically feasible, such an assurance is consistent with the spirit of work cultures such as Topeka's. If it is not feasible, it will be very difficult, if not impossible, to build a system where workers are spontaneously committed to unusually high productivity goals.

Participation in work design. In Topeka, because the plant was a new start-up, there was no worker participation in the initial design of the compensation system and other planning. In existing plants, heavy worker and union involvement are essential in work redesign.

Even if innovations have potentially wide application, diffusion does not follow automatically. Significant diffusion depends upon a growing commitment to *both quality of work life and productivity goals* — dual and balanced commitment by all participants in the work place, including managers, workers, and unions. If these goals are understood, then progress toward them can be seen as *relative*: the aspiration level in any particular work situation can be conditioned by the constraints inherent in the technology and economics of that situation. Thus, we would recognize that what is feasible and desirable with assembly tasks may be different in continuous process operations. But that fact would not deter us from making the improvements that are possible.

A final point. Some constraints need not be viewed as absolute and may better be viewed in a *spirit of inventiveness*. For example, the very nature of assembly tasks may be reconceived to accommodate a preferred social organization — rather than fit an organization to standard assembly patterns. Similarly, large facilities may be structured in ways that permit the development of the extraordinary type of work culture which exists in the small Topeka plant.

"AWAKENING A SLEEPING GIANT . . ."
FORD'S EMPLOYEE INVOLVEMENT PROGRAM
Gerard Tavernier

The Ford Motor Company's Dearborn Engine Plant at Dearborn, Michigan — where 1.6 liter engines for the company's world cars are manufactured — had a serious scrap problem caused by broken timing belts on cylinder head milling machines. One broken-belt incident caused a $24,000 loss in damaged parts, broken tooling, and lost production.

An employee problem-solving team, consisting of machine operators and job setters, solved the problem by redesigning the machine controls to shut down automatically when a timing belt breaks while the machine is operating.

The cost for fixing each machine: $252.

As a result of improvements suggested by an employee group at Ford's plant in Indianapolis, the reject rate for parts processed through the valve-centering machines has been reduced by about 37 percent. With the sustained increase in first run valve production capability, an approved project for the purchase of a $500,000 centering retest machine has been placed on hold.

At Ford's metal-stamping plant in Buffalo, New York, one of four rear-door assembly lines was rearranged, in line with a problem-solving group's suggestions, substantially reducing surface defects (fit and finish) caused by the in-process automatic handling system. The changes are being extended to the remaining three assembly lines.

At Ford's assembly plant in Chicago, Illinois, a telephone hot line has been installed so that any employee can report quality problems. Signs are posted throughout the plant encouraging them to do so and giving the telephone number 333.

"We've received about 160 calls so far and we've acted on each one," says Steve Adams, quality control manager. "We had lots of good suggestions on how to do better inspections, how to build better assemblies, and how to improve an assembly operation."

The plant also brought local dealership service people into the plant and asked them for feedback on the cars being delivered. "We ask them to identify potential customer concerns very early in the model year so we can act before many cars get to the dealers," explains Adams.

THE FORD-UAW PROGRAM

More than 250 employee problem-solving teams, involving 2,500 employees, are currently tackling similar work-related problems at Ford Motor Comapny as part of a new program called Employee Involvement (EI) introduced by Ford working with the United Auto Workers (UAW).

The cooperative effort is a major step in a process of employee participation in decisions that affect their work and the overall work environment. It is broad in scope and encompasses improvements in product quality, operational efficiency, job satisfaction, and employee relations.

"We're all in this together," declares Peter J. Pestillo, vice-president, labor relations at Ford. "The success of the company depends on our employees and management working together in the most effective ways."

The Ford-UAW program reaches from small problem-solving groups in the smallest departmental units in Ford plants to top management/union levels. It aims to give every interested employee the opportunity to participate in decisions that affect him and his job.

Comments Donald F. Ephlin, a UAW vice-president and director of its National Ford Department, "We know how to strike . . . how to fight . . . how to bargain. We don't have to prove those things anymore. What we do have to prove now is that we can solve problems. We believe the union has a positive role to play in the future of the company. We're convinced that Ford is going to make it. But it's going to make it better because of our involvement."

Although the EI program is still in its early stages, the evidence so far indicates it is working well. Not in every instance to be sure, but the great majority of the time.

Significant improvements have been made in employee-supervisor and management-union relations, as well as in product quality and operational efficiency. Also, there is now greater cooperation and more open communications. And there are already signs that those involved in EI projects feel their jobs are more meaningful because of such involvement.

Employees and managers alike are starting to ask themselves, "Why did we wait so long to do this?"

Ford credits its 18-month-old EI concept as a contributing factor in the quality improvement on every single line of its 1981 vehicles. New vehicle owners surveyed report that "things gone wrong" on 1981 Fords, Lincolns, and Mercurys have declined substantially. Customer satisfaction with 1981 model trucks has risen appreciably also.

While the company and the union do not attempt to pinpoint savings, EI is clearly paying off for employees, for the union, and for the company. "But there's a certain risk in examining the EI process with a balance sheet approach," warns Pestillo. "That sort of viewpoint tends to overemphasize the short range. There's a tendency then to expect quick results. EI is really a long-range concept. Its real value is what it does for attitudes and motivation over the long haul."

And while the EI process is not intended as a substitute for the grievance procedure, or for collective bargaining, both company and union officials point out that the number and level of shop-floor complaints and grievances have declined — considerably in some locations — as a result of the improved relations that EI fosters.

"We found there is a common ground that doesn't have to be negotiated," says Bill Stevenson, bargaining unit chairman for the UAW local union at Ford's front suspension plant in Sterling Heights, Michigan.

"On the whole, progress so far has been impressive," Pestillo told *Manage-*

ment Review. "Over the last 18 months, EI projects have gotten underway at nearly 45 Ford locations. We hope to have 90 by the end of 1982."

LEADERSHIP FOR THE EFFORT

Pestillo and Ephlin are co-chairmen of the UAW-Ford National Joint Committee on Employee Involvement (NJCEI) set up to provide leadership and guidance for the overall EI effort. They and other top Ford and UAW officials are currently visiting Ford locations around the country to promote and encourage the development of EI. In addition, the company has issued a policy statement directing that all employees be encouraged to become involved in and provided the opportunity to contribute to the success of the company. This has been followed up by strong letters of support from operating executives.

Where there is interest in starting an EI project, members of the NJCEI provide guidance and visit the plant to assist the local managers and union officials. Assistance is also available from other representatives of Ford's labor relations and personnel and organization staffs and from members of the UAW's National Ford Department.

"We provide suggestions and support," explains Ernest J. Savoie, director of Ford's Labor Relations Planning and Employment Office, "But we do not tell them how to run their projects."

It is up to the managers and union leaders at each location to tailor their EI activity to suit their individual needs. Of nearly 45 EI projects now under way, no two are exactly the same.

THREE BASIC APPROACHES

There are basically three types of approaches to EI within Ford. The first emphasizes problem-solving groups. These usually are comprised of a small number of employees who are engaged in the same type of work and who meet periodically to solve work-related problems that the group has identified and assigned a priority.

EI quality circles, although they are also involved in problem solving, stress the use of more formal quality control and statistical techniques.

EI team-building groups are set up to accomplish common objectives. These groups work at improving group functions so that group objectives may be achieved. They focus on the interpersonal as well as on the analytical aspects of problem solving — improving communications, for example.

When a Ford plant decides to start an EI project, the first step is to set up a local union-management steering committee. This committee plans, implements, guides, and monitors the EI activity at that location.

A steering committee usually consists of plant management representatives and key local union officials. Typically, it includes, for example, the UAW unit chairman and bargaining committee members, the plant manager, and representatives of the quality control and industrial relations departments. Experience has shown that the most effective EI steering committees consist of three or four representatives from management and three or four from the union. Larger committees proved to be slow and unwieldy. Smaller committees, it is felt, may be inadequate to ensure that differing views are heard and that varied experience is available for overall guidance.

The steering committee identifies potential projects and objectives. It usually undertakes a diagnosis to determine what types of EI activities are most appropriate to the organization. This may involve gathering relevant information about the organizational environment through discussions, interviews, opinion surveys, and performance indicators. The diagnosis may also identify the factors that might facilitate or impede the attainment of EI objectives and provide data that can be used later to evaluate the effectiveness of the EI effort.

As a general rule, initial EI activity is limited to carefully selected pilot groups confined to specific departments or work areas, and it is gradually expanded from there. The pace of expansion is determined solely by the local steering committee.

Before any pilot project is started, extensive training and general education is required for all participants. The type and amount of training is largely determined by the results of the steering committee's determination of the particular type of E1 activity, such as problem-solving groups or team building, to be undertaken.

TRAINING UNION AND MANAGEMENT LEADERS

Education and training for the union leadership and management are usually directed at a participative philosophy and improved interpersonal and communication skills. Supervisors are trained in participative problem-solving methods, group leadership techniques, and employee performance feedback skills. Training for shop-floor employees focuses on group problem-solving methods and problem identification-solution presentation skills.

Once an EI project is underway, it is monitored by the steering committee. The committee must make certain that the expectations of the employee problem-solving teams are realistic. If the groups need any special information or assistance, from engineers, cost analysts, or maintenance personnel, for instance it is made readily available to them.

Employee groups report their progress, make recommendations to management, and publish — in conjunction with the steering committee — the results of their activities. In reviewing the EI projects, steering committees may consider such matters as: Do employees actually feel this experience is useful to them? Are both employee and organizational problems being addressed? Are the solutions developed by the problem-solving groups being implemented? Are these solutions making an impact on the work situation? Is communication and cooperation between employees, union, and management improving?

If necessary, projects are modified and revitalized to maintain or increase employee interest and participation and ensure success. Some projects may need an extended period of time to show results.

The NJCEI expects that some groups will encounter roadblocks or temporary setbacks or that some proposed solutions may not be practical. This can happen because the cost of a proposed solution may be prohibitive or it may adversely affect other operations. In such cases, the group is told why its solution cannot be accepted or must be modified. The NJCEI also believes that problems and failures should be used as valuable learning opportunities for the groups. Such experience can give a project fresh insight and impetus.

"This has been one of my best learning experiences of my 24 years with Ford," exults one shop-floor employee, a member of a group that managed to solve a nagging machine-operation problem.

The National Committee is also concerned about creating the right climate in which EI can grow. "Much of our planning and hard work right now has to do with changing the attitudes of everyone concerned — managers, employees, supervisors, and union officials," says Pestillo.

"AWARENESS" CONFERENCES

Numerous "awareness" conferences are being held to brief managers and supervisors on the concepts and principles of EI. "This is not just another management gimmick," Pestillo recently told a meeting of Ford plant managers. "It's a totally new and different way of managing and doing business. Unless we all understand that, believe me, EI won't work."

"Our employees are listening to us. Watching us. And giving us a chance to prove ourselves."

"I never thought they would let me work with employees in solving shopfloor problems," comments one Ford supervisor, "But just the opposite is happening. They are now encouraging me to do it."

Employees, too, are encouraged by the change in supervisors' and managers' attitudes. "It's about time we recognized the need for each other," says Ron J. Neppi, an employee at Ford's Twin Cities Assembly Plant in St. Paul, Minnesota.

"The company is letting the workers feel they are part of the team," comments an employee at Ford's Lorain, Ohio, Assembly Plant. "Working together, we're making cars that we are all proud of."

And the UAW's National Ford Department under Ephlin's active leadership has also been holding awareness and learning sessions for local union representatives and officials. Late last year, for example, over 150 local union leaders and Ford managers gathered at the union's Walter and May Reuther Educational Center at Black Lake, Michigan, to participate in a joint conference on Employee Involvement. At UAW regional meetings throughout the country, EI is on the agenda as well.

EI project teams are tackling problems in the area of scrap downtime, work procedures and arrangements, and housekeeping.

At the Saline, Michigan, plastics plant, for example, one problem solving group investigated ways to eliminate instrument panel defects and recommended several actions that affected not only product quality but the work environment as well. The group suggested — and management agreed — that operators on a certain operation should use hand tools, that lights should be installed on presses, and that equipment cleaning should occur more frequently.

At the Ford Truck Plant, near Avon Lake, Ohio, a problem-solving group tackled a problem of water leaks in a certain section of the vehicle and determined that changes in the application of weld sealer would improve subsequent welding operations. Incorporating the group's recommendation resulted in improved first-run capability at the plant.

At Ford's aluminum-casting plant in Sheffield, Alabama, an employee problem-solving team focused its efforts on reducing transmission case scrap caused by off-location die cast machine slides. As a result of improvements recommended by the team, made on the control machine, foundry scrap was reduced by between 4 and 5 percent. The result is an annual saving of $12,000. Extending the recommendation to nine other die cast machines has the potential for annual savings of over $100,000.

At Ford's engine plant in Lima, Ohio, various manufacturing and assembly areas have accomplished several days' production with zero defects. One day all of the manufacturing and assembly areas succeeded in building 2,400 engines with zero defects. This means that every one of the operations was performed perfectly the first time with no repairs necessary.

"Our reject level has improved by 500 percent since EI began," reports George Dalton, a production manager at Lima. "The real credit for this improvement must go to the employees," he asserts. "They're really getting behind this program."

THE BIG DIFFERENCE: COOPERATION

"Cooperation. That's the big difference around here," declares one production employee. "When a problem comes up, we work together to solve it. There's no finger pointing or buck passing anymore. It's no longer your problem or my problem. It's *our* problem."

One reason for the improvement in cooperation, not surprisingly, is the more open communication between supervisors and employees. "We've always had two-way communication here," says Dan Camper, the local union president at the Lima Engine Plant. "But now, it means much more than it used to."

A departmental manager at another plant puts it this way: "The more we talk, the more we understand each other. That's a big step forward."

Norm Slonsky, the bargaining unit chairman at Ford's Chesterfield Trim Plant near Mt. Clemens, Michigan, credits EI "for bringing dignity" to the employees.

Lou Borges, bargaining unit chairman at the San Francisco Parts Distribution Center agrees. "The important thing is that it (EI) makes the worker on the floor feel like somebody."

As part of the EI effort, last October, as an experiment, nine supervisors, two general foremen, and the warehouse manager were taken away from their place of work for a day. "I think management was hoping the place would fall to pieces without them," Borges says. In fact, every employee showed up on time, left to take their break on time, and returned on time.

Often it is the little things that are important.

At Ford's Indianapolis plant, one employee group started out by working out all the individual needs of employees, down to the location and number of light bulbs in the work areas. In another section of the plant, workers had tried for years to get a three-wheeled cycle to move parts from one area to another. The parts, weighing 15 to 20 pounds each, were carried by hand. "We could never get approval for a bike," recalls one employee. "We couldn't even get the supervisor to submit a request form."

At a problem-solving group meeting, it took just one word. The next day a requisition for a tricycle was submitted, signed, and approved.

Comments Bill Skaggs, local union president at the Indianapolis plant, "What we've been telling Ford Motor Company for years, — listen to us — is finally happening."

"Until now, the company has been putting more emphasis on maintaining a machine than on maintaining an employee," says Skaggs, at one time a vociferous critic of Ford's management style.

For Skaggs and many others like him, Employee Involvement hopefully represents only the start — the start of a never-ending process that will permit employee input into decisions affecting them and their jobs. "I like to think that what we are doing at Ford is as forward thinking as anything taking place between management and labor in any corporation in America today," says UAW's Ephlin.

PARTICIPATIVE MANAGEMENT AT MOTOROLA — THE RESULTS
Walter B. Scott

The decline in our nation's productivity didn't happen overnight. In fact, significant changes in employee attitudes that have affected productivity began to occur during the mid-1960s. Unfortunately, they took place so gradually that they went largely unnoticed. But now we are feeling the full impact of these changes, and they are sending shock waves through the corridors of corporate power.

How have employee attitudes changed? First, and perhaps most importantly, workers are less tolerant of dictatorial authority. At the same time, workers' expectations are rising. This is a result of generally higher levels of knowledge and understanding acquired not only from higher levels of formal education, but also through the influence of television and travel. And, another significant change has been in the matter of employee rights, primarily as a result of equal rights legislation.

The question facing management is: Have we changed our management style to meet the new demands of the workplace? The evidence indicates that in most companies we have not. A recent Gallup Poll conducted among a cross section of employees in different industries suggests that there are great opportunities for improving productivity in the workplace through improved managerial sensitivity to employees and their needs and expectations. Here are some of the more revealing of the study findings:

– Fifty-three percent of those polled named workers' attitudes as one of the areas of possible change that could bring about a major improvement in productivity.

– Forty-four percent of those interviewed say they think a lot about work changes that could improve their company's performance, and 65 percent consider it likely that their suggestions would be adopted if they were solicited.

– Seventy percent believe their fellow workers are enthusiastic or somewhat enthusiastic about doing a good job for their companies.

– Eighty-four percent say they would work harder and do a better job if they were involved in the decisions affecting their work.

– Sixty-five percent believe that their hard work makes — or could make — a big difference to the success of their organization.

– Eighty-six percent are somewhat or very concerned about providing top quality goods and services.

– Eighty-eight percent recognize the importance of quality to the customer.

– Seventy percent agree that improved productivity would reduce the rate of inflation.

THE ROLE OF MANAGEMENT

The results of the survey, then, indicate that most employees are eager to function effectively and productively. They want to be proud of the quality of goods and services they produce. But they also want to participate in the decisions that affect their work.

Unfortunately, many managers tend to view labor as a cost of doing business rather than as a valuable resource. Perhaps one of the key reasons for the success of Japanese managers is that they do not share this attitude. They value their employees and work with them as a critical resource. In their view, when employees are not as productive as they should be, it is because management has abdicated its proper role.

Measurement Dimension	Points	
	Maximum	Minimum
1. Quality of product	+ 5%	− Unlimited
2. Delivery of product	+ 0%	− Unlimited
3. Housekeeping and safety	+ 0%	− 1%
4. Inventory	+ 0%	− Unlimited
5. Current costs	+ 24%	− 17%
6. Buy-back	+ 12%	0%

Figure 1. Six Costs Subject to Employee Influence.

Think about it. If you are in a restaurant and you receive poor service, who is really to blame? In restaurants that are run properly, the owner or manager is generally highly visible. He is there to support his employees and to ensure that they are operating as they should. The point is that managers must be dedicated and involved. If they don't care about their business, why should their subordinates?

Employees, for the most part, rate their company on the basis of what they see occurring — in their line of sight. The CEO may write a very fine policy paper on human relations, have it printed in an elegant, expensive booklet, embellish it with his picture and signature, and circulate it to all his employees. But if the company's employees see departmental politics and observe capricious, arbitrary actions on the part of department heads, they won't believe the president and they will lose respect for the organization. In fact, the gulf between what management says it believes in and what employees actually see in management behavior is often responsible for employees seeking the protection of unions.

Corporations do not generate money — they earn it from their customers. Rather than chasing around the world after cheap labor, American corporations should be tapping the intelligent labor they have in the United States, giving it the advanced tools and technology it needs to produce effectively, and working with it cooperatively. It isn't so much what you pay per hour that determines unit costs, it is what you accomplish in each hour.

I shudder when I read in the business press about Company X laying off 500 people because the company's costs are too high. The company's real problem lies in its inability to attract customers. That company's management needs to tap the skill, intelligence, enthusiasm, and participation of the firm's labor force — including the sales force. Only if management and labor work together effectively will they be able to generate necessary customer demand at profitable prices.

If you provide the best customer quality, the best on-time delivery, and the best prices, you stand a good chance of maximizing your profits. Discuss the importance of quality, delivery, and price with your employees. As consumers, they are all expert customers and they will understand what you are talking about.

PARTICIPATIVE MANAGEMENT

Because management at Motorola feels so strongly about the need for cooperation between management and labor, and about management's proper role, the company developed a participative management program that currently taps the talent of about 12,000 employees. And the company's goal is to apply the program on a companywide basis.

Our trial project involved a plant with 1,200 employees. The plant manager was instructed to operate the plant as if he owned it and were spending his own money. We held many orientation sessions so everyone would be clear about the program. Once the program was operating successfully in the first plant, we moved on to another. This is how the program has grown and spread.

At the start of the program, after lengthy discussions and reviews of cost reports and trends, we identified six areas of costs employees can influence (see Figure 1). Using the line-of-sight theory — that is, what you can see you can affect — we then organized manufacturing production teams structured so that employees could see the results of *their* efforts. As the next step, we began to post ratings of the six elements of cost — the results — each week, in each area.

We organized a steering committee for the total facility to handle policy matters. This committee was comprised of representative executives. At the same time we organized an operating committee that meets to discuss cost trends and opportunities for improvement. Employees from all departments are appointed to this committee. We also developed smaller departmental teams that discuss opportunities for improvement and changes that should be made. Our participative management program is introduced in three phases: (1) the make-ready phase, (2) a simulated trial, or shakedown, run, and (3) the full program. These phases are PERT charted so that we are able to monitor progress.

In our experience, productivity improvements begin to occur during Phase One of the program's implementation. But, we believe it is vitally important to remain in constant communication with the employees, discussing, as the program unfolds, the importance of the customer and of producing at competitive costs. When we move on to Phase Three, the incentive phase of our program, we share the savings with our employees. It is important to understand, however, that this is an *eventual* goal. Before a group, which may consist of 100 to 200 people, earns its first dollar of bonus, our costs must be acceptable. Thereafter, as the group increases its earnings, it benefits — and our unit costs continue to drop.

Again, communication is essential to the program's success. One device we have used successfully is what we call the ''I Recommend'' system. In every team area, we have two large bulletin boards. One board posts the week's results;

the other is for the "I Recommend" system. Anybody in the group can write a suggestion on it related to quality, costs, the operation of his or her machinery, in-plant services, and so on. The suggestion may be anonymous or not, as the employee chooses. All recommendations are numbered and posted for everyone to see. We follow up on all of them.

We are required to post an answer on the bottom half of the "I Recommend" form within 72 hours. This is challenging and demanding, but it works. This is how you can show your employees that you are really interested in fixing the die, the machine, materials support, or basic processes. Our engineers have been amazed at the brilliance of a number of the recommendations. We feel that because we are treating our employees as a resource, they are reacting accordingly.

THE POSITIVE RESULTS

The results of our participative management program have outstripped our expectations; they certainly justify our continued faith in the concept. Here are highlights of our results:

• We are getting a minimum of 25 percent more output from our equipment, which improves our return on net assets. In many instances, output has been up by much higher percentages.
• The spirit of cooperation between employees has soared. They have extended themselves to new members of the production team and encouraged high team standards. Supervisors report that employees are learning faster and better. They also report major improvements in safety and cleanliness.
• When vacancies have occurred in an operation, the employees often have said, "We will share the work — you don't have to hire or replace that person." As supervisors have been transferred, teams have volunteered to work without a replacement. As we have reduced our operating budget, we have realized that our old system required more supervision simply because supervisors were doing many things employees now do for themselves.
• Cooperation between shifts has improved greatly. Employees leave notes for each other, overlap shifts to keep the equipment running constantly, and generally are demonstrating managerial behavior.
• Lunch breaks and rest periods are adhered to. Peer influence "self-polices" the team.
• Turnover is decreasing, presumably because jobs are more interesting and meaningful. Many employee grievances have been aired and corrected.
• Under participative management, weak supervisors have great difficulty covering their tracks. We have had to make some changes. The system is very demanding, but so are our competitors.
• Because the system is inherently a more open one, we are experiencing less trouble with shopfloor politics.
• Problems emerge quickly.

What is the greatest obstacle to participative management? Most managers think it is the employees, but that isn't true. It's the difficulty most managers have in changing from a dictatorial management style to one that is based on participation, which requires the ability to listen. Early in our effort to introduce participative management, we found we had to retrain our managers before we could make significant progress. This is a demanding program. But it has helped surface many problems, all of which require attention. And if we are to remain a top competitor, these problems demand answers — in 72 hours.

HEWLETT-PACKARD'S QUALITY TEAM PROGRAM
Ross Redeker

Quality teams at HP are a synthesis of several related concepts, including "Quality of Work Life (QWL)," Participative management, the Japanese (Quality Control Circle) philosophy and, most important, the "HP Way!" The "HP Way" is our company's interpretation of participative management and, since teamwork is an integral part of it, we felt it worth while to name our circles Quality Teams (QT's). It's very appropriate to retain the word "Quality", also, since at HP employees assume responsibility for the quality of their work, their work environment, their professional growth, and their personal development. Why then, does HP even need the QT process if it already has the "HP Way"? The answer is that even though we know what things we should be doing and know certain principles, we do not always have a vehicle to put them into practice in a way that is totally congruent. QT's at HP are such a vehicle and can directly contribute to the desired objectives: improved employee morale, development or job satisfaction, better communications, and increased quality and productivity of our products and services.

There are two basic assumptions at HP underlying the QT process: 1) People take more pride and interest in work when allowed to make contributions which influence decisions about their work, and 2) The people closest to a problem are in the best position to make decisions about that problem and to take the necessary action. I think another very basic reason for the advent of the QT ethic at HP is the nationwide growing emphasis on quality, clearly focused in June 1980, when the NBC white paper, "If Japan can why can't we?" burst on the scene. Our company's quality has generally been thought of as well above average since its founding days, over 40 years ago. A renewed emphasis has gripped us, however, as more of our top managers have realized that high quality results in lower costs, greater sales, higher profit, and continued success in our highly competitive market places.

Now, for some details of the HP program: The structure at a typical manufacturing facility includes a steering committee, made up a cross-section of all activities within it; part-time facilitators, usually one per team and often middle managers; team leaders who are for the most part first line supervisors; 3 to 15 members per team (all volunteers); and an overall coordinator for the entire facility. This coordinator is typically a part-timer but in a growing number of our facilities a full-time Quality Team Training Manager is being appointed by the division manufacturing manager to perform the QT function, along with other technical duties.

This leads us into the QT training topic, which is the most important one in any company's quality circle program. Our Corporate training department has provided a 2-day course for leaders and facilitators, since June 1980, and then these people train more of their own within a particular facility. The content of the course covers these key areas:

- Working in groups
- Framework for problem analysis
- Cause-and-effect analysis
- Data collection
- Data analysis
- The Pareto principle
- Making presentations

Our Corporate training course claims the following as necessary, but not all inclusive, elements for a successful QT program:

- Voluntary membership
- Supportive and involved management
- Member training
- Problems are identified and solved by team members
- Members work as a team
- Activities must be related to members' work area
- People building philosophy

To the extent that the growth described in the next section of this paper is a direct result of HP following all these steps carefully, our program has been an eminent success.

HISTORY AND GROWTH OF QT's AT HP

Quality Control Circles were started in Japan in 1962 after 12 years of intense training in quality techniques of their engineers and managers. After that time they realized their foreman and workers were not up to speed with this philosophy, so THEY invented QCC to solve this educational problem. About ten years later (1972?) the first HP exposure began with the hosting of some Japanese Quality Circle winners by the Loveland Instrument Division. Wayne Rieker, then at Lockheed, got them started in the U.S. in 1974; now, over 750 companies and many more service oriented functions, even school systems, have joined this movement. Some skeptics are claiming that U.S. companies are blindly jumping on the Quality Circle bandwagon, not realizing that a strong foundation of training in the quality arts is a prerequisite to success.

This may be true at some companies, but not HP! We will not pay homage to the doomsdayers who proclaim that no thought has been given to the differences between the culture of Japanese and American employees, and that quality circles in the US will go the way of other fads, like Hula-hoops. HP has the advantage of starting QCC's before they were even introduced in the US. This paradox can be explained by the fact that our division in Japan, YHP, initiated QCC's in 1973 and now has 175 circles. Contrary to the typical trend of nearly all circles in a Japanese company forming in production areas, 62% of YHP's circles today are in non-production work areas, primarily sales and service. This emphasis reflects the fact Ken Sasaoka, our YHP president, has targeted to win a Deming award in 1982. His unusual thrust into the unchartered waters of administrative circles may just be the edge he needs to win it.

Our history with QTs overseas at HP has been in three phases; the early start at YHP, a strong effort in Southeast Asia at our two factories in Penang and Singapore commencing in early 1979, and most recently, a grass roots movement in Europe. The time lag in Eruope and other factories and sales offices outside the US can be attributed to the necessity to translate all of the training materials.

The recent domestic history of QTs at HP will be the subject of most of the remainder of this paper. Four divisions, three located in Colorado and one in the San Francisco Bay Area, all started teams at the same time in late 1978 and early 1979. One division utilized an outside consultant; one embarked on the QWL concept; a third piggy-backed on another's outside training, then went their own way; and the fourth wrote their own course material. This last is worth mentioning for at least two reasons: their original training materials became solid input for our corporate leader/facilitator course in 1980, and the author of that original course, Fred Riley, is now president of IAQC, the leading US society dedicated to the QC philosophy. Also one of Fred's first teams was the star of a 17 minute video tape made at our Corporate TV studios, entitled "Quality Circles at HP." (Note: the title was generalized to QC since, in true HP fashion, not all facilities use the QT name, and because the tape is for sale outside HP and would be somewhat confusing with QT in the title.)

With that background, we are proud to announce we now have nearly 550 quality worldwide, of which well over 300 are in the US. We cannot state the number with more accuracy, because we have yet to implement a system for collecting the rapidly changing statistics. Also, we prefer to emphasize the "Quality" of our QTs rather than the quantity. A closer look at HP's QT growth in the U.S. shows a jump from 15, or so, in June of 1980 to about 220 teams in June of 1981, with another 20-30 per month now. A more interesting discussion relates to the phases of this growth, defined as follows:

1. Initiation — presentations to management, training of leaders/facilitators, setting up steering committees (usually 3 months to a year).
2. Training — Team selection and training in the pilot phase (approx. one year).
3. Development — Expansion from pilot phase, movement beyond production to administrative areas, retraining in quality techniques, like Statistical Quality Control (perhaps two more years).
4. Mature — the "self actualization" state, in Maslow terms, where competition as a form of recognition, for example, is used. Only two divisions at HP, in my opinion, have reached this lofty state.

All this activity in the past 2-3 years did not just happen by chance. What happened, to quote a quality sage this time, was that HP experienced a series of "breakthroughs" (Dr. Juran's term for a step function of improvement). The first, and most important, occurred in mid-1979 when Ray Démeré, HP's Vice-President of Manufacturing Services, took a group of Quality, and Manufacturing managers to Japan to view first hand that country's revolution in Quality. They came back inspired to try out some of the innovations observed, including QCC, automation and "on-time inventory". The next synergistic event was in mid-

1980, the broadcast of the aforementioned NBC white paper. Over 50 copies permeated our many divisions and sensitized all levels of employees with the necessity to think "Quality".

This year the pace accelerated! In March, our Company Quality Department brought out Dr. W. Edwards Deming, one of the two quality pioneers (Juran was the other) to talk to our top management about the necessity for training everyone in the concepts of statistical quality control. Secondly, and more germaine to the growth of our QT's at HP, we held our first HP International Quality Team Conference in June, at the Loveland division. The combination of these events has served to focus on not only the usefulness of Quality Teams, but also toward more quality awareness at all levels.

MANAGEMENT STRUCTURE

Today, the organization of QTs at HP is somewhat different than most companies and is still evolving. The quality team movement has been informally sanctioned. There has been a "bottoms up" acceptance of the opportunities publicized about this activity. Additionally, top management has listened to a number of QT presentations, and have gone on record as approving them. Some divisions have appointed a full-time coordinator, as mentioned earlier, and this is perceived as a temporary management training assignment. The main support for the QT movement at HP has come from a sort of a triad management consortium, consisting of the manufacturing areas (the primary end user or customer), the personnel/training areas (the teacher for behavorial techniques), and the quality areas (the teacher for quality technology). Because of this split responsibility, some of the founding fathers of QTs got together in January 1981 and formed a steering committee, whose stated purpose was to, "nurture the development of Quality Teams by operating as a QT to identify, analyze and resolve concerns of Communication and Coordination for HP managers and QT members." Starting in the San Francisco Bay Area, at HP corporate headquarters, we chose to call ourselves $BA(QT)^2$, for Bay Area Quality Team Quality Team, and have met monthly after we initially brainstormed over 150 concerns for the future of QTs at HP. The main work has been accomplished in sub-committees, which have covered additional facilitator training, the addition of statistics modules to our training courses, and a continued concern about maintaining the long-term momentum of the activity. Also, we have small groups planning for our 2nd annual QT conference in Palo Alto, next June, and we are developing a QT data base.

RECOGNITION

As we mentioned earlier, under the History/Growth section, recognition is an important ingredient of the long-term momentum recipe. After several years of operation one division, located in Loveland, Colorado, decided to host an international HP conference for all our QTs. This was held in June, 1981, and featured competition between 13 of their 45 teams there. The other 40 or so entities watched in awe as the local TV station came in to film them while they conducted their 15-minute mini-presentations. The winner, a team of five IC technicians, aptly named "Quality by Night", since they work the swing shift, gave us a very professional 35mm slide talk on how they statistically improved one of the critical processes in their Integrated Circuit fabrication shop. One of the runner-up teams was made up of six ladies whose team was called "Rant 'N' Rave," and whose project was to improve the quality of 4 front panels on similar type instruments made at that location. Our division in Japan has long used competition and this September they are sending the leaders of their four top teams to the US as a form of award. In addition, these teams will be visiting our facilities here, sharing their knowledge with our newer and less experienced QTs.

Another powerful form of recognition is publicity. The Corporate Training Department that conducts the two day training course for leaders, has available a small brochure to briefly describe our program at HP. Our company quality department issues a quarterly "Company Quality News" letter to spread the quality gospel among our 62,000 employees, 2000 quality professionals, and 5000 others involved with quality teams. In addition, most of our 50 or more divisions issue their own newsletters, many of which include quality, and regularly provide status of the QT programs there. It's also refreshing to see how innovative our various divisions have become in involving their middle managers in the QT process and then publicizing the fact in their internal house organs. For instance, one of our computer divisions has a policy, formed by their steering committee, that their facilitators will come only from the middle manager ranks and that each will only serve one team and that cannot be in their own work area.

A final area of recognition is more indirect. This is the activity of our people outside HP, both in connection with technical societies and with our vendors. First, Fred Riley, mentioned earlier, was elected President of IAQC, which stands for International Association for Quality Circles, and which is a relatively new society dedicated to furthering the QC movement. Also, several of our more active coordinators have presented papers at various functions, all of which helps recognize HP as one of the top companies in the US for quality circles.

Another facet of our activities outside HP is the recent Quality Team training sessions we have had with several vendors who supply us with raw PC boards. These firms recognized the potential gains in employee morale and improved quality of their product, so we are investing in a few "seed" projects.

FUTURE

Measurement of results of our QT program has not been a big issue, although we can see in the more advanced divisions that the results of their projects more and more are stated in monetary terms. (It's an interesting corollary of this measurement point that most of HP's QTs start out with "frustration" type projects, and then after a year or so of operation get into more "meaty" problems to solve.) The key area for the future is training, in my opinion, both in the behavioral skills as well as the analytical. Since my function covers the latter, I will dwell on our plans here next. Although our present 2 day leader course is being expanded to three days, the original one hour session for data collection and analysis remains intact. This is because the immediate need was to provide more training for facilitators, and primarily in the behavioral and motivational area. Therefore, our company quality department, working with several key quality and QT people, is developing a multi-module course, each segment two to four hours, which will train team members in production areas, primarily, to be conversant with basic statistical concepts including the capability to develop their own control charts. The list of modules follows:

1. Problem solving process
2. Basic mathematics and use of calculators
3. Data collection
4. Graphical plots
5. Basic statistics
6. Control charts

More advanced modules, for those in supporting roles to the QTs, will cover:

1. Applying control charts
2. Advanced statistics
3. Experimental design

As mentioned before, a data base of information about the status of QTs at HP and the projects solved to date, will be a valuable tool for aiding the future growth of our quality teams. In true HP tradition an EDP manager, now deeply immersed in the QT process in his division, has stepped forward and volunteered to set up such a data base. (We will use our own HP 3000 computer for collection and our new laser printer to provide reports of where we stand.)

CONCLUSION

Finally, it should be clearly stated that QTs are used at HP as only one thread in the fabric of participative management; in fact, they are most successful when they are used as part of a Quality Improvement Program (QIP) in a division.

CIRCLES
Dian Sprenger

As we enter the room, the 12 who are already seated shift their chairs to make space for two more. Conversations break off gradually until there is silence, and eyes turn curiously to me. The leader answers their unspoken question: "We have a visitor in our Circle today. She wants to learn more about what we do here each Thursday afternoon so she can tell other hospitals about it. She'd like to ask you some questions. Is that okay?

Around the Circle, the heads nod approval. The faces refelct a multitude of experiences and expectations, but the uniforms suggest a commonality of purpose. They are housekeeping employees, assigned to the surgical suites specifically. They're a team, but they just began to learn the full meaning of the word a few months ago when they volunteered to be members of a Quality Control Circle.

Quality Control Circle — the Japanese management technique which takes so much credit for the high level of productivity and worker satisfaction in that country's workforce. Will it work for American hospitals as well? It is, and it does — or so it seems — at Barnes Hospital in St. Louis where the technique was adopted almost a year ago.

There's an old saying among farmers here in the Midwest about the best chicken feed in the world not being worth a plugged nickel if the chickens won't eat it. So, yes, I had some questions for members of this housekeeping Quality Control Circle.

Why did you volunteer to be a part of this Circle?

"It sounded like a good idea, so I thought I'd take a chance."

"I had a problem that I wanted to communicate to others."

"I thought I might learn something."

"I thought it would be good to get all our minds working in the same direction — to solve problems."

"I wanted to find solutions to our work place problems."

"I wanted to know what was going on . . . and to be a part of the solution."

How has this Circle changed your attitude about Barnes Hospital as a place to work?

"When we brainstorm, we have a multitude of ideas, and we can put the best ones to work . . . that's really it, that *we* can put *our* ideas to work. I never had that feeling before we had the Circle."

"In our Circle, we not only get to know each other better, we also talk to department heads and get to know them. They *listen* to us and show an interest in us."

"I've learned that our supervisors are interested in us — in *helping* us. They sit and talk with us, and they are working with us to accomplish something."

"I've come to believe that we can make a difference. This Circle makes me aware of my part in making this hospital a nice place to work."

"So many people said nothing could be done . . . but something can be done. We can make a better tomorrow."

This Circle of housekeeping employees has been working for a number of weeks on an employee safety problem which they had lived with unhappily for years, believing nothing could be done about it: frequent puncture injuries due to handling discarded needles in the cleanup process. Soon, they will implement a plan to reduce such injuries; then, they will identify another workplace problem and work toward its solution.

Rusti Moore, director of education and training at Barnes Hospital, is responsible for the Quality Circles (QC) program — not only its day-to-day coordination, but also its original introduction to management as a worthwhile, workable concept. In the spring of 1980, she attended a local workshop dealing with the ecology of work. "There were a lot of workers there as a part of the program who talked about how 'turned on' to work they had become through Quality Circles. Their unmasked enthusiasm for the concept riveted my attention," she explains. Wayne S. Rieker, a former Lockheed executive, also participated in the workshop; he had visited Japan in the early '70s to study quality control techniques and returned to introduce a system of Quality Control Circles to the production of missiles. Moore, intrigued by what she heard at the workshop and by increasingly frequent mention of such Japanese techniques in the media, talked with several American industries about their experiences with Quality Control Circles.

Convinced that Quality Control Circles were applicable to the health care sector, Moore engaged Rieker, now a consultant in Circles-style management techniques, to make a presentation to the executives of Barnes Hospital. "The keystone of Quality Control Circles is worker involvement in increased productivity and quality," Moore explains. "Barnes' dual emphasis has always been quality patient care and cost-effectiveness, plus, we've always had a decentralized system of management. In other words, the Quality Circles concept fell on fertile ground."

Robert E. Frank, president of Barnes Hospital, made the institutional commitment to proceed with Quality Circles. "We believe people at the delivery edge of health care have a lot of good ideas about how to improve the quality and efficiency of service, but you don't get those ideas unless you actively solicit them. We need a system that allows employees to express their ideas — Quality Circles is such a system," Frank explains.

Realizing that genuine commitment all up and down the organizational chain of command would be critical to the success of Quality Circles, Frank authorized the implementation of QCs on a purely voluntary basis. In other words, if a vice president agrees that QCs are appropirate in the hospital departments within his system, then each department head will have a choice of whether or not to foster the development of one or more QCs. Even within the department, each supervisor has a choice. Those who volunteer will become Circle leaders, and the Circle itself will be composed of volunteers under his supervision. When the opportunity presented itself last winter, some of the vice presidents were eager to try the concept; others took a more cautious "wait-and-see" posture.

At Barnes, eight Quality Circles were formed originally. Five of them were established in departments which parallel industry — dietary, laboratory, housekeeping, security, and education/training. This was done intentionally, Moore says, so they could draw on the past experiences of others. Three additional QCs were formed on nursing units. A handful of hospitals in the United States have implemented QCs, but none other than Barnes have established Circles in nursing divisions. In March 1981, eight additional Circles were formed, and nine more are scheduled for startup in August 1981.

When Barnes launched its QC program, Rieker was hired as a consultant and he conducted the first leader training session and provided training materials. Today, the Barnes Education and Training Department conducts these training sessions. They run three days and give supervisors an orientation and opportunity for actual experience in small-group discussion and problem-solving techniques. "The most important thing we can teach them is to identify not only the problem but also its causes and practical solutions," Moore explains. "Initially," she says, a QC will pinpoint problems quickly, spend too little time collecting data, and end up with a solution which was derived quickly but which may be superficial. Therefore, at training sessions for supervisors, "we underscore the hazard of the too-quick solution." Future QC leaders are taught to encourage a free flow of ideas — brainstorming — before letting the group zero in on a single issue, and to emphasize data-gathering and documentation. They also become familiar with cause-and-effect diagrams, checklists, graphs and other audio-visual tools that can be used to keep discussions on a focused path.

After the three-day training session, the supervisors make a decision. Will they drop out or proceed with establishing a Quality Circle? "The question they have to ask themselves is whether or not they are truly interested in helping people in their area of the hospital solve their problems," says Moore. Once committed, they go back to their people, discuss the concept of Circles, and ask for volunteers. The optimum size of a Quality Circle is 5-12 employees. In more than half of the Circles established at Barnes, there have been too many volunteers, so some Circles must devise a plan for scaling the group down to size. The Circles at Barnes choose their meeting day and generally convene at the same time each week for one hour.

Many of the employees who volunteer for a QC are hesitant initially to speak up in front of a group. "For some of them," Moore explains, "it is the first time in their working lives they have been asked to participate in management decision making. Once they get used to the idea and begin to build confidence in the system, they relax and become involved quite naturally."

One department head admits he had doubts that the Quality Circles would work. Don Braeutigam, director of plant engineering, had served in Japan while in the military. "I know Japan well, and the Japanese people are different," he says. "Their philosophy of raising their children is different. They instill an orientation to obedience and esprit de corps which stays with them throughout their lives. I thought we were such different people that something like Quality Circles might not work here in the U.S., in St. Louis, at Barnes Hospital. But I was mistaken."

Despite his doubts, he was eager to try the concept in his own department. In March, a Circle was formed which includes ten employees in the air conditioning division; 15 employees volunteered originally, though, so they drew names. Braeutigam sees real enthusiasm for the Circle, and he hopes that another Circle will be formed in his department whenever the hospital is ready to expand the program.

The leader for the air conditioning QC had some doubts of his own: "At first, I thought the QC concept was just another gimmick . . . that someone had done a good sales job on administration. But I see why it works now. In the Circle, we start talking, and people have an opportunity to say things that might never be heard otherwise. We pick each other's brains, and we get something accomplished," says Homer Pearson.

The first problem solved by the air conditioning QC was a shift-to-shift communication gap. The problem: a new shift would come on duty and spend time unnecessarily diagnosing problems which had been discovered on the earlier shift, or just trying to figure out what repairs had been made already. Solution: a status board alerts the incoming shift to problem areas and brings them up-to-date on work done by the previous shift. "This was a simple thing which could have been done long ago if we'd just taken the time to think it through," Pearson admits. What will the Circle do next? "We've identified 28 other areas for improvement," Pearson says, "so it looks like our Circle will be busy for quite awhile."

Pearson says he can see advantages of QC all through the hospital. He and the other Circle leaders "brown bag" their lunch one day a week. "It's a time for sharing our successes, but also the problems we encounter in group dynamics. You always leave the lunch period with good ideas on handling various situations that might arise. That lunch period accomplishes a lot more, though; it opens up relationships between departments."

While the conversations of Circle meetings are regarded as confidential, the problems and the solutions being discussed are very public, Moore explains. On the nursing units, for example, QC members post large flip-chart sheets after a meeting, so the entire unit will have a chance to contribute a comment or suggestion.

"Quality Circles have brought us some control over our own destiny," one nurse says. Donna Granda, R.N., associate director for nursing at Barnes, believes that the good feeling nursing personnel derive from QCs helps build morale within nursing divisions. The process and the attitude also reduce barriers to implementation of new policies or procedures. "If the nurses themselves spend time identifying the problem and seeking a solution, and everybody knows what's happening and supports the solution, then resistance is virtually eliminated," Granda says. She also observes that QCs seem to "ease tensions" among the staff members themselves and with supervision. "I support the concept. I like it. I want it to continue. It gives people a sense of accomplishment . . . and it makes our job in management easier," Granda concludes.

What kinds of problems have the nursing QCs tackled? In the cardiothoracic operating room, the Quality Circle — they call themselves "Heart-to-Heart" —

first dealt with a problem which was contributing to low morale: overtime. The nurses resented the long and often unpredictable hours they were working as overtime. Over a period of months, they devised a flexible ten-hour shift, a proposal which they presented to management. Management accepted the plan, and now they are happy with their work schedule because it is their plan, based on their needs.

This is an example of a QC solution going full cycle. Generally, a QC will deal with problems of a nature that can be solved within the division, with the agreement of the supervisor. "Occasionally, a QC will tackle a problem and come up with a solution for which they need higher approval," explains Moore. In such a case, the QC will make a management presentation. "Management clearly has the authority to accept a QC proposal, to request additional information or to reject the proposal. But in every case, they are committed to listen," Moore says. Sometimes management presentations are made, just to report on the progress of the QC, as in the following case.

On the surgical nursing unit, QC members focused their attention on devising a plan for making the best use of personnel during the two hour overlap period when the ten hour shifts change. Duties were not clearly defined during that period, and jobs that might have been done easily with the number of personnel available sometimes were overlooked. As a result of the QC effort, a checklist of duties during the overlap period was developed and put to use. Now, the division can show an increased percentage in performance of those duties.

Enthusiasm for the Circles runs high. "The Circles are working so well that members who may not be scheduled to work on the meeting day will come in anyway for the meeting hour," Granda says. Since staffing varies somewhat from week to week in the nursing divisions, those QCs generally have a larger number of members — 14 or more — so that half or more of the group will always be available. Are there any problems? Yes. "The biggest one is being able to provide the time for people to engage in the Quality Circles activity. This is probably more of a problem in nursing than anywhere else, because of scheduling patterns," Granda admits. Currently, for the three nursing QCs, head nurses are providing coverage for staff personnel during the Circle meetings. "I can see this becoming quite a burden on head nurses if the number of Circles continues to grow," Granda says, "but the benefits of the QC activity are worthwhile, and we'll find a way to nurture them. That's *my* job — to eliminate barriers along the way so the Circles can accomplish what they'd like to."

What about the time investment? Aside from each member of the group committing one hour per week to QC, there is an intricate support system for QC which involves another whole dimension of time commitment. This is the role played by Rusti Moore and her education and training staff. "There are two real keys to successful QCs," Moore says, "One is leadership training, and the other is the ongoing facilitator relationship with each QC." Earlier, we mentioned the three-day training program which each new volunteer Circle leader completes. Before actually starting up the Quality Circle, the leader chooses a facilitator who will serve as a resource person for the group.

Walter Klein, who serves both as an instructor in the leadership course and as a facilitator to a number of QCs, talks about his role as a facilitator. "It's two-fold. First, I serve as a consultant to the Circle leader, providing one-on-one training in leadership skills and helping him work through his personal anxieties or frustrations. Second, I am a consultant to the Circle itself, providing resources, doing continuous training in problem-solving techniques, and providing feedback on the process and focus of the group's activity rather than the content of their deliberations."

So, in addition to the QC participants spending one hour per week, Moore estimates that the QC leader may commit three or four hours per week initially to the activity. Later, as the leader becomes more comfortable and capable in the role, that time commitment will be less, maybe only one hour per week. For the facilitator, the initial time investment per week, per group, is generally four hours. In time, the investment lessens to about 1½ hours. Does that sound like a lot of hours away from work? "Some might say QCs result in lost time," says Bob Frank, "but we believe the time spent in QCs *is time at work* for every employee, *important* work time where they're finding constructive ways to make the rest of their time more productive, more beneficial to the institution and to themselves as individuals and professionals. "What about the jobs these employees would have been doing during that hour?" Frank says, "The employees who are excited about being in a Quality Circle also are conscientious about their work, so maybe they push just a little harder to get their jobs done that day so they can be a part of the Circle."

For hospitals that are contemplating the use of Quality Circles, Rusti Moore has some advice:

SUPERVISION. When a Circle emerges, its leader should be a supervisor. This is important since the Circle's primary objective is to deal with problems which they can solve by themselves. In many instances, the supervisor can say "yes" to the Circle's suggestions and solve the problem immediately.

VOLUNTARISM. Quality Circles give appropriate, positive structure to participative management. For the concept to work, all levels of management need to support it. The system devised by Barnes insures this. At the Circle level, too, it's important to have individual commitment; if employees volunteer, they are professing an interest in solving work-related problems.

OPENNESS. It's important that Quality Circles not become cliques; they serve in the interest of all employees. That is why leaders and facilitators encourage QC members to talk to other employees about the Circle's current concerns, to solicit feedback from other employees.

BURNOUT. Avoid this by starting at a responsible pace. Realize that you need a strong support staff for a hospital-wide system of Circles. If you have only one facilitator, start with only two or three Circles. Remember, in the beginning, it's a one-on-one training process with Circle leaders. The reason Barnes Hospital has been able to move into the QC system so quickly is because they already had 12 trained resource people with the skills needed to work with small-group leaders. Organizations that start on a too-large scale will heat up too fast and burn out before the system has a chance to work.

245

COMMITMENT. Once you start Circles, it's an environment you must be willing to keep up forever.

CONSULTANTS. Don't try to startup Quality Circles with little or no information. Begin with a consultant who has "hands-on" experience; otherwise you can't anticipate the problems. Ask what training materials will be left with the hospital. Good training materials are essential in giving employees a uniform, ongoing orientation to QCs. If you can acquire the materials from a consultant, you will save countless hours of research and development.

Barnes Hospital recently received official designation as a licensee of Quality Control Circles, Inc., Wayne Rieker's company. As such, Barnes staff will be rewriting the training materials to make them fully applicable to the hospital setting. They also will be available to consult with hospitals in developing Quality Circles, both in the initial start-up phase and in the later follow-up stages.

What is the cost of installing a Quality Circle system? To do it right, Moore says, approximately $10,000 to $20,000. Training materials probably will cost an additional $3,500.

What is the return on the investment? Barnes Hospital believes it's still too early to evaluate the dollars and cents return on the Quality Circles program. "There are patient benefits," says Walter Klein. "A lot of them are intangible. Enthusiasm, for instance. When employee morale is up, employee enthusiasm is infectious, and it has a positive impact on patient care. There are employee benefits, too, like greater satisfaction with scheduling and workloads and communication because they are a part of the decision-making process now. And, finally, there are cost benefits to the hospital, as in the case of the nursing division which devised a plan to eliminate overtime work."

Another facilitator in the Barnes Quality Circles program puts it this way: "Hospital employees are starved for recognition. QC goes a long way in providing the communication opportunities they need. In the last few months, I've seen Circle members literally blossom. When that happens over and over again, you know you're onto something good."

BANKING ON HIGH QUALITY
Charles A. Aubrey II
Lawrence A. Eldridge

Quality Control as a well-developed body of theory and techniques has existed since World War II in product manufacturing industries. It is only relatively recently, however, that financial institutions, along with other service industries, have begun to flirt with the formal application of Quality Control along lines defined by the manufacturing model. There are obvious differences between producing physical products and handling financial transactions and these differences complicate the wholesale use of Quality Control tools in banking. Financial transactions must be processed immediately due to their value and, therefore, "delivery date" to the customer is virtually every minute of every hour of every day. Because of the emphasis on timeliness in handling banking transactions, there is little leeway for final inspection prior to delivery of the finished product — the completed transaction.

The time dimension of bank quality becomes even more critical as banking's reliance on computers and on-line, real-time systems becomes pervasive. Transactions are completed instantaneously with little opportunity for human intervention. Giving customers instant access to account information using a terminal in their office or home is the latest wrinkle in service delivery. Thus, the finished product can move directly from the bank's input clerk to the customer. The back office clerk becomes the key determinant of the bank's quality. What's more, a significant portion of our service is personal interaction between bank people — a customer service representative or a banker — and the customer, and it is tough to monitor the quality of this communications process. Finally, the basic nature of our business, with its tradition of responsibility in handling other people's money, always requires extensive financial controls which inherently tend to yield high quality.

In spite of these service complexities and an already high level of quality, in 1979 Continental Bank embarked on a formal quality control program. Several things prompted this development. For one, we were in the throes of decentralizing our operating units from a single operations department, dispersing a variety of high-volume, error-prone functions to a number of relatively autonomous departments. This tended to add impetus to the development of a centralized focus on Quality Control.

Secondly, with our rapid expansion into diverse markets we found ourselves competing actively in a widening geographic marketplace, adding large numbers of new customers and broadening our line of services. This expansion, as well as the aggressiveness of other banks and less regulated nonbanking institutions intruding onto traditional banking turf, created demanding competitive pressures. Also, customer expectations were rising and their demands becoming more insistent for innovative, high quality banking services.

In this period of rapid growth and mounting competitive pressures, the performance of our service delivery systems, which had always been important to us,
moved even closer to center stage. Out of this focus on service quality, one of
the questions that formed was: What is the proper organizational response to this
strategic concern with quality? The most obvious answer was a collective commitment to quality on the part of our entire staff, beginning with top management
and communicated clearly through all levels, expressed in demanding goals and
reflected in the way performance is rewarded. While that has the ring of unassail-
able truth, just what should a large, complex, decentralized and expanding bank
do to give quality that kind of emphasis?

MANAGEMENT SUPPORT

Any organized program to control and enhance quality in a bank requires top
management support. It must take on some of the characteristics of classical
"Quality Control," including the formal structure of a quality control unit itself,
as well as such activities as setting quality standards, measuring conformance to
standards, and reporting to management.

At Continental Bank, the top officers making up the corporate office — chairman of the board, president, and vice chairman — have provided vital support
from the outset, exhibiting a strong periodic involvement in, and concern for
quality by regularly reviewing each department's quality measures, level, trends
and objective (see Figures 1 & 2). In our strategic and annual planning process,
discussion of quality issues, strategy, decisions and measures are required as well
as an assessment of our competitors' thinking and actions in these areas.

A Quality Assurance Division was established in late 1979 as the first step in
institutionalizing the emphasis on the quality of our service. The published mission of the Quality Assurance Division was to assist management at all levels
throughout the corporation in maintaining a consistently high quality of service
in all our activities, and to make every employee keenly aware of the importance
of quality and the customer.

From the onset, our program was firmly rooted in the idea that quality is
everyone's job, that line managers are responsible for managing quality, and that
each employee has a stake in the quality of the part of the bank's service delivery
system in which he or she is involved. Consistent with this philosophy, the objectives of Quality Assurance, and the programs to carry them out, are management
oriented, and are developed and implemented using participative methodology.

GROUP PARTICIPATION

The first major objective of our Quality Assurance unit was to assist management in establishing or updating service quality performance standards and developing monitoring and feedback systems. This is now done through group participation modeled after a technique developed by Professor Everett Adams, Jr.
of the University of Missouri. Each group formed within a work unit is made up
of the first-line supervisor and other key individuals from the section.

SERVICE VOLUME IN ERROR AFFECTING CUSTOMERS
BOND DEPARTMENT

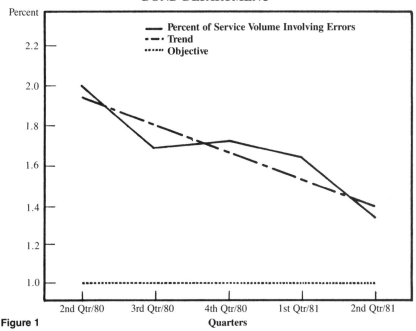

Figure 1

In the first session the group participants receive a general introduction to the concepts of quality, quality control, and quality measurement. The benefits of high quality within a basic quality control system are outlined, and participants are introduced to the methods they will be using in the following sessions to construct their section's quality control systems.

During the second session, services provided or items of output produced in the unit are identified. Then the group — or a subgroup within the section — develops a flowchart depicting the flow of work or functions performed in the unit. Developing a functional flowchart ensures that the group is in agreement as to how the work is performed.

In the third session, the group is asked to develop a list of deviations that can or do occur in the process to mar the quality of the unit's output. Controlled brainstorming is conducted; here, group members offer specific deviations they can identify in the various functions or processing steps making up the unit's work. Once an array of possible quality deviations is identified the participants choose the key quality deviations that significantly affect the customer or require substantial resources to correct.

During the fourth session, participants develop measures for the key quality deviations so that occurrences of the deviations can be recorded, monitored, and reported to management. Definitions of the measures are also developed to ensure a consensus as to the purpose of each measure (see Figure 3).

Results of the group process are reviewed and discussed by all levels of the section's management. Management further defines the relative importance of

AVERAGE INVESTIGATION TURNAROUND TIME
BOND DEPARTMENT

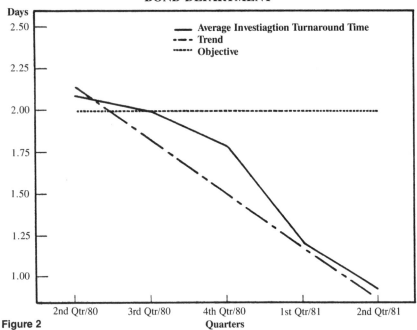

Figure 2

each measure within the Quality Control process by assigning a weight of 1 to 9 to each measure. A larger weight signifies a measure more costly to correct.

The system to capture Quality data is then implemented and feedback consisting of Quality Control reports is provided periodically to management (see Figure 4). Quality levels are monitored for a period of three months and initial performance standards are developed based on the unit's results during that time. The Quality Assurance analyst assigned to assist the unit being studied works with the area's management to formulate these standards. Once standards are in place and performance objectives are communicated down the line, based on measures developed by the people who do the work, a major step has been taken toward enhancing quality.

The group process, accompanied by management's input, provides a communication medium by which everyone is made acutely aware of, and understands, the area's commitment to quality. The participative approach to formulating the quality measures helps assure the success of the Quality program since the employees doing the work are instrumental in developing the means by which the quality of their finished product is evaluated.

The Quality Control Report is only a by-product of the actual process control that takes place. This report is available on a daily, weekly, or a monthly basis (depending on the needs of the recipient) to show actual performance results for each quality measure by work unit and by product across work units. The report helps management identify quality problems as well as track the results of quality improvement activities.

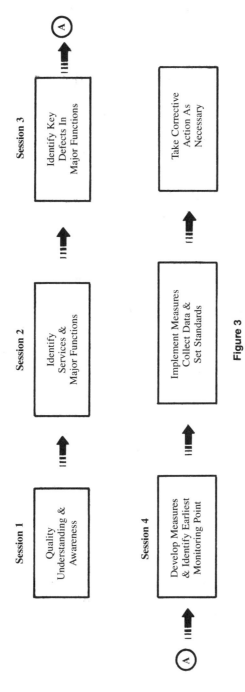

Figure 3

DEVELOPING QUALITY MEASURES

251

QUALITY CONTROL FEEDBACK SYSTEM
Bookkeeping Services

Defect/Control Subject	This Period's Defect Ratio	This Period's Defect %	Last Month's Defect %	Previous Month's Defect %	Standard	Process Capability UCL/LCL	QCI Unweighted	Weight	QCI Weighted
Wrong Account Number/Total Deposits	76/37,936	.2	.3	.1	.1	.4/.08	50		
Non-Endorsed Deposits/Total Deposits	113/37,936	.3	.2	.1	.3	.4/.1	100		
Input Quality									
Missing Items/Total Statements	60/49,538	.12*	.08	.09	.08	.1/.05	67	6	402
Stop Payment Incorrect/Total Stop Payments	6/2,376	.25	.23	.21	.26	.28/.02	104	5	520
Misfiled Items/Total Checks & Debits	24/236,799	.01	.03	.04	.01	.04/.007	100	4	400
Internal Quality Performance								(15)	1,322 88%
Wrong Statement Sent/Total Statements	14/49,538	.03	.03	.04	.02	.06/.01	67	4	268
Missing Items/Total Statements	4/49,538	.008*	.005	.002	.004	.006/.001	50	3	150
Incorrect Adjustment/Total Statements	33/49,538	.07	.08	.07	.06	.09/.05	86	5	430
External Quality Performance								(12)	848 71%
Overall Quality Performance								(27)	2,170 80%

*Out of control

Figure 4

252

All units at Continental Bank which have installed the quality measurement program have increased quality levels since implementation. Some units have cut defects in half and increased performance against standard by 100%, requiring new quality objectives and standards to keep the units' people challenged. Fifteen operating divisions with over 100 sections have gone through this process, and more than 600 quality measures have been developed to date.

QUALITY COST INFORMATION

The second major objective of our Quality Assurance program is to assist managers in developing information regarding the cost of quality for their units. Quality costs are those costs incurred to assure that high quality service is being delivered to our customers (in other words, those costs we incur to meet our customer's expectations and our own corresponding standards).

There are four categories of quality costs: 1) internal failure costs — activities devoted to correcting defects before delivery to the customer; 2) external failure costs — correcting defects or errors after delivery; 3) appraisal costs — determining the level or degree of quality; and 4) prevention costs — activities designed to keep failure and appraisal costs down by taking steps to keep defects or errors from occurring.

Quality cost data are developed using either of two approaches, depending on whether or not work measurement standards have been developed in the area under study. If such standards are already in place, those processes related to quality are identified and cost information developed based on established standards, with adjustments made for differences between actual performance and standard. If work measurement standards are not available, it is necessary to develop a list of all area activities, collect sample times of the quality-related activities, and identify hourly rates of personnel performing the relevant activities. This will provide a basis for identifying direct labor costs associated with quality. Other quality costs then are isolated by analyzing the unit's expense statements and pinpointing expenses of delivering quality services. The resulting quality cost data can then be broken into its component parts of prevention, appraisal, internal, and external failure costs.

Management becomes aware of the magnitude of quality costs, and the data immediately identify activities with significant levels of failure costs as candidates for quality improvement projects. Units with relatively low prevention and appraisal costs might be candidates for increased prevention and appraisal activities to reduce failure costs. We have found in our bank studies that about 50% of our total cost of quality results from failure. Shifting some of that cost to support prevention and appraisal activities should assure an even higher quality service delivered to our customers, ultimately enhancing productivity.

DEVELOPING UNIT EXPERTISE

Quality Assurance's third key objective is to perform quality improvement studies on significant quality weaknesses identified through Quality Control systems, cost of quality studies, or any other means. Consistent with the philosophy that line managers are responsible for managing quality, the Quality Assurance Division helps operating units develop the expertise to perform their own problem identification, analysis, and development of solutions, or at least to participate with the Quality Assurance staff in such projects. Besides being a resource in joint projects, their participation is always necessary for effective implementation of solutions. Sometimes, if line unit resources are unavailable, the Quality Assurance staff will perform an independent study as a service to a user, but such independent efforts are rarely necessary.

Therefore, the Quality Assurance staff is limited in size and provides training for line operating personnel to perform the same techniques it uses to identify, analyze and solve quality problems. In addition, quality control and quality improvement techniques are taught in the bank's Supervisory Development Program provided for all new supervisors.

The fourth broad objective is to develop and implement educational, motivational and communications programs to improve employee performance by increasing awareness of importance of high quality in delivering the bank's services. After much research the process called quality circles was determined to be the most appropriate vehicle to satisfy this objective. Not only do circles meet the specifications of this objective, but they are also in harmony with our overall Quality program philosophy which emphasizes employee participation coupled with management responsibility. Supervisors lead the circles and the appropriate level of management must approve solutions recommended by circles. But employees themselves provide the driving force of fresh ideas.

A by-product of circle activities is that circle members become more aware of their own unit's quality level, so, as active participants in developing suggestions for improvement in their area, they are more committed to proposed changes when they are put in place.

Our definition of a quality circle is a small group of people from the same work unit who meet together on a regular basis to identify, analyze, and solve service and product quality and other problems in their area. Quality circles are based on the simple concept that people will take more pride and interest in their work if they are allowed to make meaningful contributions which influence decisions made about their work. Our general objectives for the quality circles are to: 1) improve communications at all levels, 2) provide employees with an opportunity to solve problems, not just identify them, 3) build team spirit, 4) improve quality and cost awareness, 5) get people more involved in their work, 6) link different levels and functions of the organization to achieve smoother work flow and cooperation, and 7) provide professional and personal growth opportunities for participants. We think of quality circles as process, not a program, which can supplement existing managerial processes.

QUALITY CIRCLE ACTIVITIES

There are 135 quality circles in operation at Continental Bank with an average of eight members per circle. These circles have been implemented in such diverse areas as systems, check processing, operations and accounting.

Each operating unit involved with the circle process determines what individual policies, procedures, and guidelines should be set for its quality circle operation. This is achieved through individual steering committees that review implementation plans and the progress of individual circles.

Allowing all employees the opportunity for circle membership required a network of part-time facilitators who could train supervisors to be group leaders and assist with member training. Representatives from each unit's facilitator group meet on a monthly basis to share experiences, concerns, and insights regarding the circle process.

Supervisors are trained in three-day sessions for circle leadership responsibilities. This training includes the subjects of motivation, group dynamics, communications, as well as eight audio-visual modules which introduce topics such as Pareto analysis, cause-and-effect diagrams and problem prevention. Role-playing, case study exercises, and discussion periods round out the seminars. Four of the audio-visual modules are used to train all employees in a given work unit. After completing this training, the employees are given the opportunity to volunteer for Quality Circle involvement. Those individuals who volunteer are trained in the remaining four modules for which the circle meets once a week. We have found this method to be effective in orienting employees in circle operation, concepts, and responsibilities.

The projects which are worked on by our Circles are selected by the members, although any interested employee, staff person or manager can suggest topics. Examples of project themes include new procedures for handling claims, balancing with the Federal Reserve, a glossary of bank terms, reduction of paper costs and improved handling of customer inquires.

Management support of circle activities has been overwhelming. Unit managers have given immediate and positive attention to circle recommendations. They have committed people and other resources to the process. And most importantly, they are actively involved themselves with individual circles in their area.

While the jury is still out on the success of our quality circle program, we are happy with the results of our first nine months of operation. Our overall participation rate is 65% of potential circle members. Meanwhile, our Quality Control monitoring system allows us to gage the impact of quality circles on a section's quality performance. Productivity measures are already in place which may also be used to monitor the effectiveness of circles.

This then is the Quality Control "system" at Continental Bank designed to assure the delivery of high quality service to our customers (see Figure 5). With corporate office support and participation, management actively carrying out its responsibility for managing quality, and employees effectively assuming responsibility for the quality of their own work, service quality levels are increasing,

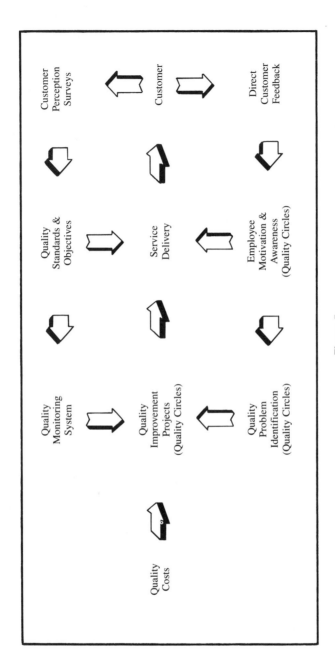

Figure 5

QUALITY CONTROL SYSTEM

256

quality costs are being reduced, and quality improvement projects are being implemented by project teams as well as quality circles. It will take months, even years, to realize the potential of a concerted emphasis on quality throughout the bank, but at least we've taken the first steps and we're banking on success!

QUALITY CIRCLES AT HUGHES AIRCRAFT

Mary T. Kohler and Everett R. Wells

INTRODUCTION

"An enormous potential source of energy — for good, for evil, for apathy or advancement — exists in the interdependencies that modern organizations create. These can be ignored, extinguished, or managed. Why not harness them to productive use?"[1]

Executives in science-based, high-technology environments have long recognized the need for flexible, comprehensive management strategies that allow continuous adaptation to changing circumstances. Successful management strategies of the past are not guaranteed to address the organizational issues of today, for contemporary organizational problems are often too complex and diversified for a single management approach. Executives are confronted with a dual challenge: to design and build products that require radically new technologies and simultaneously to develop adaptive management strategies to support these technological advances. High technology companies need a blend of skill and perspectives, and, therefore, many have established "involvement" types of management programs to achieve their goals.

Executives in the aerospace industry have been particularly affected by this dual challenge. To cope with the problem of developing more sophisticated, complex technical and human systems, they have employed a variety of group forms. Task teams, advisory committees, project teams, "tiger" teams, and interface teams are just a sample of approaches used. Generally, these temporary problem-solving or task groups have allowed executives to bring together persons, usually from middle and upper management and representing a variety of organizational perspectives and specialties, to examine problems and propose solutions.

In recent years, a new form of work group called a "quality circle" has been employed by U.S. industry to address issues of organizational improvement. An exciting feature of quality circles is that they provide an orderly approach to bringing together a number of human and technical resources with the stated goals of improving both the quality of work life and organizational efficiency. Quality circles can involve employees from any level of the company in the process of identifying, analyzing, and proposing solutions to problems or issues that affect employees' ability to successfully conduct their work activities.

In 1974, Lockheed Corporation brought quality circles into the U.S. aerospace industry. In 1976, when Hughes Aircraft Company management personnel investigated quality circles, they were impressed with what they found, and shortly thereafter the company implemented the "Hughes Circles" program.

HUGHES CIRCLES

The umbrella under which all Hughes Aircraft Company quality circles operate is Hughes Circles, whose central premise is that employee groups will take more pride and interest in their work if they have opportunities to contribute systematically to improvements in their work environment. The program is also seen as a means of motivating employees to acquire a high level of commitment to the company's goals, thereby affording the company the opportunity to maximize management-employee communication, develop a creative and responsive work force, and maintain a desirable level of productivity. According to the mission statement for Hughes Circles, as presented in "Hughes Circles — Guidelines":

It is the approach of the Hughes Aircraft Company and its management and supervision to promote and use methods that provide employees with the opportunity of participating with management in communicating, identifying, and solving problems that affect the performance of the Company. The goal of the Hughes Aircraft Company is to encourage vital communications, participation, and contributions between management and employees in meeting Hughes and customer requirements and improving products, service, quality, job performance, safety, working conditions, individual growth, company morale, productivity, and overall company success.

The philosophical assumption underlying Hughes Circles is that those who actually perform the work have a unique perspective on the problems in their work areas, are willing to share their insights in order to improve the quality of their work experience, and will respond positively when they are given the opportunity to do so. This "bubble-up" approach to organizational improvement is based on the belief that the collective knowledge of the group is greater than that of each individual.

After tracking four pilot circles for approximately one year, Hughes Corporate staff reported that the results "have been significant, showing improvement in employee morale, quality of goods and services, safety, products, job performance, working conditions, and overall productivity." With these impressive results, Hughes Circles were greatly expanded. Today, more than 500 Hughes Circles have been implemented company wide. The support of Hughes Corporate management was reiterated by John H. Richardson, president of Hughes Aircraft Company, in his State of the Company address in Spring, 1980, and in a later correspondence:

. . . [a] communication device called "Quality Circles" is now taking hold throughout the company. I strongly support this "communication upward" approach. . . . I encourage you to implement Quality Circles whenever practical.

DEVELOPMENTAL FRAMEWORK

In providing a general developmental framework for Hughes Circles, Hughes Corporate staff sought to establish principles broad enough to accommodate its highly diversified organizational arrangements and to allow each Group sufficient autonomy to structure its circles to meet its own specific needs. Some Groups have "bought in" totally to this framework, while others, such as the Radar Systems Group, have adopted variations that they consider more responsive to their specific Group needs.

Corporate staff proposed several conditions for program development. Hughes Circles were to complement existing management structures and were to be implemented in a manner that would minimize the overhead expenses involved in conducting circle activities. Each Group and/or Division was to be responsible for assigning to a senior manager the task of coordinating and encouraging that

259

Group/Division's circle activities. Each Group/Division was to employ an indigenous approach to encouraging people development, motivation, and commitment through Hughes Circles and was to be supported administratively in this effort.

According to William E. Courtright, manager, Corporate Hughes Circles:

Since management is primarily responsible for maximizing people productivity, supervisors and middle managers should be asked to make this a top priority of their job. Circles are one important way to improve communications and solve problems of quality and productivity at the same time.

GUIDELINES

Below are seven general guidelines governing the overall development and operation of Hughes Circles. Operating with so few guidelines is considered optimal, since it allows the program implementors to negotiate other key elements of the program structure with individual departmental managers in accordance with their needs and departmental objectives.

1. *Each Group is to structure its own circles within program guidelines.* The Hughes Aircraft company's diversified organizational approach gives each Group maximum autonomy to structure its circles to meet specific needs and requirements. Autonomy allows departmental "ownership" to emerge more fully and promotes prompt and thoughtful consideration by management of solutions proposed.

2. *Circle membership and participation is voluntary.* Since employees agree to devote several hours monthly to group problem-solving activities, it is essential that they do not feel coerced into joining. Anything other than purely voluntary participation would stifle the free flow of information within the circle and between it and management.

3. *The work-group supervisor is the circle leader when feasible.* Since approximately 85 percent of the problems identified by circle members are under the direct jurisdiction of the work-group supervisor, he or she should be an integral part of the circle. Also, having the supervisor serve as circle leader creates a forum in which employees and supervisors can more openly address issues that affect them both.

4. *The circle facilitator — always a company employee — is not from the same work area but may be from the same department.* The facilitators are drawn from the existing employee pool. This "grass roots" approach differs significantly from that of the many companies that hire outside facilitators. The use of "part-time" facilitators permits increased program expansion, since circles do not become dependent on one key person in this role. This system also stresses the self-sufficiency of the circle.

The benefits of having a facilitator from a different, but related, work area are threefold: (1) a unique outside perspective is provided regarding the problems discussed; (2) the facilitator's objectivity is enhanced since he or she is not affected daily by the problems under discussion; and (3) members sometimes initially feel more at ease with the facilitator than the leader who is usually also the area supervisor.

5. *Leaders and facilitators participate in training workshops before implementing their circles.* Since Hughes Circles emphasize utilizing personnel from the existing employee pool in the roles of leader and facilitator, training is viewed as an extremely important prerequisite to initiating a circle. Once the initial training is completed, ongoing coaching is provided for the leader and facilitator on an as-needed basis. Follow-up workshops stressing specific techniques are also encouraged.

6. *Circles are composed of from three to twelve members.* The leader and facilitator are not usually professionals in the field of group relations. Therefore, it is important to keep the size of the circle manageable. Social science research indicates that once a group exceeds ten to twelve members, new and complex group dynamics often begin to affect its ability to accomplish its work. Controlling group size enables circle leaders and facilitators to focus on problem-solving activities rather than group dynamics issues.

7. *Circles hold weekly one-hour meetings on company time.* Circles meet three or four times a month, depending on departmental schedules. When circles meet less frequently, continuity may be jeopardized. Since one of the major goals of Hughes Circles is to keep overhead expenses at a minimum, meetings are limited to one hour on company time. Adherence to this rule has the incidental advantage of encouraging circle members to develop realistic and timely approaches to problem solving.

IMPLEMENTING THE RADAR SYSTEMS GROUP'S QUALITY CIRCLES

In the following pages, the approach to establishing quality circles used by the Hughes Aircraft Company's Radar Systems Group (RSG) in El Segundo, California, will be presented. Special attention will be paid to how RSG has tailored its quality circle program to meet specific needs and requirements of the Group.

RSG quality circles began in 1978 with three pilot circles. By the end of 1981, a total of seventy-eight circles had been implemented. Within RSG, the quality circle program is administratively based in the Personnel Training and Development section of Human Resources Development. According to Jill King, section head and founder of quality circles in RSG:

> The major roles of the RSG Quality Circle program office are to provide training for the volunteer leaders and facilitators; to act as a resource for management and circles; and, to gather appropriate data for history, tracking, and measurement purposes. The Personnel Training and Development staff has the *skills* and *objectivity* to provide line management and circle participants with the service and support needed.

Approximately half of RSG's quality circles are located in Manufacturing areas, while others are based in (but not limited to) such white-collar areas as Finance, Drafting, Engineering, Computer-aided Operations, Planning, Quality, Receiving, Purchasing, and various administrative support services. The diversity of the divisions within RSG that have initiated circles has necessitated a thorough examination of the key elements that promote an effective circle and the design of a flexible program response that can be tailored to individual departmental requirements.

RSG PROGRAM STRUCTURE

The program structure for RSG quality circles is designed to maximize the optimistic attitudes of those participating in or touched by ongoing circles. Ingredients of the structure include:

• Cultivating and maintaining management support;
• Implementing a comprehensive training program for circle leaders and facilitators, with frequent follow-up reinforcement training;
• Assuring that those who participate in quality circles are genuinely volunteers;
• Recognizing the efforts and maintaining the interest of those who are part of the circle process, both as participants and resources;
• Fostering departmental and employee "ownership" of quality circles as a joint venture; and
• Promoting collaborative interactions among circle participants and with others in their work environments.

Before implementing a circle, there are two important steps that must be taken: (1) securing management support; and (2) training the leader and facilitator. The success of the circle hinges notably on the ability of the RSG quality circle administrative staff to lay this important foundation.

SECURING MANAGEMENT SUPPORT

Considerable emphasis is placed on assisting all concerned managers to understand and actively support circles established in their divisions. Managers who express interest in circles invite a member of the RSG quality circle administrative staff to make a brief presentation on the philosophy, techniques, and operation of RSG quality circles. Attendees are provided with examples of work by existing or past circles, and an effort is made to help them understand the role and expectations of the various parties to an RSG quality circle — including those of management. It is explained that the organizational arrangements for RSG quality circles are designed to complement and build upon their existing organizational structures, and that RSG views the support of their departmental level managers as critical to the success of the circles.

Special informational workshops are conducted to acquaint middle managers with the concepts underlying RSG quality circles, provide "hands-on" experience with a variety of the problem-solving techniques being taught to supervisors or senior employees, and give them an opportunity to ask questions about RSG's approach to quality circles. Managers are encouraged to attend these workshops even if they do not have circles in their areas.

The collaborative relationship between the departmental manager and the circle is stressed throughout the workshop. Six general requirements expected of departmental management are discussed. These are: (1) allowing the circle leader and participants the time needed to conduct circle business; (2) assisting the circle leader in identifying meeting space and other resources as needed; (3) attending circle meetings and presentations; (4) replying promptly to circle requests and inquiries; (5) giving substantive explanations of why circle recommendations are accepted or denied; and (6) recognizing the efforts of all those who are participants in the circle.

LEADER AND FACILITATOR TRAINING

Perhaps one of the most important predictors of a successful circle is the caliber of training provided the leader and facilitator as they learn to identify, research, and solve problems. Prospective leaders and facilitators are nominated by their managers to participate in a comprehensive series of workshops on a wide variety of problem-solving techniques, group dynamics, and climate-setting techniques.

RSG places special emphasis on developing the skills of all who are involved in circle activity. Therefore, once the circle is implemented, the leader and facilitator team teach these same techniques to circle members, reinforcing the ''people-building'' orientation to group problem solving that is at the heart of RSG's quality circle approach.

To assure that each technique is clearly understood and solidly reinforced, a varied training format is employed. Workshops consist of lectures, discussions, application exercises, and videotape and slide presentations.

Training of leaders and facilitators is viewed as an ongoing process. Each circle has its own culture, group dynamics, and strengths and weaknesses. Therefore, it is critical that leaders and facilitators be involved in a continual reassessment of their work with the circles. This is the function of follow-up training. RSG offers several types of follow-up training, including monthly meetings on specific topics of interest and a workshop for new leaders and facilitators to reinforce training techniques when they begin their circles.

Upon completion of training, the new leader and facilitator meet with departmental management to reconfirm their interest in beginning a circle. During this meeting, the manager's goals for the circle are discussed, expectations are clarified, and other items related to the initiation of the circle are reviewed. The leader and facilitator secure meeting space, identify the most convenient meeting time, and invite the manager to attend an orientation meeting for the whole department. We view the manager's presence as so critical that if he or she must cancel at the last minute, the meeting is rescheduled.

LIFE CYCLE OF A CIRCLE

The orientation meeting is held to acquaint all departmental employees with the history of quality circles and the RSG quality circle concept, discuss the possible benefits of having a circle in their work area, and invite them to join. The departmental manager (and *all* line management above the circle leader and facilitator's immediate boss) attends the orientation meeting, expresses support for the circle, and indicates the types of resources and support that he or she will make available to the circle. The leader and facilitator discuss their roles and give an overview of the circle problem-solving process. Ample time is allowed for

263

employees to ask questions and explore concretely the advantages that can result from participation. Those interested in volunteering for the circle contact the leader after the meeting. When a sufficient number has volunteered, the circle is ready to begin.

THE FIRST MEETING

The first meeting sets the tone for future interactions within the circle. This meeting stresses getting acquainted, indentifying circle objectives, and establishing ground rules for conduct. Volunteers are recruited to serve as circle secretary and to keep attendance. A brief overview of the techniques used in problem solving is usually given by the facilitator. Both the leader and facilitator encourage discussion, emphasizing that the circle atmosphere should be characterized by openness and trust. Finally, the agenda for the next meeting is established.

THE PROBLEM-SOLVING PROCESS

In establishing the agenda for the second meeting, circle members are asked to prepare for an extensive "brainstorming" session at which they will be asked to identify problems or issues that they, as a circle, might want to investigate and solve. They are asked to meet during the week with other employees in the work area and, if possible, with area management to collect problems and issues they might like to place on the circle's list.

RSG employs a six-step approach to the quality circle problem-solving process: (1) identify potential problems and select the most significant; (2) gather and analyze data; (3) select possible solutions; (4) define implementation strategies; (5) present possible solutions to management; and (6) follow up on implemented solutions. Each step will be discussed briefly to illustrate the flow of the problem-solving process.

1. *Identify potential problems and select the most important.* Although suggestions about possible problems or issues for circle consideration may come from any individual in the work unit, the final selection is entirely in the hands of the circle members. To decide upon which problems they wish to solve, circle members brainstorm an initial problem list and then establish priorities by considering three factors: the *significance* of the problem, the *time* needed to arrive at an effective solution of the problem, and the *payoffs* for the work area (or related areas) if the problem is solved. Presentations and discussions of perceived problems help circle participants to develop their abilities to articulate their concerns and to "lobby" for the problem they prefer to work on. The Nominal Group Technique is used to arrive at group consensus on the top two or three problems that the circle wishes to focus upon.

2. *Gather and analyze data.* It is part of the role of the leader and facilitator to make sure that solutions proposed to management are backed up by a thorough documentation of the nature and extent of the problem. The circle is urged to develop substantive plans for examining root causes of problems.

Several techniques are used. One is the Cause-and-Effect diagram. Each possible cause of a problem is analyzed, separating true causes from symptoms. "Experts'' are often invited to circle meetings to present their perspectives on the problem. Check sheets, graphs, histograms, and Pareto diagrams are typical tools at this stage.

3. *Select possible solutions.* After again reviewing the initial problem and the information gathered from data collection, the circle uses the consensus decision-making process to brainstorm and select possible solutions to the problem. Suggested solutions are ranked according to significance, time required, and payoffs. Circles are urged to present more than one viable solution for management's consideration.

4. *Define implementation strategies.* As noted in the definition of a quality circle, it is not sufficient for the circle to merely identify possible solutions. The part of the quality circle process with the most potential payoff is that aspect involving the development of workable implementation strategies for suggested solutions. The circle must consider not only its ''ideal'' solution but also what is ''realistic'' given the various constraints on the work environment. Cost, availability of resources, difficulties of implementation, impact on others, willingness of management to accept the proposed solution, and the ability of the circle to track/monitor the solution are discussed. Proposed solutions are reviewed by other knowledgeable persons to determine the likelihood of management's acceptance. Modifications are made if the circle agrees that they are necessary.

5. *Present solutions to management.* When reviewing proposed solutions, it often becomes clear that the solution can be implemented directly by the area supervisor (circle leader). In some cases, however, solutions may necessitate policy or procedural changes, call for expenditures that cannot be authorized by the supervisor, or require other special attention not within the authority of the supervisor. In such instances, the circle makes an informal presentation to management to obtain approval for its proposed solution. These informal presentations are often ''working sessions'' where there is a lively exchange of information and ideas on implementation strategies. At these presentations, management can hear all relevant information. An automatic ''go ahead'' is not sought, but a response is requested by the next circle meeting, if possible. If a proposed solution is rejected, management is asked to explain why and to suggest how the solution can be modified to make it acceptable.

Informal presentations can occur at any point in the life cycle of the circle. The only requirement is that members believe that such a meeting would help resolve their selected problems. Informal presentations provide members direct access to their managers and provide managers with the members' perspective on the work. The presentations allow members to challenge some of their personal assumptions about management while management, on the other hand, has the opportunity to examine some of its assumptions about employees' knowledge, communication skills, and commitment.

Another type of presentation to management is the formal presentation, which occurs at the end of the six-month period to which management had committed its support when it authorized a circle in the work area. Formal presentations serve as a vehicle to renew management's support of the circle and to stress to the members that the work they are doing is valued. Top as well as middle management is invited to a formal presentation — and in most cases will attend.

If the circle has completed its work and decided to close, the formal presentation recaps the activities of the past six months; each member has the opportunity to tell management what he or she learned from the experience. Certificates are presented to members by the department manager to demonstrate appreciation for their work.

If the circle has received management support to continue for another six months (and the participants wish to continue), a formal presentation is more like an "updating" on the circle's activities. This presentation allows management to observe firsthand the circle's progress, to give recognition and reinforcement for work well done, and to suggest resources that the circle may use.

6. *Follow-up tracking/monitoring*. When a circle presents proposals to management, the role of the circle is that of "recommender." Management retains its right to accept or reject the proposed solutions. Before presenting their solutions, members decide what aspects of the solution will be tracked, how and by whom the tracking will be done, and over what length of time the tracking will occur. The leader and facilitator are usually very active during this process to assure that the plan developed is realistic and that it has a reasonable chance of success.

When management accepts a circle's proposed solution, the role that the circle will play in its implementation is discussed. At management's discretion, the circle may take an active role in the implementation of the solution, or it may simply monitor the impact of the solution after management has initiated its implementation.

CASE STUDIES

The following are examples of problems worked by RSG quality circles. We have included brief discussions indicating the process by which a circle handled those problems. These reports reflect observations made by circle members, leaders, facilitators, and administrative representatives. Four cases have been chosen — two from Manufacturing and two from nonmanufacturing environments to illustrate that the quality circle concepts can be tailored to the specific needs of the work area in which the circle operates.

• **Area:** Manufacturing — Hybrid and Microwave Devices.

Problem: Excessive assembler error, part scrappage, and rework.

Discussion: During several meetings in which circle members brainstormed possible causes of the problem, they identified inadequate lighting, dirty projector screens, warped slides, and lack of "color-coded" planning documents. In addition, circle members felt strongly that minor changes in the assembly planning documents could result in clearer assembly procedures.

Regarding the latter problem, circle participants decided to study and document the incidence of assembler error, part scrappage, and rework that appeared to be related to problems in the assembly planning documents. The circle's facilitator, an employee from Planning, taught circle members how to document their find-

266

ings and write up their recommendations in a manner that would be meaningful to the Planning Department.

Resolution: In meetings between circle participants and supervisors from the Planning Department, agreement was reached on the process for submitting the circle's documented suggestions. The new process allowed the circle leader/area supervisor more immediate access to Planning to get recommended changes reviewed. Through her, a request was made to the Environmental Health and Safety Department to conduct a lighting check. The check demonstrated a need for additional lighting to supplement overhead lighting, and replacements of existing station lighting were ordered. One of the circle members volunteered to clean screens on projectors. Warped slides have been replaced, and all assembly documents are now color-coded.

- **Area:** Computer-aided Operations — Engineering Data Control.
  Problem: Excessive computer downtime.

Discussion: Members of this circle were frustrated by the backlog of work that accummulated when the computer was down. Downtime was such a frequent occurrence that morale was affected and customer complaints were on the rise.

The circle monitored the incidence of downtime for several weeks, keeping track of the number of times per day that the computer went down as well as the specific hours it was inoperable. The circle found the highest incidence of downtime occurred between the hours of 10 a.m. and 2 p.m. The circle leader referred the members to an expert in the central computer facility. Through his investigation, the expert found that the troublesome computer shared a terminal line with another busy center in the same building. The amount of traffic on this line was simply too great to be handled effectively.

Resolution: A work order was placed to install a larger line to accommodate the volume of traffic generated by these two departments. This line has been operational for six months. Computer downtime has been reduced from approximately one full day a week to less than two hours a week, with concomitant improvement in employee morale and customer satisfaction.

- **Area:** Manufacturing — Printed Circuit Board.
  Problem: Excessive rework and scrappage of printed circuit boards.

Discussion: Excessive rework and scrappage were attributed to several causes. Among these were inadequate employee training, mishandling by employees, inadequate "move" equipment, and faulty artwork. Circle members chose to examine "artwork" and "move" equipment first.

When investigating artwork issues, the circle decided to focus on bad or distorted masters and incorrect handling of artwork by employees. It attempted to isolate the areas where the most frequent artwork problems occurred. Since the circle was composed of representatives from each phase in the assembly process, it decided to track certain assemblies as they were being built.

The first step was to inspect the artwork thoroughly when it entered the work area. From this inspection, members found that some masters arrived "bad" (damaged, with incorrect specifications, out-of-date, etc.). Other masters were "blown up" or duplicated so often that distortions occurred on the working copy.

Other problems with the artwork occurred during the assembly process. These were more difficult to uncover, since boards being built went through too many work stations for accurate follow-up. The circle felt that training of employees in the correct methods of handling artwork would eliminate some of the scrappage, but it was unable to collect concrete data. It decided to take the problem to management for assistance.

Resolution: The circle presented to management its data on high scrappage caused by bad artwork and asked for suggestions on how to proceed. Management was pleased with the amount of documentation already gathered, asked questions of circle members, and proposed several steps for implementation at the management level in collaboration with the circle. A management task team was formed with responsibility for investigating problems with artwork. Circle members have been invited to give input on this problem, and a member of the task team visits the circle regularly to receive up-to-date briefings on problems.

Masters that arrived in "bad" condition were returned to the originator for replacement and those that were distorted were remade more frequently and checked to assure that specifications were met. Regarding "move" equipment, the circle recommended that new equipment with "double wide" racks and a tighter wire mesh be purchased. This would prevent boards from falling off the racks or falling through the shelves while being transported. Management accepted this proposal and the new move racks have been ordered.

• **Area:** Engineering — Diffraction Optics Laboratory.

Problem: Difficulty in meeting research schedules.

Discussion: After brainstorming possible causes for the difficulty in meeting research schedules, the circle decided to focus on its inability to obtain needed parts and supplies in a timely fashion. Part of this problem was traced to the circle's own errors in completing paperwork and failing to adhere to Purchasing, Shipping, and Receiving "lead-in" (timetables) schedules. Other problems were traced to interdepartmental procedures that did not accommodate the engineers' need to expedite "hot" (critical) items.

The circle approached these multiple causes from several angles. It compiled a list of timetables for processing requests through the Purchasing and Receiving Departments and for its own departmental "signoffs." It obtained copies of the forms necessary for ordering parts and other supplies and met with appropriate departmental representatives to receive instruction on the correct method for completing these forms. Additionally, several members met with representatives from Purchasing and Receiving to develop a system to expedite "hot" items.

Resolution: The circle compiled a "Lab Users' Manual" that was circulated to others in the lab. The guide contained: (1) a list of pertinent deadlines; (2) samples of necessary forms (filled out correctly); (3) the names of resource persons (and their phone numbers) in various service departments; and (4) a detailing of the procedure for expediting "hot" items.

The incidence of delays in obtaining needed parts and supplies has been reduced significantly. As an ongoing check of the effectiveness of the new procedures, a circle member volunteered to conduct a follow-up check on the remaining isolated instances in which parts and supplies were delayed. To date he has reported few cases of major "roadblocks."

OBSERVABLE RESULTS

The positive results of circle problem-solving activity fall into two major categories: (1) the growth and development of individual employees; and (2) the creation of a more viable, collaborative work group. Illustrations of these two types of results follow.

1. Circle leaders report among their employees a noticeable increase in information sharing, cooperation in resolving problems, and a willingness to make an extra effort when working with other departments. They most often attribute these observed behavioral changes to (1) an increased understanding by employees of how their jobs "fit" into the total company; (2) the development of skills by employees to analyze their own needs and the needs of others; and (3) an increased appreciation by employees of those showing initiative on the job.

2. Problems are less identified with individuals. Application of action research in the work group focuses attention on the systemic sources of problems rather than the shortcomings of individuals. The orderly approach to problem solving allows members to analyze the complexities of key issues and to identify dysfunctional aspects of work procedures. Approaching perceived problems from this perspective allows members to develop new strategies for handling old problems and issues.

3. Participants regularly report that they feel less "cut off" from the company, since they are actively involved in seeking information and clarifying complex issues. The problem-solving process tends to make participants more aware of the impact of issues upon themselves and those in related units.

4. Working with departmental interface issues seems to be emerging as a strong quality circle theme. The format of the circle lends itself particularly well to creating a neutral turf where team building activities can occur between employee groups. There is clearly a skill-building process inherent in inviting outsiders to the quality circle to discuss problems of mutual importance and in negotiating specific points with the outsiders.

5. By ensuring that employees at all levels can bring their problems to the top, quality circles reduce potential conflict situations. Members state that they receive much personal satisfaction knowing that their suggestions have been adopted by the company. Circle leaders report that their employees come to them more frequently to discuss problems or issues. The leaders attribute this in part to an improvement in their own ability to take time with their employees and to really listen to what they have to say.

6. Participants report that they understand the difficulties of the management process more fully, particularly when they need to consider the most viable strategies for effecting change in their work environments. They routinely express surprise at the complexity of problems that on the surface seem quite trivial. Early in the life cycle of circles, members begin to appreciate the need to document and integrate their findings into their work area in a timely fashion.

7. Managers report that supervisors seem to have a better rapport with their employees. Supervisors and others who serve as circle leaders routinely report that they feel that their ability to work with their employees has been enhanced. They indicate that they are able to see problems from additional "angles" and that they can think through the steps needed to solve problems.

8. Managers frequently report that they view facilitator training as an excellent learning experience for their presupervisory-level employees. In several instances employees have been promoted to supervisory or group head positions upon completion of training. These newly appointed supervisors reported that they have used the quality circle techniques in their supervisory activities.

Perhaps these points can be best summed up through the statement of the facilitator for a quality circle based in the Printed Circuit Board area of Manufacturing:

> These people who are your most important asset will reward you if given the opportunity. Their problem-solving skills are being developed with each new endeavor. The process of problem identification and solving can be a very slow and frustrating experience for the circle members; however, it gives each one of them the opportunity to speak up, be heard, and see their suggestions implemented.

NOTES

1. Richard Tanner Pascale and Anthony G. Athos, *The Art of Japanese Management* (N.Y.: Simon and Schuster, 1981), p. 147.

INTRODUCTION: CHAPTER SIX

SUPPORTIVE LITERATURE FROM BEHAVIORAL SCIENCES AND HUMAN RESOURCE DEVELOPMENT

The concept of quality circles is supported by recognized leaders in the field of industrial engineering and human resource development. This chapter presents six readings describing their views.

New Patterns Of Management by Rensis Likert deals with the principle of supportive relationships. Likert says that every successful organization has within its organizational structure the dimension, or philosophy, that the mission of the organization must be seen by its members as genuinely important. He says further that to be highly motivated, each member of the organization must feel that the organization's objectives are of significance and that his own particular task contributes in an indispensable manner to the achievement of the organization's objectives. You will find references to his long-familiar linking-pin analogy. It can be used to explain how the concept of quality circles works as a management technique. He stresses the need for meaningful communication from the top down, from the bottom up, and laterally between groups. He describes how group functioning can assist with leveling out staffing peaks and valleys by utilizing labor within work groups and between groups. He cites examples that illustrate his support for the QC concepts.

In "An Improvement Cycle for Human Development," Likert states that "organizational development", or as it is known more recently, human resource development, consists all too often of uncoordinated, piecemeal efforts such as team building, job enrichment or job redesign, sensitivity training, participative decision making, and management by objectives. He goes on to describe the characteristics that should be used as a model for organizations interested in guiding human resource development efforts. He lists six steps to follow that will create an organizational improvement cycle. The article ends with a list of references that provide further information about his theories.

Richard E. Walton contributes his ideas, derived from ten years of experience, on work improvement projects. You will appreciate his objective analysis of projects bearing a variety of labels: quality of work life and work innovations. Walton sets forth his own three-level conception of work innovation and demonstrates how techniques, outcomes, and culture relate to each other. You will find his conclusions interesting.

The former vice president of the United Automobile Workers, Irving Bluestone asks, "What can be done to fulfill more responsively at the workplace the democratic concept of "self-fulfillment" and "participation" envisioned for society as a whole." He harks back to Frederick Taylor's principles of scientific management as a basis for production and presents his views of the union laborer seeking more participative roles in the corporate decision-making structure. He presents his views concisely. He challenges the Taylor concepts of humans laboring at an energy efficient production peak throughout a work period working against goals established by a stop watch.

Edwin Yager restates briefly, in his article, the history of the quality circle movement. After outlining the growth of the movement in the U.S., he refers to the "bandwagon" effect in the human resource development field. He, too, covers some of the organizational concerns and concepts of the quality circle groups and stresses the focus of the circles as being very important. In his conclusion, Yager reports some interesting ratios he has derived from evaluation studies regarding return on investment. The article is easy to read and uses work-place examples to illustrate his narrative.

Finally, this chapter deals with integrating quality control and quality of work life. Sidney P. Rubinstein begins his presentation with the statement that decision-making workers are the wave of the future. He quotes notables, referred to in other readings in this book, to illustrate his belief. He points out that "participative problem solving" has evolved from 20 years of field experience in the U.S. and abroad. He defines participative problem solving as a concept that combines the science of quality control engineering with advances in the behavioral sciences, and states that it requires an ongoing effort which seeks the resolution of inhibiting influences unique to the U.S. He reports that the American style of management is "conflict management" and the work environment as "competitive." He addresses manager mobility by corporate decision and personal volition and the effects of mobility upon work performance and job security. He offers well-developed conclusions for his point of view that quality control professionals must redefine their roles within the participation movement.

THE PRINCIPLE OF SUPPORTIVE
RELATIONSHIPS AS AN ORGANIZING CONCEPT
Rensis Likert

This general principle provides a fundamental formula for obtaining the full potential of every major motive which can be constructively harnessed in a working situation. There is impressive evidence, for example, that economic motivations will be tapped more effectively when the conditions specified by the principle of supportive relationships are met (Katz & Kahn, 1951; Krulee, 1955). In addition, as motives are used in the ways called for by this general principle, the attitudes accompanying the motives will be favorable and the different motivational forces will be cumulative and reinforcing. Under these circumstances, the full power from each of the available motives will be added to that from the others to yield a maximum of coordinated, enthusiastic effort.

The principle of supportive relationships points to a dimension essential for the success of every organization, namely, that the mission of the organization be seen by its members as genuinely important. To be highly motivated, each member of the organization must feel that the organization's objectives are of significance and that his own particular task contributes in an indispensable manner to the organization's achievement of its objectives. He should see his role as difficult, important, and meaningful. This is necessary if the individual is to achieve and maintain a sense of personal worth and importance. When jobs do not meet this specification they should be reorganized so that they do. This is likely to require the participation of those involved in the work in a manner suggested in subsequent chapters.

The term "supportive" is used frequently in subsequent chapters and also is a key word in the principle of supportive relationships. Experiences, relationships, etc., are considered to be supportive when the individual involved sees the experience (in terms of his values, goals, expectations, and aspirations) as contributing to or maintaining his sense of personal worth and importance.

The principle of supportive relationships contains within it an important clue to its effective use. To apply this general principle, a superior must take into consideration the experience and expectations of each of his subordinates. In determining what these expectations are, he cannot rely solely on his observations and impressions. It helps the superior to try to put himself in his subordinate's shoes and endeavor to see things as the subordinate sees them, but this is not enough. Too often, the superior's estimates are wrong. He needs direct evidence if he is to know how the subordinate views things and to estimate the kinds of behavior and interaction which will be seen by the subordiante as supportive. The superior needs accurate information as to how his behavior is actually seen by the subordinate. Does the subordinate, in fact, perceive the superior's behavior as supportive?

There are two major ways to obtain this evidence. In a complex organization it can be found by the use of measurements of the intervening variables, as

273

suggested in Chapter 5 and discussed at greater length in Chapter 13. It can also be obtained by the development of work group relationships, which not only facilitate but actually require, as part of the group building and maintenance functions, candid expressions by group members of their perceptions and reactions to the behavior of others.

THE CENTRAL ROLE OF THE WORK GROUP

An important theoretical derivation can be made from the principle of supportive relationships. This derivation is based directly on the desire to achieve and maintain a sense of personal worth, which is a central concept of the principle. The most important source of satisfaction for this desire is the response we get from the people we are close to, in whom we are interested, and whose approval and support we are eager to have. The face-to-face groups with whom we spend the bulk of our time are, consequently, the most important to us. Our work group is one in which we spend much of our time and one in which we are particularly eager to achieve and maintain a sense of personal worth. As a consequence, most persons are highly motivated to behave in ways consistent with the goals and values of their work group in order to obtain recognition, support, security, and favorable reactions from this group. It can be concluded, therefore, that *management will make full use of the potential capacities of its human resources only when each person in an organization is a member of one or more effectively functioning work groups that have a high degree of group loyalty, effective skills of interaction, and high performance goals.*

The full significance of this derivation becomes more evident when we examine the research findings that show how groups function when they are well knit and have effective interaction skills. Research shows, for example, that the greater the attraction and loyalty to the group, the more the individual is motivated to accept the goals and decisions of the group; to seek to influence the goals and decisions of the group so that they are consistent with his own experience and his own goals; to communicate fully to the members of the group; to welcome communication and influence attempts from the other members; to behave so as to help implement the goals and decisions that are seen as most important to the group; and to behave in ways calculated to receive support and favorable recognition from members of the group, especially from those who the individual feels are the more power and higher status members (Cartwright & Zander, 1960). Groups which display a high level of member attraction to the group and high levels of the above characteristics will be referred to in this volume as highly effective groups.

As our theoretical derivation has indicated, an organization will function best when its personnel function not as individuals but as members of highly effective work groups with high performance goals. Consequently, management should deliberately endeavor to build these effective groups, linking them into an overall organization by means of people who hold overlapping group membership (Figure 6-1). The superior in one group is a subordinate in the next group, and so on through the organization. If the work groups at each hierarchical level are well knit and effective, the linking process will be accomplished well. Staff as well as line should be characterized by this pattern of operation.

The dark lines in Figure 6-1 are intended to show that interaction occurs between individuals as well as in groups. The dark lines are omitted at the lowest level in the chart in order to avoid complexity. Interaction between individuals occurs there, of course, just as it does at higher levels in the organization.

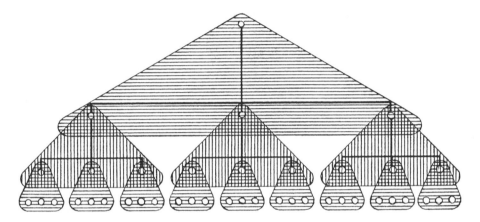

Figure 6-1. The overlapping group form of organization. Work groups vary in size as circumstances require although shown here as consisting of four persons.

In most organizations, there are also various continuing and *ad hoc* committees, committees related to staff functions, etc., which should also become highly effective groups and thereby help further to tie the many parts of the organization together. These links are in addition to the linking provided by the overlapping members in the line organization. Throughout the organization, the supervisory process should develop and strengthen group functioning. This theoretically ideal organizational structure provides the framework for the management system called for by the newer theory.

THE TRADITIONAL COMPANY ORGANIZATION

Let us examine the way an organization would function were it to apply this one derivation and establish highly effective groups with high performance goals, instead of adhering to the traditional man-to-man pattern. First, let us look briefly at how the traditional man-to-man pattern usually functions. Figure 6-2 shows the top of an ordinary organization chart. Such an organization ordinarily functions on a man-to-man basis as shown in Figure 6-3a. In Figure 6-3a, the president, vice presidents, and others reporting to the president are represented by 0's.

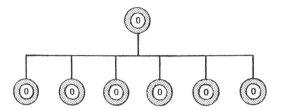

Figure 6-2. Typical organization chart.

The solid lines in Figure 6-3a indicate the boundaries of well-defined areas of responsibility.

The president of such a man-to-man organization has said to us, "I have been made president of this company by the board of directors because they believe I am more intelligent or better trained or have more relevant experience than my fellow managers. Therefore, it is my responsibility to make the top-level decisions" He regularly holds meetings of the people who report to him for purposes of sharing information, but *not* for decision-making.

What happens? The vice president in charge of manufcturing, for example, may go to the president with a problem and a recommendation. Because it involves a model change, the vice president in charge of sales is called in. On the basis of the discussion with the two vice presidents and the recommendations they make, the president arrives at a decision. However, in any organization larger than a few hundred employes, that decision usually will affect other vice presidents and subordinates whose interests were not represented in it. Under the circumstances, they are not likely to accept this decision wholeheartedly nor strive hard to implement it. Instead, they usually begin to plan how they can get decisions from the president which are going to be beneficial to them but not necessarily to sales and manufacturing.

And what happens to the communication process? This president, it will be recalled, holds meetings for the primary purpose of sharing information. But if the manufcturing vice president, for example, has some important facts bearing on an action which he wants the president to approve, does he reveal them at these meetings? No, he does not. He waits until he is alone with the president and can use the information to obtain the decision he seeks. Each vice president is careful to share in these communication meetings only trivial information. The motivational pressures are against sharing anything of importance.

The man-to-man pattern of operation enables a vice president or manager to benefit by keeping as much information as possible to himself. Not only can he obtain decisions from his superior beneficial to himself, but he can use his knowledge secretly to connive with peers or subordinates or to pit one peer or subordinate against the other. In these ways, he often is able to increase his own power

276

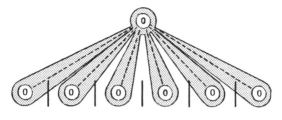

(a) Man-to-man pattern of organization

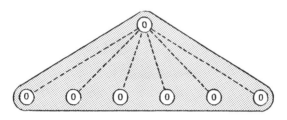

(b) Group pattern of organization

Figure 6-3. Man-to-man and group patterns of organization.

and influence. He does this, however, at the expense of the total organization. The distrust and fear created by his behavior adversely affect the amount of influence which the organization can exert in coordinating the activities of its members. Measures of the amount of influence an organization can exert on its members show that distrust of superiors, colleagues, and subordinates adversely affects the amount of influence that can be exercised.

Another serious weakness of the communication process in the man-to-man method of operating is that communications upward are highly filtered and correspondingly inaccurate. Orders and instructions flow down through the organization, at times with some distortion. But when management asks for information on the execution of orders and on difficulties encountered, incomplete and partially inaccurate information is often forthcoming. With these items and wtih other kinds of communication as well, those below the boss study him carefully to discover what he is interested in, what he approves and disapproves of, and what he wants to hear and does not want to hear. They then tend to feed him the material he wants. It is difficult and often hazardous for an individual subordinate in man-to-man discussion to tell the boss something which he needs to know but which runs counter to the boss's desires, convictions, or prejudices. A subordinate's future in an organization often is influenced appreciably by how well he senses and communicates to his boss material which fits the latter's orientation.

277

Another characteristic of the man-to-man pattern concerns the point of view from which problems are solved. When a problem is brought to the president, each vice president usually states and discusses the problem from a departmental orientation, despite efforts by the president to deal with it from a company-wide point of view. This operates to the disadvantage of the entire organization. Problems tend to be solved in terms of what is best for a department, not what is best for the company as a whole.

EFFECT OF COMPETITION BETWEEN FUNCTIONS

In the man-to-man situation it is clear that sharply defined lines of responsiblity are necessary (Figure 6-3a) because of the nature of the promotion process and because the men involved are able people who want promotion.

Now, what are the chances of having one's competence so visible that one moves up in such an organization or receives offers elsewhere? Two factors are important: the magnitude of one's responsibility and the definition of one's functions so as to assure successful performance. For example, if you are head of sales and can get the president to order the manufacturing department to make a product or to price it in such a way that it is highly competitive, that will be to your advantage, even though it imposes excessive difficulties and cost problems on the manufacturing operation.

Each man, in short, is trying to enlarge his area of responsibility, thereby encroaching on the other's territory. He is also trying to get decisions from the president which set easily attained goals for him and enable him to achieve excellent performance. Thus, the sales vice president may get prices set which make his job easy but which put undue pressure on the manufacturing vice president to cut production costs.

One consequence of this struggle for power is that each department or operation has to be staffed for peak loads, and job responsibilities and boundaries have to be precisely defined. No one dares let anybody else take over any part of his activity temporarily for fear that the line of responsibility will be moved over permanently.

The tighter the hierarchical control in an organization, in the sense that decisions are made at the top and orders flow down, the greater tends to be the hostility among subordinates. In autocratic organizations, subordinates bow down to superiors and fight among themselves for power and status. Consequently, the greater the extent to which the president makes the decisions, the greater is the probability that competition, hostility, and conflict will exist between his vice presidents and staff members.

THE GROUP SYSTEM OF OPERATION

Figure 6-3b represents a company patterned on the group system of organization. One of the presidents we interviewed follows this pattern. He will not permit an organization chart to be drawn because he does not want people to think in terms of man-to-man hierarchy. He wants to build working groups. He holds meetings of his top staff regularly to solve problems and make decisions. Any member of his staff can propose problems for consideration, but each problem is viewed from a company-wide point of view. It is virtually impossible for one department to force a decision beneficial to it but detrimental to other departments if the group, as a whole, makes the decisions.

An effectively functioning group pressing for solutions in the best interest of *all* the members and refusing to accept solutions which unduly favor a particular member or segment of the group is an important characteristic of the group pattern of organization. It also provides the president, or the superior at any level in an organization, with a powerful managerial tool for dealing with special requests or favors from subordinates. Often the subordinate may feel that the request is legitimate even though it may not be in the best interest of the organization. In the man-to-man operation (Figure 6-3a), the chief sometimes finds it difficult to turn down such requests. With the group pattern of operation, however, the superior can suggest that the subordinate submit his proposal to the group at their next staff meeting. If the request is legitimate and in the best interest of the organization, the group will grant the request. If the request is unreasonable, an effectively functioning group can skillfully turn it down by analyzing it in relation to what is best for the entire organization. Subordinates in this situation soon find they cannot get special favors or preferred treatment from the chief. This leads to a tradition that one does not ask for any treatment or decision which is recognized as unfair to one's colleagues.

The capacity of effective groups to press for decisions and action in the best interest of all members can be applied in other ways. An example is provided by the president of a subsidiary of a large corporation. He was younger (age 42) than most of his staff and much younger than two of his vice presidents (age 61 and 62). The subsidiary had done quite well under its previous president, but the young president was eager to have it do still better. In his first two years as president, his company showed substantial improvement. He found, however, that the two older vice presidents were not effectively handling their responsibilities. Better results were needed from them if the company was to achieve the record performance which the president and the other vice presidents sought.

The president met the situation by using his regular staff meetings to analyze the company's present position, evaluate its potential, and decide on goals and on the action required to reach them. The president had no need to put pressure on his coasting vice presidents. The other vice presidents did it for him. One vice president, in particular, slightly younger but with more years of experience than the two who were dragging their feet, gently but effectively pushed them to commit themselves to higher performance goals. In the regular staff meetings, progress toward objectives was watched and new short-term goals were set as needed. Using this group process, steady progress was made. The two oldest vice presidents became as much involved and worked as enthusiastically as did the rest of the staff.

GROUP DECISION MAKING

With the model of organization shown in Figure 6-3b, persons reporting to the president, such as vice presidents for sales, research, and manufacturing, contribute their technical knowledge in the decision making process. They also make other contributions. One member of the group, for example, may be an imaginative person who comes up rapidly with many stimulating and original ideas. Others, such as the general counsel or the head of research, may make the group do a rigorous job of sifting ideas. In this way, the different contributions required for a competent job of thinking and decision making are introduced.

In addition, these people become experienced in effective group functioning. They know what leadership involves. If the president grows absorbed in some detail and fails to keep the group focused on the topic for discussion, the members will help by performing appropriate leadership functions, such as asking, "Where are we? What have we decided so far? Why don't we summarize?"

There are other advantages to this sort of group action. The motivation is high to communicate accurately all relevant and important information. If any one of these men holds back important facts affecting the company so that he can take it to the president later, the president is likely to ask him why he withheld the information and request him to report it to the group at the next session. The group also is apt to be hard on any member who withholds important information from them. Moreover, the group can get ideas across to the boss that no subordinate dares tell him As a consequence, there is better communication, which brings a better awareness of problems, and better decision making than with the man-to-man system

Another important advantage of effective group action is the high degree of motivation on the part of each member to do his best to implement decisions and to achieve the group goals. Since the goals of the group are arrived at through group decisions, each individual group member tends to have a high level of ego identification with the goals because of his involvement in the decisions.

Finally, there are indications that an organization operating in this way can be staffed for less than peak loads at each point. When one man is overburdened, some of his colleagues can pick up part of the load temporarily. This is possible with group methods of supervision because the struggle for power and status is less. Everybody recognizes his broad area of responsibility and is not alarmed by occasional shifts in one direction or the other. Moreover, he knows that his for promotion depend not upon the width of his responsibility, but upon his total performance, of which his work in the group is an important part. The group, including the president, comes to know the strengths and weaknesses of each member well as a result of working closely with him.

A few years ago a department of fifteen people in a medium-sized company shifted from a man-to-man pattern of supervision to the group pattern. Each operation under the man-to-man system was staffed to carry adequately the peak loads encountered, but these peaks virtually never occurred for all jobs at the same time. In shifting to group supervision, the department studied how the work was being done. They concluded that seven persons instead of fifteen could carry the load except in emergencies. Gradually, over several months, the persons not needed transferred to other departments and the income of those doing the work was increased 50%. The work is being done well, peak loads are handled, those doing it have more favorable attitudes, and there is less absence and turnover than under the man-to-man system.

RESPONSIBILITY AND SITUATIONAL REQUIREMENTS

In every organization there are many basic facts of life which cannot be ignored if the organization is to achieve its objectives. For example, there are often deadlines or minimum financial conditions as to earnings and reserves to be met. These hard, objective realities are the *situational requirements* which impose limitations on the decision making processes.

The supervisor of every work group must be fully aware of the situational requirements which apply to the operation of his group. In making decisions, he and his group should never lose sight of them. If the group is so divided in opinion that there is not time to reach decisions by consensus which adequately meet these requirements, the superior has the responsibility of making a decision which does meet them. In this event, the superior may be wise to accept the solution preferred by the individuals in the group who will have the major responsibility for implementing the decision, provided, of course, the superior himself feels that the solution is reasonably sound.

Sometimes the differences of opinion exist not between members of the work group, but between the superior and his subordinates. In this event, the superior should participate fully in the discussion and present clearly the evidence which makes him hold another point of view. If after further discussion, the group still prefers a course of action different from that which the chief favors, the superior faces a tough decision. He can overrule the group and take the action he favors. This is likely to affect adversely group loyalties and the capacity of his work group to function well as a group. Or he can go along with the group and accept the decision they prefer. If he overrules the group, the superior usually reduces the amount of work group loyalty which has "in the bank." If the costs of a mistake are not too great, he may prefer to accept the group's decision in order to strengthen the group as a group and to provide an opportunity for his group to learn from its mistakes. If the costs of a mistake are likely to be excessive, the superior may feel that he has no choice but to do what his own experience indicates is best. But whatever course of action is taken, he is responsible and must accept full responsibility for what occurs.

THE "LINKING PIN" FUNCTION

Figure 6-3 and the preceding discussion have been concerned with the group pattern of organization at the very top of a company. Our theoretical derivation indicates, however, that this pattern is equally applicable at all levels of an organization. If an organization is to apply this system effectively at all organizational levels, an important linking function must be performed.

281

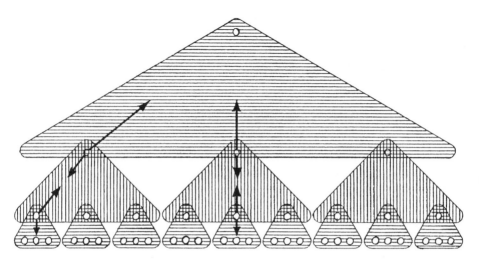

(The arrows indicate the linking pin function)

Figure 6-4. The linking pin.

The concept of the ''linking pin'' is shown by the arrows in Figure 6-4. The research pointing to the importance of upward influence in an organization has already been described before. The study by Pelz (1951; 1952) showed that there was only a slight relationship between some 50 different measures of supervisory practices and points of view, as reported by the supervisors, and the attitudes and morale of the subordinates. Pelz found that an important variable was responsible for the absence of more marked relationships. This variable proved to be the amount of influence which a supervisor felt he had with his supervisor. To function effectively, a supervisor must have sufficient influence with his own superior to be able to affect the superior's decisions. Subordinates expect their supervisors to be able to exercise an influence upward in dealing with problems on the job and in handling problems which affect them and their well being. As Pelz's analysis shows, when a supervisor cannot exert sufficient influence upward in the hierarchy to handle these problems constructively, an unfavorable reaction to the supervisor and to the organization is likely to occur.

Other research confirms the importance of Pelz's findings and also indicates that the ability to exert an influence upward affects not only morale and motivation but also productivity and performance variables (Katz et al., 1950; Likert & Willits, 1940). Ronken and Sawrence (1952) summarize their findings on this matter as follows:

> An additional complication for the foreman was the necessity of learning how to work with new supervisors and a new group of subordinates. When the foreman experienced difficulty in communicating with his superior, he was not able to understand his subordinates' problems or to gain their spontaneous cooperation, and the work suffered. When he felt more confident of his relations upward, he administered his own group with greater skill. During such periods his operators showed considerable initiative in their work, contributed more useful suggestions, and raced with themselves and each other to increase output.

These results demonstrate that *the capacity to exert influence upward is essential if a supervisor (or manager) is to perform his supervisory functions successfully*. To be effective in leading his own work group, a superior must be able to influence his own boss; that is, he needs to be skilled both as a supervisor and as a subordinate. In terms of group functioning, he must be skilled in both leadership and membership functions and roles.

Effective groups with high group loyalty are characterized by efficient and full communication and by the fact that their members respect each other, welcome attempts by the other members to influence them, and are influenced in their thinking and behavior when they believe that the evidence submitteed by the other members warrants it. The linking pin function, consequently, will be performed well in an organization when each work group at all the different hierarchical levels above the nonsupervisory level is functioning effectively as a group and when every member of each group is performing his functions and roles well. Whenever an individual member of one of these groups fails in his leadership and membership roles, the group or groups under him will not be linked into the organization effectively and will fail in the performance of their tasks. When an entire work group ceases to function effectively as a group, the activities and performance of all the work groups below such a group will be correspondingly adversely affected.

The linking pin function requires effective group processes and points to the following:

- An organization will not derive the full benefit from its highly effective groups unless they are linked to the total organization by means of equally effective overlapping groups such as those illustrated in Figures 6-1 and 6-4. The use of highly effective groups in only one part or in scattered portions of an organization will fail, therefore, to achieve the full potential value of such groups.
- The potential power of the overlapping group form of organization will not be approached until all the groups in the organization are functioning reasonably well. The failure of any group will adversely affect the performance of the total organization.
- The higher an ineffective group is in the hierarchy, the greater is the adverse effect of its failure on the performance of the organization. The linking process is more important at high levels in an organization than at low because the policies and problems dealt with are more important to the total organization and affect more people.
- To help maintain an effective organization, it is desirable for superiors not only to hold group meetings of their own subordinates, but also to have occasional meetings over two hierarchical levels. This enables the superior to observe any breakdown in the linking pin process as performed by the subordinates reporting to him. If in such meetings the subordinates under one of his subordinates are reluctant to talk, never question any procedure or policy, or give other evidence of fear, the superior can conclude that he has a coaching job to do with his own subordinate, who is failing both as a leader and in his performance of the linking pin function. This subordinate needs help in learning how to build

his own subordinates into a work group with high group loyalty and with confidence and trust in their supervisor.

• An organization takes a serious risk when it relies on a single linking pin or single linking process to tie the organization together. As will be discussed further in subsequent chapters, an organization is strengthened by having staff groups and *ad hoc* committees provide multiple overlapping groups through which linking functions are performed and the organization bound together.

ORGANIZATIONAL OBJECTIVES AND GOALS OF UNITS

The ability of a supervisor to behave in a supportive manner is circumscribed by the degree of compatibility between the objectives of the organization and the needs of the individuals comprising it. If the objectives of the organization are in basic conflict with the needs and desires of the individual members, it is virtually impossible for superior to be supportive to subordinates and at the same time serve the objectives of the organization. The principle of supportive relationships, consequently, points to the necessity for an adequate degree of harmony between organizational objectives and the needs and desires of its individual members.

This conclusion is applicable to every kind of organization: industrial, governmental, or voluntary. A business organization, if it is to function well, needs to have objectives which represent a satisfactory integration of the needs and desires of all the major segments involved: its shareowners, its suppliers, its consumers, its employes (including all levels of supervisory and nonsupervisory personnel), and its union(s). If governmental agencies are to function effectively, their objectives similarly must be a satisfactory integration of the needs and desires of all the different segments involved in their activities: employes, citizens, and legislators.

Neither the needs and desires of individuals nor the objectives of organizations are stable and unchanging. The desires of individuals grow and change as people interact with other people. Similarly, the objectives of organizations must change continuously to meet the requirements of changed technologies, changed conditions, and the changes in needs and desires of those involved in the organization or served by it. The interaction process of the organization must be capable of dealing effectively with these requirements for continuous change.

In every healthy organization there is, consequently, an unending process of examining and modifying individual goals and organizational objectives as well as consideration of the methods for achieving them. The newer theory specifies that:

• The objectives of the entire organization and of its component parts must be in satisfactory harmony with the relevant needs and desires of the great majority, if not all, of the members of the organization and of the persons served by it.

• The goals and assignments of each member of the organization must be established in such a way that he is highly motivated to achieve them.

• The methods and procedures used by the organization and its subunits to achieve the agreed-upon objectives must be developed and adopted in such a way that the members are highly motivated to use these methods to their maximum potentiality.

- The members of the organization and the persons related to it must feel that the reward system of the organization — salaries, wages, bonuses, dividends, interest payments — yields them equitable compensation for their efforts and contributions.

The overlapping group form of organization offers a structure which, in conjunction with a high level of group interactional skills, is particularly effective in performing the processes necessary to meet these requirements.

CONSTRUCTIVE USE OF CONFLICT

An organization operating under the newer theory is not free from conflict. Conflict and differences of opinion always exist in a healthy, virile organization, for it is usually from such differences that new and better objectives and methods emerge. Differences are essential to progress, but bitter, unresolved differences can immobilize an organization. The central problem, consequently, becomes not how to reduce or eliminate conflict, but how to deal constructively with it. Effective organizations have extraordinary capacity to handle conflict. Their success is due to three very important characteristics:

1. They possess the machinery to deal constructively with conflict. They have an organizational structure which facilitates constructive interaction between individuals and between work groups.

2. The personnel of the organization are skilled in the processes of effective interaction and mutual influence.

3. There is high confidence and trust among the members of the organization in each other, high loyalty to the work group and to the organization, and high motivation to achieve the organization's objecties. Confidence, loyalty, and cooperative motivation produce earnest, sincere, and determined efforts to find solutions to conflict. There is greater motivation to find a constructive solution than to maintain an irreconcilable conflict. The solutions reached are often highly creative and represent a far better solution than any initially proposed by the conflicting interests (Metcalf & Urwick, 1940).

The discussion in this chapter has deliberately focused on and emphasized the group aspects of organization and management. This has been done to make clear some of the major differences between the classical and the newer theories of management. It should also sharpen the awareness of the kind of changes needed to start applying the newer theory.

Any organization which bases its operation on this theory will necessarily make use of individual counseling and coaching by superiors of subordinates. There is need in every situation for a balanced use of both procedures, individual and group. Here, as with other aspects of supervision, the balance which will be most appropriate and work best will depend upon the experience, expectations, and skills of the poeple involved.

AN IMPROVEMENT CYCLE FOR
HUMAN RESOURCE DEVELOPMENT
Rensis Likert

Organizational Development (OD) or, as it has been labeled more recently, Human Resource Development (HRD), consists all too often of uncoordinated, piecemeal efforts such as team building, job enrichment or job redesign, sensitivity training, participative decision making, and management by objectives. These activities would be much more effective if they were an integral part of a well-defined, overall plan. An important factor, for example, in the failure of organizational development to produce improvement in medical centers, as described by Weisbord (1976), appears to have been the absence of an effective model to guide the change effort.

Walton has pointed to the necessity of using a systematically unified approach in seeking to bring about organizational improvement. He shows that if used in an uncoordinated manner, various specific OD devices yield disappointing results (Walton, 1972). What is needed is a total system of management into which these parts, if compatible with the overall effort, can fit.

What should be the characteristics of a management system that can be used as a model to guide HRD efforts?

- The system should have been discovered by rigorous, quantitative research. This research should have demonstrated that this management system yields the best performance and other desirable results in most working situations.
- It should be possible to define this management system by means of a limited number of measurable dimensions.
- These dimensions should have been demonstrated through extensive research to be those that, on the average, have closer relationships than do other organizational dimensions to desired results such as productivity and employee satisfaction.
- Efficient procedures and instruments to measure these key organizational dimensions should be available.
- There should be ample research findings to show that as organizations shift toward this management system, there is a corresponding improvement in performance and other desired outcomes. The research should demonstrate that these results occur in different kinds of industries and working situations.

These are demanding specifications. There appears, however, to be at least one management system which meets all of these specifications and which can be used as a model to guide and coordinate HRD efforts. This is the *System 4* model which, very briefly stated, is a *participative group* system. System 1 is a punitive, authoritarian system; System 2 is benevolent, authoritarian; System 3 is consultative (Likert and Likert, 1976).

The System 1-4 continuum was discovered by extensive research over a 25-year period and with the expenditure of more than $15 million by the Institute

286

for Social Research of The University of Michigan. These systems can be defined by using a limited number of key human organizational dimensions. These dimensions are those that have been found through extensive research to correlate highest with performance across a wide variety of different kinds of organizations (Likert, 1977a; Taylor and Bowers, 1972).

Efficient instruments are available to measure these key dimensions of any human organization (Taylor and Bowers, 1972). A short questionnaire also is available which yields useful approximations of these key dimensions. This is the *Profile of Organizational Characteristics – Form S* (Likert, 1977b). A sizable number of studies on different kinds of work situations have found that as an organization shifts closer to System 4, there is a corresponding improvement in performance and an increase in other desired results (Likert, 1977a).

Another useful aspect of the System 1-4 models for HRD purposes is the recognition that certain of the human organizational dimensions are causal in character and others are symptomatic or intervening in character. Causal variables are those which are capable of being influenced or altered by the organization's leadership and which, when altered, produce corresponding changes in the symptomatic (intervening) variables and, in turn, in the results that the organization achieves (Likert and Likert, 1976).

An organizational improvement cycle that can be used in any HRD effort is shown in Figure 1. As will be observed, it makes use of the System 1-4 model. The process described in Figure 1 is the survey feedback method of HRD. This has been found to be a particularly effective method for producing organizational improvement (Bowers, 1973; Bowers and Franklin, 1976).

6 STEPS TO FOLLOW

In using the organizational improvement cycle, the organization must be guided by the following steps (Likert and Likert, 1976).

1. *Focus the action efforts on the causal variables*, such as leadership behavior and structure. Do not try to change by direct action the intervening variables such as motivation and control. If the causal variables are improved, there will be subsequent gains in the intervening variables. But if efforts to improve the intervening variables are made by focusing direct action on them, any improvement that occurs is likely to be minor and transitory, and there often is a deterioration in the causal variables with long-range, adverse consequences (Likert, 1973).

2. *Move to the System 4 model gradually*. Do not attempt one big jump such as from System 1 to System 4. Move, rather, from System 1 to System 2, from System 2 to System 3, from System 3 to System 4. Both leaders and members lack the skills and find it difficult to make a sudden, sizable shift to System 4.

In moving toward it, a leader should make no greater shift at any one time than subordinates or members can adjust to comfortably and respond to positively. If a leader suddenly makes a sizable shift, the members do not have the interaction skills to respond appropriately and usually are made insecure or frightened by the shift, responding to it negatively.

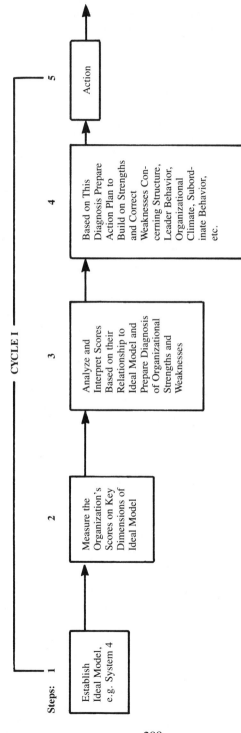

Figure 1.

ORGANIZATIONAL IMPROVEMENT CYCLE

3. *In planning the action to be taken, involve those whose behavior has to change to bring the desired improvement.* It is, of course, important to involve all the persons affected in all the steps of the improvement cycle, but it is especially important to involve them in planning the action effort.

4. *Use objective, impersonal evidence as much as possible in the action-planning process.* This includes using ''situational requirements,'' that is, the hard facts of organizational life such as budgets, time and legal restrictions. It also includes the discrepancies between the measurements describing the current situation and the desired model.

5. *Insofar as the circumstances permit, have those persons who are in the most powerful and influential positions take the most initiative and become most active in the improvement program.* In a corporation, for example, the change programs that are initiated and supported by top management are more likely to be successful than are those started by a middle-level manager. These programs often encounter top management's displeasure and typically come to a halt.

6. *Conduct the action planning in a supportive, helpful atmosphere.* HRD is much more likely to realize the desired improvement when it is guided by a highly effective management system serving as a model than when it is not.

Casey Stengel is quoted as saying, *''If you don't know where you're going, you'll wind up somewhere else.''* HRD projects which lack an ideal model as a coordinating guide may well ''wind up somewhere else.''

REFERENCES

Bowers, D.G., OD Techniques and Their Results in 23 Organizations: The Michigan-ICL Study, *Journal of Applied Behavioral Science*, 1973, 9, 21-43.

Bowers, D.G. and J.L. Franklin, *Survey Guided Development: Data Based on Organizational Change*, LaJolla, California University Associates, 1977.

Likert, R., Human Resource Accounting: Building and Assessing Productive Organizations, *Personnel*, May/June, 1973, 8-24.

Likert, R., *Past and Future Perspectives on System 4*, Rensis Likert Associates, Ann Arbor, Michigan, 1977a.

Likert, R., *Profile of Organizational Characteristics: Form S*, Rensis Likert Associates, Ann Arbor, Michigan, 1977b.

Likert, R. and J.G. Likert, *New Ways of Managing Conflict*, N.Y. McGraw-Hill, 1976.

Taylor, J.C. and D.G. Bowers, *Survey of Organizations: A Machine-Scored Standardized Questionnaire Instrument*, Ann Arbor, Michigan, 1972.

Walton, R.E., ''How to Counter Alienation in the Plant,'' *Harvard Business Review*, November-December, 1972, p.70-81.

Weisbord, M.R., Why Organizational Development Hasn't Worked (So Far) in Medical Centers, *Health Management Review*, Spring, 1976, p. 17-28.

WORK INNOVATIONS IN
THE UNITED STATES
Richard E. Walton

Americans tend to do things by trial and error and in dealing with changes in the way they work, they are no different. Whereas changes in European workplaces tend to be guided by government intervention and ideological rationalizations and involve an explicit transfer of authority, innovations in American workplaces are voluntary and pragmatic and involve no such transfer.[1] Despite its random nature, however, much change that has been planned has occurred in American workplaces during the past ten years.

Observers differ about whether work improvement is a fad or a long-term transformation in the nature of work organizations. Scientists differ in their theoretical explanations of why it works or when the conditions are right for it. Managers invariably wonder whether it has application in their organizations, and some union officials are concerned about its implications for the union as an institution. These concerns imply varying conceptions of work innovation and hence indicate the amount of confusion that exists about what work improvement is.

In this article, I want to look at what has actually changed in workplaces, find out what we can learn from these work improvement activities, and derive some principles from what is reflected in the most successful ones. First, though, let us clarify what "work improvement" means and how I will be using it in the remainder of this article.

WHAT WORK IMPROVEMENT IS

The planned changes called "work improvements" have appeared in workplaces in many guises — as "quality of work life," "humanization of work," "work reform," "work restructuring," "work design," and "sociotechnical systems."

Although some of these terms have special connotations for the professionals who employ them, in method and goals the actual activities pursued under the various labels are not very different. I find it useful to distinguish three separate aspects of a work improvement effort.

1. DESIGN TECHNIQUES

The element of work improvement activities that is most apparent is the specific changes in the way work is organized and managed. For instance, the content of tasks changes when jobs are enriched, work teams affect the way tasks are organized and how they relate to each other, and consultative management gives workers the opportunity to influence decisions that affect them. The techniques may also affect the information provided workers as well as their compensation, security, physical environment, and access to due process.

The techniques employed and their possible combinations are many. For example, in changing assembly methods, auto plants have assigned related tasks to work teams, allowed them to decide how to allocate the work among themselves (provided they meet quality and quantity requirements), and created buffer inventories between adjacent work teams to increase latitude in the rhythm of their work. Also, management and unions in competitive manufacturing situations have designed plantwide schemes to share productivity increases and have structured mechanisms to ensure that workers' ideas for improvement are considered.

2. INTENDED RESULTS

Another aspect of work improvement is the results it is intended to produce. They can be either economic (for the benefit of the organization) or human (for the benefit of employees). The business benefits can take many forms — quality, delivery, materials usage, machine capacity utilization, and labor efficiency. The human benefits can take form as real income, security, challenge, variety, advancement opportunity, dignity, equity, and sense of community. The relative importance of these depends on the needs and aspirations of the employees in question.

Most of the work improvement labels focus narrowly on either techniques or results. For example, "job enrichment" directs attention to the techniques level and only to one technique. The connotation of "job design" is only slightly broader. "Quality of work life" has the same limitations. If refers directly to an objective that can be served in innumerable ways. Moreover, as labels, "quality of work life" and its first cousin, "humanization of work," have serious drawbacks; they refer only to human gains, which in today's business environment need to be closely coupled with improved competitive performance.

In my experience, I have found that organizations can improve business results in a humane way and improve the quality of the human experience in a businesslike manner by identifying the work cultures that promote both improvements simultaneously. Such work cultures are the links between technique and results in my three-level conception of work improvements.

3. WORK CULTURE: THE INTERMEDIATE EFFECTS

The combination of attitudes, relationships, developed capabilities, habits, and other behavioral patterns that characterize the dynamics of an organization is a work culture.

Some changes in the culture, such as high-cost consciousness, responsiveness to authority, and high activity norms, may promote performance but do little or nothing for people. Conversely, under some circumstances, high sensitivity to feelings and concern for the personal growth of the individual are cultural attributes that may be appreciated by the people affected but may not by themselves contribute to business performance.

In the most successful work improvement efforts, the culture simultaneously enhances business performance and the quality of human experience. In one food plant, for instance, management sought to promote employee identification with goals. Such positive identification increases not only workers' motivation to work but also their sense of belonging in the workplace and their pride in the plant's achievement. Similarly, a behavior pattern that influences both employee self-esteem and the soundness of business decisions is another desirable cultural attribute.

Identification and mutual influence are ideals common to many work improvement projects, but no single culture is ideal for all businesses or all people. What particular set of attitudes, capabilities, and relationships a company should emphasize will depend on its industry's strategic performance indexes and its employees' work life values. Whatever the work culture sought, it cannot be mandated by anyone. It can only be shaped over time by a combination of things — including the techniques by which work is organized and managed.

Exhibit
Three-level conception work improvement

Level I Design techniques	Level II Work culture ideals	Level III intended results
Job design	High skill levels and flexibility in using them	*For business:*
Pay	Identification with product, process, and total business viewpoint	Low cost
Supervisor's role	Problem solving instead of finger pointing	Quick delivery
Training	Influence by information and expertise instead of by position	High-quality products
Performance feedback	Mutual influence	Low turnover
Goal setting	Openness	Low absenteeism
Communication	Responsiveness	Equipment utilization
Employment stability policies	Trust	*For quality of work life:*
Status symbols	Egalitarian climate	Self-esteem
Leadership patterns	Equity	Economic well being Security

Note: The design techniques, cultural ideals, and intended results listed above are presented as illustrative, not as comprehensive or even universally applicable. Also, the items in the three columns are not horizontally lined up to relate to each other. The arrows indicate influence.

Let us review how these three aspects of work improvement activities relate to each other.

Techniques are the elements of the work organization that people can alter directly; intended results are the fundamental business and human criteria by which to judge effectiveness; and the work culture mediates the impact of the former on the latter. The techniques create the culture, which strongly influences business performance and the human experience at work.

According to this conception, one's choice of techniques is guided by continuously referring to the type of work culture that they promote, and in turn to projected business and human outcomes. For example, in a paper manufacturing plant, the business ends required that the manpower be flexible, and employees wanted the opportunity to acquire new skills. The plant adopted a design in which teams are responsible for a cluster of tasks and members are rewarded for acquiring the skills to perform all the team tasks. Such a design promotes both flexibility and opportunity. (The three-level conception of work improvement is shown in the Exhibit; the arrows indicate influence.)

The Exhibit illustrates how important it is to specify the proper business and work life outcomes for a particular company.

Applying this concept, one is also guided in the quality of choice one should make at each level. As one moves backward in the exhibit from intended results through work culture to design techniques, one's stance should become increasingly pragmatic. If the desired outcomes are clear and one's commitment to both business and human values is firm, then one can evaluate cultural attributes and in turn design techniques in terms of their efficacy in achieving the desired results.

INTEREST IN WORK INNOVATION

Over the past decade, media attention has gradually shifted from focusing on the symptoms of disaffection with work to possible solutions. The amount of work improvement activity in plants and offices throughout the U.S. has grown steadily, appearing to be on the path of a classical S growth curve, in which growth climbs slowly at first, accelerates, and then slows again. Today, the rate of growth in these experiments continues to increase annually, suggesting that we are approaching the steeper portion of the curve.

Extrapolating from available information, I estimate that an important minority of the *Fortune "500"* companies are attempting some significant work improvement projects. And, not surprisingly, the companies that have greater commitment to and experience with such projects are among the leaders in their respective industries: General Motors, Procter & Gamble, Exxon, General Foods, TRW, and Cummins Engine. Less prominent but similarly well-managed manufacturing companies such as Butler Manufacturing and Mars, Inc. have also become increasingly active in this area. Citibank is one company with major work improvement efforts in the office environment.[2] Prudential Insurance is another.

All of the manufacturing companies I have listed have regarded new plant start-ups as opportunities to introduce major new work structures. In recent years, major projects have begun in organizations of various sizes (from 100 to over 3,000), with varying technologies (from simple hand assembly to sophisticated continuous flow processes) and in different geographical locations (from upstate New York to the deep South and the West). As these companies extend their innovative work systems to other new plant sites, managers learn from the experience of the pioneers, and the systems cease to be regarded as experimental. Although the diffusion generally occurs slowly, the principles that underlie these new designs usually spread to companies' established plants as well. Let us look at some of these work innovations in detail.

INDIVIDUAL PROJECTS

HBR readers have been exposed to a number of accounts of individual efforts (e.g., the Topeka Pet Food Plant) and to the distinctive approaches of several U.S. companies (e.g., Donnelly Mirrors and Eaton Corporation).[3] Although not fully representative of the diverse practices that one can observe, these experiments do illustrate the growing work improvement activity in the U.S.

To my knowledge, the activity of General Motors is the most extensive of any company in the U.S. and may be more extensive than that of Volvo, whose pioneering efforts have been well publicized internationally. GM's dozens of projects take a variety of forms. One long-term effort at GM began in the early 1970s in an assembly plant in Tarrytown, N.Y. What began as a "What-have-we-got-to-lose?" experiment in which workers and the union were involved in redesigning the hard- and soft-trim departments' facilities has blossomed into a plantwide quality of work life program involving over 3,500 people.

A different type of project at GM began in 1974 at a new battery plant in Fitzgerald, Ga., where the pay system was set up to reward knowledge and skills acquisition. After four years, almost all workers there have become familiar with a wide range of jobs and have detailed knowledge of the production process. Initially, inspectors evaluated the workers' performance, but eventually the production teams themselves acquired the responsibility to ensure high-quality performance. Since 1977, work teams have prepared their own departmental budgets for materials and supplies. Managers provide workers with information such as cost data, which is traditionally not shown to them. The sparse and functional offices reveal the prevailing attitude about status symbols.

The pay system, self-supervision, and other design techniques have been combined at the Fitzgerald plant to create a work culture characterized by flexibility, mutual trust, informality, equality, and commitment. Reportedly, the Fitzgerald plant's performance has been very favorable, compared both with other plants and with its own plan. Those familiar with the plant attribute much of its superior performance to the work structure and to the fact that workers take pride in establishing new levels of output and quality.

Another innovator in this field is as much a leader in nondurable consumer goods as GM is in durable goods but shuns publicity of any of its work improvements. It regards the knowledge it has developed about implementing innovative work systems as proprietary, similar to other types of know-how that give it a competitive edge.

In the late 1960s in one plant of a major division, this company introduced a new work system designed around the idea that workers would be paid according to their skill levels. Under this system, the company does not impose quotas to limit the number who could advance to higher levels. The work system promotes the development of relatively self-supervising work teams. The basic features of this system have been adapted to the six new plants built subsequently as well as to departments in the preexisting, unionized plants of the division.

Because successful work improvement approaches have not always spread to other plants within the same company, it is worth noting why transfer did occur in this case. The acceptance of change in the existing plants has been fueled by their need to remain competitive with the newer plants, which employ more productive work structures. The change has been facilitated by transferring managers with experience from the innovative plants to the established ones. Also, whenever a new technology or project has been launched or major physical renovations planned, work innovations have been introduced in the old plants.

I have observed many of the plants in this company. Without a doubt, their innovative work systems have contributed significantly to the impressive performance of these plants and to the fact that by a wide margin the plants are usually regarded as the best places to work in their respective communities.

Although GM and the manufacturer of nondurable goods are leaders in the field of work improvements, they are not typical. Most companies, such as Butler Manufacturing, have only a few projects. In 1976, Butler introduced innovative work structures similar to the one at GM's Fitzgerald plant in two new plants. In one plant, the program is working exceptionally well; participants are enthusiastic about the work system and think it contributes strongly to their performance. According to pertinent internal criteria, this plant is 20% more productive and 35% more profitable than comparable plants in the same company.

The other new plant has experienced difficulties, and it is less clear that it has benefited from the work innovations.

The experience of a large paper company is also typical. With encouragement and support from the company's chairman, management launched two major facility wide projects at the time of the plants' start-ups. When I last heard, the paper mill project was regarded as successful, but the other, in a converting plant, was not. Extenuating circumstances in the marketplace have contributed to the lack of profitability of the converting plant. Also, misjudgments in design reportedly have not been remedied, and optimism is declining.

Most companies experience both success and failure. One large company with four major plantwide projects has experienced almost the full spectrum. A plant that started up with a bold and imaginative work structure three and a half years ago has been very disappointing in terms of economic performance and the work system itself. Local management and union officials judge a second plant to be only somewhat more effective than it would have been without the innovations. A third is solidly effective, and a fourth is a big success according to both human and economic criteria.

The examples I have discussed so far are plant projects, but comparably conceived work improvement efforts have been occurring in office settings as well. In 1972, the clerical work in the Group Policyholders' Service Department of the Guardian Life Insurance Company was fragmented. To process a case file required several steps, each performed by a different person at a different desk in assembly line fashion. Files were hard to find, and response to client inquiries were delayed. No one person performed or had responsibility for a whole job. Consequently, there was little basis for meaningful recognition of achievement, and morale was low.

The work improvement effort created natural units of work by combining policyholder services and accounting functions for a particular geographic area.

The new "account analyst" became identified with a limited and stable set of clients with whom he or she maintained contact and for whom he or she provided a number of services previously assigned to different desks. Control over individual aspects of the work was removed, and individual accountability for overall results was increased.

Although the new system at Guardian required people to go through complex training, with the result that 6 out of 120 employees could now meet the demands of the redesigned jobs, management reports that the system was effective in producing cumulative increases in productivity of about 33% in four years.

TOP MANAGEMENT INTEREST

Part of the evidence supporting my projection of a continued acceleration of the growth rate of new projects goes beyond concrete activities; it is found in the trend toward increased top management attention to work innovation. Whereas five years ago it was plant or division level managers who invariably sought educational or consultative assistance for potential projects, today it is equally likely that inquiries will come from top corporate managers who are interested in advancing their own understanding of the field, formulating appropriate policies, and promoting constructive corporate activity.

Also, whereas before managers would invite professors to meet with them and report on developments in the field, today it is equally likely that managers with direct experience in promoting work innovations will address these management groups. For example, the chairman of the board of a major packaging company recently assembled his top corporate and divisional executives to learn about the work innovations of a major automobile company by a firsthand report of the auto company's vice chairman.

A particularly striking example of the trend toward top management interest in work innovations and toward more manager-to-manager consultation on the subject is provided by a November 1977 conference sponsored by the American Center for the Quality of Working Life. Convened for the purpose of exchanging experiences and examining from the "practical viewpoint of operating executives the principles underlying quality of work life efforts and their efficacy in society," the conference was attended by 40 senior executives from Xerox, General Motors, Nabisco, and Weyerhaeuser.

The "blue collar blues" may promote the adoption and diffusion of innovative work designs in a wide range of industries, from blue collar manufacturing work to white collar and service work and in both the private and the public sector, but a major reason companies are trying work improvement projects is competition. Another is the changing expectations of workers, whose consciousness of quality of work life issues continues to rise. Another is the implicit threat of legislation that might set new, more embracing quality of work environment standards or that might require workers to participate in the governance of private industry.

ASKING THE RIGHT QUESTIONS

Despite the many good reasons for attempting work improvement systems, their future depends on how managers approach some fundamental issues and whether they reject the myths surrounding these efforts. Some misconceptions yield easily to more valid assumptions; others appear to need more direct challenge.

HAVE WORK IMPROVEMENTS BEEN EFFECTIVE?

There has been a tendency for people to assume that work innovation projects are either spectacular successes or abject failures. At the expense of some widely held myths, however, people active in the field have become increasingly realistic, recognizing that, in fact, projects can and do fall at every point along a broad spectrum of effectiveness.

I have been deeply involved in 4 major projects and am familiar with aspects of another 30 or so. In terms of their effectiveness in achieving excellence in business and quality of work life outcomes, my impression is that these three dozen projects represent roughly a normal distribution around the mean, just as the effectiveness of more conventionally organized plants would be expected to form a normal distribution.

I believe that the average effectiveness of these innovative work systems is higher than the average of more conventionally organized but otherwise comparable plants. Certainly, however, the poorly managed innovative plants are less effective than the better managed conventional ones. I cannot offer proof that these assumptions are valid, but the mixed experiences of the companies I have discussed illustrate my observations.

Despite the evidence, the myths persist. I have visited a few innovative plants that were advertised as significantly successful, only to discover that they were at best marginally more effective than they would have been without the work innovations. And I have read reports of the "failures" of previously publicized projects, which, on investigation, I found were faulty. People had blown some difficulties encountered in the design or implementation of the projects way out of proportion.

Why these exaggerations? First, people view such efforts with emotion — some being deeply committed to work improvement activities, others being basically hostile to them. Second, where they are involved, the media deem dramatic successes and failures to be newsworthy. Third, because their expectations are high, people readily see any shortfall as a failure.

Even assuming that work innovations have merit, managers and researchers need to have the realistic expectation that their effectiveness will conform to some normal distribution.

WHAT ARE THE SPONSORS' MOTIVES?

Myths have surrounded the motives of those promoting or undertaking work improvement activities. People see sponsors as narrowly interested in either productivity or the human condition, each at the expense of the other. During the early 1970s, when much interest in work improvement was stimulated by one of the two objectives, these beliefs had some basis in reality, but the situation has gradually changed.

In the successful innovations, managers behave as if both economic and human values count. I am familiar with several major innovative work systems that have taken a long time to become effective (and in one plant remain not very effective today) because management's choices were too heavily influenced by quality of work life considerations in the beginning.

In one case, for example, while stability of assignments and mastery of jobs was necessary to get the plant's new technology under control, employees were permitted to move among jobs and learn multiple skills that would advance their pay. Management later recognized that it had erred in not continuously keeping economic as well as human considerations in mind.

Conversely, I am aware of some abortive job redesign efforts in which management strictly viewed worker satisfaction either as a means to improve productivity or as an incidental by-product. Not surprisingly, management's orientation affected not only what changes were made but also workers' attitudes toward the changes. Many union officials believe it unwise to be publicly committed to productivity as well as to quality of work life goals lest the former be identified with speedups and other activities that achieve productivity at the workers' expense. Nevertheless, union officials often implicitly acknowledge the legitimacy of improved business results.

A commitment to dual outcomes is congruent with the values increasingly held by knowledgeable people, but also it has proved to be the most practical approach to making significant advances toward either end. Consider the point negatively. When changes in the work structure do not improve the work environment from a human perspective, they will not increase employees' contribution to the business; likewise, changes in work structure that require managers to relate differently to workers but do not also benefit the business are not as likely to be sustained by those managers over time.

One should not confuse a dedication to achieving both results with the assumption that meeting one will guarantee the other; morale and productivity are not necessarily linked. Morale can be enhanced in any number of ways. Rather, a commitment to dual objectives sets in motion a search for the limited set of changes that will promote both human and economic ends.

Some issues will inevitably not yield to dual orientation. Planners and managers will have to make trade-off decisions in areas where achieving human goals can occur only at the expense of the business, and vice versa. Nevertheless, it is more important for those involved in work improvement to recognize that in most work structures there is an abundance of opportunities to make changes that will advance both objectives.

WHAT DO WORKERS REALLY WANT FROM WORK?

Individuals and groups will always express broad differences in the types of work structure they prefer. Therefore, as the multiple-level framework indicates, the ideal culture and the design features of the work structure need to be responsive to the employee population at a given location. Even though researchers and managers are learning which questions about employees' needs and preferences will provide good guidelines to practice, they continue to ask a few either-or questions, which are more confusing than helpful.

Observers often ask variations of the following question. "Are people motivated more by intrinsic factors, such as tasks that use and develop their skills, or by extrinsic factors, such as variable pay for performance and the prospect of advancement?" Both kinds of factors are important, albeit one may be more important to any one group at any one time. The most significant question is how to integrate both extrinsic and intrinsic factors in a practical way.

My observation is that workers in innovative systems have not had to choose between more interesting work and more pay; and that where intrinsic satisfaction has increased, the pay has been improved, reflecting the workers' greater contribution. As Irving Bluestone of the UAW has said of the American worker, "While his rate of pay may dominate his relationship to his job, he can be responsive to the opportunity for playing an innovative, creative, and imaginative role in the production process."[4]

A related question people often ask is: "Are people more interested in finding meaning in the workplace or in minimizing the time spent there?" While the answer to this question may add to our understanding of the sociology of work today, it is not a productive question for improving current practice. It is better to assume that the work force as a whole would like both in some measure.

But, even if some workers care more about time off than a meaningful work life, it may still pay to heed the lower priority issue because improving the meaning of the workplace may be much more feasible than reducing the workweek. Speculating about workers' desires also leads to the related myths about regional differences and the need for selective hiring. Each myth is built on the assumption that a relatively small subset of the work force has attitudes and talents compatible with work restructuring. I have heard managers assert, "It may work in a plant located in a small town in the Midwest, but workers in the South (or the Northeast, California, big cities, and so on) are different."

If an innovative plant is located in an abundant labor market where supervisors screen, say, six times as many applicants as they actually hire, then their myth may be: "Only one in six is a high achiever who will be receptive to the new work structure. It is okay to redesign work if you can be selective but not if you are in a tight labor market."

Fortunately, since projects are launched in all regions of the country, in both rural and urban areas, in both tight and abundant labor markets, and appear to have a degree of effectiveness not determined by these factors, belief in these myths is weakening.

WHAT ECONOMIC BENEFITS CAN ONE EXPECT?

Managers frequently ask, "How much productivity gain can one expect from work redesign?" Unfortunately, some advocates answer, "One should be able to achieve 15% to 20% improvement in productivity." The question itself is emphatically misdirected, and the response just cited is meaningless without knowing what index of productivity the questioner has in mind and whether it is appropriate. For example, the number of output units per man-hour may not be an important index when labor is a low fraction of total costs. Moreover, prior to analysis of the operations in question, one cannot assume a basis for the estimates.

An inquiry and response should focus on methods by which managers can answer the question for themselves. The form of potential gains will vary significantly according to the technology used. The magnitude of possible gains will depend on how well the unit is already performing and on whether the aspects of performance that can be improved are strongly influenced by employees' attitudes and skills. Finally, whether potential gains ever materialize depends on the quality of redesign ideas and their implementation.

The following examples illustrate how productivity indexes can take different forms.

- A facility that warehouses and supplies engine parts to dealers and dealer chains could gain new accounts by speeding up its delivery response; it could add very profitable business if it could promise certain large national chains 48 hours versus 72 hours for delivery.
- In a capital-intensive plant that machines casted parts, management determined that it was technically feasible to increase by 15% the maximum throughput of a $10 million segment of the technology manned by 10 employees. This rate has, however, been achieved only for brief periods of time because of the limitations of operating personnel. Running speeds and machine downtime play a similarly important role in other parts of this plant and strongly affect its competitiveness.
- In a relatively high labor-intensive business, management was experiencing a high rate of turnover. The particular tasks, mostly assembly line jobs, did not require great skill, but learning the idiosyncrasies of the company's many different products took a lot of time. While the new employees were learning to deal with these peculiarities, their higher scrap rates and lower labor efficiency significantly affected unit costs. As a result, the turnover costs were significant.

To assess the potential of work improvements in the foregoing operations, one should ask: "How much difference would it make if workers cared more and knew more about this work?" Let us examine the first example in light of this question to show how one can begin to analyze the situation.

First, one needs some facts: the replacement engine parts center employs about 100 hourly workers; the pay is good for this type of work in the area; turnover is relatively low; and labor relations are amicable. While workers do not especially identify with management and many are known to goof off whenever possible, they are not antagonistic.

After a preliminary analysis of the various ways in which performance is sensitive to employee motivation and knowledge, the management of the center estimated that:

1. Employees could reasonably handle a 10% additional volume, even allowing for increased time to be devoted to training and regular meetings. But the 10% savings would not create a net economic benefit because the wage increases reflecting greater job scope and skills would offset them.

2. The cost of errors (orders lost, wrong parts pulled, overages, underages, or damages in shipment due to carelessness) could be reduced by $100,000 per year.

3. The work system could reliably handle up to 25% of the facility's volume within a 48-hour response time, enabling the management to win over some additional accounts and increase the margin on some existing ones and thereby to add an estimated $200,000 more profit per year.

4. The potential benefits of $300,000 assumes a work force that cares more and knows more and that is amenable to flexibility in work assignments based on the needs of the business, the latter point being especially critical to reducing the central response time.

The foregoing analysis illustrates good practice.

First, management identified particular points in the system where poor labor utilization, errors, and limitations in response time occurred. It did not rely on global hunches.

Second, by converting potential gains to annual dollar amounts, management could see the relative importance of error reduction and improved response time. Moreover, management could relate the benefits to other factors; for example, $300,000 would be a savings equal to 25% of the annual payroll.

Third, management understood these were potential benefits and not certain gains that would automatically flow from the adoption of some set of design techniques. Its ability to achieve any of these benefits depended on its ingenuity and skill. It aways ran the risk that it would not be able to modify the work culture as intended.

Fourth, management knew that for any changes to be effective from a business standpoint, it would also have to improve the work from the workers' point of view.

Managers in the machining operation and assembly unit followed procedures similar to the one just outlined. However, their estimate of benefits took a different form. Because they could spread the large fixed interest and depreciated expenses, managers in the capital-intensive machining operation figured that increasing the output rate of finished parts by 15% would result in lower unit costs. The estimated annual savings represented 150% of the $140,000 payroll for the unit — that is, $210,000.

In the assembly line unit, the managers concluded that it was not feasible to reduce turnover significantly, that only modest improvements in scrap and labor efficiency were possible, and that costs associated with any changes contemplated would largely offset the estimated gains.

In cases such as those just described, management's analyses are limited by the same difficulties encountered in estimating the costs and benefits of untried technologies or management systems — that is, the estimates can prove to be incomplete, too optimistic, too conservative, and so on. Nevertheless, the analytic approach presented here illustrates the systematic and realistic efforts managers should make to assess the potential performance gains.

Which procedures a manager actually uses and the level of detail of the analysis is not the point. The important point is that planners have some systematic approach for assessing potential benefits that might accrue if the cultural ideals are actually realized. The methodology need not be elaborate.

SOME LESSONS FROM EXPERIENCE

For those who consider undertaking new initiatives and promoting the spread of successful innovations to other units in the organization, I offer the following guidelines. Though not comprehensive, they are nonetheless derived from observations of the contrasts between relatively effective work improvement efforts and less effective ones.

1. *Attempt work improvement because of its intrinsic positive values, not because it might be a way to avoid unionization.* Apart from the fact that I believe in the institution of collective bargaining, trying to avoid unionization has several drawbacks. One is that unions are more likely to join in efforts to adapt innovations to existing facilities if work patterns are not being used as an anti-union device in the new plants. Another is that, although most projects in the U.S. have been in nonunionized offices and plants, the amount of joint union-management cooperation is increasing. Such projects as Harman Industries, Weyerhaeuser, Tennessee Valley Authority, the Rushton Coal Mines, and Rockwell International attest to the benefit of cooperation.

As I stated earlier, GM and UAW have a very active program of work improvement. The approach contractually agreed on by the parties is oriented to quality of work life, but as the Tarrytown experience illustrates, management, union officials, and workers are all genuinely interested in the business results. Irving Bluestone, international vice president of the UAW, describes the joint GM-UAW program as follows:

"The objective of our quality of work life program is to create a more participative and satisfying work environment. If, as a result of increased participation, unit costs are improved because turnover rates go down and product quality goes up, that is fine."

"But if a plant manager is thinking of a quality of work life project as a means for increasing productivity, we don't proceed. There are certain other constraints — people must not be compelled to work harder, changes must not result in workers getting laid off, and the local and national agreements remain inviolate. The projects must be from the ground up and participation voluntary on the part of workers. The first phase of all projects is to improve the climate of mutual respect between union and management; if this doesn't succeed, there is no basis to proceed on. Plant management and the local union must both be committed."[5]

302

During the past half dozen years, as work improvement activities have been growing in number, diversity, and visibility, both labor and management have encountered doubt within their own ranks. UAW officials have not found it easy to convince union members that the program is not a management gimmick to increase productivity and perhaps weaken the union.

At GM, managers at certain levels express concern that the program will result in a loss of authority and prestige. These fears are diminishing gradually but can flare up at any event that seems to support them. Still, the commitment at the top of both organizations has been extraordinary and is bolstered by a growing constituency of local managers and union officials who have had positive experiences.

According to Bluestone, very few projects have actually failed, but more time must pass before the majority of projects currently under way can be declared successes.

2. *Recognize the basic difference between opportunities in new facilities and opportunities in existing ones.* Once, most people assumed that the major innovations introduced in new plant start-ups could serve as inspirational and instructive examples for managements and union officials of established plants. I have concluded that providing examples of what was done in a new organization is not helpful in enabling managers of established units to visualize alternative futures for their units and is not an effective stimulus for developing a program for transforming them.

The reasons are severalfold and go beyond the fact that a particular work structure that is successful in a new plant may be inappropriate in an old one. More fundamentally, the processes of innovation (diagnosing, planning, inventing, and implementing) are significantly different for new and existing units. In established facilities, the level of aspiration for change and the time frame allotted for achieving it must be much more modest then in new facilities.

In selecting aspects of work structure that can be changed, planners need to be opportunistic — doing what they can when they can. Also, the main job of planners in old facilities is defrosting the old work culture and creating a sense of the potential for change. To do this, they need to give careful attention to the participative processes for deciding the direction and method of the change.

Fortunately, the literature is providing us with a growing number of instructive examples of productive change in established organizations. The Tarrytown plant is one such example.

3. *Avoid either-or conceptions of work organization.* An example of this faulty thinking relates to the sources and types of controls: "Traditional systems rely on hierarchical controls. The innovative system is the opposite; therefore, it must rely on individual or team self-management." Another example of this thinking is: "If we need to rely on self-discipline and peer group pressure to minimize counterproductive behavior, then there is no place for management-administered discipline."

Indeed, as managers in these work systems have sooner or later discovered, a selective emphasis and sensible mixture of management techniques are called for. A number of organizations have had to go through a period of permissiveness before management discovered the need to set and enforce certain boundaries on the behavior of members of the company.

Managers make a related mistake when they assume that an organization at start-up can be at an idealized, advanced state of development. Some plans for new plant organization neglect the important distinction between conceiving of the steady state design and designing the initial organization. These plants start up with workers and supervisors having roles and responsibilities that reflect the planners' idealized view of the mature organization. Workers lack the technical and human skills as well as the problem-solving capacities to perform effectively. Supervisors cannot merely "facilitate" — they must provide directive supervision.

Delegation is the cornerstone of new plant development. Such delegation must be rooted in careful diagnosis of the existing base of skills and capabilities in the work force and a realistic view of their ability to develop over time.

4. *Do not advocate one answer; spread a way of looking for answers.* Managers and planners need to inculcate their people with a way of thinking about the diagnosis and designing of innovative work structures, not the work structures themselves. This is a major implication of my three-level conception of work improvement activity. It is less appropriate (and sometimes counterproductive) to promote the spread of particular techniques — for example, enriched jobs, team concepts, productivity gain sharing — than it is to promote the diffusion of a diagnostic and innovative planning process.

PRINCIPLES REFLECTED IN THE THREE-LEVEL CONCEPTION OF WORK INNOVATION

Most effective work improvement efforts have reflected the following principles. I have induced them largely from experience rather than deduced them from social science theory.

1. In designing work structures, it is imperative to be absolutely committed to the results one chooses (shown on the far right of the *Exhibit*). One should become pragmatic in the choice of techniques to achieve these ends (shown on the far left of the *Exhibit*).

2. Recognize that no universally applicable set of human preferences and priorities regarding quality of work life exists. Hypotheses about what would enhance human experience at work may be useful, provided that they are tested with the people in question and are revised or discarded and replaced on the basis of that experience. The same points apply to the determination of the business results that the work culture should promote.

3. Accept that most techniques affect business and human results indirectly, altering first the culture of the organization. Even if in their designs planners ignore cultural considerations, the latter will nevertheless surface as the most important elements of the operation. Participants and visiting observers are quick to appreciate the motivation, cooperation, problem solving, openness, and candor that often mark a successful effort in practice.

4. Imagine the attitudes, relationships, and capabilities that would promote both business achievement and quality of work life in a particular setting, and then use these cultural attributes as proximate criteria for guiding the design of the work structure. In many cases, duality of goals is absent, or the step of idealizing a work culture is omitted, or both. An elaborate methodology is not required, but a certain type of thinking is advantageous.

5. Be sure that at the technique level the many different elements of design and management practice — reward scheme, division of labor performance reporting scheme, status symbols, and leadership style — are consistent with each other, each reinforcing or complementing the other. When these elements of the work structure send common or compatible signals, the culture will be internally consistent; if they send "mixed signals," people will feel ambivalent. Also, the more comprehensive the planned work structure and the more the design elements are aligned with each other, the more powerful the structure will be in shaping a distinctive work culture.

A CHANGING VIEW OF THE UNION-MANAGEMENT RELATIONSHIP: SCIENTIFIC MANAGEMENT vs. HUMAN DEVELOPMENT
Irving Bluestone

In his thoughtful exposition on modern society — "The Creative Balance" — Secretary of Commerce, Elliot Richardson, fashions his concept of democratic values in these words:

"My point of departure is a set of beliefs which seem to me not only fundamental to the values of our own society but implicit in a valid perception of what it is to be a human being. Foremost among them is the belief that every individual seeks a sense of personal identity and worth. Each person gains this partly through the development and exercise of individual capacities, partly through the sense of belonging and sharing that comes from participating in the society of others. In both cases, freedom to choose is indispensable to the opportunity to become a complete person. It is also essential to our self-esteem that we feel able to exert some control over the forces that affect our lives."

Applied to life at the workplace, this democratic ideal of human development assumes added meaning. For in the world of work the majority of millions find themselves deprived of the opportunity to seek a "sense of personal identity and worth" or "to exert some control over the forces that affect (their) lives."

Why is this so? Need it be so? What can be done to fulfill more responsively at the workplace the democratic concept of "self-fulfillment" and "participation" envisioned for society as a whole?

For about seventy years the production system has been predicated on the Frederick Taylor principles of "scientific management." It is rooted in the drive for more output per man-hour by breaking down each job to its simplest, most repetitive tasks, with the shortest possible learning period, limited to the greatest efficiency in space and time. Such a production system necessarily requires nothing more from the worker than to follow instructions to the letter and perform precisely in a manner prescribed over and over again so that each motion becomes mechanically perfect. "Scientific management" in these terms is epitomized by the techniques of the moving assembly line.

The usual and customary — though not necessarily valid — definition of productivity: output per man-hour is married naturally to the principle of "scientific management." They fit each other. Over time, reducing each task to its least common denominator became the measure of efficiency; and counting units produced by man-hour became the measure of productivity. Both together were designed to maximize profit, which, of course, is the essential purpose of business enterprise.

Times and circumstances are changing, however, and some management executives are reevaluating these more traditional concepts of efficiency and productivity. At the same time the workers are increasingly challenging the authoritarian climate of the workplace and its structure.

The purpose of union organization is to alter the human condition of the worker: improve his standard of living, provide a greater measure of job and income security; establish sensible rules of behavior governing the relationship between manager and worker; create decent working conditions. Despite the major strides made by unions in achieving these goals, for the most part they have stopped short of challenging the basic system of production.

The fact is that management authority over the methods, means and processes of production, relegating the worker substantially to the role of robot to the machine, still holds supreme.

Picture the production worker employed in the normal factory. He leaves for work betwen 5 a.m. and 6 a.m. in the morning. He arrives at the plant, walks to his clock card, punches in, and then proceeds to his workplace. There he is told precisely what his task is, a task which has been broken down into several specific elements of work. He is instructed as to the order in which these work elements are to be performed. He is told what tools to use and where his material is stacked. He is instructed in what time span he must perform his task. He is given a specific space area in which to perform it. He must perform the task over and over again, each cycle within a fixed time frame measured by stopwatch. He is subject to an array of shop rules, governing his behavior in the plant. Should he violate any of these instructions or any of the rules, he is subject to discipline. He is constantly under the watchful eye of supervision, often even when he goes to the bathroom and during relief. In moving line assembly operations, he cannot leave his work station until a reliefman is available to take over his job. After eight hours of this kind of repetitive work he leaves for home only to contemplate the next dreary day ahead of him.

Experiments, as you know, are underway both in Europe and the U.S. which are designed to escape from this deadening routine of the work process. Some appear more successful than others; some are utter failures. Important, however, is the fact that these experiments exhibit a desire to stress the fulfillment of human development as much as and sometimes even more than the achievement of productive efficiency.

Concomitant with this "new mood" in structuring the work is an equally significant challenge to the views held regarding the definition of productivity. It is not enough to define productivity simply in terms of units of production per man-hour. Dr. Michael Maccoby, for instance, suggests a broad, humanistic concept of productivity which to my mind is far more attuned to twentieth century society. He speaks of "social productivity" in contrast to "economic productivity" in these terms:

"For the economist, productivity is a measure of output per man-hour, and an increase in productivity results in a decrease in the cost per unit produced.

"But neither the general public nor policy makers define productivity in such a limited way. More generally, productivity may mean effectiveness and efficiency in the use of resources, including manpower, energy, raw materials, and technology. Productivity may also refer to generativity or creativity as in 'productive soil' or 'productive human beings.'

"Do the different definitions of productivity imply the same policies? That depends on who is the beneficiary of productivity. It may be efficient for a company to use people and resources to maximize output per man-hour, because it leads to growth and profit. But the company's productivity may be unproductive for the workers and society.

"Is it efficient to use up national resources to maintain profits in a few companies? Is it efficient to increase productivity and pollute the air and water? Is it efficient to use up workers like so many interchangeable parts and leave them to the care of welfare agencies? Most people would answer no to these questions. If we think of productivity in terms of overall social effectiveness or generativity, then any particular increase in output per man-hour might or might not turn out to be socially productive."

As we couple the idea of human development at the workplace with a humanistic definition of productivity, we must arrive at a different — if not altogether new — concept of the relationship between management and labor.

In Sweden, for instance, management is discovering that better educated workers with improved income have tended to place greater emphasis upon the availability and utilization of leisure time. Absenteeism has skyrocketed, attentiveness to the quality of product has deteriorated, the demand to have greater input in the day-to-day affairs of the company, both in the managerial and workplace functions, have combined to induce management to pay far greater attention to the human development aspects of worklife. Experiments such as that undertaken by Volvo in its Kalmar plant are apparently proving that the Frederick Taylor concept of worklife is not necessarily the most efficient. In fact, indications are that the departure from the structured, rigid format of ''scientific management'' is proving feasible and profitable.

As an increasing number of management executives either reach a similar conclusion or at least become willing to engage in demonstration projects which depart from the precepts of ''scientific management'' the opportunities become brighter for the development of a new look in the labor-management relationship, one in which workers are treated not as substitutes for machines to perform the bidding of the foreman without question but rather as ''copartners'' in the decision-making process.

U.S. management has always paid lip service to the idea that it is the people performing the work who are the most important in the productive process. As a matter of fact, however, the treatment given the workers has belied the rhetoric. Traditionally, management has called upon labor to cooperate in increasing productivity and improving the quality of the product. My view is that the other side of the coin is more appropriate; namely, that management should cooperate with the workers to find ways to enhance the human dignity of labor and to tap the creative resources of each human being in developing a more satisfying worklife, with emphasis on worker participation in the decision-making process.

In practical and realistic terms this kind of mutual cooperation is taking form in certain specific problem areas of mutual concern to management and labor.

By way of example, in the past several years in the auto industry, both management and the union have begun to embrace the advantages of joint undertakings in several areas of mutual interest.

Alcoholism, long a festering problem, was tradtitonally handled by management as a matter for progressive discipline. Yet discipline could not and did not correct the alcoholic. Succeedingly severe disciplinary measures simply aggravated the illness until discharge resulted. Thus, management lost the employee's training and skills; the employee lost his paycheck — and often his family as well. Joint alcoholism rehabilitation programs are now established which recognize in the first instance that alcoholism is an illness like other illnesses. Management and union representatives with training and expertise work together assisting the alcoholic who seeks or is induced to seek help. Thousands of ill workers have thus been restored to health, to their jobs and to their families.

A similar activity is developing with regard to the illness of drug addiction. True, the cures are still uncertain. Nevertheless, workers who seek help are being provided a measure of assistance through joint cooperative union-management programs.

This idea of cooperative effort to assist troubled employees is now expanding in some areas to cover as well family problems, emotional problems, etc.

Essentially this approach represents an endeavor to meet human problems through humane methods, jointly undertaken.

Joint programs to help orient new hires in their jobs is another cooperative undertaking. In such programs a knowledgeable management and union representative jointly meet with workers newly hired into the plant and provide them with pertinent information concerning their job, the union, etc. Thus, they enter upon a new and often strange world armed with comforting knowledge concerning the workplace and its surroundings and the people with whom they will be thrown into contact.

Joint preretirement programs have been initiated involving not only the prospective retiree but the spouse as well. Here again instruction and pertinent information are provided jointly by management and union representatives in meetings whose agenda is carefully designed to assist workers contemplating retirement.

Experiments in which union and management think through together how best to handle problems of discipline regarding individual workers are also finding their place in the labor-management scene. How successful they will be remains to be evaluated but the fact that in some instances management is willing to share its historic prerogative to discipline by seeking the assistance of the union in correcting the behavior of straying workers is an important concession to the concept of cooperative effort.

Perhaps the most important cooperative effort of recent years relates to the establishment of joint health and safety committees. The worker after all is the first-line victim of improper health and safety conditions at the workplace. The fact that management and the union undertake a copartnership in maintaining safe and healthful working conditions is of major importance to the worker. In the programs thus far undertaken in the auto industry, literally thousands of corrective actions have resulted from the joint efforts of the union-management teams at the national and local levels.

Many other areas of mutual concern can well be subject to such joint enterprise. The movement of work and workers, the subcontracting out of work, production scheduling, the introduction of technological innovation, the handling of necessary overtime are the kinds of issues which could well lend themselves to a partnership decision-making process.

Experiments in restructuring and redesigning work, or to put it in broader terms, the entire arena encompassed by the term "managing the job" is the basis for literally hundreds of demonstration projects in Europe and the U.S., adapted to fit the unique circumstances of each situation. The list of such efforts which afford workers the opportunity to participate in the decision-making process is growing steadily. And the number of management and union officials expressing interest in such projects is similarly on the increase. Management apparently is observing that with the success of such endeavors absenteeism declines, labor turnover is reduced, and the quality of the product improves. Moreover, treating workers as adults rather than as nonadults permeates the workplace with a sense of job satisfaction and self-fulfillment conducive to improving overall efficiency. My personal experience indicates, moreover, that successful experiments of this kind enhance the image of the union in the eyes of the worker and bring him to hold the union, its goals and its purposes in higher regard.

Even though more and more areas of mutual concern to management and the union may become subject to joint cooperative undertaking, the basic issues inherent in the adversarial relationship will remain matters of confrontation. Wages, fringe benefits, job security, etc. remain in the collective bargaining arena and I see no contradiction between enlarging the scope of cooperative effort where mutual interest and concern dictate this to be the best course of action while, at the same time, the parties remain adversaries with regard to subjects which lend themselves more naturally to the hard business of confrontation collective bargaining.

Over the ensuing years I would hope that the course of union-management relations will be dictated by departure from the principles of "scientific management" and by acceptance of the concept of human development, coupled with a more humanistic definition of the term productivity. In my judgment this will lend to joint endeavors to the advantage of management, the union and above all the workers. In the final analysis all of society will stand to gain.

THE QUALITY CONTROL CIRCLE EXPLOSION
Edwin G. Yager

No management process has so caught the fancy of so many organizations in such a short period of time as has the QC Circle. The impact of this concept on U.S. industry has been phenomenal! As recently as 1978, few American managers had even heard of the process. Today, its use is becoming quite common, as evidenced by the exposure received via trade and news publications as well as radio and television stations across the country.

QC Circles were born in Japan. In the period 1946 to 1950 statistical quality control methods were introduced in Japan through the U.S. occupation forces. W. E. Deming and other educators and specialists introduced these techniques throughout Japan. The Q.C. research group was formed as a part of the Union of Japanese Scientists and Engineers (JUSE). A massive effort to educate millions of workers and their supervisors in the basic Q.C. methods was introduced throughout the country. Over the years, these involved a series of seminars; radio and TV broadcasts, "at-home" courses, local, regional, national conferences, and other techniques.

The QC Circle was actually an educational tool. This is quite contrary to the myth that has grown in the U.S. that QC Circles are unique to the Japanese culture or that QC Circles were primarily developed as a participative tool related to the so-called Japanese management style. In fact, rapid industrial expansion created a work force needing basic training. Thousands of new supervisors needed training in methods of quality control and management technique. Perhaps this was a factor most unique for Japan. Quality control techniques were seen as a tool for every supervisor — not just quality control specialists. Even today Q.C. inspectors are employed in Japan at a rate of one to 1,000 compared to one to 50 in the U.S. Each supervisor is responsible for the quality in his or her own department.

In 1949, the Industrial Standardization Law was enforced in Japan. Under the provisions of this law, companies successful in meeting quality requirements, especially as related to the application of statistical quality control techniques as prescribed by law, were permitted to use the JIS symbol on their products. The period of 1951 to 1954 saw even more rapid expansion of the technique as well as the establishment of several national prizes for quality. The Deming Application Prize is now awarded nationally to companies rated excellent for their application of statistical quality control methods. The prize is based on the scrutiny of the Deming Prize Committee.

TOTAL QUALITY CONTROL

From 1955 to 1960, the country saw a growth of what they called *Total Quality Control*. In the Japanese concept, all people in the organization hierarchy, from top management to rank and file workers received exposure to statistical quality

311

control knowledge and then jointly participated in the upgrading of quality control practice. National Quality Month (November) was begun in 1960, and the "Q" symbol was adopted throughout the nation. Companies subscribing to the quality control movement flew the "Q" flag on top of their buildings or inside their factories.

In 1968 the following factors were outlined by K. Ishakawa as those contributing to the rapid growth of the Q.C. practice.[1]

1. Generally prevalent enthusiasm for further education and a general attitude in all the country to provide continuing education for *all* citizens.

2. Availability of Q.C. courses and seminars, including massive distribution of short and long courses in all media and at all hours.

3. Invitation of top-level foreign educators to provide informal stimulus and growth.

4. Adaptation of Q.C. practice to specific needs, cultural values and industries.

5. The institutionalizing and government support through the Japanese Industrial Standardization, the Deming Prize, the JUSE and similar efforts.

6. Regular audits of quality control by top management.

7. The faithful observance of November as the National Quality Month.

8. Increasingly important role of first-line supervisors and rank and file workers in quality.

9. Export laws and inspections requiring a target of world first-class quality.

Perhaps the most significant difference between Japan and the U.S. in this regard is the national and government support of business and industrial practices in Japan. This is especially true when one compares the Japanese practice to the illogical and adversarial regulations that are so prevalent in the U.S. between government and industry.

As the demand for even more intensive education of the foremen increased, a move was launched in which foremen and workers got themselves organized to discuss Q.C. techniques and to study together. As this movement grew, JUSE began encouraging such activities and the QC Circle was born. By 1967, 12,000 circles had formed and were registered with JUSE and an additional 60,000 were meeting without registration.

QC CIRCLES IN THE U.S.

Since the introduction of this concept in the U.S., primarily credited to Lockheed Industries, hundreds of organizations have formed thousands of circles. For example, the circle process is now underway in Hughes Aircraft, 3M Co., General Motors Corp., Ford Motor Co., Westinghouse, General Electric, Bank of America, Memorex Corp., Foremost Foods, Crucible Steel, Hoover NSK, Eaton Corp., Polaroid Corp., Pentel of America, Verbatim, and perhaps a hundred other organizations.

A significant interest has been shown in this country by hospitals, banks, service organizations, accounting, engineer and professional firms. This same growth in nonindustrial organizations has developed in Japan in the last few years.

Unfortunately not all news related to the growth in HRD-related efforts is good news. It has been interesting to me to observe the general "bandwagon" effect in the HRD field. Programs and concepts which have been on the market for years have suddenly become "productivity" programs. It has been all to easy for many in the field of employee and supervisory development to continue to sing the same song — simply changing or adding a few verses and calling it productivity.

It is true that there are some fundamental underlying issues common to organizational change efforts that work and to those that do not work. In fact, many programs that work in one area will not work in another seemingly similar area. The entire field of organizational development and the behavioral sciences has tried to answer the questions related to the transplant effect.

A similar problem is seen in the Quality Circle movement — that is that Circles work in some areas, but do not work in other areas. The QC Circle movement is based on known principles of the behavioral sciences but is not built on teaching those principles. Teaching organizational behavior theory may be one strategy necessary for preparing the organization in the use of Circles, but it is not an underlying factor. What appears to occur, however, is that the QC Circle as implementation of behavioral science concepts works, whether or not managers believe or understand those concepts.

Perhaps we have wasted too much time in past years training managers in concepts, and not enough in techniques.

BASIC FORMATION PRINCIPLES

Ishakawa outlines the basic underlying principles applicable to QC Circle formation. These may look familiar and are translated directly from the Japanese.

1. Managers, engineering staff, personnel, and industrial relations staff must have a thorough understanding of the importance and significance of the QC Circle movement. They must study the feasibility of implementing this practice in the company by getting data on Q.C. activities in other companies and by adequate study and preparation.

2. They must send a core of foremen, around whom the QC Circle will revolve to gain full appreciation of the process, to visit other companies with Circles. They may attend QC Circle conventions and meet with others who are already involved in the movement. (Note that those who are involved in Circles are encouraged to make this investigation, not senior management or personnel and training directors.)

3. After all such groundworks are completed and a group realization of the importance of the Q.C. movement is evident to all workers and foremen, the company approaches to permit the formation of QC Circles in a limited number of workshops which are headed by competent superiors. These superiors must understand the movement and be able to identify which foremen possess good Q.C. sense and are doing supervision. Dependent upon circumstances, it is also

313

advisable that only supervisors and service workers are first organized into a few QC Circles. Circles can then be added in other workshops in a fashion that organic cells keep on adding up while disintegrating.

4. Activity of QC Circles must be closely followed to see that the Circle is functioning, that the foreman is providing proper leadership, that workers are learning, analyzing problems and are working cooperatively with other Circles. However, a caution must be exercised that the management or staff people do not supply too much intervention with or control over the activity of QC Circles. They should refrain from telling the Circles what to do or what not to do. This tends to discourage their spontaneous wish of achieving something worthy of doing. This caution must also be exercised by the Circle leader. His or her position in the Circle is a coordinator rather than a leader. He/she tries to be inductive in stirring up thinking of members so they can come up with ideas . . . in no instance should he or she state own opinions nor force such opinions on members.

5. Now that interest in QC Control movement has grown in the workshop and that everyone begins to have keen concern over the workshop improvement, the scope of Circle activities gradually expands to include people in as many other operating departments as possible. When it has developed into this stage, the company-wide standard operating procedures of the QC Circle, regulations of QC Circle activity in relation to various other company work regulations and standards, need to be developed to avoid confusion in work responsibility and authority resulting therefrom.

But the Circles themselves depend upon — and flourish — only if the following principles are firmly in place.

1. Top management (all levels of senior management) must agree to support, encourage and listen to Circle activities — no matter how many or how few circles are operating.

2. Management must not "use" Circles to further their own pet ideas or projects. Circle members must be free to pursue their own priorities.

3. Management must be patient — Circles do not represent overnight change.

4. Managers must accept failures with no recrimination or criticism — but with encouragement.

5. The philosophy of the Circle concept (i.e., basically a Theory Y philosophy) must be present in every step of the process.

A. Managers and supervisors are given the option of being involved.

B. It is recognized that this is not a plant or organization-wide activity. It must be allowed to grow in a ripple effect — one Circle after another — and not be a sweeping, new program.

6. Circle leaders and facilitators must be carefully chosen, be well trained and be credible (i.e., not seen as management patsies).

7. Facilitators must be given time and support to carry out their activities (too many facilitators have too many other responsibilities and all the subtle messages tell him or her that this is only if and when she has nothing else to do).

8. Circle membership must be voluntary. The Circle itself will deal with membership and member effectiveness in the same way most peers affect the behaviors of others.

"NOT A TOTAL OD EFFORT"

The Circle movement is not a total effort in Organization Development. As mentioned, it was launched initially in Japan as a training effort. Many of the motivational and participative effects emerged as the process developed. Quality of Work Life, on the other hand, is much broader and is aimed specifically at a myriad of issues related to communicating, organization, job enrichment, incentives, working conditions, team building, attitudes and other human factors on the job.

Neither is the QC Circle "participative management" as we understand that concept. The Circle does not involve interdepartment efforts, "linking pins," representative forms of employee involvement or similar activity where employees participate at higher levels of management or in higher organizational decisions. (Carried to an extreme, these plans have even appointed line workers to the board of directors.)

Circle activities involve effort only at the level of application of the worker. Decision powers are limited dramatically compared to those of other participative techniques. A Circle project does not preclude these activities, however. Nearly every QWL effort (or OD effort) today uses, or at least considers, Quality Circles as *one* element of a total project.

Quality Circles also will have an impact on other forms of organizational change or development efforts, and other management practices. Some of these might be:

· *Suggestion Programs*. Most Quality Circles are installed without any changes to the existing suggestion system. Individuals will still have more suggestions that the Circle can possibly process. Any suggestions that may result in rewards coming from Circle activity are simply submitted by the Circles, and the rewards are shared by the Circle.

In many cases, Circle members do not even submit their suggestions through the formal channels, satisfied with the intrinsic rewards they have already achieved.

· *Productivity Sharing/Impro-Share or Other Incentive Programs*. Not only will the Circle program not interfere, it will dramatically increase the value of most incentive programs. One weakness of most incentive programs is that they rely too heavily on "working harder;" by Circle formation, workers are also encouraged to "work smarter."

· *Job Enrichment*. Despite the fact that the formation of a Circle is a classic example of a job enrichment technique, the Circles themselves have a history of designing work methods improvement that become enriching and do fall into the category of job design. A weakness of many job enrichment installations is that the focus of job redesign comes from the engineers instead of from the workers themselves.

FOCUS OF THE CIRCLE

Each Circle is independent. The members of the Circle focus on problems specific to their area of responsibility. Circles are formed by members who share like responsibilities. Circles may, however, call upon resources from any other place in the organization when cooperation or expertise is required. For example, a Circle might work on a problem that involves a supplier or a supplier department (perhaps the way a sub-assembly is finished, or material is being shipped). The first Circle may call upon another Circle, or an employee, in the other group. They would ask for cooperation or information. The second Circle or employees then analyze their own work process to determine the feasibility and cost to arrive at a resolution. Both Circles may find they lack the expertise needed to solve the problem and may call upon a staff engineer or another process expert to find an answer. The focus is always on *the* problem which is being solved. The Circle does not move into decisions involving pay, working conditions, product plans, etc., which may be of interest — but beyond the Circle's authority.

Some organizations have developed what they call Circles to address organizational problems. They seek volunteers from a number of areas to work together. This looks much more like participative management than a Quality Circle. It changes the focus from Quality Control measurements and statistical techniques. Seldom do the efforts of higher-level participant groups or task force groups ever use the techniques or statistical approaches which the Circle uses. Similarly, 9/9, participative or involvement programs which include employees in decisions at various levels may reflect a management style — but do not use the statistical measurements which are unique to the Quality Circle.

The uniqueness of the Quality Circle lies in its emphasis on measurement and problem solving. Circles focus on measurement . . . how much, how often, how far, where, when, etc. They also focus on problem solving . . . why, what can be done, and similar questions. And Circles also focus on experimentation . . . what if this were skipped, ignored, done less often, done more often, etc. And they focus on evaluation . . . what happened with each change, what was the result, what is the value, etc.

Because the Quality Circle process is so frequently mentioned as a part of an organizational development / organizational behavior effort, it may be interesting to relate this process to some organizational behavior thoughts. Richard Walton — in an excellent article in the *Harvard Business Review* — outlines "some lessons from experience."[2] He relates these lessons to the broad range of OD types of activities and they are especially relevant when one considers QC Circles. (As Reid Rundell of General Motors points out when discussing the controversial Tarrytown Project that has been so successful, "Remember, this process was developed *at* Tarrytown, *for* Tarrytown." This ownership is critical to any efforts of change.)

Walton warns to:

1. "Attempt work improvement because of its intrinsic positive values, not because it might be the way to avoid unionization."

And, we add, to increase quality or productivity. We have found unions to be extremely cooperative in the Q.C. movement. The structure and relationships within unions can be very helpful to support a good worker improvement project, if the effort is not being used against — but for the work force. Unions know as well as management the challenge that exists to increase productivity and quality in this country, and so long as adversarial relationships are avoided — the coop-eration can be a powerful asset.

2. "Recognize the basic differences between opportunities in new facilities, and opportunities in existing ones."

Much more sensitivity and professionalism, from a person knowledgeable in organizational behavior principles is necessary in instituting a work or decision-making process that interrupts existing norms, cultural attitudes or power struc-tures. It is in these situations where we believe an organizational behavior consul-tant can be of most help. The QC Circle process should not be initiated until adequate work is done to prepare the environment and the organization. The first Circle is so visible it attracts undue attention. The consultant is better able to buffer and dampen this attention than an insider in many cases. (Sometimes senior managers need to be told to stay out — and keep quiet for a while. Insiders are seldom able to do this as tenaciously as may be necessary.)

3. "Avoid either/or concepts of organization and management style."

There is not one right way to manage an organization nor to decide. Recent publications of JUSE focus on methods of organizing Quality Circle activities — and they are as varied as the organizations and work processes themselves. The organization within the business entity should emerge through the same Circle process as is inherent to the Circle itself.

Neither is there one right management style. Too much emphasis has been placed in this country on "style" and on "humanistic or nondirective" forms of com-munication as *the* way to manage. We now know that style is but a minor part of this process. We have spent much too much energy playing with personalities and not near enough on process.

4. "Do not advocate one answer; spread a way of looking for answers."

Although it is clear that employee involvement does have a positive effect in organization productivity and quality, Quality Circles are *not* the only way to accomplish this. Look carefully at the alternatives before deciding whether Cir-cles, compared to some other job enrichment, productivity sharing or goal setting process is more appropriate, and whether or not this is the best time in your or-ganization's history to initiate an effort.

IMPLEMENTING THE PROCESS

One organization's experience serves well to describe the potential and the limits of the QC Circle effort. This company is most interested in solving com-plaints and improving quality in an integrated consumer product service division. The product is processed, packaged and delivered to "at-home" customers through an extensive route delivery system. The concept of Circles was intro-duced to senior management and the middle management in two separate ses-sions. All managers participated in a workshop focusing on employee involve-ment in consensus management processes. Volunteer departments, limited to six initially, were then sought to implement Circles. (Six is a very high limit for an initial project.)

Two production, one purchasing, one long-haul trucking, and one shipping department, and one local delivery Circle were formed. A facilitator was trained, and so were Circle leaders. Once the Circles began, the facilitator worked closely with each as they got started learning the techniques of data collection, brainstorming, problem solving, cause and effect diagrams, histograms, Pareto techniques and other statistical methods.

One Circle began on the problem of "bottle caps." Discarded bottle caps in the unloading area created hazardous and inconvenient conditions. By designing a way to collect the discarded caps they also found that they could be recycled, saving hundreds of dollars per day.

A second Circle of drivers worked on some issues related to errors in the forms that they were using, especially as it related to collection of refunds and bottle deposits. The purchasing department Circle began working on paperwork errors and the truckers and delivery route workers began working on a problem of broken bottles in delivery.

In all cases, the Circles became highly motivated and highly involved. Within a matter of months, each was contributing significantly to cost reduction and improved quality within the organization.

As a second plant was brought on line in the installation of the Quality Circle process, the facilitator was not given adequate time away from the job in order to serve the Circles that had been formed. In addition, a new plant manager joined the organization during the implementation phase and was not adequately brought on board as a participating member in the Circles. His subsequent lack of support and the competitive pressure for time of the facilitator began to destroy the Circles almost before they had begun.

In one instance, a supervisor who found the Circle meeting time to be inconvenient for something that he had to do personally arbitrarily changed the meeting time. In this case, the Circle read this as a very definite signal regarding the importance of their work and immediately changed what were very productive Circle sessions into gripe sessions and general excuses for being away from work. The Circle soon folded, perhaps a victim of its own success.

SUMMARY

All the data suggests that the Quality Circle process, if installed as an organizational intervention — which it most certainly is — with the proper preparation and communication and the commitment and ownership of senior management can be an extremely valuable tool in nearly any organization. Managers and workers alike are continually amazed at the value of the intrinsic rewards that accrue from participation in the Circle, as well as the cost returns from the Circle's activities.

Nearly every evaluation study that has been done to date has demonstrated anywhere from 4:1 to 8:1 return on investment within the first year of Circle activities. Implementation of a Circle process requires patience and recognition that it is a change in the management system and is not a program or a package to bring about dramatic effects but rather is a long-term commitment aimed at significant changes over a period of time.

REFERENCES

1. Along with Dr. Juran and Dr. Deming from the U.S., K. Ishakawa is awarded much of the credit for the growth and enthusiasm of the QC method in Japan. See K. Ishakawa, QC Circle Activities, Union of Japanese Scientists and Engineers, 1968, Japan.

2. Walton, Richard. "Work Innovations in the United States," *Harvard Business Review*, July-August 1979, Boston, MA.

INTEGRATING QUALITY CONTROL AND QUALITY OF WORK LIFE

Sidney P. Rubinstein

ABSTRACT

Now that worker participation and labor/management cooperation have proven feasible, we must direct our efforts to the implementation of systems which can survive. The QC Circle movement, highly successful in Japan, has not addressed itself to inhibiting social-environmental conditions in the U.S. such as labor/management conflict, job security, and management mobility. It is therefore not a ready-made panacea. Such issues must be addressed to insure the survival of the system. Participative Problem Solving evolved from twenty years of field experience in the U.S. and abroad. It combines the science of quality control engineering with advances in the behavioral sciences. PPS requires an on-going effort which seeks the resolution of inhibiting influences unique to the U.S.

The quality work life movement in the U.S. is becoming an interdisciplinary, value-based effort directed toward greater worker participation. This effort features labor/management cooperation. The quality professional now has the unique opportunity to provide leadership for the improvement of quality performance and the quality of work life.

DETROIT FREE PRESS   FRIDAY, JANUARY 26, 1979

DECISION-MAKING WORKERS ARE WAVE OF THE FUTURE

GENERAL MOTORS CORPORATION PRESIDENT E.M. (PETE) ESTES AND UNITED AUTO WORKERS VICE-PRESIDENT IRVING BLUESTONE SAID JOINT GM-UAW "QUALITY OF WORK LIFE" EXPERIMENTS GIVING WORKERS A BIGGER SAY IN SUCH MATTERS AS WORK SCHEDULES AND SOLVING PRODUCT QUALITY PROBLEMS SO FAR HAVE MET WITH MIXED SUCCESS.

. . . ESTES SAID, NOTING THAT GM TOP MANAGEMENT REMAINS SOLIDLY BEHIND THE QUALITY OF WORK LIFE CONCEPT: "IT IS TREMENDOUSLY EXCITING . . . AND THIS IS JUST THE BAREST BEGINNING . . . WE BELIEVE THAT (IT) REALLY PAYS OFF."

IN ONE PROGRAM AT A GM ASSEMBLY PLANT IN TARRYTOWN, N.Y., FOR EXAMPLE, WORKERS WERE GIVEN TRAINING — ON COMPANY TIME — IN PROBLEM SOLVING TECHNIQUES. THEY THEN PARTICIPATED IN SESSIONS AIMED AT RESOLVING PRODUCT QUALITY PROBLEMS IN THE PLANT. BLUESTONE SAID THE RESULT WAS "A RATHER STARTLING IMPROVEMENT IN RELATIONS" BETWEEN MANAGEMENT AND WORKERS.

BLUESTONE SAID THE CONCEPT ONLY SUCCEEDS IN AN ATMOSPHERE OF MUTUAL MANAGEMENT-LABOR RESPECT AND WHERE THE COMPANY HAS A SINCERE DESIRE TO IMPROVE A WORKER'S SATISFACTION IN HIS JOB.

COMPANIES THAT ADOPT THE IDEA AS A "GIMMICK" TO IMPROVE PRODUCTIVITY, HE SAID, INVARIABLY FAIL "BECAUSE THE WORKERS QUICKLY SEE THROUGH IT."

"IT'S VITALLY IMPORTANT THAT THE QUALITY OF WORK LIFE START ON A CO-EQUAL BASIS BETWEEN UNION AND MANAGEMENT."

I had the privilege of serving as the consultant and trainer at the above mentioned Tarrytown Assembly Plant project. The success at Tarrytown resulted from integrating the know-how we had acquired in organizing and training workers to solve *quality* problems for fifteen years prior to the project, with the change in labor-management relations resulting from the Joint G.M.-U.A.W. Quality of Work Life effort. The Quality of Work Life movement's positive effect on labor-management relations provides a significant solution to one of the negative social environmental factors in our society.

Employee participation in problem solving is now a world-wide movement. It takes different forms in different environmental settings, each model responding uniquely to its specific environment. An examination of our own and others' experiences with employee participation, and an attempt to deal with the contradictions that become clear in the course of these experiences, has led to the identification of characteristics felt to be necessary for the growth and diffusion of employee participation in the United States. A comparison and analysis of the social environment in Japan was presented by the author at the International Conference for Quality Control, 1978-Tokyo[2].

IN UNDERSTANDING A COMPLEX SOCIAL SYSTEM ONE . . . "MUST INCLUDE THIS SYSTEM AND ITS IMMEDIATELY RELEVENT ENVIRONMENT"[3]

The focus of my work has shifted from how to structure and initiate such a system, to a prime concern with how to promote the environmental changes necessary to nurture and sustain the system. It is easy to start such a system, but very hard to sustain it.

Since 1969 I have worked with over 20 organizations in implementing systems of employee participation. We have also conducted numerous seminars involving hundreds of managers and union leaders. From this experience we have been able to distill the structure necessary in a system of worker and supervisor joint problem solving, as well as the environmental context that will allow such a system to be sustained.

In presenting the QC Circle movement at my seminars, I have to carefully distinguish between the Japanese system and the systems that might be developed in the home environment. I describe the structure of the circle, the role of the participants and supervisors, types of activities and training, the structure of the management and technical support activities at the plant level, and the external support structure of the JUSE and other agencies. This description explains how the QC Circle movement is organized as an effective system. I then describe the supportive environmental context for the QC Circle in Japan.

321

FIGURE I

1. An industrial environment created by concensus management, with managers promoted from within the organization and motivated to adopt and maintain a new system for achieving superior quality.[4]
2. A bonus system which can reflect productivity improvement.[5]
3. A tradition of methods improvement by the production unit.[6]
4. Lifetime employment and high labor demand.[7]
5. Union influence concentrated at the local level and union leaders interested in joint consultation and more productive use of resources.[8]
6. An engineering community willing to share its knowledge.[9]

The cost-effective results of the QC Circle movement are due to the structure of the system. The system's survival, its rate of diffusion, and its on-going maintenance can be attributed to the supportive environment.

"MOST SYSTEMS, PARTICULARLY IN THEIR EARLY STAGES, ARE INCOMPLETE. ADEQUATE SYSTEM IDENTIFICATION MUST ENUMERATE NOT ONLY THE PRESENT MEMBERS AND THEIR RELATIONS, BUT ALSO, FROM THESE THE UNFILLED POSITIONS IN THE SYSTEM AND THE STRAINS THEY CREATE."[10]

When evaluating the QC Circle system in terms of its relevance to the U.S. I found that the system was incomplete. It was incomplete because it was developed in an environmental context that would nurture it. In the U.S., the environmental context of the past 10 years in many major areas has been quite different than that in Japan. The most significant differences I have found include mobility and style of management, economic remuneration, job security and the heavy reliance on specialized departments to solve quality and production problems. The environmental context in the United States was not only different, but frequently in direct conflict with the environment required to develop a system of worker participation. It was necessary to identify new system requirements that would be needed to affect this environmental contest. This process has been slow and we can now begin to report on progress.

Participation Problem Solving has evolved as a body of knowledge tempered by field experience rooted in the consulting experience of Participative Quality Control. It has been motivated by the success of the QC Circle movement and other efforts, and has focused on developing a total system responsive to the environmental context found in the U.S. and some European countries. The body of knowledge grew out of application experiences, all of which supported the general observation that, "A system must be cost effective to survive, but being cost effective will not guarantee its survival".

I have had the privilege to work with many enlightened managers. The managers' principle concern has been to install worker participation systems that are cost effective. We have succeeded in that task, only to find the system discontinued when a new manager takes over the plant and/or company and wants to be recognized for his own system and not that of his predecessor.

The style of management has an effect on the types and growth of participation programs. Japanese managers operate in a consensus milieu. In large part, because of the tradition of lifetime employment for males in Japan, the managers of an organization learn to work cooperatively and to decide policy by a process of concensus. Value is placed on the continuation of policy from one manager to another. This atmosphere was particularly conducive to the development of the required broad-based and continuous support for the QC Circle from the management and technical staffs.

The American style is *conflict management* — competition between managers and also between labor and management. There is no denying that competition has had some very positive results. However, when the support, cooperation, interest and satisfaction of the workers is lacking, human and physical resources are being wasted. A new style of management must evolve.

It is characteristic of the United States system that *managers are moved fairly often* or move of their own volition. A manager is encouraged to change methods and to feel he has to make his own track record. He feels the safest changes are those involving no or little cost. Changes in technology, machinery, and processes are costly — discontinuing human resource programs is not. Thus, human resource programs are particularly vulnerable to changes in management.

While management interest and motivation for worker participation has continued to grow for various reasons over the past ten years, it is still primarily the interest of a small minority of enlightened managers. Until a critical mass of managers support the philosophy it will be necessary to *provide in the system a means which will encourage continuation when there is a change in management.*

There is another reason why such programs are susceptible to discontinuation. Managers are competitively evaluated on short term results and are looking for short term pay-out. When dealing with human resources we are investing in the future. Training people and building up mutual trust is a long term process with short term benefits.[11]

ENSURING JOB SECURITY

During the past decade, a number of pioneering efforts have been launched in the U.S. to improve the Quality of Work Life and Union-Management relations by establishing joint Union/Management committees on a regional, industry, corporate, or plant level. These committees have then initiated quality of work projects such as the joint G.M.-U.A.W. project at Tarrytown. A more recent effort is that of the National Quality of Work Life Committee of Chrysler Motor Company and the United Auto Workers. This committee adopted Participative Systems' training and consulting model for their first and most intensive effort.

An important element for sustaining such efforts is still lacking; that is the development of a system providing for job security. The author is currently testing a system called Job Maintenance as a means by which to provide greater flexibility in manpower allocation.

During periods of low market demand, a certain percentage of production man-hours in an organization is shifted to worker participation in improving the effectiveness of the organization by means of problem solving. For example, if five percent of the production time is not needed for production, five percent of the production worker's time would be used for training and problem-solving activity rather than laying off five percent of the production force.

The cost of maintaining the production rolls during periods of reduced income for the organization can be met, up to a certain level of maintenance, by the increased productivity that problem solving produces, by reduced payments to unemployment insurance funds in those states where payments are determined by experience-rating, by lower taxation levels because of the reduced need for services to the unemployed, and by a great reduction in the organization's costs for termination, recruitment, and new worker training. For periods when jobs need to be maintained above the level that an organization can support internally, a system of employment insurance and/or direct grants or tax benefits needs to be developed.

Breakthroughs have occurred in the past decade because of a persistent effort and the courage of managers and union leaders to undertake pioneering projects. (A summary of the environmental context and the special responsive systems are listed in Figure 2.) As these systems and others successfully respond to the remaining difficulties participative systems will be diffused. I have great expectations for the next decade. Of necessity, we must take an interdisciplinary approach to the continued diffusion of participative systems. The commitment, concepts, and vocabulary of employee participation have become more familiar to the human resource professionals such as organizers of labor/management QWL committees than they are to the quality professionals. Planning for a national movement must thus be done in conjunction with management, union leaders, and the human resource managers as well as the quality and engineering professionals from both the public and private sector.

FIGURE 2

ENVIRONMENTAL CONTEXT	RESPONSIVE SYSTEM
1. Management Mobility: causing discontinuity.	Broad based ownership of the system among managers and the union.
2. Immature Union/Management Relations: causing non-productive conflict.	Joint and equal ownership. New trade union role.
3. Practice of Cyclical Layoffs: causing unemployment, insecurity, and inadequate investment in human resources.	Job maintenance.
4. Excessive Scientific Management: causing organizational overspecialization and technical as well as managerial special interests.	Parallel strategy of change allowing those affected to participate voluntarily as they recognize the benefit of the new system for them.

The societal implications of our strategies for quality are important. A system based on self-control versus a system based on imposed inspection has a major impact on how each worker, manager, and engineer views himself and by extrapolation on how society views itself. Control provides the basis for self-respect, responsibility and accomplishment. These are critical characteristics for mental health and for a mature, self-directed populace. Conversely, where people are controlled and constantly directed at work, the society at large will assume the same characteristics. A system based on the maximum creative contribution of all members of the organization, working together, instead of a system of restricted opportunity because of oversimplification, overspecialization and rationalization is critical for developing in the individual a sense of growth, self-actualization, and confidence that problems can be solved and aspirations realized. This sense is necessary for a free, open and responsive society.

The present stage in the development of employee participation programs is the integration of the worker participation system with the total organization. Such integration was inherent in the evolution of Japanese QC Circles, where the establishment and maintenance of QC Circles have been an ongoing effort with the support of both the engineering community and management. This occurred because the efforts toward the improvement of quality were a motivating factor in the establishment of participation programs. The leadership of the QC Circles movement in Japan is provided by the quality control experts. Dr. Ishikawa and Dr. Kondo are not only proponents of QC Circles, but are also among the outstanding leadership in the quality control movement, representing the Japanese quality control professionals at the International Academy of Quality.

The Japanese quality control systems differ markedly from those of the United States. Rather than consisting of a specialized department with total responsibility for product quality, the quality control function is the responsibility of the entire organization with the QC professionals providing the required training and tackling the technical problems requiring their greater expertise.

In the U.S. we must concern ourselves with developing worker participation programs within the context of our own quality control system. We must evaluate whether or not this system is adequate to meet our competitive needs. More and more industries find it difficult to compete with regard to the quality of their products and services as well as the costs of producing them. There has been a growing realization that by involving workers in problem solving it is possible to improve quality while reducing costs. However, it is not realistic to initiate a participation effort without first evaluating how such a program will impact on the quality system and without first evaluating the changes that are required of the system in order to provide technical support to workers solving quality problems. Perhaps the advent of worker participation will provide the framework in which to review our quality control system.

An additional stimulant to that review is now developing in the personnel departments within the corporate structure. The Quality of Work Life efforts initiated by managers from organization development, personnel, and labor relations departments in conjunction with the trade unions are without input from quality control personnel. Such efforts operate in parallel to the functions of the quality control system and, therefore, do not benefit from the expertise and direction QC professionals could provide. The integration of a role for quality control personnel within such programs provides participation with a purpose. Participation is then not merely a program by which workers may provide input about their workplace, not merely a basis for labor/management cooperation, it is then a system with a purpose — to improve the quality and productivity of an organization while simultaneously improving the quality of work life.

These developments within the quality of work life movement can now stimulate quality control departments and quality control professionals to redefine their role within the corporate structure. There is now a ready audience for the quality professional's expertise and a means by which it can be integrated with that of other disciplines. And it provides a forum in which management can be asked to re-evaluate the traditional structure of its quality control system from the perspective of its contributions to improving both product quality and quality of work life.

For the quality professional, such an integrated system opens up new opportunities to use his knowledge in collaboration with that of personnel, labor relations, and organization development, engineering, operations managers, as well as that of trade union leaders. In developing the types of systems that will allow participation, it provides the opportunity for QC professionals to have access to upper-level management and a means of improving quality by broadening the base of responsibility to encompass the entire organization. Finally, such integration allows the QC professional growth opportunities whereby he can become more familiar with the roles of other disciplines and thereby expand his own expertise.

Thus, the quality control professional, in redefining his role within the participation movement, will not only respond to the danger inherent in permitting non-technical departments to organize problem-solving programs without technical input, but also he will expand and enrich the scope of his own work. These are our new opportunities and these are our challenges.

SUMMARY

As world trade becomes more complex and interwoven, the name of the game has become "competitive edge." Balance of trade, international monetary funds, international trade agreements, balance of payments, export and import quotas all become matters of concern for corporate entities both large and small.

Union leaders are becoming more vocal in the employees' demands for recognition and participation in corporate decision making related to profit and loss. Workers are becoming more concerned about maintaining their employment status quo while looking at unemployment figures and reading of business failures, massive layoffs, and corporate decisions to close unprofitable operations. The WALL STREET JOURNAL reports daily on trends and the beginning and demise of corporate entities.

Management specialists are taking a close look at management techniques that have allowed competing nations and organizations to produce competitively priced goods in foreign markets. They are trying to cope with demands for trade embargoes and other political protections for American manufacturers and American-produced goods.

Will the concept of quality circles work in the U.S. as successfully as it has in Japan? Can the concept be successfully adapted for application in the American workplaces? There are as many opinions as there are theorists, organizations, and managers. There is also great faith in the idea of American technology, ingenuity, and entrepreneurship.

The human resource development concepts will continue to be alternative approaches to the idea of conflict management. To maintain a competitive status, American industry must continue to examine management alternatives that hold promise of uniting workers and managers in a common goal of producing quality products at competitive prices resulting in a profitable venture for owners, managers, employees, customers, and peripheral contacts.